D1552840

RUSSIAN NATIONAL INCOME, 1885–1913

This book presents estimates of the growth of the tsarist economy during the "industrialization era," 1885–1913. The economic performance of the tsarist economy is compared with that of Soviet Russia during the plan era and with other industrialized countries during the late nineteenth and early twentieth centuries. Its main importance is to provide a frame of reference against which to contrast the Soviet performance. The author finds a stronger economic performance from the tsarist economy than the literature had led us to suspect, and he disputes several of the established views of economic historians concerning Russian agriculture and the Russian nineteenth-century business cycle.

Dedicated to the memory of my father

RUSSIAN NATIONAL INCOME, 1885–1913

PAUL R. GREGORY
University of Houston

ORRADRE LIBRARY
UNIVERSITY OF SANTA CLARA
SANTA CLARA, CALIFORNIA

CAMBRIDGE UNIVERSITY PRESS

Cambridge
London   New York   New Rochelle
Melbourne   Sydney

Published by the Press Syndicate for the University of Cambridge
The Pitt Building, Trumpington Street, Cambridge CB2 1RP
32 East 57th Street, New York, NY 10022, USA
296 Beaconsfield Parade, Middle Park, Melbourne 3206, Australia

© Cambridge University Press 1982

First published 1982

Printed in the United States of America

Library of Congress Cataloging in Publication Data
Gregory, Paul R.
Russian national income, 1885-
Bibliography: p.
Includes index.
1. National income - Soviet Union - History.
I. Title.
NC340.I5G73 339.347 81-21563
ISBN 0521243823

The publication of this volume was aided by a grant from the University
of Houston.

The type for this book was prepared and output at the University of Houston
using the IBM System 6.

ORRADRE LIBRARY
UNIVERSITY OF SANTA CLARA
SANTA CLARA, CALIFORNIA

349669

FIGURES

This monograph summarizes my work, begun more than a decade ago, on Russian national income. I attempt in this summary to describe the flaws, data problems, weaknesses, systematic biases, and sundry problems in the reported series. One must be realistic in these matters. These reservations most likely will be read in detail by only a few; most readers will want to turn to the summary results to answer one simple question: What was the rate of growth of the tsarist economy during its "industrialization era"? There is no simple answer to this question. What I present in this work is my "best estimate" of the tsarist growth rate. My estimates disagree with some past research; they agree with others. I would hope that my "best estimates" will be subjected to close scrutiny to determine whether they can be improved. No work of this sort is ever finished.

In the process of conducting this research, it was necessary for me to acquaint myself with the historical national income series of other countries. In reading this literature I became convinced that my series on tsarist Russia, despite its numerous flaws and weaknesses, is of comparable quality and reliability to those of the other major industrialized countries. It is this conclusion that has encouraged me to publish my results at this time.

The list of individuals and institutions that deserve my thanks and gratitude is long, and I would like to thank them all collectively. The National Science Foundation and the Humboldt Stiftung of Bonn-Bad Godesberg, Federal Republic of Germany, provided the financial support that made this project possible. Much of this research was conducted at the Institut für osteuropäische Geschichte und Landeskunde, Universität Tübingen, Dietrich Geyer, director. I wish to thank the staff of the institute collectively for their support. The Osteuropa-abteilung of the Staatsbibliotek Berlin also provided invaluable assistance, as did the interlibrary loan department of the University of Tübingen, which succeeded in obtaining valuable research materials

from the Lenin Library. The University of Houston deserves an
expression of gratitude for granting me a faculty development leave to
facilitate the preparation of this manuscript. The University of
Houston and the Minnie Stevens Piper Foundation provided financial
support for the publication of this book.

A number of individuals provided valuable advice and assistance
in the course of this project. I mention them in random order: R. W.
Davies, Eugene Zaleski, M. E. Falkus, Simon Kuznets, Bernd Bonwetsch,
Bernhard Schalhorn, Erich Klinkmueller, Steven Wheatcroft, the late
Arcadius Kahan, Jan Marcezwski, and Olga Crisp. Abram Bergson provided
the scholarly foundation for this work through his pioneering research
on Soviet national income. I wish to thank the Word Processing Center
of the University of Houston, especially Diane Salazar and Mary
Kershner, for their assistance in the preparation of this manuscript.

Paul R. Gregory

CHAPTER 1

INTRODUCTION

OBJECTIVES OF THE STUDY

The objective of this study is to estimate the real national income of tsarist Russia during its "industrialization era" from 1885 to 1913. The two major studies of Russian industrialization by Alexander Gerschenkron and Raymond Goldsmith[1] agree that an upsurge in the rate of growth of industrial output occurred in the late 1880s, after a long period of sluggish growth following the 1861 peasant emancipation. Industrial growth was retarded by the world depression at the turn of the century and again by the civil unrest of 1905 but resumed thereafter in full vigor until the outbreak of World War I.

This study of tsarist national income investigates Russia's industrialization era. My estimates take 1885 as their starting point and end in 1913, the last year of "normal" economic activity prior to the outbreak of World War I. It thus depicts the growth of Russian real national income in the most favorable possible light. The literature is in agreement that rapid and sustained growth of aggregate output would have been difficult to achieve before the abolition of serfdom and prior to the construction of a rail network in a land mass as large as that of the Russian Empire.[2] Raymond Goldsmith's national income figures for the subperiod 1860 to the mid-1880s confirm that the growth of Russian national income was indeed slow by international standards during this early period, and scholars blame both the stubborn persistence of feudal institutions and the poor transportation system for this outcome.[3]

There are two reasons for devoting attention to Russian national income. The first is that, although the empirical record of the Soviet economy during the era of centralized planning is now well established, relatively little is known about the economic base the Bolsheviks inherited from their tsarist predecessors. Our ignorance is equally profound concerning the transition period from World War I to the

1

initiation of the first five-year plan in 1928, a period that witnessed the terrible destruction of the first global war, a violent upheaval of established political and social institutions, a civil war, and tentative experiments to establish a new socialist order. It is no wonder therefore that the pre-1928 heritage of the Soviet economy remains ill defined.

EVALUATING TSARIST AND SOVIET ECONOMIC PERFORMANCE

The record shows that economic growth during the Soviet plan era has been indeed rapid by international standards, albeit declining in recent years.[4] On this point, both Western and Soviet authors agree. The record also shows that this growth was purchased at a high cost in the form of the rapid (and sometimes "forced") expansion of conventional inputs.[5] Insofar as the utilization of labor and capital inputs imposes the economic costs of sacrificed current consumption, leisure, and household production, an evaluation of the success of the Soviet economic system in accelerating the expansion of production potential must deal with the hypothetical question of "what would have been" under a capitalist regime. Answers to such counterfactual questions must be speculative in nature, but the historical behavior of real national income during the tsarist era provides at least a starting point.

If one accepts a "planners preference" utility standard in the Soviet case,[6] the rate of expansion of real output takes on primary importance in any evaluation of Soviet economic performance, for a consistent theme of the Soviet leadership has been the primacy of the growth objective. To this end, resource allocation mechanisms and policies were adopted for the expressed purpose of accelerating growth above what would have been under a market allocation system. The magnitude (or existence) of this growth acceleration must therefore serve as the principal measure of the payoff of adopting the Soviet economic system, and the costs of the system must be weighed against this payoff.

The transitional era from the 1917 revolution to 1928 also plays a prominent, but to this point unheralded, role in the evaluation of Soviet economic performance. The October Revolution set into motion a process of violent and disruptive transition that caused a substantial loss of real output. The established political order was overturned, ownership of property, with the exception of agriculture, was transferred from individuals, the crown, and the church to the Bolshevik state. Opposition to these changes prompted a bloody civil war, the outcome of which was by no means predetermined. Even after the termination of civil hostilities, an additional seven years of experimentation (and recovery) were required before the formulas of centralized planning and collectivization were adopted.

If, as Simon Kuznets has argued,[7] economic disruption is an inevitable concomitant of the transition from capitalism to planned socialism, the loss of output and of foregone economic growth during the transition must be incorporated in the assessment of Soviet growth. Adding a decade of zero growth to a half century of rapid growth, for example, can markedly affect the assessment of the Soviet growth performance. Should the economic upheaval of the transition period be regarded as a historical curiosity or as an integral and inevitable feature of the transition to planned socialism?

There is yet another reason for interest in the transition period. Received doctrine, as handed down by Soviet and Western scholars,[8] maintains that the five-year plans were initiated at a time when the labor and capital resources, intact from the tsarist era, were stretched to the limits of utilization. As the story goes, the recovery to prewar output levels was completed in the mid-1920s. Much physical capital had been destroyed during the war and civil war, and the Soviet economy was confronted in the late 1920s with a severe "capital replacement crisis."[9] In fact, this was the subject matter of the "Soviet industrialization debate" of the mid-1920s: How to expand the industrial capital stock at a rapid rate (to "build socialism") without sowing the seeds of a destructive hyperinflation? The answer proffered by the Soviet leadership under Stalin was a massive infusion of investment into heavy industry accompanied by a precipitous decline in the share of consumption, and it was this investment drive that enabled the Soviet Union to transform itself into an industrial economy and to embark upon a path of high secular growth.

In the research presented in this book, I reopen the issue of the transition period because I feel that the evidence supporting the conventional interpretation is not convincing. It is based largely upon official Soviet calculations made in the late 1920s,[10] which, although most likely superior to the statistical pronouncements of the 1930s, suffer from serious deficiencies. This matter is important because the speed of recovery is at issue as is the interpretation of the early five-year-plan era. If the economic recovery to prewar levels was not complete at the beginning of the first five-year plan, then a portion of output growth during the 1930s must be attributed to economic recovery rather than to the more difficult expansion of the production possibilities frontier.

THE TSARIST ECONOMY AND THE ECONOMIC HISTORY OF EUROPE

Scholarly interest in the tsarist economy transcends its importance as a base line for evaluating Soviet performance. The Russian economy during its industrialization era is a case study of economic growth under conditions of relative backwardness. The military significance of Imperial Russia need not be emphasized. It was the Russian army that ended the Napoleonic domination of Europe, and the aura of Russian military might left its imprint on European relations from the eighteenth century to 1917. The Russian Empire had a population of some 162 million on the eve of World War I, some 2.5 times that of its largest European neighbor, Germany, and larger than the United States by a factor of 1.6. In terms of volume of industrial production, Russia ranked fifth in the world, behind the United States, Germany, the United Kingdom, and France. Russia was the world's fourth largest steel producer and was in second place in petroleum production. In 1913 Russia produced 123 million metric tons of cereal products against Germany's 85 million and France's 31 million. Russia's major competitor in the world cereal market, the United States, produced approximately 150 million metric tons of cereals,[11] a figure that illustrates the much higher per capita cereal output of the United States and the relative backwardness of Russian agriculture.

Although the Russian Empire ranked high on the world's economic and military ladder, this ranking was due to its sheer size. According to Soviet estimates made in 1927, Russia's 1913 per capita income was 15% of United States, 22% of British, 33% of German, 50% of Italian and Austro-Hungarian per capita income, and was roughly equal to that of

Bulgaria and Rumania.[12] Independent estimates made by the author for
earlier years confirm these rankings,[13] and Russia's low per capita income ranking relative to the major industrialized countries is really
not subject to dispute.

The low per capita income ranking is indicative of Russia's
relative technological backwardness, a deficiency thought to be more
striking in agriculture than in industry. This theme is prominent in
the writings of Alexander Gerschenkron,[14] who singled out the retention
of communal agriculture and restrictions on agricultural labor mobility
as the major culprits. The Gerschenkronian view of the strictures on
Russian peasant agriculture may ultimately prove to be exaggerated, for
this study shows that income (and productivity) differentials between
the city and countryside were likely less extreme and the performance
of agriculture was likely better than those depicted by Gerschenkron.[15]

The growing technological backwardness of the Russian economy is
reflected in both statistical and military events. Although one cannot
document this with any precision, the best assumption is that very
large disparities in per capita income (and output per worker) did not
exist between Petrine Russia and Europe.[16] By the time of the 1861
peasant emancipation, however, Russian per capita income was somewhere
between one-third and one-half that of Great Britain, and by 1913 it
was approximately one-fifth.[17] What underlies this trend is not the
stagnation of the Russian economy as is commonly assumed[18] but the more
rapid relative per capita growth of Russia's European competitors as
they entered the process of modern economic growth. Russia's relative
decline can also be seen from its waning military fortunes. From the
repulsing of the Napoleonic invasion in 1812 to humiliating losses to
smaller but technologically superior foes in the Crimean War (1855) and
the Russo-Japanese War (1904-5), Russia's declining military fortunes
paralleled its relative economic fortunes.

Thus Russia, like Japan, entered the second half of the nineteenth century increasingly cognizant of its growing economic backwardness, and it was the Russian response to this backwardness that has
attracted the attention of economic historians. As formulated by
Alexander Gerschenkron in his noted theory of relative backwardness,[19]
the Russian state is pictured as being compelled by the growing disadvantages of technological inferiority to embark after the Crimean

defeat upon a deliberate program of forced industrialization, a program that, according to Gerschenkron, bears some resemblance to Stalinist policies of the 1930s. Before this, the Russian state had been content to forgo industrialization. Mass education and railroad construction were viewed as possible threats to the established political order and were even discouraged. Now forced into a pro-industrialization stance, the Russian bureaucracy turned to the promotion of industrialization. Lacking an indigent entrepreneurial class, the state (more accurately, the Ministry of Finance) fostered railroad construction through loan and profit guarantees and direct state ownership. Markets for Russian heavy industry were guaranteed by protective tariffs and government purchases. Foreign capital and foreign entrepreneurs were actively courted, and the Ministry of Finance, by pursuing a consistent policy of balanced budgets and the withdrawal of fiat money (credit rubles) from circulation, achieved its goal of convertibility in 1897.

The stability brought about by the gold standard, the continued fiscal conservatism of budgetary authorities, export surpluses, and tax concessions granted to foreign businesses facilitated an influx of foreign capital into Russian industry, attracted principally by the higher rates of return in technologically backward Russian industry. Foreign investment was concentrated in metallurgy, chemicals, mining, and petroleum, and these industries adopted the modern capital-intensive techniques of the day, leading Lenin to refer to tsarist Russia as a "dual economy" of modern heavy industry and backward agriculture and artisan manufacturing.[20] By 1914, the Russian Empire was the world's largest net debtor.

This coordinated program to accelerate industrialization through a mix of government participation, guarantees, concessions, and the enticement of foreign capital was best exemplified during Sergei Witte's tenure as finance minister (1892-1903), although the foundation of the "Witte system" was laid by his predecessors. Witte's own policy statement, justifying his program to the tsar, documents the deliberate nature of the program.[21] The description and assessment of the Witte system has occupied numerous scholars, and there is disagreement concerning how and how well it worked.[22] There is agreement, however, that the Witte system had its costs: The peasant community was thought to be burdened by oppressive indirect taxes and land payments to guar-

antee revenue for government programs and to force agricultural exports, and the restrictive monetary policies required to attain convertibility are said to have led to losses of real output.[23] The main
point is that the literature represents Russia as a case, similar to
Japan, where the state embarked upon a deliberate and consistent program to accelerate industrialization and to reduce the technology gap
between it and its advanced neighbors.

     If this was the case, two revelant questions must be addressed:
The first is whether the Russian experience did indeed differ significantly from those other countries undergoing modern economic
growth? The second issue is the degree of success of the Russian
model. Is there something either unique or unusual about the Russian
industrialization experience that requires the special attention of the
economic historian? Are there parallels between the tsarist industrialization era and the Soviet industrialization of the 1930s?

     The study of Russian national income permits the researcher to
come to grips with these issues. Although working at a high degree of
aggregation, he can examine the general pattern of resource allocation
during the era of attempted forced industrialization. Insofar as the
stated objectives of state economic policy were to raise the investment
rate (through depressed peasant consumption and enhanced foreign investment), to raise the foreign savings share of national income, and
to promote (force?) agricultural exports,[24] the behavior of these
variables can be observed in aggregate analysis, as can the government
resources devoted to developing human and physical capital resources.

     The major advantage of observing changes in resource allocation
is that one is dealing with *actual* rather than *intended* outcomes. Much
of the literature on tsarist economic history has been based, because
of the absence of a firmer empirical footing, upon intended government
action, such as that enunciated in Witte's noted policy statement.
There is little doubt that the intent of state action was to depress
peasant consumption, to raise the investment rate, and so on above
rates that would have prevailed without such state action. The much
more important issue is whether these intended actions were actually
implemented to create end-use distributions of national income "different" from other European countries at a similar stage of development. This, in my opinion, is the more useful test of the Russian
model.

Soviet economic historians, employing Marx's dialectical materialism, have sought to extract from the tsarist economic experience those features that culminated in the socialist revolution in Russia. The Marxist interpretation argues that the growing immiserization of the peasantry and the industrial worker, the "dual economy" growth of modern factory industry, the influx of foreign monopoly capital, and so on rendered Imperial Russia the "weak link" in the capitalist chain, ripe for a socialist revolution.[25] One objective of this study must be to evaluate this Soviet-Marxist literature in light of the quantitative history of tsarist Russia to establish whether the posited correlation between economic and revolutionary events exists.

In sum, there are two reasons for studying the real national income of tsarist Russia. The first is that it establishes a base line for assessing the economic performance of the Soviet economy during the plan era. The key issue, given the dominance of the growth objective throughout the Soviet era, is the extent to which the advent of centralized planning did succeed in accelerating economic growth. The second reason is that it allows the researcher to elaborate the tsarist model of economic development under conditions of relative backwardness. Moreover, the traditional Soviet historiographic interpretation of the Russian revolutionary process as caused by economic forces can be reexamined.

METHODOLOGY: SOME PRELIMINARY OBSERVATIONS

The bulk of this monograph is devoted to describing my estimates of the real national income of the Russian Empire for the period 1885 to 1913. Without detailed discussion of the calculations, the reader is in no position to assess their value. National income estimation has been called an art rather than a science, and after working on this project for a number of years, I am inclined to agree, at least in part. In some instances, crucial assumptions must be made, and it is these assumptions that are often swept under the rug out of sight of the unsuspecting user of the series. I believe it is the responsibility of the national income investigator to relate openly the important assumptions that underlie his calculations. This is necessary because analytical models used to supply components of various series may build specific relationships into the aggregate series that later users may cite as an important finding.[26]

The raw material of national income calculations is never per-
fect, and the more remote the time period and the more underdeveloped
the country, the less satisfactory is the underlying statistical material. National income calculations are conditioned by the stock of
data produced by the country investigated. Data are gathered in an
uncoordinated fashion by various governmental agencies with authority
to compel responses. The stock of data collected reflects the political, cultural, and social institutions of the nation. In the Russian
case, thanks to the fortuitous need to find public employment for the
intelligentsia, the tsarist government's interest in tax collections,
the official concern over agricultural exports and foreign capital, and
the genuine social concern and public controversy over the agrarian
question, the statistical data base is much better than is typically
recognized, even by established authorities in the field.[27] It is, in
fact, my contention that the national income series reported here is
comparable to the historical series of most of the major industrialized
countries, and in some instances it may even be superior.

For any national income series to be of value, it must be comparable conceptually to the series against which contrasts are desired.
My overriding concern is to supply a series that is conceptually and
practically consistent with Western recalculations of Soviet national
income. As the recalculations were either prepared by Abram Bergson or
patterned after his methodology, I have chosen to design my calculations after Bergson's *The Real National Income of Soviet Russia Since
1928*. Bergson himself patterned his calculations after the United
States Department of Commerce methodology, and this is generally consistent with the methodology underlying the historical series of the
major industrialized countries that I cite later in this book.

Although historical series usually estimate national income by
aggregating sector-of-origin production series, I, like Bergson, emphasize the end-use methodology, that is, real national income is calculated as the sum of the end uses of national output: final household
consumption, government final expenditures, and investment. The choice
of the end-use method is based upon three considerations. First, the
impact of planners' preferences upon Soviet resource allocation has
been best revealed through shifts in end-use patterns, and it is therefore important to establish a similar frame of reference for the

tsarist period. Second, the impact of the Witte system upon tsarist resource allocation patterns is best discerned from the end-use data. Third and surprisingly, it is my view that the end-use series is more reliable than sector-of-origin aggregations in the Russian case.

A SURVEY OF ALTERNATIVE ESTIMATES

Soviet statistical authorities have yet to publish independent esti-mates of the real national income of tsarist Russia. Instead, they have been content to rely upon the estimates of an expatriate Russian scholar, S. N. Prokopovich, who did much of his research in Prague after leaving the Soviet Union.[28] Soviet publications also cite the earlier estimates of M. G. Mullhall,[29] but these are little more than casual guesses of Russian per capita income. The 1913 national income figure accepted by Soviet officialdom (Gosplan) for comparison with the plan era is basically that which Prokopovich prepared in 1918. I shall discuss in some detail the Prokopovich estimates later in this book.

The extant estimates of Russian national income are surveyed by the prominent Soviet statistician A. L. Vainshtein;[30] so the Russian-reading student is referred to his informative survey. The lack of independent Soviet estimates for the tsarist era is a puzzling feature of this field, insofar as much work, particularly that by S. G. Strumilin, G. A. Dikhtiar, P. A. Ol, and A. L. Vainshtein, has gone into the derivation of subcomponent series. For some unexplained reason, Soviet statistical authorities during the late 1920s locked themselves into accepting a modified version of the Prokopovich esti-mate. As far as I can establish, the issue has never been reopened.

Serious work on reevaluating tsarist national income has been undertaken by Western economists. M. E. Falkus has published a major revision of the original (and revised) Prokopovich sector-of-origin estimates, finding them to be substantially understated.[31] I have prepared a 1913 estimate by end use that is supportive of Falkus's assessment of the Prokopovich figures.[32] The most important work on Russian national income is the much-cited 1961 study by Raymond Gold-smith.[33] Goldsmith has estimated agricultural and factory industrial production for the entire post-emancipation era (1860-1913), which he expands into an aggregate output series by adding more casual estimates of handicraft production, livestock production, and services. Later in this work, I will make detailed comparisons of my series with that of Goldsmith for the overlapping 1885 to 1913 period. Prokopovich provides the only alternate serial data for 1900 and 1913 benchmarks, and these data will also be examined in later chapters.

A brief word is in order concerning the conclusions that emerge from the Goldsmith study: The per annum growth rate of total output between 1860 and 1913 was approximately 2.5% which, combined with a population growth rate of 1.5%, yields a per capita rate of 1.0%. According to Goldsmith, the per capita growth rate was around three-quarters of 1% per annum between 1860 and the 1880s and then rose to slightly over 1% from the 1880s to 1913. If one accepts Goldsmith's results, Russian per capita growth was well below the European average and significantly below that of Japan, the other nation attempting to overcome its relative backwardness. Thus Russia belonged to the group of more slowly growing European countries (Britain, the Netherlands, and Italy), even considering its more rapid growth beginning in the 1880s.[34]

The inevitable conclusion follows that the growth performance of tsarist Russia was disappointing, especially so for a relatively backward country seeking through deliberate means (the Witte system) to reduce its per capita income gap. In fact, the per capita income gap, according to the Goldsmith study, increased vis-à-vis Europe throughout the post-emancipation era and even during the "industrialization era." Analysts have laid the blame on agriculture's doorstep, following Gerschenkron's lead, and cite the slow per capita growth and slow pace of structural change as indicators that Russia had failed to experience modern economic growth prior to the revolution.[35] The image of economic failure that emerges rather clearly from the Goldsmith work has lent weight to Soviet claims of success for the plan era.

DATA SOURCES

I estimate Russian real national income primarily by the procedure of deflating current price series on end uses of output with relevent price indexes. Price data were not of sufficient quality to allow experimentation with different price weights as did Bergson in his study of Soviet national income. Instead, only one series that approximates the constant prices of 1913 is compiled. I feel that the lack of alternate price weighted series is not a serious drawback, as I believe that index number relativity is a less significant factor here than in the Soviet case. I shall discuss this matter in detail in the following chapter. In important instances (e.g., farm consumption in kind) physical output series weighted by 1913 prices are used.

The statistical raw material for this study is drawn from a wide variety of sources. I shall describe these sources here without supplying the references as they will be reported in detail in the course of this book. In almost all instances the data are drawn from official tsarist statistical publications, either from primary or secondary sources.

The crucial estimates of retail sales are based upon trade turnover data reported to Finance Ministry authorities by trade establishments. Government expenditure data are taken from the official (and quite detailed) annual budgetary reports of the Finance Ministry. Farm income in kind is calculated from the Agricultural Ministry net farm output series and from rail and water shipments data reported by the Ministry of Transportation.

Net investment in industrial plant is taken from Arcadius Kahan's study of industrial capital structures,[36] which he calculated principally from fire insurance data. Net investment in residential structures is also taken from Kahan with adjustments for later years. Inventory investment is calculated from corporate balance sheet data reported by the Ministry of Finance and adjusted for inventory accumulation of noncorporate enterprises. Net investment in equipment is based upon series of domestic machinery production, principally by L. B. Kafengauz and V. E. Varzar,[37] and of machinery imports, the latter reported in great detail by the tariff department of the Finance Ministry. Net investment in agricultural structures is calculated from information on the compulsory insurance of peasant structures, administered by local government, and net investment in railroad construction and equipment is drawn from the capital expenditure data reported by the Ministry of Transportation. Livestock investment is calculated from the Ministry of the Interior and veterinary department series on livestock herds.

Net foreign investment is calculated from tariff department data on Russia's merchandise balance, from information provided by the

Ministry of the Interior on foreign travel, and from Finance Ministry and banking data on interest and dividend payments to foreigners.

A variety of data sources are used to prepare the relevant price deflators. The major source of price information is the annual *Survey of Commodity Prices* series (*Svod tovarnykh tsen*) published by the Ministry of Trade and Industry. From 1890 on, the *Svod* series gives monthly and annual wholesale price quotations for sixty-eight industrial and agricultural commodities in various regional markets along with freight and insurance rates. M. N. Sobolev[38] has gathered wholesale price quotations for sixty-seven commodities for the period 1850 to 1894 from commodity exchanges, and these can be used to supplement the *Svod* prices. Two retail price indexes are available. The Petersburg Institute for Economic Research compiled retail price indexes for Petersburg for the period 1867 to 1917, and M. P. Kokhna has calculated retail price indexes for both Moscow and Petersburg for the period 1885 to 1914.[39] In both series, weights are based upon surveys of worker expenditures in the two cities.

Wage series are also required for deflation, and I use three sources of wage information in this study. First, the Ministry of Transportation reported in considerable detail the annual wages earned by full-time railroad employees in various occupations, and this is the most reliable information on wages in tsarist Russia. The Ministry of Agriculture supplied serial data on the daily and weekly earnings of hired agricultural labor (broken down by season and category), and wage series of workers in factories subject to factory inspection (compiled by Varzar) provide the third source of wage information.

The most difficult price information to obtain and analyze is that on equipment prices and construction costs. The latter are derived from construction input (materials and labor) prices. Equipment prices are drawn from a variety of sources. The average costs (per ton) of railroad rolling stock were reported by the Ministry of Transportation. Unit prices of selected equipment used in agriculture and industry (ploughs, tractors, locomobiles) can be derived from the import prices and tariffs reported by the tariff department. In most instances unit equipment prices are entirely lacking, and input prices from the *Svod* series are employed.

The deflation of current price investment series raises serious conceptual issues over and above the problem of finding appropriate price quotations. I deal with these conceptual matters in the following chapter.

SECONDARY SOURCES: TSARIST, SOVIET, AND WESTERN

This study of Russian national income owes a considerable debt to the work of a number of scholars, Russian, Soviet, and Western. The estimation of net investment was made possible in large part by the capital stock studies of A. L. Vainshtein, the noted Soviet statistician, and the late Arcadius Kahan, the University of Chicago economic historian.[40] Both rely heavily upon constructing net capital stock series through the adjustment of the insured values of structures and equipment, a painstaking undertaking, as the reader might imagine.

For the estimation of retail sales, my study is indebted to the research efforts of two Soviet scholars, S. G. Strumilin, the venerable Gosplan economist, and G. A. Dikhtiar, for their analyses of the Finance Ministry's trade turnover data. Their contribution is the netting out of non-trade establishments from trade turnover and the segregation of retail from wholesale trade turnover. Strumilin's compilation of corporate balance sheet data from Ministry of Finance publications, many not readily accessible to the Western researcher, also greatly facilitated the estimation of inventory investment.[41]

A further debt of gratitude must be expressed for the research of P. V. Ol', for his studies of Russia's foreign indebtedness, initiated in the 1890s and completed only in the 1920s.[42] Also V. I. Bovykin's and I. F. Gindin's works on net foreign indebtedness are worthy of mention.[43] T. K. Engeev's noted calculation of the Russian balance of payments prepared in 1928 was also a valuable research aid.[44]

My work on the consumption of farm products in kind benefited considerably from the pioneering studies of grain marketings by R. W. Davis, S. G. Wheatcroft, and Jerzy Karcz.[45] Finally, M. E. Falkus's study of 1913 Russian national income proved an invaluable reference source throughout this study. I have benefited from a number of other secondary studies, too numerous to mention at this juncture, that will be noted in the course of this monograph.

Without these studies, many of which date back to the late tsarist era and to the Soviet 1920s, the task of deriving a national

income series would have been too immense for one researcher, working
essentially alone. One advantage of working on the tsarist period is
the relatively high quality of the statistical work undertaken during
the early 1920s, prior to the politicization of the Soviet statistical
apparatus in the late 1920s and 1930s.

RELIABILITY OF THE DATA, MISSING DATA AND IMPUTATIONS
The usefulness of my national income series depends ultimately upon the
reliability of the statistical raw material from which it is constructed and upon its adherence to the basic principles of proper index
number construction. Discussion of this second matter is reserved for
the following chapter, but I note here that certain conceptual com-
promises and approximations are dictated by data considerations. In
the following paragraphs I discuss the relative reliability of the
component series of the national income estimates. As this material
summarizes later more detailed discussions, I do not supply references
at this point.

The statistical raw material is of varying coverage and reliability. I judge the data on final government expenditures to have the
smallest margin of error, although data on local government expenditure
are, by no means, of comparable quality to the imperial budget data.
In any case, I believe that the government expenditure series in prevailing prices is subject to only small margins of error. The deflation of government expenditures is hampered by the lack of wage series
for government employees, but the use of surrogate series (such as for
quasi-administrative personnel of the state railroads) is not likely to
introduce much measurement error.

The major issue concerning the retail sales series is the reliability of the trade turnover data reported by the trade establishments to the tax authorities. The obvious potential flaw in such data
is that enterprises will be tempted to underreport trade volume to
reduce their tax liabilities, but there are offsetting factors as well.
First, in the Russian case, the tax rate on trade turnover was a minus-
cule percentage of profits. Second, there was the offsetting desire of
the tax authorities to collect the tax. Third, if the incidence of
underreporting remained fairly constant, then the tax information would
be serially reliable. I discuss these matters in more detail in my

discussion of the retail sales figures (Appendix A).

The estimation of farm consumption in kind is a difficult undertaking because farm products consumed directly on the farm are calculated as residuals. The value of farm products marketed outside the countryside or used for productive purposes on the farm (for seed and feed) must be subtracted from the value of gross farm output. Errors can enter either through the mismeasurement of gross output or of deductions from gross output. In the Russian case, the official grain output series have been subjected to considerable scrutiny (see Appendix D), and my judgment is that the official series do capture intertemporal trends reasonably well. Debate centers more on the degree of correction in the absolute figures required for the base-year observation. On this point, I have concluded that the correction coefficient is not likely to be larger than 7%.

The necessary deductions from gross grain output cannot be measured with great precision, but I would again doubt that large intertemporal errors are involved in my calculations. The problem of feed grains is eliminated by my dealing only with food grains, leaving only deductions for seed. Net and gross grain outputs were estimated by tsarist statistical authorities, and I see no reason to expect serious serial errors in their figures. Grain marketings outside the village are estimated from rail and water transport data, which I believe to be reliable. The major source of intertemporal error is the omission of grains transported by roads to their final destination. Insofar as road transport likely declined in relative importance throughout this period, I would imagine that its omission yields, if anything, an overestimate of the growth of marketings and hence an underestimate of the growth of peasant in-kind consumption of grains. The main evidence in support of my grain farm consumption estimates is that they appear to be generally consistent with independent estimates based upon export and budgetary data.

Retained food grain products accounted for approximately one-half of all retained farm products, with meat, dairy products, technical crops, and hunting and fishing accounting for the remainder. Marketing data are simply not available for these other products, and I was forced to make the assumption that the retained shares of these products remained constant, for example, that the retained product grew at the same rate as output in each instance. In the case of food grains, the retained portion did indeed remain essentially constant, but there is no assurance that this was also true for other farm products. This assumption is an important one, but I doubt that my final results are much in error as a result because substantial marketing share changes would be required to exert a significant effect on national income.

It is difficult to assess the reliability of the net investment series because its subcomponents are derived from a wide variety of data sources using different methodologies. Net investments in urban housing, rural structures, and industrial plants are calculated by taking first differences in their respective net capital stocks valued in 1913 prices. The urban housing and industrial plant net capital stock series are those of Arcadius Kahan, who describes their derivation only in barest detail. Thus, I cannot assess their reliability independently. The net series on rural structures was derived by the author[46] from the values of peasant structures insured under compulsory insurance programs. My basic assumption is that these insured values are indicative of intertemporal trends in the entire net stock of rural structures, without adjusting for possible changes in insurance coverage. Despite evidence that this compulsory coverage was comprehensive of all peasant structures throughout the period investigated, I cannot rule out the possibility that substantial errors are involved.

The inventory investment figures are, I believe, reliable as applied to the corporate sector of industry and trade, but errors are introduced by the need to impute noncorporate inventory accumulation. For this imputation, I follow the procedures set out by S. G. Strumilin, who imputes noncorporate inventories from the distributions of capital stock (and profits) between the corporate and noncorporate sector. I believe that these imputations introduce only minor errors in the case of industrial establishments because of the predominance of the corporate form, but in the trade sector, corporate establishments accounted for only a minor portion of capital stock and profits. I calculate noncorporate trade capital stock by applying the corporate ratio of profits to capital to noncorporate profits. If profit rates were equal between the corporate and noncorporate trade sectors (and this appears to be a reasonable assumption), the errors introduced by this procedure would be small.

Finally, there is the matter of the reliability of the net equipment investment series. This series is calculated by applying an intertemporal index to Vainshtein's estimates of 1913 net investment in equipment. The intertemporal index is compiled by summing together domestic machinery production and machinery imports, both in prevailing prices. The import data are quite reliable, in my opinion, and account on average for about one-third of the total. The domestic production series are based primarily upon the machinery (metalworking) production series of Varzar and Kafengauz, and some adjustments must be made for semifabricates that enter into the production of final machinery output. This matter is handled by assuming that the ratio of final to "gross" machinery production remained roughly constant and that the gross series is indicative of serial trends in the final machinery series. The reliability of this assumption cannot be tested, but the estimates that emerge are at least broadly consistent with Kahan's series on net equipment stocks.

If the net equipment series is subject to wide margins of error, they are most likely the result of the deflation of the current price series. The problem of deflating equipment expenditures is a serious one, both from its data and conceptual perspectives. I therefore reserve discussion of this issue for the next chapter.

I could discuss the potential measurement errors in the other accounts, but I believe the major issues have already been covered. My own judgment, to be discussed later in this book, is that major systematic errors are not present, except possibly in the case of net investment in equipment, but even here, this category accounts for a small percentage of national income. It would be foolhardy to wager a guess on the margin of error incorporated in the national income series, for this is essentially an insoluble task. As Simon Kuznets writes in reference to his national income estimates for the American economy: "Were we able to ascertain the sign and size of the error for any given estimates, we could, of course, correct for this error, and there would be no need to retain it."[47] The best one can do is to assess the relative reliability of each subcomponent account and form subjective opinions about the relative reliability of one's own series vis-à-vis other historical series. I shall return to this latter issue in Chapter 7.

One important point should be emphasized. In those instances where it was necessary to make assumptions to compensate for the lack of data or to adjust other data, I sought to make "conservative" assumptions, namely, assumptions that, if anything, would understate the rate of growth of the particular account. This point should be emphasized because an important finding of this study is that the growth of Russian national income was higher than that suggested by previous studies. Thus in making my assumptions, I wanted to be sure that this result was not the consequence of arbitrary assumptions.

CONTINUOUS ANNUAL ESTIMATES

In the summary tables I provide annual estimates of Russian national income. As is common in the case of continuous series, the construction of annual observations requires considerable interpolation for missing observations, and one might question their advantages over a series of firmer benchmark observations. In the Russian case, reliance upon widely dispersed benchmarks would involve some risk because of the susceptibility of the industrial sector to international business cycles and, more important, because of the enormous annual fluctuations in agricultural output.[48] Thus, one can never know whether a particular benchmark year is "normal" in some sense. In fact, "normality" is best understood in such an environment in a moving average sense.

An examination of my estimates reveals that the more important national income components are indeed based upon annual data and that the smaller sectors (local government, components of construction, some services, etc.) must be interpolated between benchmarks. The reader should not be lulled into a false sense of security by this fact, for the various annual figures likely conceal a great deal of interpolation in the underlying series, "behind the scenes" so to speak. There is no way for me to know whether a particular series reported by a governmental agency on an annual basis (say, agricultural output, trade volume) is itself the product of interpolation.

Nevertheless, the benefits yielded by the existence of annual series far outweigh the disadvantages introduced by measurement error through interpolation. The major component series, retail sales and grain output, do suggest considerable annual fluctuation and are likely reflective of real annual fluctuations. Because government expenditures appear to be much more stable than these two series, interpolations for government expenditures (primarily at the local level) should not introduce large errors. The major benefit of an annual series is that it allows the researcher to compile averages, which, for agriculture in particular, are more indicative of intertemporal trends than annual or benchmark observations.

ORGANIZATION OF THE REMAINDER OF THE BOOK

The bulk of this manuscript is devoted to explaining my estimates of Russian national income for the period 1885 to 1913. My task is to measure the expansion of the productive capacity of the tsarist economy and to compare this expansion with that of the Soviet plan era. Thus I must adopt as my conceptual frame of reference an "efficiency standard" approach to real national income indexes. Insofar as the measurement of shifts in production possibilities schedules involves a series of analytical and conceptual difficulties, I devote Chapter 2 to a discussion of methodology. In addition to dealing with the problem of index number relativity, I deal as well with the conceptual problems of deflating net investment.

Chapter 3 presents the basic results of this study in the form of two summary tables of Russian national income in 1913 and current prices. These results are compared with other estimates, primarily with those of Goldsmith and Prokopovich.

Chapter 4 describes in general terms the derivation of personal consumption expenditures, final government expenditures, net investment outlays, and net foreign investment. In this chapter only broad outlines of computational procedures and sources are supplied. The actual details of these calculations are contained in the technical appendixes.

In Chapter 5 I attempt to compare the real national income of the Soviet Union on the eve of the first five-year plan with the level prevailing in 1913. Substantial differences between my estimates and the official Soviet estimates are noted. I should emphasize that these findings are tentative. Their reliability must be tested eventually against ongoing research using alternate data and procedures.

Chapter 6 summarizes the economic growth and structural change of the tsarist economy from 1885 to 1913. The frame of reference is provided by Gerschenkron's model of relative backwardness. Moreover, the impact of external forces on the Russian economy is examined. This chapter addresses the issue of the Russian business cycle and its relation to cycles in other countries. The traditional thesis of a strong linkage between the depression of 1900 and the 1905 revolution is investigated and rejected.

In Chapter 7 I contrast the growth of the Russian economy and its structural change with the experiences of the major industrialized countries in the late nineteenth and early twentieth centuries. The principal question being asked is how did Russian economic growth and structural change compare with those countries that had experienced or were experiencing modern economic growth? Is the conventional interpretation of tsarist Russia as the European laggard in terms of growth and structural change an accurate picture? The format is again provided by Gerschenkron's theory of relative backwardness.

Chapter 8 is devoted to a comparison of the real national income of tsarist Russia with that of the Soviet Union during the plan era. Patterns of resource allocation during the tsarist industrialization era are constrasted with the dramatic resource shifts of the 1930s, and an effort is made to link Russian real national income in 1913 with Soviet real national income on the eve of the first five-year plan. In this manner a better understanding of the economic base with which the Soviets embarked upon their industrialization program is gained, and an attempt to assess the success of the Soviet system in accelerating the historical tsarist growth rate is undertaken.

Chapter 9 is devoted to some concluding remarks concerning the major findings and conclusions of this study. The major conclusions are listed in descending order of importance.

NOTES TO CHAPTER 1

1   Alexander Gerschenkron, "The Rate of Growth of Industrial Production in Russia
    Since 1885," *Journal of Economic History*, 7, Supplement (1947); Raymond Gold-
    smith, "The Economic Growth of Tsarist Russia, 1860-1913," *Economic Development
    and Cultural Change* 9, No. 3 (April 1961):441-475.

2   I have discussed the controversy over the causes of Russian backwardness in a
    survey paper: "Russian Industrialization and Economic Growth: Results and
    Perspectives of Western Research," *Jahrbücher für die Geschichte Osteuropas* 2,
    No. 25 (1977):214-17.

3   The traditional Soviet explanation for Russia's relative backwardness is the
    persistence of feudalism in agriculture, a position shared by Alexander
    Gerschenkron in his paper "Agrarian Policies and Industrialization: Russia,
    1861-1917," in *Cambridge Economic History of Europe*, Vol. 6, pt. 2 (Cambridge
    University Press, 1965). The backward transport system is blamed as the cause
    of Russia's backwardness by Alexander Baykov in "The Economic Development of
    Russia," *Economic History Review* 7 (1954):137-49.

4   The Soviet growth record is best adduced from Abram Bergson, *The Real National
    Income of Soviet Russia Since 1928* (Cambridge: Harvard University Press, 1961);
    Simon Kuznets, "A Comparative Appraisal," in Abram Bergson and Simon Kuznets,
    eds., *Economic Trends in the Soviet Union* (Cambridge: Harvard University
    Press, 1963), pp. 333-82; Rush Greenslade, "The Real Gross National Product of
    the USSR, 1950-1975," in Joint Economic Committee, *Soviet Economy in a New
    Perspective* (Washington, D.C.: U.S. Government Printing Office, 1976), p. 271.

5   Paul Gregory and Robert Stuart, *Soviet Economic Structure and Performance* (New
    York: Harper and Row, 1974), chap. 10; Stanley Cohn, "The Soviet Path to
    Economic Growth: A Comparative Analysis," *Review of Income and Wealth* ser. 22,
    No. 1 (March 1976):49-59; Abram Bergson, "Conclusions," *The USSR in the 1980s*
    (Brussels: NATO Directorate of Economic Affairs, 1978), pp. 231-42.

6   See the discussion in chapter 2.

7   Kuznets, "A Comparative Appraisal," p. 334.

8   This position is argued by such diverse scholars as Maurice Dobb, *Soviet
    Economic Development Since 1917* (London: International Publishers, 1948), and
    Bergson, *Real National Income*, pp. 6-7. Soviet statistical publications claim
    that aggregate output in 1928 was 17% higher than in 1913. On this, see the
    discussion in Chapter 5.

9   For an account of the discussion of the capital replacement crisis, see
    Alexander Erlich, *The Soviet Industrialization Debate, 1924-1928* (Cambridge:
    Harvard University Press, 1960).

10 The Gosplan comparisons of 1927-28 with 1913 are cited in M. E. Falkus,
    "Russia's National Income, 1913: A Revaluation," *Economica* 35, No. 137
    (February 1968):60.

11 These figures are from Table 7.1.

12 M. E. Falkus, *The Industrialization of Russia, 1700-1914* (London and
    Basingstoke: Macmillan, 1972), p. 12.

13 Paul Gregory, "Economic Growth and Structural Change in Tsarist Russia: A Case

of Modern Economic Growth?" *Soviet Studies* 23, No. 3 (January 1972):423.

14   Gerschenkron, "Agrarian Policies" and "The Early Phases of Industrialization of Russia: Afterthoughts and Counterthoughts," W. W. Rostow, ed., *The Economics of Takeoff into Sustained Growth* (New York: St. Martin's, 1963).

15   Paul Gregory, "1913 Russian National Income: Some Insights into Russian Economic Development," *Quarterly Journal of Economics* 90, No. 3 (August 1976):452-3; Paul Gregory, "Grain Marketing and Peasant Consumption, Russia, 1885-1913," *Explorations in Economic History* 17, No. 2 (March 1979):135-164.

16   For a discussion of the Petrine era, see Falkus, *The Industrialization of Russia*, Chap. 2. There are no estimates of per capita income during the reign of Peter the Great. As a rough indicator of the absence of significant disparities between Russia and Europe, one might note that per capita iron output in Russia was not notably different from French and English levels. On this see S. G. Strumilin, *Ocherki ekonomicheskoi istorii Rossii i SSSR* (Moscow: Nauka, 1966), pp. 315-25.

17   Gregory, "Economic Growth and Structural Change," p. 423.

18   Arcadius Kahan, "Continuity in Economic Activity and Policy During the Post-Petrine Period in Russia," *Journal of Economic History* 23, No. 4 (December 1967):460-77.

19   Alexander Gerschenkron, *Economic Backwardness in Historical Perspective* (Cambridge: Harvard University Press, 1962), essay 1.

20   V. I. Lenin, *The Development of Capitalism in Russia* (Moscow: Foreign Languages Publishing House, 1956).

21   Theodore H. von Laue, "A Secret Memorandum of Sergei Witte on the Industrialization of Imperial Russia," *Journal of Modern History* 26, No. 1 (March 1954).

22   For a survey of the controversy over the workings of the Witte system, see Gregory, "Russian Industrialization and Economic Growth," pp. 206-14.

23   The burden on the agricultural population has been stressed in the writings of Gerschenkron, "Agrarian Policies." The loss of potential output resulting from restrictive monetary policy has been emphasized by Haim Barkai in "The Macro-Economics of Tsarist Russia in the Industrialization Era: Monetary Developments, the Balance of Payments and the Gold Standard," *Journal of Economic History* 33 (June 1973):339-71 and by Arcadius Kahan, "Government Policies and the Industrialization of Russia," *Journal of Economic History* 27, No. 4 (December 1967):460-77. The Barkai and Kahan positions are challenged in Paul Gregory and Joel Sailors, "Russian Monetary Policy and Industrialization, 1861-1913," *Journal of Economic History* 36 (December 1976):836-51.

24   Von Laue, "Secret Memorandum of Sergei Witte."

25   Dietrich Geyer, *Der russische Imperialismus* (Göttingen: Vandenhoeck and Ruprecht, 1977).

26   Arcadius Kahan, e.g., expresses skepticism over the possibility of ever deriving reliable estimates of Russian national income. On this, see Kahan, "Capital Formation During the Period of Early Industrialization in Russia, 1890-1913," *Cambridge Economic History of Europe*, vol. 7, pt. 2 (Cambridge University Press, 1978), pp. 265-95. Falkus is equally pessimistic in his

Industrialization of Russia, pp. 15-16.

27 S. N. Prokopovich, *Opyt ischisleniia narodnogo dokhoda 50 gubernii Evropeiskoi Rossii v 1900-1913 gg.* (Moscow: Sovet Vserossiskikh Kooperativnykh Sezdov, 1918). Prokopovich's "Birmingham Memorandum" results are cited by Falkus in "Russia's National Income, 1913."

28 M. G. Mulhall, *Dictionary of Statistics*, various editions, 1884-99.

29 A. L. Vainshtein, "Ischisleniia i otsenka narodnogo dokhoda Rossii v do-revoliutsionnoe vremia," Akademiia nauk, vol. 7, *Ocherki po istorii statistiki SSSR,* (Moscow: Gosstatizdat, 1961), pp. 60-93.

30 Falkus, "Russia's National Income."

31 Gregory, "Russian National Income in 1913."

32 Goldsmith, "Rate of Growth in Tsarist Russia."

33 Goldsmith concludes (p. 443) that the growth of real per capita income in Russia from 1860 to 1913 "was close to the European average" but considerably below the rates of the United States, Germany and Japan. I believe Goldsmith to be in error on this point. I cite data in Chapter 7 from Simon Kuznets, published after Goldsmith's study, that show the Russian per capita growth rate calculated by Goldsmith to be well below the European average.

34 Jürgen Nötzold, *Wirtschaftspolitische Alternativen der Entwicklung Russlands in der Ära Witte und Stolypin* (Berlin: Duncker and Humblot, 1965), Chap. 7; Olga Crisp, *Studies in the Russian Economy Before 1914* (London and Basingstoke: Macmillan, 1976), Chap. 1; Gregory, "Economic Growth and Structural Change."

35 Kahan, "Capital Formation During the Period of Early Industrialization," statistical appendix, pp. 296-307.

36 The Varzar-Kafengauz indexes are cited in Strumilin, *Ocherki*, pp. 442-53.

37 M. N. Sobolev, *Tamozhennaia politika Rossii vo vtoroi polovine XIX veka* (Tomsk: Tipografiia sibirskoe toverichestvo pechatnago dela, 1911), statistical appendix.

38 The Petersburg and Kokhna price indexes are reported and discussed in Strumilin, *Ocherki*, pp. 88-91.

39 A. L. Vainshtein, *Narodnoe bogatstvo i narodnokhoziaistvennoe nakoplenie pre-drevoliutsionnoi Rossi* (Moscow: Gosstatizdat, 1960); Kahan, "Capital Formation During the Period of Early Industrialization."

40 S. G. Strumilin, *Statistika i ekonomika* (Moscow: Nauka, 1963), pp. 433-79; G. A. Dikhtiar, *Vnutrenniai torgovlia v dorevoliutsionnoi Rossi* (Moscow: Nauka, 1960).

41 Strumilin, *Statistika i ekonomika* pp. 325-46, 433-44.

42 P. V. Ol', *Inostrannye kapitaly v narodnom khoziaistve dovoennoi Rossii, Materialy dlia izucheniia estestvennykh proizvoditel'nykh sil SSSR*, no. 53 Leningrad: N. P. 1925.

43 V. I. Bovykin, "K voprosu o roli innostranogo kapitala v Rossii," *Vestnik Moskovskogo Universiteta*, no. 1 (1964); I. F. Gindin, *Russkie kommercheskie banki* (Moscow: Gosfinizdat, 1948).

44 T. K. Engeev, "O platezhnom balanse dovoennoi Rossii," *Vestnik finansov*, no. 5 (1928).

45   R. W. Davies, "A Note on Grain Statistics," *Soviet Studies* 21, no. 3 (January
      1970):314-330; S. G. Wheatcroft, "The Reliability of Russian Prewar Grain
      Output Statistics," *Soviet Studies* 36, no. 2 (April 1974):157-80; Jerzy Karcz,
      "Back on the Grain Front," *Soviet Studies* 22, no. 2 (October 1970):262-94.

46   With the assistance of Anna Kuniansky.

47   Simon Kuznets, *National Income and Its Composition, 1919-1938* (New York:
      National Bureau of Economic Research, 1954), p. 535.

48   The major study of the Russian business cycle prior to World War I is A. A.
      Mendel'son, *Teoriia i istorii ekonomicheskikh krizisov i tsiklov*, 3 vols.
      (Moscow: Sotseklit, 1959).

CHAPTER 2

PROBLEMS OF MEASUREMENT OF REAL NATIONAL INCOME: TSARIST RUSSIA

The sensitivity of Soviet real national income measurements to "index number relativity" requires that we devote more attention to methodology than is usual in a study of historical national income.   Index number relativity, or the "Gerschenkron effect," denotes the statistical phenomenon whereby more rapid national income growth rates are obtained when early year valuation weights are used.[1]   This effect is explained by the inverse correlation between the growth rates of outputs and relative prices normally observed as an economy experiences economic development. Typically, remote historical series are constructed from crude data using prices and other value weights that, at best, approximate the underlying theoretical standard.   They are, with few exceptions, calculated in "late year" prices;[2] that is, in prices prevailing after the industrial transformation of the country has taken place.   Alternate "early year" series cannot be compiled because of the lack of data, and even when alternate series are calculated, the statistical raw material is so insensitive that anticipated results may not obtain.[3]

Moreover, there is evidence that index number relativity has a less significant impact on the national income measures of the industrialized capitalist countries, at least during the time span that can be conceivably reconstructed from the historical record.[4]   Such countries simply have not had the cataclysmic structural transformations experienced in the Soviet Union during the early five-year plans.[5] Thus national income measures spanning even a long time period will not be as seriously confounded by index number problems as in the Soviet case.

My interest, however, focuses upon national income comparisons with the Soviet era, and, as the Soviet period figures are markedly affected by the choice of weights used to aggregate outputs, the effects of different weighting schemes upon tsarist national income must be considered. Only in this manner can relevant comparisons with the Soviet period be undertaken.

The following discussion of methodology is divided into three parts. The first deals with the mechanical issues of calculating index numbers of real national income from historical data. The second part is devoted to a discussion of the pricing of capital. In the final section, the deeper issues of the methodology of measuring changes in production potential within and between the tsarist and Soviet eras are addressed.

Much of this material is well established in the literature, but it bears a brief repetition in this context. I shall forgo discussion of the concept of national income - matters of grossness and netness, marketed versus nonmarketed goods, Marxist and Western concepts, and soon - for this territory has been covered adequately in the past literature.[6] For now, I should note that I employ the Western concept of national income and reject the Marxist-Soviet "material production" scheme. The material production concept will be discussed later in this book when I evaluate different estimates of tsarist national income based upon the material production concept.

INDEX NUMBERS: PROBLEMS OF DEFLATING HISTORICAL SERIES

National income is comprised of the totality of final goods and services produced by the economy during a designated time interval. Non-market production (typically within the household) is normally excluded from measured national income with the important exceptions of farm consumption in kind and rental services of owner-occupied dwellings. In compiling national income indexes, final outputs must be valued in terms of prices prevailing at particular points in time. If only two periods of observation are considered, designated as periods 0 and 1, then four aggregations can be calculated:

(1) $\Sigma\ P_0 Q_0$

(2) $\Sigma\ P_1 Q_1$

(3) $\Sigma\ P_0 Q_1$

(4) $\Sigma\ P_1 Q_0$

The first two represent the final outputs in period 0 and 1
valued in the prices prevailing in each period. These aggregations are
called national income in "current prices." The last two aggregations
represent the final outputs of one period valued in the prices of the
other period. Formula 3 represents the late period (1) outputs valued
in the early year (0) prices, and formula 4 measures the early period
outputs valued in late year prices. I will refer to formula 3 as
national income in "early prices" and to formula 4 as national income
in "late prices."

If the underlying prices conform to the efficiency standard by
reflecting the marginal rates of transformation among outputs (the
rates at which one final product can be technically transformed into
the other at the margin by a reallocation of resources),[7] then the
various indexes can be interpreted as follows: Insofar as prevailing
prices reflect the marginal opportunity costs of transforming each
final product into a designated numeraire commodity, national income in
current prices translates the individual final products into specific
quantities of "numeraire units." Real national income in "early" and
"late" prices is subject to a similar interpretation. National income
in early prices represents a translation of the final products produced
in period 1 into numeraire units using the marginal transformation
rates prevailing in period 0. National income in late prices translates the final outputs produced in period 0 into numeraire units using
the marginal transformation rates prevailing in period 1.

The growth of real national income is typically calculated by
combining formulas 1-4. Biases are introduced by the use of constant
transformation rates in formulas 3 and 4 that fail to reflect changing
marginal rates of transformation as different output mixes are produced. These biases will be the subject of discussion at the end of
this chapter. For now, we turn to the alternate growth measures that
emerge from formulas 1-4.

Two real growth variants are commonly calculated in national
income analysis. They are the early year price formula, or the
well-known "Laspeyres formula," denoted as λ:

$$(5) \quad \lambda = \frac{\Sigma P_0 Q_1}{\Sigma P_0 Q_0}$$

and the late year price formula, or the well-known "Paasche formula," denoted as π:

$$(6) \quad \pi = \frac{\Sigma \ P_1 Q_1}{\Sigma \ P_1 Q_0}$$

The λ index measures the increased ability of the economy in period 1 to produce period 0's output mix, transforming period 1 outputs into numeraire units at the transformation rates prevailing in period 0. A λ index of "2," for example, would indicate that in period 1 the economy has the productive capacity to produce twice the amount of each commodity produced in period 0, *assuming* it can transform its output mix at the fixed transformation rates of period 0. The π index measures the (typically reduced) ability of the economy to produce the period 1 output mix in period 0. This is true because the final outputs of period 0 are translated into numeraire units using marginal transformation rates prevailing in period 1. Both formulas are subject to potentially substantial biases because they assume the output mix of one period can be transformed into the other period's output mix at *constant rates*. Insofar as transformation rates will vary as an economy moves along its production possibilities frontier, both λ and π will fail to measure the "true" shift in productive capacity.[8]

With rare exceptions, the π formula has been used to calculate remote historical national income series. Late year price weights are applied to physical production series,[9] and these aggregated series are assumed to be representative of missing series for which price and output data are not available. The λ formula is more difficult to apply to historical series because less information is available concerning prices or value added in early years. In any case, π or λ indexes, calculated by aggregating production indexes, are direct applications of the respective late and early year formulas.

In this work I calculate national income by final expenditure category. In theory, late or early year price weights could be applied to relevant physical series of final outputs (consumption, investment, services), but in practice the major components of final expenditures (retail sales, investment, government services) can only be calculated by deflating component series in prevailing prices by relevant price deflators.

Insofar as the component end-use series are themselves comprised of a variety of products, individual prices must be aggregated into component price indexes by weighting them with relevant quantities. In a two-period model, two options exist:

$$(7) \quad \lambda_p = \frac{\Sigma \ P_1 Q_0}{\Sigma \ P_0 Q_0}$$

$$(8) \quad \pi_p = \frac{\Sigma \ P_1 Q_1}{\Sigma \ P_0 Q_1}$$

The λ_p index is the price index equivalent to λ only with early year quantities serving as weights; the π_p index is equivalent to π only with late year quantities serving as weights.

If three or more periods are observed, a third "variable weight" price index can be constructed according to the formula:

$$(9) \quad P = \frac{\Sigma \ P_i Q_i}{\Sigma \ P_o Q_i}$$

where the o refers to the year designated as the base year (be it an early, middle, or late year) and the i refers to the given year.

The variable weight price index is difficult to assemble as different quantity weights must be calculated for each year observed; yet it is the only deflator that will yield λ or π for each year:

$$(10) \quad \frac{\dfrac{\Sigma \ P_i Q_i}{\Sigma \ P_o Q_o}}{P} = \frac{\Sigma \ P_o Q_i}{\Sigma \ P_o Q_o} \qquad \begin{array}{l} \lambda, \text{ when } o = 0 \\ \Pi, \text{ when } o = 1 \end{array}$$

If component series in current prices are deflated by either λ_p of π_p, one obtains:

$$(11) \quad \frac{\dfrac{\Sigma \ P_i Q_i}{\Sigma \ P_0 Q_0}}{\lambda_p} = \frac{\Sigma \ P_i Q_i}{\Sigma \ P_i Q_0}$$

or:

$$(12) \quad \frac{\dfrac{\Sigma\, P_i Q_i}{\Sigma\, P_1 Q_1}}{\pi_p} = \frac{\Sigma\, P_i Q_i}{\Sigma\, P_i Q_1}$$

Thus, deflation by either λ_p or π_p yields a quantity index weighted by prices of the given year, and this growth index is difficult to evaluate because of the changing price weights.

One peculiarity of formulas 11 and 12 is that if i equals 1, then deflation by λ_p yields π; if i equals 0, then deflation by π_p yields $1/\lambda$. Even if one does not have the preferred variable weight price index p, one can still calculate π and λ for the early and late year observations.

This appears to be an obscure technical characteristic,[10] but it is essential to interpreting my results. Some price deflators used in this study are (or approximate) fixed weight series of the π_p variety; the calculation of the more appropriate p index is beyond the capacity of the already limited data base on quantity weights. The relative values yielded by deflation for the early years of the study may approximate the λ index. The intermediate year values defy simple interpretation as they involve changing current year price weights. However, the λ and π indexes for the Soviet period are calculated using the appropriate p index.[11]

Given these complications, it is relevant to consider under what conditions deflation by π_p would yield a consistent set of national income indexes of either the λ or π variety. If the proportions of the quantity weights remain stable between 0 and 1, then $\lambda_p = \pi_p = p$, and deflation would yield identical λ and π indexes. If all prices move together proportionally between 0 and 1, then the choice of quantity weights is irrelevant and $\lambda_p = \pi_p = p$, and $\lambda = \pi$. Third, if the final use categories are finely broken down into current price series, individually deflated by appropriate π_p indexes, and then reaggregated using late year value weights, the result should approximate the π index.[12] If *within* individually disaggregated-use categories, prices move proportionally or relative quantity weights are stable, then the π index is again approximated.

Is it realistic to assume that one of these four conditions will be realized in this study? The third condition is not likely to hold. Retail sales are deflated by a single price index of the π_p variety. Investment is broken down into component series, yet the categories are quite broad (machinery, residential construction, inventories, railroad equipment). Nevertheless, the aggregated investment series does fulfill some aspects of the third condition. The first and second conditions, however, appear to be approximated in the case of retail sales, where notable changes in relative prices are not evident,[13] and family budget data suggest a relatively invariant market basket for worker and peasant families.[14] The first condition should hold reasonably well in the case of final government expenditures, insofar as they are typically deflated by indexes of input prices and input proportions, most likely, did not change substantially. The major question mark is the deflation of investment, for it is in the investment area that significant changes in relative prices and relative quantities are anticipated. I reserve discussion of this point for the next section.

Several important national income components (retained farm products, livestock investment, many services) are calculated by applying late year prices to physical series. In fact, component series calculated in this manner account for approximately one-half of late year national income.

Putting aside for the moment the matter of deflation of investment, what is the appropriate interpretation of the real national income series calculated in this study? Obviously, the series represents a mixture of late and early price weights. The various aggregated physical series (about 50% of 1913 national income) are in late year prices; some deflated series should be in early prices, but it is likely that deflated retail sales and government expenditures are not significantly affected by the choice of price weights anyway. For this reason, I believe that the resulting series approximates the π growth index, although it should be emphasized that this is a subjective judgment.

THE PRICING OF CAPITAL GOODS

In this study, net investments in plant, equipment, inventories, transportation equipment and transportation construction, and residential construction are calculated by deflating expenditure series expressed

in current prices. The current price series are drawn from machinery
production series and machinery imports, corporate book value data,
insured values of residential and farm structures, and other sources,
and these values should approximate the prevailing market values of the
capital assets.[15]

The fundamental issue that must be addressed is the type of price
index that is to be employed to translate investment series in current
prices into constant prices. This issue is of great theoretical importance, "for the very nature of capital is at stake,"[16] and it is complicated by the large number and technical variety of capital goods
that must be considered.

There are two basic approaches to the measurement of changes in
the real capital stock: The first is to measure the change in the
capacity of the stock to produce output; the second is to measure
changes in the stock in terms of the resources embodied in the stock.[17]
The second measure can be expressed either in terms of the actual
inputs (valued in constant prices) used to produce the capital goods or
in terms of the inputs (valued in constant prices) required to produce
the capital goods, using the technology of a base year.

The first concept, although a theoretically valid approach to
capital measurement, is difficult to implement empirically because
quality adjusted price deflators are required. It will not be used in
this study, although there may be a tendency for some of the constant
price investment series to tend toward this concept.[18] Rather, the
constant price investment series aim toward the factor input concept.

Input price biases
To illustrate the input approach, we begin with real capital goods
produced in periods 0 and 1, (I_0, I_1), and selling at market prices P_0
and P_1. Only the current price investment outlays ($\Sigma P_0 I_0$ and $\Sigma P_1 P_1$)
are observed in the two periods, and we must estimate "real" investment
outlays from this information. If the vectors P_0 and P_1 were known,
current price investment outlays could be deflated using the formulas
discussed earlier. However, capital goods are, by nature, heterogene-
ous, possessing differing technical characteristics, and it is
difficult to establish price series for individual capital goods of
constant quality.[19] This is particularly true of capital price series

that extend over a long remote historical period. More typically, the
prices of the inputs used to produce the capital goods are known along
with their cost shares. To simplify further, we assume that the
"quality" of the capital goods produced in 0 and 1 remains constant,
that is, that no embodied technical change has occurred between 0
and 1.

The capital goods prices, P_0 and P_1, will equal:

$$(13) \quad P_i = \Sigma \, a_i w_i \qquad i = 0,1$$

where the a's refer to the input of each factor required to produce one
unit of real capital in period i and the w's denote the factor prices
in each period.

From 13, it is apparent that real investment in the two periods
can be calculated in one of three ways:

$$(14) \quad I_1 = \frac{\Sigma \, P_1 I_1}{\Sigma\Sigma \, a_0 w_1}$$

$$(15) \quad I_0 = \frac{\Sigma \, P_0 I_0}{\Sigma\Sigma \, a_1 w_0}$$

$$(16) \quad I_i = \frac{\Sigma \, P_i I_i}{\Sigma\Sigma \, a_i w_i} \qquad i = 0,1$$

Formula 14 measures real investment in period 1 assuming that the
inputs were combined according to the production technology of period
0. Insofar as the productivities of factor inputs likely have
increased between 0 and 1 (the $a_1 < a_0$), this formula would tend to bias
the measure of period 1 real investment *downward*. Formula 15 measures
real investment in period 0 assuming the technology of period 1 is used
in its production. For reasons similar to those noted immediately
above, this measure would *overstate* real investment in period 0.
Formula 16 measures real investment in the given year using the given
year technology and thus avoids the biases introduced by productivity
improvements between 0 and 1.

In sum, if current investment expenditures are deflated using an index of input prices aggregated using the production technology of another period, the growth of the volume of actual inputs used to produce the capital goods will be understated if productivity advances have occurred *within* the capital goods producing sector.[20]

Quality problems

The discussion to this point has assumed that capital goods of successive "vintages" are of constant "quality." This assumption is unrealistic, especially when a long time span is being considered and improved technology is being embodied in newer capital goods.[21] As successive vintages of capital goods are produced, the market values of capital goods of previous vintages will decline relatively and will fall short of the relative value of factor resources required to produce the earlier vintage with the given year technology.

Therefore, if a price deflator is employed that captures the impact of quality improvements upon early vintages, a smaller price increase will be registered, and the deflated real value index will be larger than if input price indexes are used. The real investment index will thus incorporate the technological advance embodied in the newer vintage capital goods. Price indexes constructed from serial market price observations on homogeneous capital goods will likely reflect the impact of embodied technological progress on capital goods prices. If, however, under conditions of quality improvement, a factor cost deflator (the cost of producing capital with the given year technology) is used, then embodied technological improvements will be netted out of the real investment series, for quality changes will be captured only if they impact on the quantities of resources embodied in the capital goods.

The capital goods price deflators employed in this study largely do not reflect quality improvements. Although there is some controversy about the handling of quality improvements,[22] this particular approach to capital pricing is justified on the grounds that price changes should be reflected in such a manner "that a new unit of a given type of plant and equipment is accorded the same base year value, or weight, in all periods. Changes in the productive efficiency of new models . . . are not reflected in real value of the item (unless more resources are used). This is desirable from the viewpoint of productivity analysis, for increased efficiency should show up in the output-input ratio."[23]

The point of this discussion is that the appropriate measurement of capital goods price deflators and hence of real investment expenditures represents a substantive gray area of national income analysis.[24] There are two reasons for this: The first is that the amount of data required to make quality adjustments either for the vintage problem or for changing technical characteristics is enormous, even for modern economies with well-developed statistical apparatuses; the second reason is that there is little agreement on the theoretical principles of quality adjustment of capital goods prices. One can imagine the extent to which these problems are compounded when applied to historical investment series, where substantial quality changes can be expected and where the statistical raw material is strictly limited.

This technical discussion of alternate measures of real investment is important to understanding the investment series reported in this study in terms of its comparability with other historical series, most notably those of the Soviet Union. The standard adopted here is that capital goods should be measured in terms of the real factor inputs used to produce them with the technology of the *given year*. In other words, productivity improvements *within* the capital goods producing sector should be reflected in the capital goods price deflators but quality improvements should not.

This study, like most studies of historical and even contemporary real investment series,[25] is hampered by the paucity of data on capital goods prices, although the amount of information on prices is about average relative to the other major European countries.[26] Two types of price information can be utilized. The first is data on the unit prices of specific capital goods, such as railroad rolling stock, steam engines, locomobiles, and farm hand tools. In the case of these prices, it is difficult to establish to what degree the average prices reflect quality changes, the changing product mix, or more general factors. The second type of price information is data on the prices of the major inputs into the capital goods industry, that is, wages in heavy industry and construction, prices of metals and steel rails and of construction materials.

Let us consider the implications of using unit price observations, on the one hand, and input price observations, on the other, in light of the above discussion. In the case of unit prices, one must deal with two problems. The first is that the product mix (say the mix of steam locomotives or of steam engines) is changing in an unobserved manner, and one does not know whether the relative change is in the direction of lower or higher priced items. One would think that the tendency would be toward an increasing weight of higher priced (quality) items, but this is not necessarily the case.[27] The second problem is the vintage problem: Insofar as one is observing market prices (assuming a constant product mix), the impact of embodied technological progress on older vintage (traditional?) capital goods would be to depress their relative market prices. There is very little chance of sorting out these divergent effects, especially in historical data.

If one uses input prices to construct the capital goods price deflator, the calculated price index will diverge from the desired formula when productivity improvements within the capital goods industries occur. If productivity improvements are substantial for inputs that have a large weight in the index, then the calculated price index will overstate the "true" growth of capital goods prices. If, on the other hand, input-output ratios remain fairly stable for important factor inputs, the divergence between the estimated and the desired price deflators would be small. If the rate of productivity change for each factor were known, then downward corrections could be made in the fixed weighted index, but one must know real investment (the desired end product) in order to make such adjustments.

Capital goods and tsarist and Soviet period comparisons
Like most historical studies of capital goods prices, this work combines fixed weighted indexes of input prices (wage indexes in the capital goods sectors, metals, building materials) with the more sparse information on the unit prices of specific capital goods. The latter prices are problematic because they must be assumed to be representative of omitted categories of capital goods and, more important, because they are average prices of nonhomogeneous models of capital equipment (steam engines, for example). Such prices are confounded by both vintage-quality and assortment problems, so that one cannot inter-

pret them directly.[28] It is my judgment that the capital goods price
deflators used in this study for fixed capital investment (construction
and equipment) will *overstate* the rate of increase in capital goods
prices because of the predominant use of input prices. Insofar as the
biases present in this study also afflict most other real investment
series calculated for the nineteenth century, my results should not be
"biased" relative to the other historical series. The major issue is
the degree to which these real investment estimates (and by implication
the historical series of other industrialized countries) are "biased"
relative to the corresponding figures for the Soviet period.

If a "bias" exists, it would be concentrated in the fixed investment figures. The Soviet period machinery estimates are calculated by
deflating current price machinery investment by a price index compiled
from actual price observations of standardized machinery types.[29]
Also, the individual price series are aggregated using the desired
variable weight (formula 9) method. Thus, the Soviet period machinery
figures should approximate the desired method of deflation (e.g.,
productivity improvements within the capital goods sector will be
reflected in the capital goods price deflator). Moreover, the problem
of adjusting for quality changes is likely not as serious in the Soviet
period case (at least for the critical early years of centralized
planning) because of the industrialization strategy of mass producing
standardized models over protracted periods.[30]

Between 1928 and 1940 enormous changes in the relative prices of
Soviet machinery types have been noted. The prices of "modern" goods
entering into mass production after 1928 experienced substantial declines relative to those of "traditional" equipment accorded low
priority by the first five-year plans. This phenomenon was first observed by Alexander Gerschenkron and then confirmed in the voluminous
study of Richard Moorsteen,[31] and it is a major factor in the substantial discrepancy between the growth rates of Soviet real national
income in "early" and "late" year prices.[32]

Size of capital goods bias

If Soviet period equipment investment had been estimated according to
the same procedures employed in this study, what results would have
emerged? Fortunately, the data required for such a calculation are

supplied by Moorsteen,[33] who calculates machinery input prices for the purpose of estimating "real" machinery costs. From this information, I can calculate an alternate Soviet real machinery output series using virtually the same procedures as those applied to the tsarist period.

The annual growth rate of new investment in domestically produced machinery (1928-37) was 28% in 1937 prices, 38% in 1928 prices, and 22% if deflated with an index of machinery input prices.[34] This finding illustrates the possible magnitude of understatement of investment growth introduced by the use of input price deflators under conditions of rapid productivity advances within the capital goods sector. In the Soviet case, the input price deflator yields a rate of growth less than 60% of the 1928 figure, but it yields a result much closer to the 1937 "late" year weighted index. The explanation for this latter result is that the major productivity improvements within the machinery sector took place between 1928 and 1937,[35] although real cost reductions continued after 1937, albeit at a slower annual rate.

Like most historical series, this study computes real investment in construction by deflating construction outlays using a material input price deflator. Construction wages enter the deflator with a weight equal to labor's share of construction costs. The Soviet period series, on the other hand, is based upon Raymond Powell's index of physical material inputs (excluding labor) into construction (cited by Bergson, 1961, p. 80).

There is no solid evidence supporting one calculation method over the other, although Bergson argues that the relation of material inputs to the volume of output in construction should not be highly volatile. The fact is, however, that different calculation procedures were used, and one must ask whether this imparts a "bias" to the tsarist period figures.

Fortunately, Powell has prepared an alternate real construction series. This alternate index is calculated by deflating construction outlays by prices of material and labor inputs and is thus conceptually identical to the tsarist period series. According to Powell's calculations the use of the materials input index (in 1937 prices) *raises* the annual growth rate of construction by approximately 25% above that yielded by the deflation method (1928-40). Thus, the adjustment coefficient suggested for construction is similar to that for equipment.

Implications for tsarist-Soviet period comparison

What implications should be drawn from such recalculations? The *first* is that if Soviet period investment had been calculated according to the procedures applied to most historical studies of nineteenth-century national income, investment growth would have been less rapid, especially so if early prices are used. The second question is the most significant; namely, if it had been possible to recalculate tsarist (or German, French, or English) fixed investment using the same procedures applied to the Soviet period calculations, would markedly different results have emerged? An answer to this question cannot be supplied because it depends upon the reduction of real costs within the capital goods sector. In the Soviet case, the rate of reduction was extremely rapid between 1928 and 1940; thus, the large discrepancy between the two methods. One cannot establish whether real cost reductions of this magnitude were experienced by other countries at a similar stage of development, but my subjective opinion is that real cost reductions were less dramatic (but still substantial) because of the lesser emphasis on capital goods and the lesser increase in mass production of standardized product models.

The upper limit adjustment required to bring Soviet period and tsarist period fixed investment estimates into line with each other is that suggested by the 1937 weighted figures. The use of input prices to deflate equipment and construction causes a reduction in the annual growth rate (1928-1940) by a factor of approximately .8; thus a 25% increase in the estimated tsarist period growth rate of fixed investment is implied. This, I emphasize, is an upper limit adjustment. In the next chapter I will attempt to correct downward biases in the tsarist period real investment series using this adjustment coefficient.

These comparisons also support the use of "late" year price weights for the Soviet period estimates in comparisons with the tsarist and other historical series because the Soviet late year figures appear to approximate better the factor input standard used for other countries.

One final point deserves emphasis: the unlikelihood of detecting significant index number relativity effects in remote historical investment series. The reliance on capital goods input price deflators and on generalized unit prices, where the mix of goods is changing, more or less rules out significant relative price changes within the capital goods industry. This fact is confirmed by examining the available historical series and comparing early investment proportions in late year and in current prices.[36] Such effects apparently can be picked up by applying early and late year price weights to physical production series of machinery (at least for the United States),[37] but here one must question the use of physical output series that are almost impossible to standardize.[38] Nevertheless, the point remains valid that the fixed investment series that enter into the historical national income series of the industrialized countries are derived primarily by deflation using the procedures applied in this work. Moorsteen may be correct in noting that the process of dramatic relative price changes may indeed be confined to a limited period in a nation's economic history.[39] If so, the analyst must possess the appropriate statistical data to detect these effects. If the episode occurred prior to the development of a fine-tuned statistical apparatus, then the chance of detecting it appears to be small.

RELATIVE PRICES AND TSARIST-SOVIET PERIOD COMPARISONS

The conceptual problems of estimating the increase in the production potential of an economy experiencing dramatic change in the structure of output have been discussed exhaustively elsewhere,[40] and I need only apply standard results to the problem at hand. The basic results of this literature are that index numbers of real national income in "early" prices will yield a higher rate of growth than index numbers in "late" year prices if changes in relative prices and relative quantities are inversely correlated. This result is well known to observers of national income. If the production possibilities schedules are nonlinear (marginal rates of transformation, or MRTs, decline as the product mix changes), the early year index will overstate the "true" increase in the production possibilities frontier, whereas the late year index will understate the "true" increase. These results apply when early and late year output mixes are employed respectively to measure composite commodity output in fixed prices, and the degree of bias can be reduced in each case by employing the composite commodity of the other period. These results are standard and do not require further explanation in this text.

In this study I am interested primarily in measuring the rate of change in production potential during four periods: 1885-1913, to capture the expansion of production possibilities during the late tsarist era; 1913-28, to capture the expansion (or perhaps contraction) of production possibilities during the "transitional" period from World War I to the first five-year plan; 1928-40, to measure the expansion of productive potential during the early five-year-plan era; finally, 1928 to the present, to capture the long-term growth of productive potential during the era of Soviet central planning.

To illustrate the conceptual procedures involved in making such measurements, I present (Fig. 2.1) a stylized version in two dimensions of real national income index number measurements during three of the periods under consideration. Following standard procedures, I depict the economy as producing two generalized commodities - a consumption good C and an investment good I. At the various points in time, the actual physical outputs of C and I can be observed, and illustrative output combinations for four benchmark years (1885, 1913, 1928, and 1937) are given in Figure 2.1. I draw these points according to a stylized version of Soviet economic history to show that in 1913 more of both C and I were produced than in 1885 (an unambiguous increase in production potential); that more I but less C was produced in 1928 than in 1913; and that more of both I and C were produced in 1937 than in both 1913 and 1928, although the relative increase was greater for I. According to the results reported below, this picture is roughly illustrative of Soviet economic reality.

To measure the expansion of productive potential between any two points in time, one set of relative prices must be applied to the two observed output combinations. Throughout, we assume that the relative prices observed for each benchmark year will correspond to the marginal rates of transformation of one product into another through a reallocation of available resources. Thus I assume that prices conform to the "efficiency standard" and that the economy is on its production possibilities frontier.

Let us now take inventory of the price information at our disposal for valuing the output of one year in the prices of another year. I have sufficient information on 1913 prices to value the outputs of

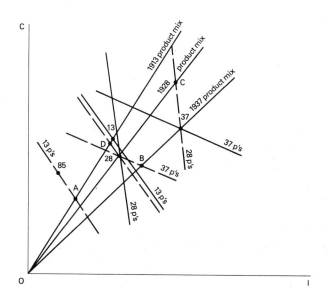

2.1 *Alternate indexes of real national income, tsarist and Soviet period prices*

both 1885 and 1928 in the prices of 1913. We have sufficient information (from Bergson) to value 1937 output in 1928 prices and 1928 output
in 1937 prices but not enough information to value 1913 output either
in 1928 or in 1937 prices.

There is firm empirical support for the proposition that the
relative price of *I* in 1937 was much lower than in 1928,[41] and I assume
for now that the shift in the output mix between 1913 and 1928 in favor
of *I* (under conditions of a declining MRT of *C* into *I*) caused an increase in the relative price of *I* between 1913 and 1928. The relationship between 1913 and 1937 relative prices is not known a priori, but I
assume for now a lower relative price of *I* in 1937. All these proposi-
tions are incorporated in the price lines (labeled according to benchmark years) shown in Figure 2.1.

With Figure 2.1, I illustrate the alternate indexes of real national income that can be calculated with the data at hand.   The
relative prices of 1913, 1928, and 1937 are drawn as slopes through the
appropriate output combinations (where the slope indicates the MRT for
the benchmark year), and these price lines are drawn as solid lines
when they pass through the actual output combination and as broken
lines when they pass through the output combination of another year.
The various real national income growth indexes can be summarized as
follows:

Period	Prices	Growth index
1913/1885	1913	O13/OA
1928/1913	1913	OD/O13
1937/1928	1928	OC/O28
1937/1928	1937	O37/OB

These growth indexes show the standard result that the 1937/1928
index is larger when early prices are used.   They also show, in the
stylized version presented here, that 1928/1913 growth is negative, but
that this is due to a reversal of the typical index number relativity
effect, as relative prices and quantities are assumed to move together.
        These calculated indexes will fail to capture the "true" ex-
pansion in productive capacity if MRTs are indeed declining because
they transform the given year output at a constant rate into that of
the base year using the (fixed) transformation rates prevailing in the
base year.   The degree of bias will depend upon the curvature of the
underlying production possibilities schedules, the degree of structural
change, and the choice of price weights.[42]   Unfortunately, we are not
able to shed further light on the measurement of these biases; all we
can do is to reiterate their existence.
        Figure 1 also allows us to speculate on what growth indexes would
have emerged had sufficient data been available to prepare calculations
in alternate prices.   Little is known about 1885 prices.   The results
presented in later chapters suggest that 1885 relative prices were not

much different from those of 1913, but (as the preceding discussion indicated) this may be the consequence of measurement bias in the capital goods sector. It is safe to assume, however, that the relative price of I was higher in 1885 than in 1913. Thus, if the 1913/1885 growth index could have been calculated in 1885 prices, the growth rate would increase.

Assuming my speculations about 1928 and 1913 relative prices are correct, the application of 1928 prices to the 1928/1913 index would raise the growth index (as drawn from negative to positive). The application of 1928 prices to the 1913/1885 index would raise it above the index in 1913 prices, whereas the use of 1937 prices (assuming my assumption about relative 1937 and 1913 prices is correct) would lower the 1913/1885 index. Thus the 1913/1885 index in 1913 prices is likely *intermediate* between the two hypothetical indexes employing Soviet period prices. Conversely, if 1913 prices were applied to calculate the Soviet period growth rates, the calculated rate would be *inter-mediate* between the 1928 and 1937 price weighted indexes. If 1885 prices were used to calculate Soviet period growth, the calculated rate would be higher than if 1913 prices were used. If the relative price of I in 1928 was higher than in 1885, this index would be intermediate between the 1913 and 1928 price weighted indexes.

Not knowing the relative price structure of 1885 and not being able to apply Soviet period prices to the tsarist period indexes (and vice versa), we can only speculate about these hypothetical growth indexes expressed in alternate prices. They do, however, provide us with some guidance concerning the appropriate comparisons between tsarist and Soviet period growth indexes. They suggest that the application of "late" tsarist prices to Soviet period indexes would yield results intermediate between indexes calculated in "late" Soviet prices (1937, 1955) and in "early" (1928) prices. The same applies to the calculation of tsarist period growth indexes in terms of Soviet period prices. Combining this result with the downward "biases" in the tsarist investment series, I conclude that it is more appropriate to compare tsarist period growth indexes in "late" prices with Soviet period indexes in "late" prices than to use early (late) prices for one period and late (early) prices for another. This conclusion must be hedged by the fact that relatively little is known about relative price structures and by the fact that these indexes do not (because of the biases discussed above) measure the "true" expansion in productive capacity. As Simon Kuznets writes in support of the use of late year prices:

> But . . . recent year price weights should be used, since our historical records, insofar as they involve measurement, necessarily represent an observer of today looking backward rather than an observer of a century ago looking forward. Only the observer of today has weights to apply to goods that were not in existence a century or half century ago. Any judgment of growth must be made from the standpoint of a later phase, because in the earlier phase of the economy the subsequent stages cannot be seen even in embryo.[43]

As applied to the case at hand, we must regard the year 1913 as the culmination or final phase of capitalism in Russia, and the output mix of 1913 must be perceived in this light. One could perhaps speculate on what the output mix of a capitalist Russia would have been (and the market valuations of these outputs) in the mid and late twentieth century, but these speculations would not bring us far in terms of our empirical analysis. Conversely, the price and output structures attained by the Soviet economy immediately before World War II and thereafter can be regarded as indicating the desired output mix (dictated by planners' preferences) of the mature Soviet economy.

SUMMARY

The topic of this chapter was the appropriate interpretation of the real national income series of tsarist Russia and the comparability of this series with the historical series of the industrialized capitalist countries and with the Soviet Union.

It was noted that the national income estimates represent a mixture of physical series, weighted by 1913 prices, and deflated current price series. In important instances (e.g., retail sales) the appropriate variable weight deflator could not be applied, but it was argued that in such instances this technique would approximate the desired result. Thus the real national income indexes presented in this study are to be interpreted as approximating a Paasche index (in the "late" prices of 1913).

Special attention was devoted to the matter of the pricing (deflation) of capital goods. This issue is particularly important because different techniques were used to calculate real investment outlays for the Soviet period estimates, and the possibility therefore exists that the tsarist and Soviet period investment figures are not comparable. The crux of the problem is that the tsarist equipment series (like almost all historical series) has been deflated by a combination of input prices and unit prices of nonhomogeneous capital equipment. The use of an input price index, however, will overstate the increase in machinery prices (and understate the increase in real investment) whenever productivity advances have occurred within the capital goods sector. When unit prices are used, the direction of bias is ambiguous because of unobservable movements in the output mix and the effects of embodied technological change upon unit prices.

If the Soviet period experience is at all representative, the overall direction of bias is toward overstatement of the rate of increase in capital goods prices in the tsarist figures relative to the Soviet period figures, and this bias appears to be shared by the historical series of other industrialized countries. The bias appears to be greater when "early" prices are used, and this finding caused me to argue that late year comparisons are more appropriate in contrasting tsarist and Soviet period growth. Moreover, an upper limit correction of approximately 20% was suggested for the tsarist period equipment investment figures.

Some standard results of index number theory were then applied to the analysis of growth index comparisons of the tsarist and Soviet periods. This analysis was based upon a stylized model of changes in relative prices and quantities. It was noted that the data at hand would not permit the estimation of Soviet period growth in tsarist period prices (or vice versa), but that certain conclusions concerning these hypothetical growth indexes could be drawn (assuming the underlying assumptions concerning relative prices are correct). It was concluded that the use of late tsarist period prices (1913) to value Soviet period outputs would result in a growth index that would likely be intermediate between the growth indexes calculated using "early" and "late" Soviet period prices. Conversely, the 1913 price weighted index would be intermediate between the early and late year price indexes if

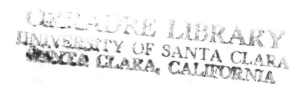
ORRADRE LIBRARY
UNIVERSITY OF SANTA CLARA
SANTA CLARA, CALIFORNIA

tsarist period national income were valued in the prices of the Soviet
period.

NOTES TO CHAPTER 2

1   For an authoritative theoretical discussion of index number relativity, see
    Abram Bergson, *The Real National Income of Soviet Russia Since 1928* (Cambridge:
    Harvard University Press, 1961), pp. 25-41.

2   The available historical national income series are summarized in B. R.
    Mitchell, *European Historical Statistics, 1750-1970* (New York: Columbia Univer-
    sity Press, 1976), table K, and in Ben J. Wattenberg, ed., *The Statistical
    History of the United States From Colonial Times to the Present* (New York:
    Basic Books, 1976), Chap. F. For the earliest periods covered by national
    income statistics, prices from the period 1900-38 are used, although estimates
    are available for the United States in the prices of 1860. The latter are
    summarized in Robert Gallman, "Gross National Product in the United States,
    1834-1909," in National Bureau of Economic Research, *Output, Employment and
    Productivity in the United States after 1800*, vol. 30, Studies in Income and
    Wealth (New York: Columbia University Press, 1966), pp. 3-90.

3   E.g. comparison of overlapping periods of American national income series, one
    in 1860, the other in 1929, prices, fails to reveal a higher growth rate for
    the figures in the early prices. The two sets of estimates are by Simon
    Kuznets (1929 prices) and Robert Gallman (1860 prices) and are reported in
    Wattenberg *Statistical History*, Chap. F. This result may be the consequence
    of differences in the underlying current price figures used by Kuznets and
    Gallman. See Gallman, "Gross National Product," p. 40.

4   See note 3.

5   For comparisons of structural changes in the United States and the Soviet
    Union, see Bergson, *Real National Income*, Chap. 14.

6   Paul Studenski, *The Income of Nations; Theory, Measurement and Analysis, Past
    and Present* (New York: New York University Press, 1958), pp. 21-5, 183-7,
    349-373.

7   For a discussion of the efficiency versus the welfare standard, see Bergson,
    Real National Income, pp. 25-41.

8   Richard Moorsteen, "On Measuring Productive Potential and Relative Efficiency,"
    Quarterly Journal of Economics 75, no. 3 (August 1961):451-67.

9   Studenski, *Income of Nations*, Chap. 10, esp. pp. 156-67.

10 This characteristic is obscure, but its implications have been well analyzed by
    Bergson, *Real National Income*, p. 36, and by Richard Moorsteen, *Prices and Pro-
    duction of Machinery in the Soviet Union, 1928-1958* (Cambridge: Harvard Uni-
    versity Press, 1962), pp. 38-42.

11 The Soviet real national income figures are calculated primarily by deflating
    expenditure series in current prices. The major price deflators, consumer
    prices, and producer goods prices employ given year quantity weights.

12 This point is emphasized by Bergson, *Real National Income*, pp.262-3 in his
    comparisons of the Soviet period estimates with Kuznets's estimates of American
    national income.

13 This judgment is based upon inspection of price indexes and individual price
    series reported in the following sources: S. G. Strumilin, *Ocherki*

ekonomicheskoi istorii Rossii i SSSR (Moscow: Nauka, 1966), p. 90 and Ministerstvo torgovli i promyshlennost, *Svod tovarnykh tsen na glavnykh russkikh i inostrannykh rynkakh za 1913 god* (Petersburg: Ministerstvo finansov, 1914), pp. II-VII.

14 The available data on worker and peasant budgetary expenditures are supplied in G. A. Dikhtiar, *Vnutrenniaia torgovlia v dorevoliutsionnoi Rossii* (Moscow: Nauka, 1960), Chap. 2; S. N. Prokopovich, *Krestianskoe khoziaistvo po dannym biudzhetnykh isledovanii i dinamicheskikh perepisei* (Berlin: Kooperativenaia mysl', 1924), Chap. 3.

15 The assets of the Russian railroads were apparently updated frequently to reflect market values (see Appendix L). The other major use of corporate asset data is to calculate inventories. The insured value data should also reflect current market values.

16 Robert Solow and Peter Temin, "Introduction: The Inputs for Growth," *Cambridge Economic History of Europe*, vol. 7, pt. 1 (Cambridge University Press, 1978), p. 17.

17 This discussion is based upon: Solow and Temin, "Introduction," pp. 16-21; Lance Davis and Robert Gallman, "Capital Formation in the United States during the Nineteenth Century," *Cambridge Economic History of Europe*, vol. 7, pt. 2 (Cambridge University Press, 1978), pp.7-9; Edward Denison, *Why Growth Rates Differ, Postwar Experiences in Nine Western Countries* (Washington, D.C.: Brookings, 1967), pp. 134-5; Edward Denison, "Theoretical Aspects of Quality Change, Capital Consumption and Net Capital Formation," National Bureau for Economic Research, *Problems of Capital Formation*, vol.19, Studies in Income and Wealth (Princeton: Princeton University Press, 1957), pp. 215-260. Edward Denison, *Accounting for United States Economic Growth 1929-1969* (Washington, D.C.: Brookings, 1974), pp. 52-58.

18 E.g. take a standardized type of equipment whose value declines relatively in later years as new technology is embodied in equipment of more recent vintage. This price decline will occur independently of the resources required to re-produce this equipment using the base-year technology.

19 Typically, price series for general categories of capital equipment, such as lathes, steam engines, locomotives, etc., are recorded. Under ideal conditions, the individual price series will be for capital goods of a standardized quality, but this condition is rarely met in reality, especially when the price series covers a long period of time. Thus, it is difficult to determine to what extent the price is rising (falling) because of quality changes, mix changes, or more general price changes.

20 The calculation of growth indexes from formulas 14 and 15 reduces to deflation by a weighted average index of input prices, where factor cost shares serve as weights:

$$17) \quad \frac{\dfrac{\Sigma\, P_1 I_1}{\Sigma\, P_0 I_0}}{\dfrac{\Sigma\Sigma\, A_0 w_0 (w_1/w_0)}{\Sigma\Sigma\, A_0 w_0}}$$

for formula 14, and

$$18) \quad \frac{\dfrac{\Sigma\, P_1 I_1}{\Sigma\, P_0 I_0}}{\dfrac{\Sigma\Sigma\, A_1 w_1}{\Sigma\Sigma\, A_1 w_0 (w_0/w_1)}}$$

for formula 15, where the A's refer to factor inputs. The two indexes will be identical if factor cost shares remain constant between periods 0 and 1, a condition that will hold if the elasticity of substitution among inputs is unitary. If the elasticity of substitution between factors equals unity, relative price changes are offset by relative quantity changes and factor shares remain constant. If the elasticity of substitution is other than unity, factor shares will change as relative prices change.

The calculation of growth indexes from formula 16 requires a complicated computation that cannot typically be calculated with the data at hand.

$$(19) \quad \frac{\dfrac{\Sigma\, P_1 I_1}{\Sigma\, P_0 I_0}}{\dfrac{\Sigma\Sigma\, a_1 w_1}{\Sigma\Sigma\, a_0 w_0}} = \frac{\dfrac{\Sigma\, P_1 I_1}{\Sigma\, P_0 I_0}}{\dfrac{\Sigma\Sigma\, \mu A_0 w_0 (w_1/w_0)}{\Sigma\Sigma\, A_0 w_0}}$$

where μ denotes the change in input-output ratios between 0 and 1 for each factor input. Comparison of this index with 17 and 18 indicates that the investment growth index calculated from 19 will be larger than those calculated using 17 and 18 if productivity improvements within the capital goods producing sectors have occurred. This is easy to demonstrate, for

$$(20) \quad \frac{\Sigma a_1 w_1}{\Sigma a_0 w_0} < \frac{\Sigma a_0 w_1}{\Sigma a_0 w_0} \quad \text{and} \quad \frac{\Sigma a_0 w_0}{\Sigma a_1 w_1} > \frac{\Sigma a_0 w_0}{\Sigma a_0 w_1} \quad \text{if} \quad a_1 < a^0$$

Thus the use of input indexes weighted by early or late year factor shares will understate the growth rate of real investment, if one wishes to measure capital in terms of actual inputs rather than hypothetical inputs required by the technology of another year. One surprising feature of deflation by input prices is that (if elasticities of substitution among factor inputs equal unity) there will be little difference between the use of early or late year factor shares, insofar as the factor shares will be constant.

21 The original statement of the vintage argument is given in Robert Solow, "Investment and Technical Progress," in Kenneth Arrow et al., eds., *Mathematical Methods in the Social Sciences* (Stanford: Stanford University Press, 1960).

22 For a discussion of the controversy over the treatment of quality changes in the measurement of capital stock, see Daniel Creamer, "Measuring Capital Input for Total Factor Productivity Analysis: Comments of a Sometime Estimator," *Review of Income and Wealth* 18, no. 1 (March 1972):55-79.

23 John W. Kendrick, *Productivity Trends in the United States* (Princeton: Princeton University Press, 1961), p. 35.

24 The quality problem arises in yet another context: the statistical problem of constructing capital goods price indexes under conditions of changing product mixes and changing specifications of capital goods. The technical characteristics of capital goods change over time and it is difficult to assemble serial indexes that, in effect, hold technical ("quality") characteristics "constant" and thus yield price movements of capital goods of hypothetical "constant quality." This problem, I must emphasize, is different from the vintage-quality problem discussed above and has attracted considerable attention in the contemporary literature. For a survey and evaluation of this literature, see Robert Gordon, "Measurement Bias in Price Indexes for Capital Goods," *Review of Income and Wealth*, ser. 17, no. 2 (June 1971):121-174.

There are two approaches to resolving the problem of changing technical characteristics. The first is the "specification price" approach, whereby an attempt is made to classify capital goods into distinct and homogeneous categories and thus to observe, in effect, price changes of capital goods of uniform technical specifications over time. This approach requires a substantial amount of information on prices and technical characteristics, and its principal weakness is that only a few technical characteristics can be held constant, whereas in reality a multitude of technical characteristics must be used to hold quality constant. The second approach is econometric: the hedonic regression approach, whereby the relationships between unit prices and a series of measurable technical characteristics are estimated econometrically and the estimated coefficients are then employed to estimate hypothetical capital goods price changes holding technical characteristics constant. The drawbacks of the hedonic regression approach are that the number of technical characteristics that can enter into the regression equations is strictly limited (the same problem as the specification price approach) and that substantial changes in the product mix can seriously distort the results.

Joel Popkin and Robert Gillingham, in: "Comments on 'Recent Developments in the Measurement of Price Indexes for Fixed Capital Goods,'" *Review of Income* and Wealth, ser. 17, no. 3 (September 1971):307-309, demonstrate that even within very narrowly defined product categories the product mix can seriously affect unit prices, and this is their principal criticism of the unit price approach to the measurement of capital goods prices.

25   Most studies of historical national income employ input price indexes to deflate capital investment.   See e.g., Walther Hoffmann, *Das Wachstum der Deutschen Wirtschaft seit der Mitte des 19. Jahrhunderts* (Berlin: Springer, 1965), pp. 571-4;   Charles Feinstein, *National Income, Expenditure and Output of the United Kingdom, 1855-1965* (Cambridge University Press, 1972), pp. 191-6; Maurice Levy-Leboyer, "Capital Investment and Economic Growth in France, 1820-1930," *Cambridge Economic History of Europe*, vol. 7, pt. 1 (Cambridge University Press, 1978), p. 277; B. J. Emery and G. J. Garsten, "The Measurement of Constant Price Aggregates in Canada," *Review of Income and Wealth*, ser. 15 (1969) pp.16-21.   The U.S. historical series appear to be constructed from the firmest information on capital goods prices.   On this, see the contributions by Robert Gallman in National Bureau of Economic Research, *Output, Employment and Productivity in the United States After 1800*, vol. 30, (New York: Columbia University Press, 1966), pp.3-75, 91-116.

26   A.K. Cairncross, *Home and Foreign Investment, 1870-1913* (Cambridge University Press, 1953), writes (p. 58) on his attempt to estimate a British machinery series in which he had to manufacture an index of output without any figures of machinery produced and an index of machinery prices without any price quotations.

27   Popkin and Gillingham, "Comments" (p. 308) note the tendency for the capital goods product mix to shift within categories in favor of lower priced goods in the United States in the postwar period.

28   I have, however, made one quasi-hedonic quality adjustment of the unit price series: I have standardized each unit price by weight (locomotive unit price per ton, unit price of farm hand tools per lb., etc.), but this, as is evident, represents a very crude quality adjustment. The magnitude of the product mix problem can be illustrated by my inability to employ plough prices in this study.   Product mix changes were so substantial that the unit prices were meaningless;   yet specification price information was not available.

29   Moorsteen, *Prices and Production of Machinery*, Chap. 8.

30   Moorsteen, *Prices and Production of Machinery*, Chap. 2.

31   Moorsteen, *Prices and Production of Machinery*, Chap. 8;   Alexander Gerschenkron, *A Dollar Index of Soviet Machinery Output, 1927-28 to 1937*, Rand, Report R-197, April 1961.

32   Bergson, *Real National Income*, p. 225.

33   Moorsteen, *Prices and Production of Machinery*, p. 138.

34   This is calculated by applying Moorsteen's material input price data to Bergson's data on fixed investment (Appendix F).

35   Moorsteen, *Prices and Production of Machinery*, pp. 131-138.

36   This information is summarized in Mitchell, *European Historical Statistics*,

Chap. K.

37   Gerschenkron's study of U.S. machinery in late and early prices is summarized
     by Moorsteen, *Prices and Production of Machinery*, pp. 132-3.

38   F. B. Horner, "The Effect of Grouping Data on the Divergence Between Laspeyres
     and Paasche Forms of Quantum Indexes," *Review of Income and Wealth*, Ser. 17,
     no. 3 (September 1971):263-7, shows that index number relativity effects are
     best picked up from disaggregated data. The greater the degree of aggregation,
     the lower the probability of finding significant index number relativity ef-
     fects.

39   Moorsteen, *Prices and Production of Machinery*, p. 133.

40   Bergson, *Real National Income*, Chap. 3; Abram Bergson, "Index Numbers and the
     Computation of Factor Productivity," *Review of Income and Wealth*, Ser. 21, no.
     3 (September 1975):259-78; Moorsteen, "On Measuring Productive Potential and
     Relative Efficiency," pp. 451-67; G. Warren Nutter, "On Economic Size and
     Growth," *Journal of Law and Economics* 9 (October 1966):163-88.

41   Bergson, *Real National Income*, p. 237.

42   Bergson, "Index Numbers," pp. 259-271.

43   Simon Kuznets, *Capital in the American Economy* (Princeton: Princeton University
     Press, 1961), p. 509.

CHAPTER 3

SUMMARY RESULTS: NATIONAL INCOME OF TSARIST RUSSIA, 1885-1913

This chapter is devoted to a summary presentation of my calculations of Russian national income by end use for the period 1885 to 1913. These results are summarized in two tables. Table 3.1 supplies annual esti- mates of net national product (NNP) in constant 1913 prices; Table 3.2 gives NNP in prices of the current year. Chapter 4 provides an over- view of estimation techniques and data sources; the actual details of the calculations are given in Appendixes A-M at the end of this book.

The organization of this chapter is as follows: First, the annual estimates themselves are presented. Second, the various potential biases discussed in the preceding chapter are considered. Third, the national income figures are compared with the estimates of Raymond Goldsmith and of S. N. Prokopovich for overlapping periods (1885-1913 for Goldsmith and 1900 and 1913 for Prokopovich). They are also compared with the "production indexes" of V. E. Varzar for the years 1887, 1900, and 1913. Fourth, an alternate calculation of NNP by sector of origin is offered. This alternate national income index involves a substantive revaluation of the Goldsmith series using the more recent evidence on agricultural production and services uncovered in the course of this study. First, let me turn to the estimates themselves.

THE NNP ESTIMATES, 1885-1913
Annual estimates of tsarist NNP are given in Tables 3.1 and 3.2. The major items in these tables are drawn from annual, rather than inter- polated, data, although one can never be sure that the raw data itself does not conceal some hidden interpolation. The most important inter- polations are made between benchmarks for government final expendi- tures. The interpolated figures are given in parentheses in the two tables but should not have a significant effect on the global figures because such expenditures did not appear to be subject to significant

Table 3.1. *Net national product Russian Empire, 1885-1913 (millions of rubles, 1913 prices)*

	1885	1886	1887	1888	1889	1890	1891	1892	1893	1894	1895	1896	1897
1. Retail sales													
Variant 1: Moscow-Petersburg price index	2559	2791	3203	3090	2969	3135	3028	2960	3226	3688	4173	4374	4473
Variant 2: Podtiagin price index	2722	2869	3251	3135	3185	3358	2763	2731	3283	4232	4870	5021	4511
2. Housing rents, total	639	649	643	676	698	720	724	736	732	726	760	776	772
a. urban	466	475	484	494	504	513	522	528	524	518	534	550	560
b. rural	173	174	158	182	194	207	202	208	208	208	226	226	212
3. Services, total	364	(377)	(390)	404	(410)	(417)	435	(431)	(437)	444	(461)	481	(484)
a. passenger rail	27			33			38			45		62	
b. communications	12			14			16			17		19	
c. utilities	72			80			86			88		96	
d. domestic service	209			218			230			225		228	
e. medical expenditures	44			59			65			69		76	
4. Consumption of farm products in kind, total	3025	2864	3299	3223	2777	3064	2478	3142	3834	3969	3912	4096	3702
a. grain products	1183	1058	1322	1198	842	1074	669	1183	1680	1758	1556	1591	1307
b. meat products	437	438	439	479	480	487	471	459	462	467	490	545	555
c. technical crops	108	100	125	149	138	133	110	131	172	179	195	223	187
d. dairy products	673	677	732	732	744	738	717	721	729	746	859	887	885
e. omitted products, forestry, hunting, fishing	624	591	681	665	573	632	511	648	791	819	812	850	768
5. Military subsistence	74	(72)	(69)	67	(62)	(57)	52	(66)	(80)	95	(101)	107	(104)
A. PERSONAL CONSUMPTION													
Variant 1 (1a + 2 + 3 + 4 + 5)	6661	(6753)	(7604)	7460	(6916)	(7393)	6705	(7335)	8309	8922	(9407)	9834	(9535)
Variant 2 (1b + 2 + 3 + 4 + 5)	6824	(6931)	(7652)	7505	(7132)	(7616)	6440	(7106)	8366	9466	(10104)	10481	(9573)
6. Imperial government expenditures, total	566	(593)	(592)	588	(601)	(652)	719	(704)	(705)	795	(910)	873	(836)
a. administration	249			262			329			342		399	
b. health and education	28			26			33			39		40	
c. defense	289			300			357			414		434	
7. Local government expenditures, total	145	(149)	(153)	157	(164)	(173)	180	(192)	(204)	217	(234)	250	(261)
a. administration	109			110			129			160		173	
b. health and education	31			41			45			51		69	
c. defense	5			3			6			6		8	
8. Government capital expenditures, excluding defense capital	47	(49)	(51)	54	(57)	(60)	64	(65)	(66)	68	(78)	88	(97)
B. GOVERNMENT													
Including government capital (6 + 7)	711	(742)	(745)	745	(765)	(825)	899	(896)	(909)	1012	(1144)	1123	(1097)
Excluding capital (6 + 7 - 8)	644	(693)	(694)	691	(708)	(765)	835	(831)	(843)	944	(1066)	1035	(1000)
9. Investment in livestock	14	7	399	42	42	-161	-126	35	42	238	553	105	0
10. Net investment in equipment, total	52	53	56	66	69	62	61	63	89	105	120	168	191
a. agriculture	6	6	6	9	6	6	5	7	8	12	12	13	13
b. nonagriculture	46	47	50	57	63	56	56	56	81	93	108	155	178
11. Net investment, structures, total	344	235	242	256	217	353	143	147	41	265	403	197	400
a. industry	74	82	82	89	94	99	-7	60	84	25	119	77	198
b. agriculture	198	89	89	89	58	187	105	121	0	120	172	40	36
c. urban residential	72	64	71	78	65	67	45	-34	-43	120	112	80	166
12. Inventories, total	167	31	36	97	289	-57	47	257	553	1053	-865	538	478
a. industry	-4	53	40	62	-6	20	34	80	102	117	-20	91	133
b. trade	171	-22	-4	35	295	-77	13	177	451	936	-845	447	345
13. Net investment, transportation and communication	69	93	98	100	96	49	36	185	255	123	162	213	349
C. NET INVESTMENT (8 + 9 + 10 + 11 + 12 + 13)	693	468	882	615	770	306	225	752	1046	1852	451	1309	1515
D. NET FOREIGN INVESTMENT	-114	-182	31	246	133	108	142	-179	-129	-185	-158	-228	-208
NET NATIONAL PRODUCT (A + B + C + D)													
Variant 1	7904	7732	9210	9012	8527	8572	7917	8739	10069	11533	10766	11950	11842
Variant 2	8067	7810	9258	9057	8743	8795	7654	8510	10126	12077	11463	12597	11880
Population (million)	109	111	113	115	117	118	119	120	122	123	124	125	126
Per capita income (rubles)													
Variant 1	72.5	69.7	81.5	78.4	72.9	72.6	66.5	72.8	82.5	93.8	86.8	95.6	94.0

1898	1899	1900	1901	1902	1903	1904	1905	1906	1907	1908	1909	1910	1911	1912	1913	Source Appendix
4559	5719	5454	5573	5573	5861	5841	5973	5562	5351	5289	5623	6215	6611	6705	7141	A
4450	5697	5647	5644	5622	5951	5899	5881	5391	4851	5002	5492	6209	6576	6567	7141	
803	814	830	868	939	982	1008	1081	1127	1154	1185	1220	1285	1354	1412	1465	B
583	593	591	610	660	702	722	761	800	808	818	832	876	931	983	1035	
220	221	239	258	279	280	286	320	327	346	367	388	409	423	429	430	
(491)	(497)	504	(519)	(534)	549	(573)	(597)	(623)	650	(677)	(706)	736	(756)	(776)	799	C
		95			112				149			188			222	
		25			29				38			52			65	
		83			94				118			125			118	
		218			225				244			254			268	
		83			89				101			117			126	
4115	4454	4444	4058	4857	4704	5258	4675	4096	4494	4881	5392	5658	4908	6209	6726	D
1588	1869	1885	1588	2143	2079	2437	1979	1517	1830	2014	2327	2479	1914	2821	3228	
555	569	576	567	579	578	569	603	587	572	570	657	688	701	679	720	
213	164	169	149	215	195	192	192	230	251	238	184	202	215	246	256	
905	928	891	912	912	876	968	931	912	908	1046	1105	1115	1059	1174	1126	
854	924	923	842	1008	976	1092	970	850	933	1013	1119	1174	1019	1289	1396	
(101)	(99)	97	(100)	(102)	105	(111)	(117)	(123)	129	(139)	(149)	159	(164)	(169)	175	E
(10069)	(11583)	11329	(11118)	(12005)	12201	(12791)	(12443)	(11531)	11778	(12171)	(13090)	14053	(13793)	(15271)	16306	
(9960)	(11561)	11522	(11189)	(12054)	12291	(12849)	(12351)	(11360)	11278	(11884)	(12959)	14047	(13758)	(15133)	16306	
(965)	(946)	991	(961)	(1120)	1147	(1331)	(1560)	(1582)	1139	(1190)	(1250)	1293	(1294)	(1371)	1707	F
		408				508			476			583			583	
		58				73			63			110			154	
		525				566			600			600			970	
(271)	(283)	294	(319)	(347)	375	(374)	(373)	(372)	370	(402)	(436)	475	(525)	(580)	643	G
		193			230				222			275			357	
		91			132				135			179			256	
		10			13				13			21			30	
(106)	(115)	125	(127)	(129)	131	(128)	(126)	(124)	122	(138)	(154)	171	(156)	(141)	126	
(1236)	(1229)	1285	(1280)	(1467)	1522	(1705)	(1933)	(1954)	1509	(1592)	(1686)	1768	(1819)	(1951)	2350	
(1130)	(1114)	1160	(1153)	(1338)	1391	(1577)	(1807)	(1830)	1387	(1454)	(1532)	1597	(1663)	(1810)	2224	
140	70	-98	126	-7	-98	349	-161	-147	-34	881	322	125	-223	154	112	H
237	248	222	224	210	226	244	255	248	226	235	247	286	321	360	454	I
15	17	18	28	25	35	36	42	37	33	42	55	61	73	81	73	
222	231	204	196	185	191	208	213	211	193	193	192	225	248	279	381	
430	424	682	771	556	483	719	865	224	429	580	786	1246	1018	976	1043	J
87	181	211	94	-77	-20	89	226	-151	37	112	87	139	320	285	248	
266	226	331	312	325	350	350	350	315	322	364	372	705	315	308	392	
77	17	140	365	308	153	280	289	61	70	104	327	402	383	383	403	
226	-72	-127	281	940		110	-991	264	199	177	395	593	263	378	-371	K
69	14	19	21	162	120	-125	130	77	57	85	122	274	96	177	152	
157	-86	-146	260	778	-119	235	-1121	187	142	92	273	319	167	201	219	
260	260	361	268	192	138	260	257	262	177	209	67	337	320	185	208	L
1399	1045	1165	1797	2020	881	1810	351	976	1119	2220	1971	2758	1855	2194	2314	
-242	-430	-327	-199	-70	-35	18	45	-153	-369	-393	30	-214	-185	-322	-578	M
12356	13312	13327	13869	15293	14438	16196	14646	14184	13915	15452	16623	18194	17126	18953	20266	
12247	13290	13520	13940	15342	14528	16254	14554	14013	13415	15165	16492	18188	17091	18815	20266	
128	130	133	135	137	139	141	144	146	149	153	157	161	164	168	171	
96.5	102.4	100.2	102.7	111.6	103.9	114.9	101.7	97.2	93.4	101.0	105.9	113.0	104.4	112.8	118.5	

Table 3.2. *Net national product Russian Empire, 1885-1913, current year prices (millions of credit rubles)*

	1885	1886	1887	1888	1889	1890	1891	1892	1893	1894	1895	1896	1897
1. Retail sales	2052	2096	2409	2364	2319	2364	2365	2409	2587	2810	3034	3123	3257
2. Housing rents, total	456	456	439	472	483	491	504	523	532	535	565	585	604
a. urban	313	312	309	318	326	328	336	351	360	358	381	400	417
b. rural	143	144	130	154	157	163	168	172	172	177	184	185	187
3. Services total	266	(276)	(286)	297	(306)	(316)	326	(329)	(332)	336	(345)	353	(367)
a. passenger rail	42			47			51			57		66	
b. communications	12			14			16			17		19	
c. utilities	37			45			51			53		60	
d. domestic service	140			147			155			153		151	
e. medical expenditures	35			44			53			56		57	
4. Consumption of farm products in kind, total	2477	2219	2699	2932	2471	2573	2364	2991	3151	2715	2679	2696	2779
a. grain products	1100	899	1084	1138	790	913	829	1336	1411	1037	825	843	954
b. meat products	310	315	360	431	418	395	405	381	402	388	333	343	411
c. technical crops	65	60	76	92	91	85	68	87	134	141	240	156	125
d. dairy products	491	487	622	666	662	649	574	570	554	589	696	674	637
e. omitted products	511	458	557	605	510	531	488	617	650	560	585	680	652
5. Military subsistence	65	(63)	(62)	60	(59)	(58)	57	(59)	(60)	62	(63)	64	(69)
A. PERSONAL CONSUMPTION (1 + 2 + 3 + 4 + 5)	5316	(5110)	(5895)	6125	(5638)	(5802)	5616	(6311)	(6662)	(6458)	(6686)	6821	(7076)
6. Imperial government	457			477			569			611		673	
7. Local government	114			125			138			162		187	
8. Government capital expenditures, excluding defense capital	37	(39)	(42)	45	(47)	(49)	53	(54)	(58)	62	(66)	72	(77)
B. GOVERNMENT, EXCLUDING CAPITAL (6 + 7 – 8)	534	(541)	(548)	557	(587)	(620)	654	674	692	711	749	788	(838)
9. Investment in livestock	-8	4	235	243	27	-98	-76	19	26	143	331	61	0
10. Net investment, equipment, total	49	55	55	66	70	65	64	65	89	111	120	170	182
a. agriculture	6	6	6	9	6	6	5	7	8	12	12	13	12
b. nonagriculture	43	49	49	57	64	59	59	58	81	99	108	157	170
11. Net investment, structures, total	285	189	193	210	176	279	118	122	34	225	326	162	352
a. industry	61	68	67	76	76	78	-6	50	70	21	96	63	174
b. agriculture	164	68	68	68	47	148	87	100	0	102	139	33	32
c. urban residential	60	53	58	66	53	53	37	-28	-36	102	91	66	146
12. Inventories, total	108	47	140	47	74	-45	-2	270	291	753	-582	458	497
a. industry	8	38	77	58	-23	-3	20	87	104	75	-36	81	118
b. trade	100	9	63	-11	97	-42	-22	183	187	678	-546	377	379
13. Net investment, transportation and communication	54	74	85	86	85	44	32	159	222	107	141	186	311
C. NET INVESTMENT (8 + 9 + 10 + 11 + 12 + 13)	525	408	750	697	479	294	189	689	720	1401	402	1109	1419
14. Net merchandise account	102	54	216	395	313	282	329	71	138	100	150	72	125
15. Net dividend, interest payments and repatriated profits	-151	-155	-158	-162	-166	-162	-155	-161	-174	-177	-194	-184	-200
16. Net tourist expenditures and miscellaneous items	-40	-38	-34	-36	-48	-36	-59	-61	-65	-60	-68	-75	-86
D. NET FOREIGN INVESTMENT (14 + 15 + 16)	-89	-139	24	197	99	84	115	-151	-101	-137	-112	-187	-161
NET NATIONAL PRODUCT (A + B + C + D)	6286	5920	7217	7576	6803	6800	6574	7523	7973	8433	7725	8531	9172

1898	1899	1900	1901	1902	1903	1904	1905	1906	1907	1908	1909	1910	1911	1912	1913
3524	4461	4292	4397	4441	4630	4725	4975	4906	4982	5167	5415	5861	6221	6665	7141
713	691	707	735	790	849	854	914	975	1003	1031	1057	1130	1232	1362	1465
517	482	485	500	541	586	591	620	667	681	694	704	746	834	950	1035
196	209	222	235	249	263	263	294	308	322	337	353	384	398	412	430
(382)	(397)	414	(436)	(460)	486	(511)	(537)	(564)	593	(625)	(659)	697	(732)	(768)	799
		102		122					146			186			222
		25		29					38			52			65
		66		76					97			111			118
		158		200					222			240			268
		35		59					90			108			126
3594	3875	3776	3519	4189	3937	4323	4118	3810	4666	5252	5655	5448	5076	6769	6726
1525	1663	1376	1239	1736	1580	1852	1742	1456	2196	2538	2606	2281	2086	3272	3228
511	484	518	533	533	457	461	567	581	549	570	696	743	743	788	720
136	108	157	156	206	185	190	173	232	256	207	251	191	201	222	256
670	761	802	766	766	710	794	782	793	844	1046	1061	1059	1027	1198	1126
752	859	923	825	948	1005	1026	854	748	821	891	1041	1174	1019	1289	1396
(72)	(74)	76	(78)	(80)	82	(95)	(110)	(127)	147	(154)	(161)	169	(171)	(173)	175
(8285)	(9498)	9265	(9165)	(9960)	9984	(10508)	(10654)	(10382)	11391	(12229)	(12947)	13305	(13432)	(15737)	16306
		855			879				1070			1195			1707
		236			283				341			437			643
(85)	(93)	104	(104)	(104)	105	(105)	(105)	(105)	105	(117)	(133)	144	(138)	(132)	126
(887)	(939)	987	(1009)	(1032)	1057	(1112)	(1171)	(1235)	1306	(1351)	(1402)	1488	(1682)	(1934)	2224
83	43	−63	81	−5	−66	237	−116	−104	−27	749	280	109	−187	143	112
223	234	211	215	209	219	227	237	230	238	230	248	282	320	358	454
14	16	17	27	33	33	32	38	32	35	42	54	60	72	77	73
209	218	194	188	176	186	195	199	198	203	188	194	222	248	281	381
386	396	634	702	494	449	664	798	211	398	534	716	1172	938	937	1043
78	168	196	86	−69	−19	82	208	−142	34	103	79	131	282	273	248
239	212	308	284	289	324	324	324	296	299	335	339	663	296	296	392
69	16	130	332	274	144	258	266	57	65	96	298	378	360	368	403
329	86	−225	48	769	121	158	−617	522	157	47	315	607	526	506	371
109	60	19	−29	137	95	−114	88	196	55	31	114	194	243	222	152
220	26	−244	77	632	26	272	−705	326	102	16	201	413	283	284	219
235	235	317	233	173	123	229	232	241	161	186	60	300	291	188	208
1341	1087	978	1383	1744	951	1620	639	1205	1032	1863	1752	2614	2026	2264	2314
91	−56	71	164	261	314	371	425	285	198	77	510	353	416	329	128
−212	−216	−220	−211	−230	−237	−230	−243	−232	−290	−309	−322	−345	−367	−394	−401
−84	−89	−119	−120	−99	−117	−126	−143	−191	−167	−149	−159	−211	−232	−267	−305
−205	−361	−268	−167	−58	−40	15	39	−138	−259	−381	29	−203	−183	−332	−578
10308	11163	10962	11390	12678	11952	13255	12503	12684	13470	15062	16130	17204	16957	19603	20266

annual fluctuations and the interpolations of imperial government expenditures should be fairly accurate anyway.[1]

Net national product is expressed in market prices with no adjustments made at this point for indirect taxes and subsidies. The investment series have been calculated net of depreciation; so no independent estimates of depreciation are available from which one could construct gross national product. Government investment is included under investment outlays rather than under government expenditures.[2]

The figures presented in Tables 3.1 and 3.2 are self-explanatory with the important exception of the constant price retail sales figures. In this study, real retail sales (and hence real NNP) is given in two variants: variant 1, labeled the "Moscow-Petersburg" index, and variant 2, labeled the "Podtiagin" index. These two variants correspond to retail sales in current prices deflated by the Moscow-Petersburg retail price index, on the one hand, and by the Podtiagin price index, on the other. Both price indexes are discussed in detail in Appendix A.

Although it may seem premature at this point, I think it important for the reader that I indicate a preference for one variant over the other. Fortunately, for the period as a whole, the two variants yield quite similar results, but for specific subperiods, especially for the early 1890s and the early twentieth century, the two indexes diverge.

The principal difference between the two deflators is that the Moscow-Petersburg index is an index of retail prices in the two major cities, Moscow and Petersburg. Weights are supplied by investigations of worker family budgets of residents of the two cities. The Podtiagin index, on the other hand, is a quasi-retail price index, compiled (by Professor M. E. Podtiagin) by applying worker budget weights to wholesale prices observed in various regional and metropolitan markets (including ports and even some foreign prices).[3]

The advantage of the Podtiagin index is that, if one can assume fairly constant retail margins over time, trends in retail prices for the Russian Empire as a whole may be better related by observations from a series of regional markets rather than from the retail markets of the two major cities. In the Russian case, regional price variation, especially for agricultural products, was indeed substantial, and thus Moscow-Petersburg prices may not have been representative of the empire as a whole.

I judge, however, the advantages of the Moscow-Petersburg index to outweigh these advantages; thus I shall use the variant 1 results in my evaluation of Russian national income. Nevertheless, the variant 2 figures are valuable as a check on the first set of figures. My reasons for preferring the Moscow-Petersburg variant are as follows: First, in an intertemporal study of this sort it is valuable to have serial price observations from a uniform market, as these will better capture serial price movements than an index assembled from various regional markets weighted in a necessarily arbitrary manner. Second, one should deflate retail sales by retail, rather than by wholesale, prices, and divergences between the two can be substantial. This is true of the period 1913 to 1928 (Chap. 5), and it is true for the tsarist period as well. Comparisons of the two indexes reveal that wholesale prices were subject to much more significant annual fluc-tuations than were retail prices, even though the trend over the full period was not all that different. Thus it would seem more appropriate to rely on retail price observations than on wholesale prices. Third, the Moscow-Petersburg variant gives results for the various subperiods that appear to be more plausible than the Podtiagin variant, which often yields enormous year-to-year fluctuations in end-use proportions. Finally, most of the historical series against which this study will be compared (Chap. 7) are based upon major city retail price deflators, much like those used in this study.

A CONSIDERATION OF BIASES AND INDEX NUMBER EFFECTS

Chapter 2 was devoted to a theoretical analysis of the types of biases that may be present in these calculations, and particular attention was accorded the problem of calculating real fixed investment. It was noted that the use of input price deflators and unit prices of nonhomo-geneous capital goods likely imparted a downward bias to the calculated growth rates of real investment. This bias, it was noted, is shared by most of the historical studies of real national income but is likely not present in the Soviet period calculations. The further point was made that significant index number relativity effects are unlikely to

reveal themselves when input price deflators are applied to the deflation of investment expenditures.

The magnitude of index number relativity effects present in these
calculations can be assessed, at least partially, by comparing investment proportions in current and in constant prices. If the measured
index number effects are large, they will reveal themselves as divergences of the current price proportions from their constant price
counterparts.

In Table 3.3 I compare early year (1885-89) net investment proportions (fixed investment plus inventories and livestock) and net
fixed investment proportions in 1913 prices and in current prices to
investigate these effects. As Table 3.3 indicates, the 1885-89 investment proportions in current and in 1913 prices do reveal the anticipated relationship between current and constant ("late") prices: The
current price proportions exceed the constant price proportions (but
only slightly), thus indicating a decline in the relative price of
investment goods over the period.

In Chapter 2 it was established that had Soviet fixed investment
been calculated using material input prices, the annual growth of fixed
investment (in 1937 prices) would have been less by a factor of .8.
This coefficient was taken as the maximum possible adjustment for the
tsarist fixed investment index, for it was felt that real cost reductions within the capital goods sector in tsarist Russia between 1885
and 1913 likely were not as rapid as during the early five-year-plan
era of the Soviet Union.

If one applies the maximal 25% adjustment to the real equipment
investment series of Table 3.1, and then calculates the resulting
investment proportions (col. 2), the constant price early investment
proportion for equipment falls from 0.7 of 1% to .45 of 1% (row B.2).
The effect on the overall net investment proportion of this adjustment
is small (it falls from 7.6% to 7.45%) because of the small weight of
equipment investment during this early period (row A.2). The effect on
overall economic growth of this adjustment, although substantial for
equipment, is indistinguishable from zero because of the small share of
equipment investment in the early period. If one were to apply the
same 25% adjustment coefficient to *fixed* investment (row C.2), the
overall effect would be to lower the constant price investment propor-

Table 3.3. *Investment proportions in current prices and in 1913 prices (%)*

	(1) Unadjusted (1885-9)	(2) Adjusted (1885-9)	(3) Current prices (1909-3)
A. Net investment/NNP			
1. Current prices	7.8	-	13.5
2. Constant prices (from B)	7.6	7.1	-
3. Constant prices (from C)	-	6.7	-
B. Net equipment investment/NNP			
1. Current prices	0.9	-	1.9
2. Constant prices	0.7	0.45	-
C. Net fixed investment/NNP			
1. Current prices	5.2	-	8.6
2. Constant prices	4.6	3.7	-

Note: Dash indicates not applicable.

tion from 7.6% to 6.7% (row A.3). The impact on economic growth of this adjustment would be to raise the NNP annual growth rate by a maximum of 0.05% per annum. This overstates the correct adjustment by a large margin for the reasons given above.

I judge therefore that the growth bias introduced by the use of input prices is small because of the small weight of fixed investment. For the 1885 to 1913 period the adjustment would raise the annual growth rate at most from 3.25% to 3.3%.

My estimate of the late year investment proportion can be compared with the earlier calculations of M. N. Sobolev and S. N. Prokopovich.[4] The Sobolev and Prokopovich calculations are for the year 1913, and for this year my calculated net investment proportion is 11.4%. Sobolev and Prokopovich both arrive independently at a 10%

proportion. Because the exact contents of these alternate calculations cannot be established with the material available, I cannot say whether they support or deny the validity of my own investment ratio calculation; however, that the alternate calculations are close to my own is a comforting finding. Strumilin has made a third alternate estimation of the 1911-13 investment proportion, based on his own calculation of 1913 national income (16.4 billion rubles) and Vainshtein's estimate of the increment of "national wealth" (*narodnoe bogatstvo*) between 1911 and 1913.[5] Strumilin arrives at an investment proportion of 16% but this high figure is generally consistent with my own (13.5%) because his estimate of national income is well below the current figure and because he includes the increment in consumer durables in the investment figure.[6] I cannot, however, cite the Strumilin-Vainshtein investment proportion in support of my own calculation as my own 1913 investment estimates are based in large part on those of Vainshtein.

COMPARISON WITH OTHER NATIONAL INCOME ESTIMATES

My national income series should be compared with the extant studies of Russian national income, the most important being those of Raymond Goldsmith and S. N. Prokopovich. The 1913 NNP estimate should also be compared with the 1913 estimates of Prokopovich, Nikitski, Falkus, and Gosplan to establish the degree of agreement in levels as well as growth rates.

The 1913 estimates: Prokopovich, Nikitski, Falkus, Gosplan

Let us begin by comparing my 1913 figure with the national income estimates of other researchers (Table 3.4). The estimate that has come to be accepted by Soviet officialdom for 1913 is that by Gosplan under the direction of S. G. Strumilin (14.5 billion gold rubles). We refer to this as the "Gosplan-Strumilin" estimate.

An alternate measure was also prepared by A. Nikitski in 1927 for Gosplan and was published in *Planovoe khoziaistvo*, but it differs only slightly from the Gosplan-Strumilin estimate. Two non-Soviet estimates of 1913 Russian national income are also available. The first, prepared in 1931 by the émigré economist S. N. Prokopovich, indicates a much lower level of 1913 national income (13.9 billion rubles) than the Gosplan-Strumilin and Nikitski studies, whereas the second estimate, by

the English economist M. E. Falkus (published in 1968), is generally
consistent with, but slightly higher than, the Gosplan-Strumilin estimate, at least in Falkus's USSR territory figures.

As these estimates will be discussed in Chapter 5, I will not go
into the details here. The question raised at this juncture is the
degree of agreement of my estimate for 1913 with the other estimates
given in Table 3.4. To render the two sets of estimates comparable, I
must omit indirect taxes from my figure and add surpluses of government
enterprises to obtain national income. As the other estimates employ
the narrower "material product" concept of national income, I must add
to them categories omitted to make them comparable to my national
income figure. These adjustments are shown in Table 3.4, and the
comparable figures are located in row IB (my estimate) and IIIA.2, B.2,
C.2, and D.2. (adjusted estimates of other researchers).

What conclusions can be drawn from these comparisons? The first
is that the Prokopovich 1931 estimate appears to be too low and that
the Falkus empire estimate appears to be too high relative to my own.
My figure agrees with Vainshtein's assessment of both Prokopovich and
Falkus.[7] Vainshtein believes both have understated depreciation deductions. My figures are reasonably close to the Gosplan-Strumilin,
Nikitski, and Falkus (USSR territory) estimates. They are almost
identical to the Falkus USSR territory estimate but slightly (3%) above
the official Gosplan-Strumilin estimates later used to link prewar
national income to the 1920s. The major finding is the surprising
degree of agreement between my 1913 estimates and those of earlier
researchers. The only substantive disagreement is with the apparently
low 1931 Prokopovich figures. In this regard, it must be noted that
the 1931 Prokopovich estimate represents a downward revision of his
1918 work for the 50 European provinces (upon which Gosplan based its
estimates for 1913).[8] If one applies Prokopovich's own territorial
adjustment in his 1931 study (the ration of USSR territory national
income to the 50 European provinces) to his earlier 1918 estimates, one
obtains a close approximation of the Gosplan 1913 figure. In general,
I would have to emphasize that the available estimates tend to be
supportive of each other (if one accepts the eary Prokopovich study),
and this agreement provides important support for the accuracy of my
1913 estimate insofar as it was derived quite independently.

Table 3.4. *1913 Russian net national product, national income, current and other estimates (Empire and USSR pre-1939 territory)*

		Million rubles	
		USSR pre-1939 territory	Empire
I.	Current estimates		
	A. Net national product	17,408	20,266
	- Indirect business taxes	-783	-921
	+ State subsidies to private		
	sector	+83	+98
	- Current surplus of government	-631	-742
	enterprises		
	B. National income	16,077	18,701
II.	Omissions resulting from narrow Marxian national income concept	+1,058	+1,244
	A. Product originating in rest of world	-339	-399
	B. Net government product	+290	+341
	C. Domestic and medical services	+335	+394
	D. Net housing product	+772	+908
III.	Previous national income estimates, Russia, 1913		
	A. 1. Falkus 1968 original	14,987	18,476
	2. Falkus 1968 expanded (original + II)	16,045	19,720
	B. 1. Prokopovich 1931 original	13,896	14,700
	2. Prokopovich 1931 expanded (original + II)	14,954	15,944
	C. 1. Gosplan-Strumilin 1927 original	14,538	17,108
	2. Gosplan-Strumilin 1927 expanded (original + II)	15,596	18,352
	D. 1. Nikitski 1927 original	14,800	17,725
	2. Nikitski 1927 expanded (original + II)	15,858	18,969

Table 3.4 (*cont.*)

Source: I. Derivation of national income from NNP, current estimate:
Indirect business taxes and subsidies: Imperial budget indirect taxes
are taken from *Entwurf des Reichsbudgets für das Jahr 1914*, part 1.
(Petersburg: Bohnke, 1913), p. 3 (Entwurf). Indirect taxes collected
by *zemstvos* are calculated from material supplied by Margaret Miller,
The Economic Development of Russia, 1905-1917, 2nd ed. (London: Cass,
1967), p. 169. Indirect taxes collected by municipal governments are
estimated from Miller (pp. 144, 170). State subsidies to the private
sector are taken from Iu. Shebalin, "Gosudarstvenny biudzhet tsarskoi
Rossii," *Istoricheskie zapiski* 62 (1959); 190.
   Current surpluses of government enterprises: The current surplus
of government enterprises is estimated as the sum of the current surpluses from state railroads and the spirits monopoly. I then check
this figure using general budgetary aggregates on expenditures and
revenues on government enterprises and state property. According to
Entwurf 1914 (pp. 4, 14, 15), the state spirits monopoly generated a
gross income of 838 million rubles and required gross expenditures of
217 million rubles in 1913, yielding a current surplus of 621 million
rubles. From S. G. Strumilin, *Statistika i ekonomika* (Moscow: Nauka,
1963), pp. 399-407 and Shebalin (p. 190), I estimate the current surplus of the state railroads in the following manner: According to
Strumilin (p. 407), gross profits of state and private railroads in
1913 equaled 398 million rubles. To this, I apply the ratio of state
railroad profit to total railroad profits during the 1909-13 period of
66% (Strumilin, p. 405) to yield the state railroad's share of total
profits of 263 million rubles. The above figure does not include state
interest payments on railroad debt of 142 million rubles (Shebalin, p.
190), which we subtract from the 263 million ruble figure to yield a
net state profit (surplus) of 121 million rubles for 1913. In this
manner I estimate that the total 1913 current surplus of state enterprises equaled 742 million rubles (the sum of spirit monopoly and state
railroad surpluses). I check this figure for general consistency by
subtracting reported aggregate 1913 budgetary expenditures on government enterprises and state property including expenditures on railroad
debt service (equaling 1250 million rubles, from Miller, pp. 126-31,
Shebalin, p. 190) from aggregate state revenues derived from state
enterprises and state property (Miller, pp. 126-31), which equaled 1946
million rubles in 1913. In this way I calculate a surplus of 696
million rubles in 1913, which is 42 million rubles less than the first
estimate. I use the first estimate because I believe that the current
surplus can be more accurately estimated in this manner, rather than
relying on reported budgetary aggregates on revenues and expenditures.
For example, I have no way of knowing how to apportion interest payments (which are often not included in operating expenditures) among
state enterprises and other operations, and I suspect that some
expenditures on state enterprises may enter under administrative outlays.
   I have no information on current surpluses of *zemstvo* and
municipal enterprises, and I doubt that they were of consequence. They
are thus ignored in the surplus calculations.
   USSR pre-1939 territory figures have been calculated by applying
the USSR empire population ratio to the above figures with the exception of the state railroad surplus, which is calculated by applying the
ratio of USSR territory track to empire territory track.

Table 3.4 (*cont.*)

II. Additions to narrow Marxian national income concept: The four available estimates of Russian 1913 national income by sector of origin (Falkus 1968, Prokopovich 1931, Gosplan 1929, and Nikitski 1927) all employ the narrow Marxian concept of national income, which omits government and private sector services not directly related to the production process and net product originating in the rest of the world. In this section I detail my estimation of these omitted categories for Russia in 1913:

A. *Product originating in the rest of the world:* The 399 million ruble figure is explained in my discussion of net foreign investment (Appendix M). This figure represents the net outflow of interest and dividend payments in 1913 to foreigners.

B. *Net government product:* The 1913 value added of the government sector, which is estimated at 565 and 480 million rubles for empire and USSR territory, is measured as the sum of wages and salaries of government employees. I follow U.S. Department of Commerce practices by not including interest paid by government in value added, which in the Russian case is a substantial sum. I can only crudely approximate net government product by multiplying 1913 employment in the government sector by the assumed 1913 average annual wage. I estimate employment in government service in 1913 at 2.2 million as the sum of armed forces personnel (appendix E) and government employment (.7 million). The latter figure is calculated in the absence of detailed information on government employment beyond that of the 1897 census by applying the 1897 ratio of government employment to total labor force from *Russian Yearbook 1912*, Howard Kennard, ed. (London: Eyre, 1912), pp. 48-9, of 1.4% to an estimate of total 1913 labor force (50.4 million) from Paul Gregory, "Economic Growth and Structural Change in Tsarist Russia: A Case of Modern Economic Growth?" *Soviet Studies* 23, No. 3 (January 1972): 433. I chose the 1913 average annual industrial wage of 257 rubles from S. G. Strumilin, *Ocherki ekonomicheskoi istorii Rossii i SSSR* (Moscow: Nauka, 1966), p. 121, as a rough aproximation of average annual wages in the government sector. I stress that this calculation of government net product is a gross approximation subject to a wide margin of error. I arbitrarily take 100 rubles per year as the average annual wage for military personnel.

C. *Domestic and medical services:* The value added estimates for the domestic and medical-care sectors are from appendix C.

D. *Net housing product:* The value added of the housing sector (estimated at 743 and 651 million rubles for empire and USSR territory) is calculated by applying the ratio of value added to gross output of the urban housing stock in 1912 (62% Strumilin, p. 308) to the actual and imputed rental values in table 3.2.

III. Previous national income estimates: M. E. Falkus, "Russia's National Income, 1913: A Revaluation," *Economica*, N.S. 35, No. 137 (February 1968): 60; A. L. Vainshtein, *Narodny dokhod Rossii i SSSR* (Moscow: Nauka, 1969), pp. 66-8.

THE TIME SERIES RESULTS: GOLDSMITH, VARZAR, AND PROKOPOVICH
The general compatability of my estimate for 1913 and the other
available estimates for 1913 (by sector of origin) is a comforting
finding, for major errors in my estimate may be revealed by divergences
from the sector-of-origin estimates. The same sort of comparison can
be made with the available time series studies of tsarist national
income.

Let me begin by summarizing previous time series studies of
aggregate Russian output between 1885 and 1913. The most well known
and frequently cited study is that of Raymond Goldsmith,[9] covering the
period 1860 to 1913. Goldsmith attempts to measure aggregate Russian
output during this period in constant prices. Alternate price weights
are used to measure industrial output, but Goldsmith finds that the
choice of price weights has little impact on the growth indexes. In
the following figures cited for Goldsmith, I use late year price
weights (wherever possible), but the reader should note that this is
not important as far as the growth indexes are concerned. In
actuality, Goldsmith's GNP index consists of a factory production index
and a crop production index, which he expands into an aggregate production index by means of assumptions concerning the omitted indexes
(livestock, services, and handicraft industry). The Goldsmith figures
cited for the period 1900-13 are taken from a recalculation prepared by
me in 1972 for the purpose of breaking the Goldsmith study down into
subperiods.

The second major study of the growth of Russian national income
is S. N. Prokopovich's study published in 1918 of 1900 and 1913
national income (Marxian concept).[10] Prokopovich applied 1900 prices
to the physical outputs of 1900 and 1913 and then netted out intermediate expenditures. In this way, Prokopovich avoided the necessity
of deflating one set of figures with some type of national income
deflator. A serious evaluation of Prokopovich's 1918 study is given by
Vainshtein, who argues against the viewpoint that the Prokopovich
estimate is too high.[11]

One can combine Prokopovich's 1918 study with M. E. Falkus's
reevaluation of Prokopovich's estimate for 1913 to obtain yet another
index of the growth of Russian national income between 1900 and 1913.[12]
As Falkus notes, Prokopovich's estimate for 1913 in many instances

(most important agricultural production) used 1909-13 averages rather than actual 1913 output. Insofar as 1913 was the best year for Russian agriculture of the entire tsarist period, Prokopovich would have understated 1913 national income. As noted in Table 3.4, Falkus has revised the 1913 Prokopovich estimate upward and has recalculated growth between 1900 and 1913 in light of this revision.

The third study against which my time series results can be compared is not an estimate of national income per se but, rather, an ad hoc aggregation of a series of thirty-five physical production series (both consumer and producer goods) weighted by 1913 prices. This series was compiled by the noted Russian statistician V. E. Varzar and was apparently completed in the late 1920s but never published.[13] Although, as is readily evident, such an index deviates substantially from the net or final product concepts required for a national income series, it should nevertheless provide an interesting check on the alternate series.

In Table 3.5, I supply the annual growth rates for selected subperiods yielded by the alternate estimates of Russian aggregate output. These annual growth rates can then be compared with those presented in this work.

As Table 3.5 indicates, my estimates are higher than the two estimates that have traditionally been cited in the literature for the growth of Russian aggregate output, namely, those of Goldsmith and Prokopovich. For instance, for the entire period (1885-1913) my estimated annual growth rate is 3.25%; whereas, Goldsmith's is 2.75% with a suggested error interval of ±0.25%. For the period 1900 to 1913, Prokopovich and Goldsmith are in general agreement, both estimating an annual growth rate of approximately 2.5%. My own figure is 3.25%. It should be noted, however, that my estimates are in general agreement with those of Varzar and with Falkus's revision of the 1918 Prokopovich study. In general, if my estimates are to be believed, Russian national income grew at a rate some 25% faster than that suggested by Prokopovich and Goldsmith.

A REEVALUATION OF THE GOLDSMITH STUDY

Raymond Goldsmith's study of Russian national income was completed in 1961 and has not been subjected to a serious reevaluation. As I noted

Table 3.5. *Comparison of alternate growth rates and alternate national income studies with current estimates*

Period	Author/Pub. date	Description	Annual growth
1900-1913	Prokopovich (1918)	National income, Marxian concept, 1900 prices	2.6
	Falkus-Prokopovich (1968)	Upward revision of Prokopovich's 1913 estimate	3.1
	Goldsmith[a] (1961-[1972])	GNP in 1900 prices, Goldsmith assumptions[b]	2.4
	Varzar (1929?)	Aggregation of 35 physical production series, 1913 prices	3.1
	Current estimate (1982)	NNP in 1913 prices	3.25
1885-1913	Goldsmith[c]		2.75 (±0.25)
	Varzar[d]		3.25
	Current estimate		3.4

[a] 1901-03 to 1911-13.
[b] Service sector assumed to grow at the rate of employment in commerce. 1% annual growth of livestock.
[c] 1883-1913.
[d] The Varzar figure is extrapolated from 1887 to 1885 using my national income index (table 3.1).

Sources: S. N. Prokopovich, *Opyt ischisleniia narodnogo dokhoda 50 gub. Evropeiskoi Rossii v 1900-1913 gg.* (Moscow: Sovet Vserossiiskikh Kooperativnykh Sezdov, 1918), preface, p. 5; M. E. Falkus, "Russia's National Income, 1913: A Revaluation," *Economica*, N.S. 35, No. 137 (February 1968): 58; Paul Gregory, "Economic Growth and Structural Change in Tsarist Russia: A Case of Modern Economic Growth?" *Soviet Studies* 23, No. 3 (January 1972): 433; Raymond Goldsmith, "The Economic Growth of Tsarist Russia, 1860-1913," *Economic Development and Cultural Change* 9, No. 3 (April 1961): 441-3. The Varzar index is given in P. P. Maslov, *Kriticheski analiz burzhuaznykh statisticheskikh publikatsii* (Moscow: Nauka, 1955), p. 459.

above, the Goldsmith series is founded on two major subindexes: an index of industrial factory production and an index of agricultural production (net of livestock). The industrial production index is simply that of N. D. Kondratiev, recalculated with a series of alternate early, middle, and late year weights. The agricultural production index is a production index of grain and technical products. Because relatively little information is provided by Goldsmith concerning the important questions of regional adjustments and price weights, I am not in a good position to assess his agricultural production series. The remaining series are constructed by means of various assumptions (Goldsmith assumed that the handicraft industry grew at two-thirds the rate of factory industry, livestock grew at 1% per annum, etc.).

In Table 3.6, I supply my recalculation of Russian national income by sector of origin. From the original Goldsmith study I have retained his index of factory industrial production (1908 weights) and I employ his assumption that handicraft output grew at two-thirds the rate of factory production. For agriculture, I also use Goldsmith's index for technical crops. For sector weights, I use 1913 value added as estimated by Falkus. The remaining sector indexes are drawn either directly from this study (trade, net housing product, domestic service, and utilities) or from various physical production series (transport and communication, medical services). Because of the absence of information on construction, I was forced to assume that the share of construction remained stable over the entire period. The details of my recalculation of the sector-of-origin series are provided in the notes to Table 3.6.

The most important result that emerges from Table 3.6 is a higher rate of growth than that of the original Goldsmith study. The recalculated rate of growth for the entire period (1883-7 to 1909-13) is 3.3% per annum compared with Goldsmith's 2.75%. This recalculated figure is quite consistent with my final expenditure series. Thus, I would say that the recalculated sector-of-origin index supports the finding of a higher rate of growth than that suggested by the original Goldsmith and Prokopovich studies of Russian national income. The higher growth finding is, as noted, also supported by the Varzar and Falkus indexes.

A few words are called for to explain why my calculated growth

Table 3.6. *Russian national income by sector of origin, 1883-87 to 1909-13 (1913 value added weights)*

Indexes of sector growth	1883-87	1897-1901	1909-13	1913 value added (1913 rubles) Million rubles	%
1. Agriculture (including forestry and fishing)	49	70	100	10,294	50.7
2. Industry, factory	28	65	100	3,023	14.9
3. Industry, handicraft	42	74	100	1,311	6.5
4. Transport, communication	17	54	100	1,173	5.8
5. Construction	43	69	100	1,035	5.1
6. Trade	53	80	100	1,640	8.1
7. Net government product	33	63	100	565	2.8
8. Net housing product	52	61	100	743	3.7
9. Personal medical services	37	69	100	126	.6
10. Domestic service	78	81	100	264	1.3
11. Utilities	60	69	100	118	.6
National income	43.2	69.2	100	20,292	100

Sources: 1913 value added weights: Rows 1-6, M. E. Falkus, "Russia's National Income, 1913: A Revaluation," *Economica*, N.S. 35, No. 137 (February 1968): 55. Rows 7, 8, 10, 11: Paul Gregory, unpublished statistical appendix to the article "1913 Russian National Income: Some Insights into Russian Economic Development," *Quarterly Journal of Economics* 90, No. 3 (August 1976): 445-60. The figure in row 9 is the estimated annual 1913 earnings of physicians and paramedical personnel from appendix C.

Sectoral growth indexes: Agriculture: Individual indexes of technical crop production, livestock producton, and grain production are aggregated using the value added weights of Falkus, "Russia's National Income," p. 64. For grains, I include major grains (wheat, rye, barley, oats, and potatoes), which accounted for 88% of non-technical crop production in 1913. Omitted minor grains and vegetables are assumed to grow at the same rate as major grains. The technical crop index is that used by Raymond Goldsmith in "The Economic Growth of Tsarist Russia, 1860-1913," *Economic Development and Cultural Change* 9, No. 3 (April 1961): 448-50. Prior to 1895, an index for the 50 European provinces is used. The net grain production data are taken from *Bulletin Russe de statistique financiere et de legislation*, 5th ed., 1898: 222-31 (which cites estimates by M. E. Kuhn). The remaining figures are from *Ezhegodnik ministerstva finansov* 1905: 494-7 and from *Statisticheski ezhegodnik Rossii*, annual editions 1904 to 1913. Appropriate territorial adjustments are made in the pre-1897 figures which cover the 50 European provinces and the Polish provinces. To weight the individual crop figures, 1913 prices are used. A complete description of the grain series can be found in appendix D. The livestock series is taken from Appendix H.

Industry, factory: Goldsmith, "Economic Growth of Tsarist Russia," pp. 462-3 (1908 base, imputed weights).

Industry, handicraft: I use here the same assumption as Goldsmith, based upon earlier studies by S. G. Strumilin, that handicraft production grew at two-thirds the rate of factory production.

Transportation, communication: This is a physical index of freight and passenger rail hauls (ton/km and passenger/km, where the cost of transporting one ton/km of freight is roughly equivalent to one passenger/km). The series is cited in S. G. Strumilin, *Statistika i ekonomika* (Moscow: Nauka, 1963), p. 409, and is drawn from the *Statisticheski sbornik Ministerstva putei soobshcheniia* series. A separate series for communications is not derived (weight 0.6 of 1% of national income), but series on numbers of letters, packages, and telegrams from various official publications suggest similar, but slightly slower, rates of growth of communications.

Construction: No information is available on the output of the construction sector. After consulting the long-term statistics of other countries on national income shares of construction, primarily Simon Kuznets, *Economic Growth of Nations* (Cambridge: Harvard University Press, 1971), pp. 144-62, I concluded that the assumption of no change in the national income share of construction would be reasonable. Thus the growth rate of construction is computed so as to maintain a constant construction share.

Trade: The value added series of the trade sector is a weighted index of employment in wholesale and retail trade from Strumilin, *Statistika*, p. 436, and a deflated index of capital stock in trade establishments (also from Strumilin, *Statistika*, p. 441). The price deflator is Podtiagin's index of retail prices cited in Strumilin's *Ocherki ekonomicheskoi istorii Rossii i SSSR* (Moscow: Nauka, 1966), p. 89. The labor weight is calculated to be 85% of the total by multiplying 1913 trade employment by the 1913 average industrial wage of 250 rubles.

Net government product: This is a constant price series of government expenditures for final goods and services at the imperial and local level (Appendixes F and G).

Net housing product: This series is based upon the series on residential capital stock in constant prices described in Appendix J.

Personal medical services: The index is based upon the number of physicians, nurses, and feldshers in the Russian Empire, where rough earnings weights are used to aggregate the three series. The raw data are drawn from *Statisticheski ezhegodnik Rossii*, annual series 1904 to 1914, and from *Sbornik svedenii po Rossii*, 1884-5, 1890, and 1896 editions, section *organizatsiia vrachebnoi pomoshchi*.

Table 3.6 (cont.)

   Domestic service: Domestic service employment is calculated by
applying the combined Moscow-Petersburg ratios of domestic servants to
population to the urban population of the 50 European provinces to
obtain an index of service employment. Annual service employment is
calculated by applying this index to Rashin's figure of service employment in 1913 (1.55 million), cited in Gregory, "1913 Russian National
Income," statistical appendix. The figures on Moscow-Petersburg service employment are from A. G. Rashin, *Naselenie Rossii 3a 100 let*
(Moscow: Gosstatizdat, 1956), pp. 114, 115, 323-5. The urban population series is from V. Zaitsev and V. G. Groman, eds., *Vliianie
neurozhaev na narodnoe khoziaistvo Rossii* (Petersburg: 1927), part 2,
p. 65. The approximate ratios of domestic servants to urban population
are: 1885-90: 11%; 1894 and 1896: 10%; 1900: 8.5%; 1903: 8.3%; 1907:
8%; 1910: 7.9%; 1913: 7.7%. These ratios are rough and involve interpolations between benchmarks, but one would imagine that changes in the
ratios would be relatively slow and orderly.
   Utilities: This series has been derived laboriously from data on
utility capital stock and expenditures of municipally owned utilities.
Its derivation is described in Appendix C. This is likely the most
unreliable series in Table 3.6, but its weight is only 0.6 of 1%.

rate is higher than that of Goldsmith. There are three explanations:
The first is that the growth rate of omitted service sectors (including
a slightly different estimate for trade), which accounted for slightly
less than 20% of 1913 national income, is much higher (2.8%) than that
incorporated into the Goldsmith figures. Second, my calculated 1.5%
annual growth rate of livestock production is substantially higher than
Goldsmith's figure. Third, and most important, I calculate the growth
rate of grain production at 3.1% annually, as compared with Goldsmith's
rate of 2.5%. As grain production accounted for some one-third of 1913
national income, this difference alone will yield an annual growth rate
one-fifth of 1% higher than Goldsmith's. Although Goldsmith is not too
specific about his method of calculating grain production, it appears
that he employed *gross* output figures weighted by average grain prices
near the turn of the century. Because of lack of better data, he used
a series for the 50 provinces alone (which accounted for 78% of empire
wheat production, 90% of rye production, and 82% of barley production
in 1895) to calculate the growth of grain production prior to 1895.
   According to my calculations, empire grain production grew at a
slightly more rapid rate than production in the 50 provinces throughout
the period. Moreover, my grain production figures are based (prior to
1898) on unpublished net production figures for 63 provinces, prepared

within the Ministry of Interior by M. E. Kuhn,[14] a contemporary
authority on grain statistics, which I then link to net production
figures after 1898 cited in various official statistical publications.
According to my data, the ratios of net to gross grain output increased
by some 10% between 1885-90 and 1909-13, and this alone accounts for
almost one-half of the growth rate differential.

The increase in the ratios of net to gross crop production reported in the tsarist grain statistics is thus a crucial ingredient in
my recalculation. It is important to establish whether this was a real
or statistical phenomenon. Unfortunately, historical statistics on
this matter are rare, but the one set of statistics I have been able to
find (for Prussia, 1816-64) suggest a similar pattern of development of
net and gross ratios.[15]

The difference in grain production figures raises a troublesome
conflict, which I am unable to resolve because I know little of the
details of Goldsmith's calculations and the sources of his data. Part
of the difference is explained by his use of gross, and my use of net,
production figures, and another part is explained by my use of the Kuhn
figures, which cover much more empire grain production (about 7% more
for grains and 50% more for potatoes) than Goldsmith. Moreover, the
question of weighting is an important one. It is not clear whether
Goldsmith deals with tons of grain and potato equivalents or weights
the individual grains by their prices. This is important because of
the more rapid growth of high priced wheat than of barley and potatoes.

It may be true that the official growth rates of grain production
should be lowered because of better coverage for later periods, but I
have no evidence to this effect, and the adjustment that Goldsmith
makes for increasing coverage is very small anyway. For other sectors,
such as factory production and handicraft, I accept Goldsmith's indexes
and assumptions; so differences in growth rates of industrial production cannot explain the divergence between the two calculated national
income growth rates. Thus, the most important difference between my
series and that of Goldsmith is a much higher growth rate of grain
production, which accounts for more than 50% of the difference in
aggregate growth rates. The more favorable performance of agriculture
than that admitted by Goldsmith is an important finding, for it suggests a more viable agriculture than that generally assumed, and I

believe that the differences between my findings and those of Goldsmith should be subjected to scrutiny by other researchers.

SUMMARY

In this chapter, annual estimates of Russian national income by final expenditure in current and in constant 1913 prices were presented (Tables 3.1, 3.2). These figures will be analyzed in Chapters 7 and 8. In Chapter 7 the pattern of economic development and rate of growth of the tsarist economy in the late nineteenth and early twentieth centuries will be contrasted with the experiences of other industrialized countries undergoing modern economic growth, and in Chapter 8 the tsarist period and Soviet period growth experiences will be compared.

In Chapter 2, the effects of estimation biases and of index number relativity were considered in a theoretical framework. In this chapter, their possible impacts on these estimates were deliberated. It was decided that the impact of using input price deflators on investment ratios and overall economic growth was likely not significant, although the effect on real investment expenditures alone could be significant. This conclusion was based upon alternate calculations of real fixed investment (following the Soviet period studies of Moorsteen and Powell) and was due, quite simply, to the small weight of fixed investment in tsarist national income.

Finally, the current national income series was compared with previous studies of tsarist aggregate output. Comparisons with other estimates for the year 1913 (after adjustment for conceptual differences) indicated that there was a surprising degree of agreement between the current estimates and those of Gosplan, Nikitski, and Falkus. The only substantive disagreement was with Prokopovich's 1931 estimate, which appeared to be low relative to the current estimates.

The current series was also contrasted with available time series studies of Russian national output. Here it was found that the current estimate yields substantially higher growth rates than those indicated by the much cited studies of Raymond Goldsmith and S. N. Prokopovich. In fact, the current estimates suggested an annual rate of growth some 25% above that of Goldsmith. This finding is supported by the studies of Falkus and of Varzar, who calculate the growth rate of aggregate output nearly as high as those of the current study.

As a check on the current estimates, an alternate national income series by sector of origin was prepared, which retained Goldsmith's factory production index and several of his assumptions. This independent index also suggested a higher growth rate and proved to be fully consistent with the final expenditure series. The principal differences between the revised sector-of-origin series and that of Goldsmith were differences in value added weights, the inclusion of service sectors including government, more complete territorial adjustments for agriculture, and the use of net, rather than gross, agricultural output. For the period as a whole (1885-1913) both the final expenditure series and the sector-of-origin series suggest an annual rate of growth of output of around 3.25% per annum versus Goldsmith's 2.75%. If one applies a liberal adjustment for the use of material input price deflators to calculate fixed investment, the tsarist period figure would be raised at most from 3.25% to 3.3% per annum.

NOTES TO CHAPTER 3

1   Imperial government expenditures were estimated for various benchmark years by
    netting out intermediate expenditures on public enterprises and transfers and
    subsidies. This was a rather laborious process and could only be undertaken
    for a limited number of benchmark years. The intervening years were inter-
    polated by an index of imperial government expenditures. As the ratios of
    items to be netted out to total expenditures remained fairly constant, this
    interpolation should be fairly accurate.

2   Investment expenditures on state railroads are included under railroad in-
    vestment. Other government investment expenditures are primarily on government
    enterprises and government buildings. Defense capital outlays are not
    included.

3   I have not been able to obtain the original Podtiagin study. Instead, I have
    used his results as described and cited by S. G. Strumilin in *Ocherki
    ekonomicheskoi istorii Rossii i SSSR* (Moscow: Nauka, 1966), p. 89.

4   These figures are cited by S. N. Prokopovich, "The National Income of the
    USSR," Memorandum No. 3, Birmingham Bureau of Research on Russian Economic
    Conditions (November 1931), pp. 6-7. The Sobolev estimate ("prewar" invest-
    ments equal 1500 million rubles) is given in M. N. Sobolev, "Nakoplenie
    kapitalov v Sovetskom Soiuze," *Ekonomicheskoe obozrenie* 3 (1925). Sobolev sums
    the emissions of bonds and equities, the increment in savings bank deposits,
    and the savings of the "non-capitalist" classes.

5   A. L. Vainshtein, *Narodnoe bogatstvo i narodnokhoziaistvennoe nakoplenie
    predrevoliutsionnoi Rossii* (Moscow: Gosstatizdat, 1960), introduction by S. G.
    Strumilin, p. 8.

6   Vainshtein, *Narodnoe bogatstvo*, pp. 370-1.

7   A. L. Vainshtein, *Narodny dokhod Rossii i SSSR* (Moscow: Nauka, 1969), pp.
    64-72.

8   Vainshtein, *Narodny dokhod*, p. 65.

9   Raymond Goldsmith, "The Economic Growth of Tsarst Russia, 1860-1913," *Economic
    Development and Cultural Change* 9, No. 3 (April 1961).

10 S. N. Prokopovich, *Opyt ischisleniia narodnogo dokhoda 50 gubernii Evropeiskoi
    Rossii v 1900-1913 gg.* (Moscow: Sovet Vserossiiskikh Kooperativnykh Sezdov,
    1918).

11 Vainshtein, *Narodny dokhod*, pp. 64-70.

12 M. E. Falkus, "Russia's National Income, 1913: A Revaluation," *Economica* N.S.
    35, No. 137 (February 1968):58.

13 The Varzar study was found in Varzar's personal papers after his death in 1940.
    The index is described in P. P. Maslov, *Kriticheski analiz burzhauznykh
    statisticheskikh publikatsii* (Moscow: Nauka, 1955), pp. 448-63.

14 The Kuhn estimates are published in *Bulletin russe de statistique financiere et
    de legislation*, 5th ed. (1898), pp. 222-31.

15 R. H. Tilly, "Capital Formation in Germany in the Nineteenth Century," *Cam-
    bridge Economic History of Europe*, vol. 7, pt. 2 (Cambridge University Press,
    1978), p. 390.

CHAPTER 4

AN OVERVIEW OF THE COMPONENT ACCOUNTS

The full details of my calculations are provided in the technical appendixes. In this chapter I provide an overview of the methods and sources used to estimate the major components of the national income series. In this way I seek to provide the reader with a flavor of the strengths and weaknesses of each component series without going through the technical details of each appendix. I do not discuss the derivation of minor series in this chapter, with the exception of net foreign investment, a series that has little affect on net national product but is of interest in its own right.

PERSONAL CONSUMPTION EXPENDITURES

Personal consumption expenditures are estimated as the sum of retail sales, housing rental outlays, outlays for personal services, consumption of farm products in kind, and military subsistence. The accounts in current and in 1913 constant prices are given in Tables 3.1 and 3.2. Their estimation is described in detail in Appendixes A through E. In this chapter only a flavor of the most important calculations can be provided and only a limited number of references are supplied. Critical assumptions and possible biases form the focus of this discussion; the more routine details are reserved for the technical appendixes.

The two principal component of the consumption series are retail sales and the consumption of farm products in kind. Together, they accounted for 85% of consumption expenditures in 1913. The reliability of the personal consumption series hinges primarily upon these two series, and they are discussed in some detail in this chapter. The minor accounts are described in the technical appendixes.

Retail sales (Appendix A)

The retail sales figures are drawn from a study by G. A. Dikhtiar[1] and from S. G. Strumilin's reporting of trade turnover by the Ministry of

Finance for 1885 to 1913.[2] The Strumilin-Dikhtiar series is based upon
trade turnover data reported to tax authorities. A supplementary tax
(*dopol'nite'ny nalog*) was levied on establishments along with a basic
"patent" tax and varied with the annual turnover and profits of the
establishment.[3] This supplementary tax was levied on larger establishments; small or nonprofitable establishments were, in certain
cases, exempted, as were other establishments already subject to an
excise tax.[4] A 3% tax on enterprise profits was levied on trade corporations; thus the sales of corporate trade establishments had to be
estimated by Strumilin using coefficients of profits to turnover. The
major exemption from indirect taxes was the state spirit monopoly. The
system of supplementary taxation was extremely complicated, and fifty
pages of text are required in the official Ministry of Finance publication to describe the system.[5]

Dikhtiar extracts retail trade volume from tax data series by
excluding wholesale trade establishments. The tax data are not detailed enough to segregate wholesale and retail trade with great
precision, but Dikhtiar's estimates appear to be reasonably accurate.
State sales of spirits were reported regularly by the Ministry of
Finance.[6] Total retail sales are then the sum of sales of retail
establishments (estimated from tax data) and of spirit sales by the
state monopoly. Dikhtiar's figures cover only the period 1899 to 1913.
I backcast them to 1885 by duplicating Dikhtiar's methodology.

Retail sales account for 38% of 1913 national income, thus it is
important to have some evaluation of the accuracy of the Dikhtiar-
Strumilin estimates. Strumilin himself writes that his own figures
must be regarded as "approximative."[7]

Two major sources of measurement errors must be considered:
significant tax evasion and the inclusion of some wholesale sales. In
the case of tax evasions, two countervailing forces should be present:
the enterprise's desire to avoid paying versus the desire of the state
to collect. One cannot argue a priori that one force outweighs the
other, but I believe that official tax data should provide a reasonable
approximation of trade turnover, especially as an index over time.
This is also the conclusion reached by B. V. Avilov, the authoritative
compiler of the statistical appendix of the *Granat* encyclopedia.[8] My
own suspicion is that underreporting would be most serious in remote

areas, where markets operated on a more informal basis, for example, intrapeasant markets in villages. But such sales will be captured by the farm consumption figures.

For the deflation of retail expenditures, three alternate price indexes are available.[9] Two are retail price indexes: the Petersburg index of the Institute of Economic Research and the retail price index for Petersburg and Moscow prepared by M. E. Kokhna. In both indexes, the underlying weights were based upon the structure of average budget expenditures of industrial workers in the two cities. The Petersburg portion of the combined Kokhna index coincides closely with the Institute of Economic Research index. There are, however, moderate discrepancies between the two Petersburg price indexes and the Moscow price index, which could be either the product of divergent regional prices or of different product coverage.

A third price index is the index compiled by Podtiagin. The Podtiagin index is a pseudo-retail price index as its weights are based on average worker budgets, but it uses wholesale prices, taken from price publications of the Ministry of Trade and Industry. The Podtiagin index covers 66 commodities from various regional and metropolitan markets. It is better suited to capture national price trends, but it does employ wholesale prices and, in some instances, even includes world market prices.

Fortunately, the choice of the appropriate price index is not crucial, especially if one is interested in long-term trends. According to all three price indexes, the annual rate of growth of real retail sales for 1885 to 1913 was slightly over 3.5%, and all three round to 4%. For the subperiods 1885 to 1900 and 1900 to 1913, the rate varies from 4% to 5% for the earlier period and rounds in all three cases to 2% in the later period. For the industrialization decade (1891-1900), the growth rate rounds to 7% in the case of the major city indexes and to 8% for the Podtiagin index. The greatest discrepancy among the indexes is for the subperiods 1900-07 and 1907-13. The Podtiagin index reveals a substantial (14%) decline between 1900 and 1907 and then a dramatic increase (47%) from 1907 to 1913. The major city indexes, on the other hand, reveal a stagnant level of real retail sales between 1900 and 1907 and a less substantial increase between 1907 and 1913.[10]

Retained agricultural products (Appendix D)

In 1913 retained agricultural products (defined to include hunting and fishing) accounted for one-third of NNP; so special attention should be accorded the difficult estimation of this final expenditure category. To estimate the consumption of farm products in kind, I subtract marketings from net output. Only data on the marketings of grain products were available. Yet grain products, according to my calculations, accounted for one-half of retained farm products, and I was forced to estimate the remaining product categories from production data alone, assuming that the ratios of retained products to net outputs remained constant over the period. This assumption is supported by the finding that the ratio of marketings to net output remained fairly constant for grain products, but there is no direct evidence that the same was true of other farm products.

Because of data lacunae on farm marketings other than grain products, I consider the nongrain retained agricultural products series the weakest major component of the NNP series. Yet I would doubt that serious errors are involved, for very substantial changes in the ratios of marketings to net outputs for nongrain products would be required to introduce large errors.

The estimation of the consumption of grain products in kind proceeds as follows: What I seek to measure conceptually is the consumption of grain products by the immediate producer *within the producing village*. Marketings external to the producing village should be subtracted from net output (gross output minus seed), and marketings should be net of intravillage sales. Intravillage sales are not likely to be captured in the retail sales figures, and this definition allows such sales to enter through retained farm products.

For the net grain production data, I use the official Ministry of Interior figures, including some important "unpublished" estimates prepared for internal use covering the period 1885 to 1897.[11] The official published Ministry of Interior net production figures for net grain production are used for the period after 1896. "Net production" is defined as gross production minus output retained for seed purposes (and likely some provision for harvesting losses).

The Ministry of Interior figures indicate a 10% increase in the ratio of net to gross production for major grains between 1885-90 and

1906-13, and this increase explains much of the difference between my estimate of grain output and that of Goldsmith. The early data cover only the 50 European provinces and Poland and data for the West Caucasian and Asian provinces are available only after 1896, I have had to make a series of territorial adjustments to arrive at territorially consistent estimates.

There has been considerable controversy over the reliability of the Central Statistical Committee's (of the Ministry of Interior) estimates of Russian grain output, but there appears to be a reasonable consensus that they capture intertemporal trends rather well after 1885. The main controversy has focused instead upon the correction in the level, and after reading this literature, I have chosen to use a rather modest (7%) upward correction for 1913.

The major source of data on grain marketings was published by the Ministry of Transportation for shipments of major grains by rail and water (netting out transshipments between the types of carriers).[12] I believe these data to be quite accurate. The major omission is shipments from the producer to the end user by road (without entering either the rail or water transport system). If such deliveries were largely for the local peasant (intravillage) market, such road shipments should not be counted anyway, but there is some information that road shipments of grains to southern ports was consequential.

I have proceeded from a 1913 benchmark of retained grain products that is consistent with independent budgetary studies of grain marketings. To the 1913 figure, I apply the indexes of net production and marketings, the latter supplied by data on rail and water shipments. The omission of grains transported by road will likely bias this series, but it should bias it in the direction of *understating* the rate of growth of retained grains because the share of road transport should be declining over the period. My finding of an unexpectedly high rate of growth of retained grain products does not depend upon the treatment of road transport. Experimental calculations also suggest that this result is not likely to depend upon improving coverage in the production indexes.

Retained grains are estimated in both constant 1913 prices and in current prices. In both cases, the individual physical series of retained grains are multiplied by the appropriate prices of the individual products. These prices are drawn from the wealth of data on agricultural prices. The prices used are average prices from a large number of urban and regional markets.

For grain products as a whole, the resulting series reveals a fairly constant ratio of grain marketings to net output from 1885 to 1913. I lacked data on the marketings of nongrain agricultural products (including hunting and fishing), except for the year 1913.[13] I assumed therefore that the marketings of these products grew at the same rate as net output. The output data of nongrain products are of varying quality, ranging from reasonably good (technical crops) to virtually nonexistent (hunting and fishing). In the case of nonexistent production data, I had to assume that these categories grew at the same rate as the included categories. For meat and dairy products, I assumed that output grew at the same rate as livestock herds (cattle); that is, I assume constant capital output ratios for these products. I would think that this assumption would result in the understatement of dairy product growth with improving husbandry techniques.

As noted above, the consumption in kind of nongrain agricultural products is likely the weakest element in this study. It should be emphasized that other retained agricultural products grew at a much slower pace than did retained grain products; so the finding of an unexpectedly rapid growth of retained farm products follows from the firmer grain data and not from the weaker nongrain estimates.

IMPERIAL BUDGET EXPENDITURES (APPENDIX F)

A wealth of information on imperial government expenditures is supplied in the various budgetary reports of the Ministry of Finance on the magnitude and distribution of imperial government expenditures;[14] moreover, the accounting system remained relatively uniform throughout the 1885 to 1913 period. Intermediate government expenditures were substantial, as the imperial government operated the state-owned railroads, the state spirits monopoly, various metallurgical enterprises, the telephone company, and some agricultural and timber enterprises. Subsidies and transfers were less important; the most significant subsidy went to the private railroads in the form of profit guarantees, but even at their peak around the turn of the century, such subsidies accounted for only 6% of imperial government expenditures.

The most important deduction from total outlays is interest and principal payments on the state debt. In the later years (after the adoption of the gold standard in 1897), one can deduct directly the official debt service figures reported by the imperial comptroller's office. For earlier years, gold ruble obligations must be converted into credit rubles using the prevailing gold-ruble credit-ruble exchange rate.

The distribution of imperial government expenditures among administrative expenditures, defense, and health and education can be taken directly from the detailed annual budgetary reports. Several minor adjustments must be made. Some "hidden" defense expenditures are included in the budgets of ministries other than the Marine and War ministries, and the Ministry of Finance and the Holy Synod operated some schools. Schools and hospitals belonging to the Marine and War ministries have been left in the defense budget.

Capital expenditures on administration, education and health are calculated separately and are added (Tables 3.1 and 3.2) to total investment outlays. Such expenditures were minor, and their inclusion under investment outlays does not alter the picture of government expenditures (or of net investment).

To deflate imperial government expenditures, I constructed separate deflators for administration, health and education, and defense. In each case, input price deflators are used, and the major component of each deflator is the presumed wage index for employees in each category. The tsarist government did not publish wage series for its employees, and the official salary schedules reported in the various editions of the imperial law codes fail to shed much light on this question. In the absence of direct information on wage indexes, I employ the average earnings of full-time workers and employees of the telegraph service of the state railroads and an index of average earnings of factory workers. The first is assumed to be indicative of earnings of the middle ranks of the bureaucracy; the second is assumed to be representative of the lower ranks. Other price indexes that enter into the government price deflator are the index of wholesale prices and an index of construction prices.

The imperial government expenditure series in current prices is probably the most accurate component of the NNP series. I would judge the deflated series to be reasonably reliable as well. Although direct wage series for government employees are not available, the surrogate wage series should adequately reflect wage movements as should the materials deflators employed in the three separate deflators. The use of input price deflators assumes the absence of productivity improvements within the government sector. Although this assumption may not be accurate, it is nevertheless typically employed in historical and contemporary national income studies. Insufficient detail on government employment was available to calculate an alternate real expenditure series based on government employment.[15]

EXPENDITURES OF LOCAL GOVERNMENT (APPENDIX G)

In contrast to imperial expenditures, the amount of information on local government expenditures is disappointing. Moreover, the administrative organization of local government was quite confusing,[16] and the amount of budgetary information provided by each organization differed widely. The *guberniia* administration stood at the highest level of local government with the *gubernator* serving as the chief administrative officer. A parallel representative government body, the *zemstvo*, existed in 34 *guberniia*, but was lacking in the more remote provinces. The Polish provinces were administered separately. At the local level, government consisted of a municipal government (for cities and towns) and of collective peasant organizations (the *mirs* and *volosti*).

The greatest amount of detail is provided on the expenditures at the *guberniia* level, and one can estimate such expenditures and their distribution between administration and health and education (and in some cases, even defense) at least for selected benchmark years.

There is much less detail on municipal expenditures, where significant intermediate outlays (municipal utilities, slaughterhouses, public transportation, etc.) must be netted out. In fact, data on the distribution of municipal expenditures are available only for three benchmarks (1885, 1895, and 1913), and intermediate years had to be interpolated from these three distributions.

There is even less information on the expenditures of the *mir* and *volost* organizations, especially after 1905.[17] The distribution of these expenditures is known only for 1895, and I had to assume that this distribution prevailed for the entire period. Thus, it is obvious that the weakest figures in the local government series are for the *mir* and *volost* organizations, although this weakness applies more to the distribution of expenditures among the final outlay categories than to the overall figures.

Capital expenditure data of local government organizations were also gathered. For all three levels, the major capital expenditure was for road construction, and such expenditures are itemized separately in the *guberniia* budgets. For municipal government and the *mir* and *volost* organizations, capital expenditures had to be estimated from much weaker data.

Local government expenditures for administration, health and education, and defense are deflated by the same deflators used for imperial government outlays.

AN OVERVIEW OF THE INVESTMENT SERIES

The equipment and structures estimates should directly approximate net fixed investment; estimates of depreciation have not been used to calculate net investment (from gross figures) except for railroad investment. For structures, net investment is derived by taking increments in the *net* stock of structures. I conclude that it is the net stock that is being measured because the estimates of structures are derived from their current insured values (with adjustments for coverage and for uninsured foundations), and it is assumed that the insured value will reflect the net, not the gross, value of the structure. In the case of equipment, an index of gross investment is applied to 1913 *net* equipment investment outlays.[18] In doing so, I assume that the gross and net equipment series move together. If anything, this assumption will understate net investment for early years because of the tendency for the growth of gross investment to outpace that of net investment.[19] For railroad investment, depreciation outlays are deducted from gross investment to calculate net investment.

Because investment in structures accounted for slightly under 50% of total net investment in 1913, some general comments concerning this category are in order. The estimates of net investment in structures are based upon data on the insured values of structures, and it is important to give some consideration to the interpretation of insurance

data. Two polar assumptions can be made concerning the behavior of
insurers, and different calculation methods are implied by each assumption. First, one can assume that the owners of structures updated
their insurance coverage annually to reflect depreciation and inflation
(deflation). The other polar assumption is that owners of structures
insured only the net increment in structures at current prices, leaving
the remaining stock insured at acquisition prices. If one accepts the
first assumption, net investment is estimated by deflating the insured
values and then taking first differences. The second behavioral
assumption requires taking first differences from the insured values
(to obtain net investment in current prices) and then deflating the
investment series. The resulting series can be quite different and we
do not know a priori which assumption is correct.

   An attempt was made to provide alternate calculations based upon
the two polar insurance assumptions and then to use those series that
appeared most realistic. The industry structure and the residential
structure indexes are taken from Arcadius Kahan's study of Russian
capital stock[20] and are applied to A. L. Vainshtein's estimates of 1913
investments.[21] The urban residential structure series is taken directly from Kahan for the period 1885 to 1910. For the period 1910 to
1913, I do not accept Kahan's finding of significant net disinvestment
and accept instead Vainshtein's apparently more realistic finding of
substantial growth. For rural structures, I have conducted an independent study using insurance data.

   The investment goods deflators are described in Appendixes I-L.
For structures and railroad construction, price indexes are constructed
from the material inputs into construction. For the deflation of
inventory investment, wholesale price indexes are used. The equipment
price deflator is constructed from material input prices and from unit
prices of machinery.

Investment in livestock (Appendix H)
The livestock investment (and stock) series is based upon the official
data on livestock herds in agriculture reported by the Central Statistical Committee and by veterinary authorities. From these official
series stated in physical terms, I calculate serial livestock indexes
in both current and constant prices, which I then apply to Vainshtein's

estimates of the stock of livestock (and investment in livestock) for
the year 1913.[22] Vainshtein's own reevaluation of the official statistics is based upon the agricultural census of 1916, which shows the
earlier figures to be understated.

In these calculations I follow Vainshtein's conclusion that the
official series, although they understate the total, are reasonably
reliable intertemporaly. The official series, however, have to be
adjusted for territorial coverage. Prior to 1900, livestock herds were
given for only the 50 European provinces and the Polish provinces.
After 1900, they were given for the entire empire. However, because a
specialized study of Siberian livestock casts doubt on the Siberian
figures,[23] I have had to adjust those figures.

An alternate series on livestock herds in constant 1913 prices is
provided by Kahan for the period 1890 to 1913,[24] and this series is in
marked disagreement with my own. According to my series, the real
stock grew by a factor of 1.45 between 1890 and 1913; according to
Kahan, it grew by a factor of 1.07. Because Kahan does not provide a
detailed description of his methodology and sources, it is difficult to
isolate the source of disagreement.

I would argue that my series is more plausible than Kahan's.
First, Kahan's study implies a drop in per capita livestock holdings of
approximately 40% over a twenty-three-year period, and there is no
evidence of such a drastic decline. Second, feed grains grew in real
terms at a rate close to my livestock series.

An examination of the resulting net investment and capital stock
series for livestock reveals a relatively slow rate of growth of the
stock in 1913 prices of 1.8% per annum, or a rate of livestock growth
roughly equal to that of the population. The livestock investment
series reveal erratic annual movements, some of which may be the consequence of statistical errors, others the consequence of epidemics.
The erratic nature of the annual series suggests that a smoothed investment series may be more useful in evaluating livestock investment
and points toward the use of long moving averages in evaluating livestock. One finds similarly erratic movements in the annual investment
series of the other investment categories. These erratic movements
warn against the use of single benchmark years in evaluating Russian
economic growth and speak in favor of three-to-five-year moving aver-

ages. Rather than smooth the individual series at this point, I have
decided to perform this smoothing when evaluating the national income
series in later chapters.

Investment in agricultural and industrial equipment (Appendix I)
To obtain a net investment series for agricultural and industrial
equipment (including transportation equipment), I begin by estimating
gross equipment investment in current prices for the period 1885 to
1913. Gross investment is taken to be the sum of domestic production
and imports. The machinery import data should be fairly reliable, but
the domestic production series should be much less reliable, first,
because of the difficulty of estimating machinery produced by the
handicraft industry, and second, because of the unreliability of the
factory production series for equipment.[25] From independent data on
the production and importation of agricultural machinery, the current
price series is broken down into agricultural and nonagricultural
equipment.

The resulting series in current prices are deflated using separate equipment price deflators for industrial and agricultural equipment. The deflated series are converted to index form and are then
applied to Vainshtein's estimate of 1913 net investment in agricultural
and nonagricultural equipment. The intertemporal series should capture
gross rather than net equipment investment; therefore, the rate of
increase in the net series may be slightly overstated. However, it is
difficult to come to any firm judgment about the direction of bias in
this series because of the large margins of errors in the equipment
price deflators. As argued in Chapters 2 and 3, the use of these
deflators will likely understate the rate of increase of net equipment
investment. I judge this bias to be more serious than the use of a
gross series.

My constant price series can be compared with Kahan's series on
net investment in industrial and agricultural equipment. The industrial equipment series are not directly comparable because of Kahan's
omission of transportation equipment, but an adjustment for this omission indicates a general agreement between the two series. Kahan's net
investment series for agricultural investment grows at a rate well
above my own series (13% per annum versus 9%).

Net investment, rural structures

I do not use Kahan's series on the net stock of rural structures in
this study, as it appears to be based on the assumption that this stock
grew at the same rate as the number of peasant households.[26] Employing
this assumption, Kahan arrives at a rate of growth of the stock below
the rate of growth of the rural population and thus finds implicitly
that the per capita stock of real rural structures was declining between 1890 and 1913. I find this result implausible, as the evidence
points to rising rural per capita incomes during this period, especially after 1905.

In place of the Kahan series, I have prepared an alternate series
on rural structures derived from data on the compulsory insurance of
peasant structures.[27] First, a pre-1910 series on the value of the net
stock of rural structures in current prices is calculated from data on
insured values and then this series is applied to Vainshtein's estimates of the stock of rural structures for the period 1910 to 1913. A
comparison of the current study with that of Vainshtein indicates that
they are compatible and can be linked together to form a current price
series for the entire 1885 to 1913 period.

The net investment series is calculated in two variants, corresponding to the two polar assumptions concerning the behavior of insurers. The first variant assumes that only new net investment in
rural structures was insured (valued) at current prices and that the
remainder of the stock was valued at original cost. The second variant
assumes that the insured value was at all times equal to the current
market value of the net stock. As indicated above, I use the first
variant in the summary tables because it appears to yield more plausible results. Nevertheless, I should note that differences between
the two variants will not change the overall rate of growth of net
investment substantially.

The investment and capital stock series of rural structures are
deflated using an index of material input prices into construction.

In effect, our methodology really involves the backcasting of
Vainshtein's 1910 estimate of rural structures using an index of the
insured value of peasant structures. This procedure raises two crucial
questions. The first is that one would expect the rate of coverage of
insured peasant structures to be rising over time in a backward rural

society like that of prerevolutionary Russia. I, on the other hand, assume that the rate of coverage (the ratio of insured value to actual value) remained constant over the period covered. The principal argument in support of this assumption is the pervasive system of compulsory insurance of peasant structures that had been in effect in Russia since 1864.[28] This compulsory insurance program was administered by provincial governments, which were financially responsible for losses whether or not the peasant household had paid its insurance premium. Premiums were collected by the *mir* organizations. In my opinion, the imperial government imposed compulsory insurance legislation upon local government so early because of the the state's interest in the financial solvency of the village commune and because of the high incidence of fire damage in the Russian countryside.

The other issue is whether the value of nonpeasant structures can be assumed to grow at the same rate as peasant structures insured under compulsory programs. Nonpeasant structures were insured under "voluntary" insurance programs, and the insurance data indicates that the insured value of such property grew at a more rapid rate than that of peasant structures. There is no way to determine whether this more rapid growth was due to improving insurance coverage or to the real growth of nonpeasant structures; so we adopt the conservative assumption that the two types of structures grew at the same rate.[29]

I should emphasize that my study of rural structures yields a real rate of growth of rural structures (3.5% per annum) almost three times that of Kahan (1.3% per annum). Thus, I find the stock of rural structures to be growing on a per capita basis, whereas Kahan finds it to be declining per capita. The basic argument in favor of my series is that it is based upon data that should yield some approximation of capital stock; whereas the Kahan series is based upon the rate of household formation in the Russian countryside.

Inventory stocks and inventory investment (Appendix K)
Inventory investment (and inventory stocks) are calculated primarily from studies of balance sheets of corporations and mutual associations.[30] In these balance sheet data, corporate assets were broken down into property and inventories. The major problem in calculating total inventory accumulation is that only corporate inventories are

covered, and the inventories of nonincorporated enterprises must some-
how be calculated indirectly. The estimation of the inventory accumulation of nonincorporated enterprises follows the procedures used by
S. G. Strumilin,[31] who estimates the inventories of nonincorporated
enterprises from data on the distribution of capital stock and profits
between the corporate and nonincorporated sector. For industry, corporations accounted for 70% of total capital stock; so the adjustments
for nonincorporated enterprises are not as consequential as they are
for trade, where incorporated enterprises accounted for only 5% of
total trade profits. To calculate the inventories of nonincorporated
trade enterprises, I have assumed that profit-capitalization factors
were equal in both the corporate and noncorporate sectors, and I have
applied the corporate ratios to capitalize the profits of nonincorporated trade enterprises.

There is virtually no serial information on the inventories of
farm products held by producers, but from the little evidence at hand,
I concluded that such inventories likely did not grow at all during the
period investigated and that net inventory investment would therefore
be zero.

The inventory investment series in current prices are deflated by
separate price deflators for industrial inventories and for trade
organization inventories. These deflators are discussed in Appendix K.

Contrary to many of the other investment categories reported in
this chapter, my estimates of real inventory investment are in general
agreement with those of Kahan.[32]

*Net investment, railroad construction, and other forms of transporta-
tion and communication excluding equipment investment (Appendix L)*
To calculate net investment in railroads, I begin with the official
figures on gross cumulated capital expenditures of state and private
railroads,[33] which I convert (using a fairly complicated conversion
procedure for gold ruble obligations) into a consistent series in
credit rubles. These gross investment series are converted into a net
series (excluding land) by using Strumilin's calculations of depreciation.[34] Net investment in current year prices is then calculated by
taking first differences. The net investment series is deflated using
the deflator of railroad construction costs and railroad equipment

described in Appendix L. The resulting series is applied to Vainshtein's estimate of 1913 net investment in structures and inventories in transportation and communication.[35]

ALTERNATIVE INVESTMENT SERIES: GREGORY AND KAHAN

I have sought to describe my estimates of net investment in Russia. In many cases I have contrasted my findings with those of Kahan, noting areas of agreement and disagreement. It may be useful to make some overall comparisons. Kahan concludes that total private capital in 1913 prices grew at an annual rate of 1.7% between 1890 and 1913, that is, at a rate well below all estimates of the rate of growth of output (see Chapter 3). If my estimates of national income are to be accepted, private capital grew at only one-half the rate of output, according to Kahan, or, stated otherwise, the capital-output ratio was declining at about the same rate that capital was increasing. Over a twenty-three-year period, this represents a decline in the capital-output ratio of almost 40%. Even if one accepts the slower growth rates calculated by Goldsmith, one still obtains a 25% reduction in the capital-output ratio. I believe that changes in the capital-output ratio of this magnitude are unlikely.

If one takes my capital stock series in constant 1913 prices, an annual growth rate of net capital stock 1890 to 1913 of 3.6% is obtained, a rate that implies a stable or slightly rising capital-output ratio. This appears to be a more plausible result and seems to lend support to my capital stock series.

NET FOREIGN INVESTMENT

The estimation of net foreign investment calls for the calculation of three balances: the merchandise balance, the dividend and interest balance, and the service and net transfer balance. The details of the estimation of each balance are supplied in Appendix M. Here I provide a brief overview of sources and techniques. Because of the intense interest in the question of foreign capital in Russia, I provide a summary table (4.1) of the Russian balance on current account. The reader may wish to consult a paper written by the author on these results.[36]

The dividend and interest balance is constructed from the wealth of data published by the Ministry of Finance and the banking system on payments to foreigners of dividends, interest, and repatriated profits. The data on the debt service of public debt abroad is quite detailed, and I have had to rely heavily on the work of P. V. Ol' to calculate dividend and interest payments abroad by private enterprises.[37] Net tourist expenditures represent the weakest element of the net foreign investment series, but at least it is based upon fairly firm figures on the number of travelers and length of stay abroad.

As a check on my estimates of net foreign investment, I also calculated net foreign investment directly from the available data on annual increases in indebtedness to foreigners and stocks of monetary reserves. Comparison of these "direct" estimates with the "indirect" estimates of Table 4.1 reveals only minor discrepancies. I take this as an indication that my net foreign investment series is reasonably accurate.

Table 4.1. *Net foreign investment (balance on current account), Russia, 1881 to 1913 (million credit rubles), current year prices*

	1) Merchandise account	2) Interest payments on public debt abroad	3) Interest & dividend payments abroad, corp.	4) Repatriated profits foreign-owned nonincorp. enterprises & interest paid abroad by cities	5) Net tourist expenditures	6) Misc. Items[a]	7) Net foreign investment
1881	- 12	(- 99)	- 8	(- 4)	(- 26)	(- 5)	(-154)
1882	+ 51	(-120)	- 9	(- 4)	(- 27)	(- 5)	(-114)
1883	+ 78	(-102)	- 10	(- 5)	(- 28)	(- 6)	(- 73)
1884	+ 53	(-107)	- 10	(- 5)	(- 29)	(- 6)	(-104)
1885	+102	-134	- 11	- 6	- 33	- 7	- 89
1886	+ 54	-136	- 13	- 6	- 29	- 9	-139
1887	+216	-137	- 13	- 8	- 25	- 9	+ 24
1888	+395	- 141	- 14	- 7	- 28	- 8	+197
1889	+313	-143	- 15	- 8	- 47	- 1	+ 99
1890	+282	-140	- 15	- 7	- 39	+ 3	+ 84
1891	+329	-132	- 15	- 8	- 55	- 4	+115
1892	+ 71	-136	- 17	- 8	- 54	- 7	-151
1893	+138	-146	- 19	- 9	- 54	-11	-101
1894	+100	-145	- 21	-11	- 46	-14	-137

Year							
1895	+150	-155	- 27	-12	- 58	-10	-112
1896	+ 72	-141	- 31	-12	- 63	-12	-187
1897	+125	-153	- 35	-12	- 75	-11	-161
1898	+ 91	-153	- 46	-13	- 76	- 8	-205
1899	- 56	-153	- 51	-12	- 80	- 9	-361
1900	+ 71	-156	- 53	-11	-106	-13	-168
1901	+164	-153	- 48	-10	-107	-13	-167
1902	+261	-160	- 50	-10	- 98	- 1	- 58
1903	+314	-174	- 53	-10	-104	-13	- 30
1904	+371	-165	- 53	-12	-117	- 9	+ 15
1905	+425	-177	- 54	-12	-130	-13	+ 39
1906	+285	-163	- 56	-13	-175	-16	-138
1907	+198	-213	- 63	-14	-155	-12	-259
1908	+ 77	-227	- 66	-16	-137	-12	-381
1909	+510	-225	- 78	-19	-147	-12	+ 29
1910	+353	-229	- 93	-23	-195	-16	-203
1911	+416	-226	-114	-27	-220	-12	-183
1912	+329	-221	-139	-34	-257	-10	-332
1913	+128	-221	-150	-30	-292	-13	-578

Note: Figures in parentheses are guesses and extrapolations.
a Interest receipts, insurance, freight, foreign military equipment.

NOTES TO CHAPTER 4

1   G. A. Dikhtiar, *Vnutrenniaia torgovlia v dorevoliutsionnoi Rossii* (Moscow: Nauka, 1960), p. 73.

2   S. G. Strumilin, *Statistiko-ekonomicheskie ocherki* (Moscow: Gosstatizdat, 1958), p. 680.

3   E.g., *Ezhegodnik ministerstva finansov, vypusk 1909 goda* (Petersburg: Izdania Ministerstva finansov, 1909), pp. 654-77, and Ministerstvo finansov, *Istoricheski ocherk oblozheniia torgovli i promyslov v Rossii* (Petersburg: Kirschbaum, 1893).

4   The original trade turnover figures are reported in *Entsiklopedicheski slovar' Granat, 7th ed., vol. 36, pt. IV, statistical appendix.*

5   *Istoricheski ocherk.*

6   The annual publication *Ezhegodnik ministerstva finansov,* published an entire section on state sales and production of spirits *(kazennaia prodazha pitei).*

7   S. G. Strumilin, *Statistika i ekonomika* (Moscow: Nauka, 1963), p. 437.

8   B. V. Avilov, ed., "Statisticheski obzor razvitiia narodnogo khoziaistva v dorevoliutsionnoi Rossii," *Entsiklopedicheski slovar' Granat,* 7th ed., vol. 36, pt. 4, p. 56.

9   The three price indexes discussed in this section are duplicated in S. G. Strumilin, *Ocherki ekonomicheskoi istorii Rosii i SSSR* (Moscow: Nauka, 1966), p. 89.

10 An indirect test of the accuracy of the real retail trade figures is to calculate them as residuals by subtracting all final expenditures in 1913 constant prices except retail sales from NNP in 1913 prices calculated by sector of origin. These series are given in Tables 3.1, 3.3, and 3.6. This is a very poor test as one would expect the statistical discrepancy between the two types of global estimates to be large, but major errors in the retail sales figures may reveal themselves through this procedure. For the year 1913, as Table 3.3 indicates, the two series yield quite similar results, and this finding supports the reliability of the retail sales figures. For 1898-1902, the sector-of-origin calculation yields an indirect estimate of retail sales 12% *below* the direct estimate, and for the period 1883-7, the indirectly estimated retail sales figure is virtually identical to the direct estimate. Thus, the sector-of-origin estimates fail to reveal substantive measurement errors in the retail sales estimates, but this may be simply a result of chance.

11 These estimates, prepared by M. Kuhn, a contemporary authority on grain statistics, are published in *Bulletin russe de statistique financiere et de legislation,* 5th ed. (1898), pp. 222-31.

12 The annual statistical yearbook of the Ministry of Transportation, entitled *Statisticheski sbornik ministerstva putei soobshcheniia,* consists of just under 150 volumes and covers almost every detail of rail and water transport during this period.

13 The 1913 ratios are described in Paul Gregory, "1913 Russian National Income: Some Insights into Russian Economic Development," *Quarterly Journal of*

Economics 90, No. 3 (August 1976):445-59.

14 The major official publications of the Ministry of Finance on the imperial budget are: *Otchety gosudarstvennogo kontrolia po ispol'neniiu gosudarstvennoi i finansovykh smet* (annual editions); *Entwurf des Reichsbudgets für das Jahr* (annual editions); *Bericht des Finanzministers über das Reichsbudgets für das Jahr* (annual editions). Various French editions were published as well, some of which are referenced in Appendix F.

15 There is a surprising lack of information on employment in government service during this period. The data that are available are given in P. A. Zaionchkovski, *Pravitel'stvenny apparat samoderzhavnoi Rossii v XIX v.* (Moscow: Mysl', 1978).

16 George Yaney, *The Systematization of Russian Government* (Urbana: University of Illinois Press, 1973), Chap. 9; Wiatscheslaw Gribowski, *Das Staatsrecht des Russischen Reiches* (Tübingen: Mohr, 1913), Chap. 7.

17 The major sources of data on *mir* and *volost* expenditures are: *Statistika Rossiiskoi Imperii, sbronik svedenii,* 1884-5 and 1896 editions (pp. 230-1, 1884-5; pp. 302-9, 1896), and V. I. Kovalevski, ed., *Rossiia v Kontse XIX veka* (Petersburg: Ministerstvo finansov, 1900), pp. 785-9.

18 The domestic production series is based primarily on the V. E. Varzar and L. B. Kafengauz studies of factory production cited by S. G. Strumilin, *Ocherki ekonomicheskoi istorii Rossii i SSSR* (Moscow: Nauka, 1966), pp. 442-53 and Appendix 2. The Vainshtein 1913 estimates are from A. L. Vainshtein, *Narodnoe bogatstvo i narodnokhoziaistvennoe nakoplenie predrevoliutsionnoi Rossii* (Moscow: Gosstatizdat, 1960), pp. 368-9.

19 Simon Kuznets, *Modern Economic Growth* (New Haven: Yale University Press, 1966), pp. 245-6.

20 Arcadius Kahan, "Capital Formation during the Period of Early Industrialization in Russia, 1890-1913," *Cambridge Economic History of Europe,* vol. 7, Pt. 2 (Cambridge University Press, 1978), pp. 265-307.

21 Vainshtein, *Narodnoe bogatstvo,* p. 420.

22 A. L. Vainshtein, "Iz istorii predrevoliutsionnoi statistiki zhivotnovodstva," *Ocherki po istorii statistiki SSSR,* (Moscow: Gosstatizdat, 1960), 3:86-115, and Vainshtein, *Narodnoe bogatstvo,* pp. 185-9.

23 I. A. Asalkhanov, *Sel'skoe khoziaistvo Sibiri kontsa XIX do nachala XX v.* (Novosibirsk: Nauka, Sibirskoe otdelenie, 1975), pp. 190-5.

24 Kahan, "Capital Formation," p. 300.

25 The factory production series for equipment have had to be linked together from series on "machinery and foundry production" and "metalworking." See Appendix I.

26 Kahan, "Capital Formation," p. 278.

27 This study is described in a typescript manuscript: Paul Gregory and Anna Kuniansky, "The Value of Agricultural Structures in Russia, 1885-1913," mimeographed, 1978. The basic research on this study was done by Anna Kuniansky.

28 The rural fire insurance system is decribed by V. V. Veselovski, *Istoriia*

zemstva za sorok let, 4 vols. (Petersburg: Popov, 1909), vol. 4.

29 The inclusion of nonpeasant structures would raise the rate of growth of the stock of rural structures by a maximum of 11% according to calculations in Appendix J.

30 These data were reported regularly in the *Ezhegodnik ministerstvo finansov* series under the heading *aktsionernye obshchestva*. They were also reported in various editions of *Vestnik finansov*.

31 S. G. Strumilin, *Statistika i ekonomika* (Moscow: Nauka, 1963), p. 334.

32 Kahan, "Capital Formation," p. 302.

33 The cumulated capital expenditure data were reported regularly (in gold and credit rubles) in *Statisticheski sbornik Ministerstva putei soobshcheniia*, section *zatrata kapitalov na ustroistvo set' zheleznykh dorog*.

34 Strumilin, *Statistika i ekonomikia*, p. 406.

35 Vainshtein, *Narodnoe bogatstvo*, pp. 368, 420.

36 Paul Gregory, "The Russian Balance of Payments, the Gold Standard, and Monetary Policy: A Historical Example of Foreign Capital Movements," *Journal of Economic History*, 39, No. 2 (June 1979):379-400.

37 Ol's estimates are found in S. F. Sharapov, *Tsifrovoi analiz raschetnogo balansa Rossii za 15-letie, Doklad obshchestvu dlia sodeistviia russkoi promyshlennosti i torgovli na osnovanii tsifrovykh dannykh P. V. Olem* (Petersburgh: Bernshtein, 1897), introduction.

CHAPTER 5

NATIONAL INCOME, USSR TERRITORY, 1913 AND 1928

To complete the record of Russian long-term growth, national income estimates linking 1913 with 1928 are required. Although one could, with great effort, compile benchmark estimates for a number of years intermediate between 1913 and 1928, the costs appear to outweigh the benefits of such calculations. This period witnessed the ravages of World War I, the revolution and civil war, and then the economic recovery from these traumatic political events during the 1920s. The official Soviet figures (Table 5.1) testify to these upheavals. An investigation of the impacts of these political events upon economic output would be an interesting project, but its relationship to the task at hand, assessing tsarist and Soviet long-term growth performance, may be remote. For this reason, I have chosen to deal with only two benchmarks: 1913, the last year of "normal" economic activity before World War I, and 1928, the initial year of the five-year-plan era.

The principal reason for interest in 1913 and 1928 comparisons is the need to determine the relative starting point of Soviet forced industrialization. The Soviet and Western literatures appear to be in general agreement that the Soviet economy had completed (or nearly completed) its recovery from the losses of war and civil war by the mid-1920s[1] and argue that massive infusions of capital were required to generate rapid long-term growth. This was the rationale for imposing sacrifices on the Russian population in the form of forced collectivization and reduced consumption shares starting in 1928, and the rapid growth after 1928 is often attributed to these sacrifices.[2]

The case for a recovered (or even overextended) Soviet economy in 1928 is based on the national income and industrial production statistics that have been cited by Soviet statistical authorities since the late 1920s.[3] These figures are cited in Table 5.2 along with selected physical output indicators.

As Table 5.2 indicates, the aggregate production series show increases in real national income and industrial and agricultural production but a decline in grain production. The individual physical series yield a more mixed picture, with some indicators increasing, others decreasing, relative to 1913.

Western analysts, in dealing with the official Soviet series, have either accepted the Soviet claims[4] or concluded that, at a minimum, the recovery was essentially complete by 1928.[5] The case for accepting the official national income and industrial production series is not weak, as the quality of statistical work in the mid and late 1920s done by Gosplan and the Koniunkturny Institut was much higher than that of the 1930s, and the series cited were calculated prior to the politicization of the statistical apparatus in the 1930s. Even more cautious Western analysts of the Soviet economy have failed to uncover evidence of a noticeable relative decline in aggregate production between 1913 and 1928. In fact, G. W. Nutter, whose recalculations of Soviet series call for substantial downward adjustments, concluded that Russian aggregate production in 1928 was some 4% above its 1913 level.[6]

Challenges to the official Soviet position that the recovery was completed before 1928 have been mounted by several scholars. The Russian emigre economist S. N. Prokopovich, whose estimates for 1913 are used by Soviet authorities in their comparisons with the prewar period, has claimed that the Gosplan estimates for the late 1920s overstate national income by ignoring quality deterioration and that Russia did not regain its 1913 level of per capita income until after 1930.[7] This position is also advanced by M. E. Falkus, but on different grounds.[8] Falkus has revised Prokopovich's 1913 estimates and found them to understate national income by about 25%. From this adjustment, Falkus concludes that the 1913 level of per capita national income was not achieved until after 1930.

Contrary to Prokopovich, Falkus accepts the official figures for the late 1920s, arguing that these figures were calculated by able Soviet statisticians without conscious distortion of the results.[9]

The leading Soviet authority on Russian and Soviet national income, A. L. Vainshtein, has also expressed his implicit disagreement with the official series on the grounds that they are improperly

Table 5.1. *Index of national income, 1926/27
prices, from official Soviet statistics, 1913-28*

1913	100
1917	75
1920	40
1921	38
1925	80
1926	103
1927	110
1928	119

Source: A. L. Vainshtein, *Narodny dokhod Rossii
i SSSR* (Moscow: Nauka, 1969), p. 119.

deflated. Vainshtein argues that the implicit national income deflator
of slightly less than 1.6 used by Gosplan to deflate 1928 national
income grossly understates the increase in prices between 1913 and
1928. Vainshtein maintains that a national income deflator of
approximately 2.0 would be more appropriate;[10] he points out that such
a deflator would yield real national income in 1928 some 10% below that
of 1913.[11] I shall return to these points later in this chapter.

*A COMPARISON OF THE 1913 NATIONAL INCOME ESTIMATES WITH
BERGSON'S 1928 FIGURES*

As the above discussion suggests, the relative level of Soviet national
income on the eve of the five-year-plan era has yet to be established.
There are two reasons for disagreement. The first is confusion over
the comparability of the current price figures for 1913 (based upon
Prokopovich) and the 1928 Gosplan figures cited by Soviet statistical
authorities. Although Prokopovich described his 1913 estimates in some
detail,[12] there is little discussion of the Gosplan figures for the
late 1920s.[13] Thus it is unclear whether adjustments of the original
Prokopovich figures (such as those attempted by Falkus) should be made
or whether the Gosplan estimates for the late 1920s should be adjusted
(such as the adjustments suggested by Prokopovich). Insofar as Falkus

favors a substantial upward adjustment in the 1913 figure and Prokopovich argues for a substantial downward adjustment of the 1928 figure,
quite different results emerge depending upon the type of adjustment.
The second area of confusion relates to the deflation of the current
price benchmarks, and this is as important to the final outcome as is
the comparability of the current price figures.

My estimates for 1913 were consciously patterned after those of
Abram Bergson for 1928 for just this purpose: to have two benchmark
figures in current prices that are conceptually comparable. It appears
more productive, therefore, to deal with 1913 and 1928 national incomes
using the "Bergson-Gregory" figures than to attempt to adjust the
Prokopovich-Gosplan estimates. In the following paragraphs I seek to
convert Bergson's 1928 figures into 1913 prices to obtain a real
national income index for the period 1913 to 1928.

In Table 5.3, I supply Bergson's 1928 figures in two variants:
in current market prices and in "adjusted factor costs." The adjusted
factor cost figures differ from those in market prices in that the
former are adjusted for indirect taxes (primarily on consumer goods),
subsidies (primarily for investment goods), and for differential profits. The adjusted factor cost standard values national income in
terms of factor costs of production by removing discrepancies between
market prices and factor costs caused by subsidies and differential
sales taxes. The factor cost adjustment is less substantial for 1928
than in later years when turnover taxes and industrial subsidies were
more prominent.[14]

To convert the Bergson GNP figures into net national product and
national income figures comparable conceptually to my 1913 figures,
depreciation charges must be deducted. In addition, questions have
been raised about whether capital repairs properly belong in investment
expenditures; thus I supply Bergson's adjustment for capital repairs.
As Table 5.3 indicates, Soviet 1928 net national product was circa 30
billion rubles in market prices and 27.5 billion rubles in adjusted
factor cost.

Price indexes, 1913 and 1928
The major task is to convert the 1928 current price NNP figure into
1913 prices. This requires first a discussion of the price indexes

Table 5.2. *Selected indicators of Soviet output levels in 1928*
relative to 1913 (1913 = 100)

National income	
1913 prices	117
1926/27 prices	119
Industrial production	
1913 prices	129
1926/27 prices	134-139
Agricultural production	
1926/27 prices	111
Selected physical production series	
Grain production	87
Pig iron	79
Steel	102
Coal	122
Cotton cloth	104
Freight turnover	104
Electric power	203

Sources: A. L. Vainshtein, *Narodny dokhod Rossii i SSSR* (Moscow: Nauka, 1969), p. 102; Gosplan SSSR, *Kontrol'nye tsifry narodnogo khoziaistva SSSR na 1928/29 g.* (Moscow: Izdatel'stvo Planovoe Khoziaistvo, 1929, p. 68; R. W. Davies, "Soviet Industrial Production, 1928-1937: The Rival Estimates," *Centre for Russian and East European Studies Discussion Papers,* no. 18 (University of Birmingham, 1978), p. 63; S. G. Wheatcroft, "Grain Production Statistics in the USSR in the 1920s and 1930s," *Centre for Russian and East European Studies Discussion Papers,* no. 13 (University of Birmingham, 1977), p. 23, and Wheatcroft, "Soviet Agricultural Production, 1913-1940" (mimeographed, 1979); Abram Bergson, *The Real National Income of Soviet Russia Since 1928* (Cambridge: Harvard University Press, 1961), p. 7.

available for this period.

An important point is that the price indexes of the 1920s were assembled by the most prominent Soviet economists and statisticians of the day. N. D. Kondratiev's Koniunkturny Institut played a prominent role in calculating retail and wholesale prices for the USSR and for Moscow. Other price indexes were produced by Gosplan, the Central Statistical Administration (Ts.S.U.), and the Supreme Council of the National Economy (VSNKh) under the direction of N. S. Chetverikov, A. A. Konüs, whose 1924 paper on index number theory was translated in

Econometrica,[15] and A. L. Vainshtein. The literature written during this period reveals high standards of theoretical and empirical work and a thorough knowledge of the statistical techniques used in Western countries. For this reason, it would be foolhardy to attempt any recalculation of the available indexes, insofar as there is little hope of improving upon them.

The indexes used here were published initially in the late 1920s and are summarized in Vainshtein's work on the history of prices in the USSR,[16] and most are given in *Statisticheski spravochnik 1928*[17] and in *Biulleten Koniunkturnogo Instituta*. In 1924, in anticipation of mone-tary reform (the introduction of the *chervonets* currency), Gosplan, the Central Statistical Administration, and the Koniunkturny Institut revised their price indexes and began to publish "new" indexes employ-ing weights from the years 1924 and 1925.[18] These weights were based upon shares in 1924-5 retail and wholesale trade turnover and used geometric average weighting systems. One important change introduced in 1924 is that the prewar base was shifted from 1908-12 to the year 1913.

The major price indexes were as follows: The wholesale price index of Gosplan (later designated as compiled by the Ts.S.U.) encom-passes 71 products whose prices were registered in 62 cities. The retail price index of the Ts.S.U. was based upon 34 products in 97 cities for three categories of trading establishments (state, cooperative, and private). This index apparently is the same as the all-union retail price index of the Koniunkturny Institut; so it is likely that the Central Statistical Administration later adopted the Koniunkturny Institut series as its own. The Koniunkturny Institut also published a retail price index for Moscow, but this index is virtually identical to the all-union index of the late 1920s. Finally, VSNKh published an all-union index of industry wholesale delivery (*otpusknykh*) prices, but this index is virtually identical to the industrial wholesale price index of the Ts.S.U.

In Table 5.3 I supply Bergson's 1928 market price and ruble factor cost GNP and NNP estimates in column 1. The sector price de-flators are given in column 2 in two variants. The first, labeled "best" deflator, represents the deflator I consider most suitable for deflating the appropriate end-use category in column 1; the second represents the "smallest" conceivable deflator one can find in the published price indexes, and I believe that the latter will understate the degree of price increase. They are included because the implicit national income deflator used by the Soviets is well below the "best" deflators in column 2; therefore, I use the alternate set of deflators to attempt to explain the discrepancy between my deflator and the Soviet implicit deflator, assuming that Gosplan worked with the lowest possible deflators. No price deflators are supplied for housing and services; instead, they are calculated in column 3 by applying physical production series to my 1913 housing and service categories. This process is explained in the notes to Table 5.3.

There are three major differences between the "best" and "smallest" price deflators. For retail sales and farm consumption in kind, the difference is between a deflator that is the weighted average of prices in state, cooperative, and private stores (the weights being the shares of sales of each establishment) and the state store price. Prices in private establishments were well above those in state stores, and this explains the discrepancy (2.09 vs. 1.78), as the "smallest" deflator is the state retail price. In the case of machinery, the "best" deflator is for the wholesale prices of general machinery and farm machinery; the "smallest" deflator is for metals and metalworking, where the small price increases of metals holds down the overall index.

Finally, let me note that the depreciation and capital repairs adjustment in column 3 are calculated by applying the appropriate percentages from column 1.

Results: 1928 national income in prices of 1913

The figures in column 15 are those that should be compared with my estimates of NNP in 1913 prices, as they are the closest conceptually to my own. In Table 5.4 I supply the relevant figures for such a comparison: real NNP in 1913 and 1928 in market prices and real NNP in factor costs in 1913 and 1928. I should emphasize at this point that it is an exaggeration to claim that the 1928 figures are in prices of 1913. Because fixed quantity weights of 1924-5 are used in most of the underlying price indexes, the resulting 1928 figures will only approximate 1913 prices. But I believe that the amount of change in relative weights in wholesale and retail turnover between 1925 and 1928

Table 5.3. Soviet net national product in 1928, 1928 and 1913 prices (pre-1939 boundaries) (billion rubles)

Category	(1) Bergson 1928 estimates		(2) Price deflators, 1913 = 100 (1924/25 weights)		(3) GNP, NNP in 1913 prices			
	(a) 1928 market prices (MP)	(b) 1928 ruble factor cost (FC)	(a) "Best"	(b) "Smallest"	(a) "Best" estimate		(b) "Best" estimate	
					(1) MP	(2) FC	(1) MP	(2) FC
1. Retail sales	12.10	9.42	2.09	1.78	5.79	4.50	6.80	5.29
2. Housing services	2.79	2.79	--	--	2.27	2.72	2.72	2.72
3. Consumption of farm income in king	6.60	6.70	2.16	1.69	3.10	3.10	3.97	3.97
4. Military Subsistence	.25	.23	1.78	1.78	.14	.13	.14	.13
5. Government (communal services, administration, defense)	3.13	3.05	2.22	1.41	1.41	1.37	1.41	1.37
6. Livestock investment	0.20	0.20	1.90	1.90	0.11	0.11	0.11	0.11
7. Inventory investment	0.82	0.72	1.72	1.72	0.48	0.42	0.48	0.42
8. Construction	4.38	4.48	2.08	2.08	2.11	2.15	2.11	2.15
9. Machinery and capital repairs	1.62	1.67	2.17	1.70	0.75	0.77	0.95	0.98
10. Miscellaneous investment	0.30	0.31	1.70	1.70	0.18	0.18	0.18	0.18

11. GNP	32.29	29.56				16.79	15.45	18.87	17.32
12. Depreciation	2.00	2.00				1.04	1.01	1.16	1.16
13. Capital repairs adjustment	0.30	0.30				0.15	0.13	0.17	0.16
14. NNP without capital repairs adjustment (11-12)	30.29	27.56	1.92	1.71		15.75	14.41	17.71	16.16
15. NPP with capital repairs adjustment (11-12-13)	29.99	27.26	1.92	1.71		15.60	14.28	17.54	16.00

Note: Dash indicates not available.

Sources: Column 1: Bergson 1928 estimates. Abram Bergson, The Real National Income of Soviet Russia Since 1928 (Cambridge: Harvard University Press, 1961), p. 154; Bergson, "National Income," in Abram Bergson and Simon Kuznets, eds., Economic Trends in the Soviet Union (Cambridge: Harvard University Press, 1963), p. 36.

Column 2: Price deflators. Retail Sales: This is the all-union retail price index of the Ts.S.U. described in the text, cited in Tsentral'noe Statisticheskoe Upravlenie, Statisticheski Spravochnik SSSR za 1928 (Moscow: Izdatel'stvo Ts.S.U., 1929), p. 725. The "best" deflator is the "general" retail price index, which averages prices in state, cooperative, and private outlets by shares of sales. In 1928, prices in private retail trade averaged 45% higher than in state retail outlets. The "smallest" deflator is the index of prices in state outlets alone.

Consumption of farm income in kind: The "best" deflator is the all-union Ts.S.U. retail price index of agricultural products (weighted by shares in retail trade) in the three types of trade establishments. The "smallest" deflator is the retail price index of agricultural products sold in state stores. For this series the all-union retail price index of Ts.S.U. (state stores only) is used.

Military subsistence: This is the all-union retail price index of Ts.S.U. (state stores only) is used.

Government: This is a weighted average index of the all-union wholesale price index of Gosplan (Ts.S.U.) from Statisticheski Spravochnik 1928, p. 722 (1928 = 172) and a wage index of industrial workers (1928 = 274). The 1913 and 1928 wages are from Bergson, Real National Income, p. 422, and S. G. Strumilin, Ocherki ekonomicheskoi istorii Rossii i SSSR (Moscow: Nauka, 1966), p. 94. The Bergson figure applies to all workers, the Strumilin figure to factory workers. Because Bergson's factory worker figure would have required a larger deflator, I decided to use the more conservative figure. The wage and materials indexes are combined with weights of .67 and .33, respectively.

Livestock investment: Because direct information on livestock prices is not available I used the price index of meat in state retail outlets from Statisticheski Spravochnik 1928, p. 725.

Inventory investment: For the deflation of inventory investment, the all-union wholesale price index

Construction: The index of the wholesale prices of building materials (bricks, glass, cement, plaster, lumber, construction steel) is from Gosplan's *Kontrol'nye tsifry narodnogo khoziaistva SSSR na 1928/29 g.* (Moscow: Izdatel'stvo Planovoe Khoziaistvo, 1929), p. 503.

Machinery: The "best" deflator is taken from the all-union index of delivery wholesale prices of state industry (*gospromyshlennost' SSSR*) for general machinery (1928 = 229) and for agricultural machinery (1928 = 143). These indexes are aggregated using the 1913 weights of agricultural and nonagricultural equipment (15% and 85%) to yield an equipment price index of 217. The "smallest" deflator is from the all-union wholesale price index of metals and metalworking. Both indexes are cited in *Kontrol'nye tsifry 1928/29*, p. 502.

Miscellaneous investment: The metal and metalworking index cited above is used.

Column 3: GNP and NNP in 1913 prices. In all instances except "housing and services," the column 2 deflators are applied to Bergson's 1928 figures in market prices and ruble factor cost. Because price deflators for housing rents and services are lacking, the 1928 figures in 1913 prices are established by applying physical output series to the 1913 housing and service estimates. Calculation of urban and rural rents in 1928 in 1913 prices: According to studies by Gosplan and by E. M. Tarasov (an employee of Gosplan?), the urban housing stock increased by 20% and the rural housing stock by 29% between 1913 and 1926/7. These studies are cited by S. G. Strumilin, *Statistika i ekonomika* (Moscow: *Nauka*, 1963), pp. 320-2. I accept these growth rates for 1928 and apply them to my 1913 estimates of urban and rural rental payments to obtain a figure of 1.7 billion rubles (1913 prices) in 1928, although these figures appear to be quite generous. According to *Kontrol'nye tsifry 1928/29* (p. 411), the number of passenger rail services and obtain a 1928 figure of .20 billion rubles. Again from *Kontrol'nye tsifry 1928-29* (p. 460), I calculate the increases in the number of physicians between 1913 and 1928 – an increase of 29%. I apply this index to 1913 medical expenditures and obtain a figure for 1928 of .26 billion. Utilities and personal services cannot be estimated for 1928 using physical series; so I deflate Bergson's figure in 1928 prices (approximately 1.45 billion 1928 rubles) by a weighted index of wholesale prices (1928 = 170) and wages (1928 = 300) to obtain a deflated figure of .56 billion rubles. Adding these housing and service categories together yields 2.72 billion rubles. Comparing this number with Bergson's 1928 figure yields an implicit deflator of 103, which suggests that housing and service prices were either held down considerably relative to other prices or that either my 1913 figure or Bergson's 1928 figure is in error.

must have been rather minor; so I accept the resulting figures as a reasonable approximation of 1913 prices.[19]

An examination of Table 5.4 fails to reveal evidence of the 19% increase in national income claimed by official Soviet publications. In fact, if my "best" estimates are accepted, then all variants point to a *decline* in national income ranging from 5% to 10%. Only if one is willing to accept the "highest" estimate figure, which basically excludes all private market prices, can one find a small increase in real national income between 1913 and 1928.

Let us consider briefly the sources of the discrepancy between the Gregory-Bergson 1913-28 figures and the Gosplan-Prokopovich figures. The difference lies almost entirely in the implicit deflator used. If one contrasts the current price and constant price national income figures (prewar and *chervonets* prices of the 1920s) published by Soviet official sources, it is apparent that the official figures employ an implicit national income deflator (1928 to 1913) of between 1.5 and 1.6,[20] deflators not supported by any of the available price series cited here. The implicit price deflators that emerge from Table 5.3 range from 1.92 (the "best" deflator) to 1.71, and they would have been higher except for the low implicit deflators used for services (which do not enter the official material product Soviet series anyway). If one applies the 1.92 deflator (or 2.0 deflator suggested by Vainshtein), then one obtains a result very similar to that of Table 5.4.

In sum, I would argue from this evidence that the best estimate one can make with the present information is that real national income in 1928 was between 5% and 10% below that of 1913. If one converts these findings into per capita figures, then the Falkus and Prokopovich conclusion that the 1913 per capita income level was not regained until the early 1930s, rather than in 1927, as claimed by official Soviet sources,[21] is intensified. The per capita figures, given in parentheses in Table 5.4, reveal that per capita income in 1928 was most likely between 80% and 85% of that of 1913 and at best (again using the highest estimate figures) was approximately 95% of 1913. This contrasts with the official claim of a small (7%) per capita increase between 1913 and 1928.

Table 5.4. *(National income, 1913 and 1928 in 1913 prices (pre-1939 boundaries) (billion rubles))*

	1913	"Best" estimate	1928	"Highest" estimate
A. Millions of rubles (per capita figures in parenthesis				
1. NNP, market prices (Gregory Bergson)	16.52 (118.3)	15.60 (101.3)		17.54 (113.9)
2. NNP, factor cost 1	15.89 (113.7)			
3. NNP, factor cost 2	15.22 (108.9)	14.28 (92.7)		16.00 (103.8)
4. Official Soviet estimate, national income	14.5 (103.8)		17.15 (111.4)	
5. Official Soviet estimate adjusted for "nonmaterial" production	15.5 (111.0)		18.33 (119.0)	
6. Population (millions)	139.7		154.0	
B. Growth indexes (per capita figures in parentheses)				
1. NNP, market prices	100	94.4 (85.6)		106.2 (96.3)
2. NNP, factor cost 1	100	89.9 (81.5)		100.7 (91.3)
3. NNP, factor cost 2	100	93.8 (83.1)		105.1 (95.3)
4. Official Soviet estimate, national income	100			118.3 (107.3)

Table 5.4 (cont.)

Sources: The 1928 figures are from Table 5.3. The 1913 figures are
adjusted to pre-1939 USSR territory using the ratio of .815 in M. E.
Falkus, "Russia's National Income, 1913: A Revaluation," Economica,
N.S. 35, No. 137 (February 1968); 55, 62. The factor cost 1 figures
net out indirect taxes and add subsidies. These figures are from Paul
Gregory, "1913 Russian National Income: Some Insights into Russian
Economic Development," Quarterly Journal of Economics 90, No. 3 (August
1976), statistical appendix. The factor cost 2 figures are from the
same source and net out in addition current surpluses of government
enterprises. The official Soviet figures are from Gosplan SSSR,
Kontrol'nye tsifry Narodnogo khoziajstva SSSR na 1928/9, (Moscow:
Izdatel'stvo Planovoe Khoziaistvo, 1929), p. 68. The 1928 figure is
the average 1927/8 and 1928/9 figure. The figure in row 4 is for
"material product" and excludes personal services and government. The
row 5 figures are adjusted to include missing services using the 1913
ratios in Gregory, "1913 Russian National Income," statistical appendix. The population figures are those used by Gosplan and are cited in
V. Katz, "Narodny dokhod SSSR i ego raspredelenie," Planovoe
khoziaistvo, no. 11 (1929), p. 63.

AN ATTEMPTED EXPLANATION OF GOSPLAN ESTIMATES

In view of the large differences between my estimates of relative
1928/1913 national income and those of Gosplan, it would be useful to
find an explanation for what appears to be a rather substantial deflation error in the Gosplan figures. If the Soviet estimates are to
be believed, these differences cannot be the consequence of the choice
of price weights (1913 or prices of the late 1920s), for Gosplan calculations in 1913 and 1926/27 prices yield virtually identical increases in real national income between 1913 and 1928 (see Table 5.2).
This Gosplan result notwithstanding, the possibility does exist that
the use of constant 1928 prices would have raised the 1928/1913 growth
index in the direction of the Gosplan estimate. The reasons for this
were advanced in Chapter 2, where it was assumed that the relative
price of investment goods increased between 1913 and 1928. If so, the
1928 prices would attribute larger weights to the faster growing sector
(investment goods) and the overall growth rate would be increased. It
is my suspicion, therefore, that if we could indeed estimate 1913
national income in the prices of 1928, the 1928/1913 growth index would
be raised. As Table 5.2 indicates, the 1928 relative figure is
slightly higher in 1926/27 prices than in 1913 prices, but (as already
noted) the difference is slight.

One can examine the price indexes cited in Table 5.3 for evidence of significant increases in the relative price of investment goods, but the measured rates of price increase of machinery and construction, although well above the rate of increase of wholesale prices, apparently did not diverge much from the index of retail prices. The failure of the available price indexes to reveal a dramatic shift in relative prices may be a consequence of errors in the capital goods price series, and the stylized version of the price history of the Soviet Union in the late 1920s presented in Chapter 2 may be a better description of Soviet reality. Nevertheless, with the evidence at hand, one cannot make a strong case for significant index number effects on the measurement of 1928/1913 real national income.

If the "best" estimates are used, the 1928 net investment rate is 17.2% (factor cost variant) when 1913 prices are used and 18.6% when 1928 prices are used. To obtain the largest possible index number effects (with the data on hand), one must combine the "smallest" deflators for consumer goods with the "largest" deflators for capital goods. If one does this, the 1928 investment rate in 1913 prices can be lowered to 14.6%. These results are discussed again in Chapter 8.

As I noted earlier in this chapter, the principal difference between my index and the official Soviet index does not lie in differences in current price relatives, although I do accept a higher estimate for 1913 (as does Falkus) than that used by the Soviets. In large part, this difference in 1913 estimates is due, as is recognized by both Falkus and Vainshtein, to the fact that the official Soviet estimate for 1913 (which is simply Strumilin's revision of Prokopovich's national income estimate)[22] contains several important elements that are really 1909-13 averages. The use of such averages, especially in agriculture, reduces the "1913" estimate, and Falkus, in his work, has recalculated the 1913 estimate to be representative of the year 1913. These corrections are also borne out by Nikitski's estimate of 1913 national income (prepared for Gosplan),[23] Nevertheless, the differences between my 1928/1913 estimate and Gosplan's do not hinge on the 1913 level.

The major difference between the new 1928/1913 estimate and the Gosplan estimate is Gosplan's use of a price deflator (between 1.5 and 1.6) well below any conceivable price deflator suggested by the available studies of prices for this period. I have already mentioned

Vainshtein's objection to this low implicit national income deflator. A rather extensive search of the literature failed to uncover an explanation of why Gosplan used such a low implicit deflator. Judging from Vainshtein's complaints about the lack of explanatory detail, I rather imagine that explanatory notes are simply not available.

After going through the available literature, I can advance two possible explanations for Gosplan's apparent understatement of the national income price deflator. The first is that Gosplan arbitrarily used as its national income deflator the price index of industrial products planned by VSNKh and that these prices rose much less rapidly than did other prices. There is evidence that this procedure was applied to the official estimates of industrial production[24] and may well have been applied to all estimates of national income. Contemporary articles stress the crude nature of Gosplan's calculation of national income relative to 1913 (*grubye raschety*),[25] but it is nevertheless curious why Gosplan would employ such a deflator in view of the mass of contradictory evidence on price trends, some of which had been prepared by Gosplan itself. In support of this first explanation is evidence that, as early as 1926, unrealistically low national income deflators (based on prices of primary products) were being used.[26]

As the contrast of the "best" and "highest" estimates (Table 5.3) indicated, it is possible to lower the national income deflator substantially by selecting price series that were, at least nominally, controlled by state organizations, and this may be the explanation for Gosplan's apparent error.

One interesting point should be noted: All the cited retail price series appear to give sales in private stores a weight of 40% in 1928.[27] This contradicts the government claim that private trade had been virtually eliminated by late 1928.[28] If one makes the radical assumption that all retail sales were by state and cooperative stores in 1928, then the "largest" estimate variant is approximated. Thus the choice of retail price deflators rests largely upon an empirical issue, namely, the relative volume of private trade in 1928.

The second explanation for the high Gosplan estimate of relative 1928 national income is that advanced by Prokopovich.[29] Prokopovich assumed that Gosplan's calculations of 1913 and 1928 national income in the constant prices of 1913 and 1926/27 follow Prokopovich's own procedure (applied to 1900 and 1913 national income) of applying one set of prices to the quantities of physical outputs produced in both periods. In this manner, direct estimates of relative national income in constant prices can be made without resort to deflation.

If this procedure was applied by Gosplan, argues Prokopovich, the result would be a gross overstatement of relative 1928 national income. The explanation for this phenomenon was that there had been a significant deterioration of product quality between 1913 and 1928 (about 30%, according to Prokopovich);[30] therefore, the application of 1913 prices (e.g. of shoes) to the 1928 physical output (of shoes) would grossly overstate relative 1928 shoe production insofar as the quality in 1928 was well below that of 1913. Conceivably, a well-constructed price index (which adjusted for quality changes) would have avoided this distortion.

It is difficult to assess Prokopovich's proposition primarily because we really do not know how Gosplan compiled its constant price relatives and because it is quite difficult to make empirical statements about quality change. Nevertheless, it is worthy of note that Prokopovich's quality adjusted per capita income figure for 1928[31] (three-quarters that of 1913) is rather close to my "best estimates" (80% to 85%), and I feel subjectively that my estimates likely overstate 1928 relative per capita national income.

One final word of caution: These results should be regarded as preliminary. Ultimately, they must be contrasted with the ongoing research on reconstructing physical production series for the period 1913 to 1928 being conducted by R. W. Davies at the Center for Russian and East European Studies, University of Birmingham. There are preliminary indications that Davies's finding are supportive of the official series.

SUMMARY

In this chapter I have described "new" estimates of relative 1928/1913 real national income. The new estimates involve deflating the current price estimates of Bergson for 1928 by a series of price indexes relating 1928 prices to those of 1913. It was argued that this was the best approach to the problem insofar as the two current price estimates are conceptually comparable.

The basic result of this calculation is that real national income likely decreased between 1913 and 1928, contrary to the official claims that the economic recovery was completed in 1926/1927 and real national income in 1928 was 19% above the prewar level. On a per capita basis, the 1928 relative performs less well because of the increase in population between 1913 and 1928: 1928 per capita income was calculated to be between 80% and 85% of the 1913 figure. The official Soviet claim is that it was 7% above the prewar figure, having regained the prewar level during 1927.

The finding that 1928 national income was slightly below that of 1913 and well below 1913 on a per capita basis is supported in the literature by Vainshtein and Prokopovich.

A definitive explanation of the discrepancy between the official (Gosplan) estimates and this new figure cannot be offered, primarily because little detail is provided describing the official estimates. It seems unlikely that this result is due to my use of 1913, rather than 1928 prices, although in Chapter 2 it was suggested that the application of 1928 prices would likely have raised relative 1928 income. Gosplan's alternate estimates in prewar and in 1926/27 prices and the available indexes on relative prices fail to indicate significant index number effects. Differences in 1913 and 1928 current price estimates cannot be blamed for the discrepancy, although the figure adopted for 1913 is higher than that used in the official Soviet calculations.

Instead, the discrepancy between these estimates and the Gosplan estimates is due primarily to Gosplan's use of an implicit price deflator that appears to be too low according to the various price indexes published for this period. Our suspicion is that Gosplan used some index of state controlled (industrial?) prices that well understated the rate of increase in the general price level. To support this proposition, I supplied alternate estimates calculated by selecting the smallest conceivable price increases from the available published price series. These alternate estimates were shown to be much closer to the official figures.

Prokopovich provides an alternate explanation for Gosplan's use of such a low implicit price deflator, namely, that the official estimates fail to adjust for the deterioration of product quality between

1913 and 1928. Although Prokopovich's alternate calculations (adjusting for quality differentials) are fairly close to my own, it is
difficult to assess them because of the subjective nature of his
quality adjustments.

NOTES TO CHAPTER 5

1   According to Gosplan SSSR, *Kontrol'nye tsifry narodnogo khoziaistva SSSR na 1928-29 g.* (Moscow: Izdatel'stvo Planovoe Khoziaistvo, 1929), p. 71 prewar national income in 1925-26 was roughly equal to that of 1913.

2   For differing interpretations of the necessity for the sacrifices of the 1930s, see Alexander Erlich, *The Soviet Industrialization Debate, 1924-1928* (Cambridge: Harvard University Press, 1960); Paul Gregory and Robert Stuart, *Soviet Economic Structure and Performance* (New York: Harper and Row, 1974), Chap. 3; Steven Rosefielde, "The First Great Leap Forward Reconsidered: The Lessons of Solzhenitsyn's Gulag Archipelago," *Slavic Review*, 39, No. 4 (December 1980).

3   My examination of successive statistical publications revealed that Soviet authorities have consistently used the same 1913-28 comparisons from the late 1920s to the present.

4   Prominent scholars who accept the Soviet official figures are Alec Nove, *An Economic History of the USSR* (London: Penguin, 1969), Chap. 4 and 6; Maurice Dobb, *Soviet Economic Development Since 1917*, rev. ed. (New York: International Publishers, 1966).

5   Abram Bergson, *The Real National Income of Soviet Russia Since 1928* (Cambridge: Harvard University Press, 1961), p. 7, notes that the official data that claim a 19 percent increase between 1913 and 1928 have yet to be subjected to close scrutiny. On the basis of physical output series, Bergson concludes that "the country had largely if not entirely recovered from the devastating losses suffered under the successive blows of a world war, revolution and civil war and probably was producing a total output similar to that of the Tsarist times."

6   G. Warren Nutter, "The Soviet Economy: Retrospect and Prospect," in *Conference on "Fifty Years of Communism"* (Stanford: Hoover Institution, 1976), p. 3.

7   S. N. Prokopovich, *The National Income of the USSR*, Memorandum No. 3 Birmingham Bureau of Research on Russian Economic Conditions (November 1931), p. 5.

8   M. E. Falkus, "Russia's National Income, 1913: A Revaluation," *Economica*, N.S. 35, No. 137 (February 1968):53-5.

9   Falkus, "Russia's National Income," p. 56. Among those economists and statisticians prominent in the preparation of statistics in the 1920s for Gosplan, VSNKh, and the Koniunkturny Institut were Kondratiev, Chetverikov, Konüs, and Vainshtein.

10   A. L. Vainshtein, *Narodny dokhod Rossii i SSSR* (Moscow: Nauka, 1969), p. 106.

11   Vainshtein's statement is buried in a footnote, and it would be obvious that Vainshtein was aware of the implication of changing the national income price deflator from 1.6 to 2.0, that is, 1928 national income would have been well below that of 1913.

12   S. N. Prokopovich, *Opyt ischisleniia narodnogo dokhoda 50 gubernii Evropeiskoi Rossii v 1900-1913 gg.* (Moscow: Sovet Vserossiiskikh Kooperativnykh Sezdov, 1918).

13   Gosplan SSSR, *Kontrol'nye tsifry* . . . *1928/29*, pp. 67-80, pp. 441-3.
     Vainshtein (*Narodny dokhod*, p. 100) is openly critical of Gosplan (Strumilin)
     for its failure to describe the details of its calculations.

14   Bergson, *Real National Income*, p. 130.

15   A. A. Konüs's paper "The Problem of the True Cost of Living," *Economic Bulle-
     tin of the Institute of Economic Conjuncture*, No. 9-10, Moscow, September-
     October 1924, was translated in *Econometrica* in 1939.

16   A. L. Vainshtein, *Tseny i tsenoobrazovanie v SSSR v vosstanovitel'ny period,
     1921-1928 gg.* (Moscow: Nauka, 1972).

17   Tsentral'noe Statisticheskoe Upravlenie, *Statisticheski spravochnik SSSR za
     1928* (Moscow: Izdatel'stvo Ts.S.U., 1929) Section 6. The Koniunkturny
     Institut indexes were published regularly in *Ekonomicheski Biulleten
     Koniunkturnogo Instituta*.

18   C. P. Bobrov, *Indeksy Gosplana* (Moscow: Gosplan, 1925), p. 66, gives a table
     comparing the old and new weights for wholesale turnover for 1924-5.

19   The indexes are of the type:

$$\frac{\dfrac{\Sigma\,P_{28}Q_{28}}{\Sigma\,P_{28}Q_{25}}}{\dfrac{}{\Sigma\,P_{13}Q_{25}}} \;=\; \frac{\Sigma\,P_{28}Q_{28}\Sigma\,P_{13}Q_{25}}{\Sigma\,P_{28}Q_{25}}$$

20   Vainshtein, *Narodny dokhod*, p. 102, gives 1913 national income in prices of
     1926/27 at 21 billion rubles. This, with Gosplan's estimate of 1913 national
     income in 1913 prices, yields an implicit price deflator of 1.53. *Kontrol'nye
     tsifry* (p. 68) gives 1927/28 national income in current prices as 25.9 billion
     rubles and in prewar prices at 16.4 billion rubles, yielding an implicit
     deflator of 1.58.

21   Prokopovich, Birmingham Memorandum, p. 1.

22   Vainshtein, *Narodny dokhod*, pp. 65-6.

23   The Nikitski estimate for the year 1913 is 14.8 million rubles, pre-1939 USSR
     territory, and is cited by Vainshtein, *Narodny dokhod*, p. 66. Nikitski's
     territorial adjustments are based upon his analysis of state budgetary data and
     are explained in A. Nikitski, "Dinamika biudzhetnykh postuplenii i razvitie
     narodnogo khoziaistva v otdel'nykh chastiakh Rossii v 1892-1913 godakh,"
     Planovoe khoziaistvo, no. 7 (1927).

24   A discussion of this point is found in R. W. Davies, "Soviet Industrial Produc-
     tion, 1928-1937: The Rival Estimates," *Centre for Russian and East European
     Studies Discussion Papers*, no. 18 (University of Birmingham, 1978,) p. 15; he
     also questions the use of such a low deflator to calculate prewar industrial
     production.

25   V. Katz, "Narodny dokhod SSSR i ego raspredelenie," *Planovoe khoziaistvo*, no.
     11, (1929):63.

26   Prokopovich, Birmingham Memorandum, p. 11.

27   *Statisticheski spravochnik 1928*, p. 725.

28   E. H. Carr and R. W. Davies, *Foundations of a Planned Economy, 1926-1929*, vol.

1, pt. 2 (New York: Macmillan, 1969).

29 Prokopovich, Birmingham Memorandum, pp. 1-10.

30 Prokopovich, Birmingham Memorandum, appendix 2, bases his estimate of quality deterioration upon quality control reports from the Soviet press concerning quality and durability. He bases his global figure on scattered reports, and the overall estimate is generally a subjective one.

31 Prokopovich, Birmingham Memorandum, p. 10.

CHAPTER 6

TSARIST ECONOMIC GROWTH AND STRUCTURAL CHANGE

The estimation procedures and annual national income series have been presented. Now I turn to a discussion of results. The pattern of economic growth and structural change during the late tsarist era is the subject of this chapter. In the following two chapters, this pattern will be placed in perspective by means of comparisons with the major industrialized countries prior to War War I and the Soviet Union during the plan era.

The most important question to be addressed in this and the following two chapters is the success of the Russian economy during the late tsarist era. In this study, "success" can be measured only in a restricted manner by concentrating on economic growth and the structural changes that accompany growth, and answers can be provided only through comparisons with the experiences of other countries. Other success indicators - efficiency, equity, stability - will be dealt with only in passing or not at all.

In this chapter, our focus is narrow and is restricted to the Russian data. Several issues are addressed that have occupied the literature on the economic history of tsarist Russia. The most important of these is the evaluation of the famous thesis of Alexander Gerschenkron that Russian economic development was Asian in character.[1] By "Asian," Gerschenkron meant economic growth forced by the state rather than spawned by "natural" economic forces. This is the crux of the Gerschenkronian "substitutions model" as applied to the Russian case, namely, that tsarist Russia did not possess the preconditions required for spontaneous economic growth and was therefore forced to find substitutions for missing preconditions. The most important substitutions were the use of the state bureaucracy and foreign entrepreneurs to compensate for inadequate entrepreneurial resources, foreign savings to bolster inadequate domestic savings,[2] and advanced capital-intensive technology to substitute for qualitative and quantitative deficiencies in the domestic labor force.

The peculiarly "Asian" features of tsarist economic policy cited by Gerschenkron were the heavy hand of the state in economic affairs (railroad construction, guaranteed domestic purchases, prohibitive tariffs, etc.) and most important, the practice of forcing savings from the peasant population. The latter was said to be accomplished by levying particularly oppressive direct and indirect taxes on the Russian countryside to depress peasant consumption. Another important state role was to attract foreign investment by means of interest and profit guarantees, direct recruitment of foreign capital and entrepreneurs, and conservative monetary and fiscal policy, the latter permitting Russia to join the international gold standard in 1897.

Aspects of the conventional Gerschenkronian model of Russian economic development can be "tested" using the series developed in this study. Do they reveal an extraordinary role of the state? Was the investment rate indeed accelerated relative to "normal" rates and was such an acceleration paid for through the sacrifice of peasant living standards? Did foreign capital play an extraordinary role in financing Russian economic development? Are there indeed "Asian" features in the Russian pattern of economic development, meaning an extraordinary depression of the growth of consumption for a low income country? Some evaluation of these issues will be undertaken in this chapter, but the main effort in this direction is reserved for the next chapter on international comparisons. In this chapter I shall concentrate more on laying the empirical foundations.

A second issue addressed in this chapter is the susceptibility of the Russian economy to external disturbances. This matter has not been discussed adequately in the contemporary literature, but it was an important ingredient in political-economic discussions in tsarist Russia in the late nineteenth and early twentieth centuries.[3] The point under debate was whether fluctuations in the tsarist economy were caused by external forces, for example, by business cycles in the industrialized countries, or were of domestic origin, for example, were due to agricultural disturbances. This debate had widespread policy implications: Should Russia follow a noncapitalist agrarian pattern or emulate the capitalist industrialization model of the West?

A final issue is the distribution of personal incomes in Russia.

At the end of this chapter, the limited available evidence for 1905 and 1909-10 is presented.

Although the principal focus of this study is on long-term growth, a study of short-term fluctuations is informative. First, the susceptibility of the Russian economy to short-term fluctuations in the world economy indicates the extent to which the Russian Empire was integrated into world product and capital markets. A well-integrated Russian economy would suggest then that the tsarist economy would be subject to the same international forces affecting both short and long swings in growth throughout the capitalist world. This topic cannot be pursued in appropriate depth in this study, but it appears to be an area for future study. Second, the impact of political events upon the Russian economy can be studied by investigating the Russian business cycle. In particular, the effect of the civil disorders of 1905 and 1906 on aggregate output is an important historical issue in its own right.

Third, the degree of correspondence between the tsarist price and output indexes estimated in this study and the indexes of other major countries (assuming the integration of the tsarist economy into the world economy) may serve to some degree as a primitive "test" of these calculations. One would not expect a pattern of domestic price movements, for example, quite different from that of world prices, and if significant divergences can be shown, they may be indicative of errors in the calculated series, unless explained by other forces (changes in tariff rates, political events, etc.).

TSARIST GROWTH AND THE COMPOSITION OF OUTPUT

The economic growth of the tsarist economy is best analyzed in terms of annual figures averaged over five to seven years. This is true because of the substantial annual fluctuations (primarily of agricultural output and investment) and because these averages may be more meaningful than the annual figures anyway. Livestock investment, for example, is subject to enormous year-to-year changes as are both inventory investment and equipment investment. The underlying data are such that one cannot be sure that such dramatic annual changes are real, but they have a tendency to average out over a number of years. The point is that it appears dangerous to use annual benchmark figures in the

Russian case, as one can support almost any thesis by the choice of benchmark years.[4]

In Tables 6.1 through 6.3, summary tables of Russian national income and its structure during the period 1885 to 1913 are compiled. In each case, five-year average benchmarks are used. The aggregate output concept is net national product, and these averages are calculated from the annual figures presented in Tables 3.1 and 3.6.

Growth indexes

As indicated in Chapter 3, the aggregate production series (in 1913 prices) yield an average annual growth rate of approximately 3.25% over the period 1885 to 1913, a result supported by both the end-use and sector-of-origin calculations. If one subdivides the period into two subperiods divided by the turn of the century, then growth was more rapid in the first period. This result is due primarily to the sustained decline in output between 1904 and 1907 (Figure 6.3). The first period also experienced an episode of declining output between 1887 and 1891, but this decline was less dramatic than that of 1904 to 1907 and was compensated by a sustained upsurge in output after 1891.

Looking at the growth rates over five-year intervals, one is impressed by the erratic nature of Russian national income growth even after smoothing the annual series. There were two periods of negative per capita growth (1885-9 to 1889-93 and 1901-5 to 1905-9) and of virtually zero absolute growth. The periods of peak growth were 1889-93 to 1893-7 and 1906-9 to 1909-13. The first episode of negative per capita income growth was the apparent consequence of slow growth of personal consumption expenditures and a substantial decline in net investment. The second episode (1901-5 to 1905-9) was associated with more general declines in the rates of growth of government spending and of personal consumption and a negative growth of net investment.

For the entire period, the annual rate of growth of per capita income was 1.7%. On a per capita basis, the differential between the faster growth prior to the turn of the century and the slower growth thereafter is intensified by the faster growth of population after 1900. In the first period, per capita income grew at almost 2.3% per annum, whereas per capita growth in the latter period was only 1% per annum.

Table 6.1. *National income and its composition, Russia, 1885 to 1913, 1913 prices five-year averages*

	(1) Net national product	(2) Net national product per capita	(3) Personal consumption	(4) Government	(5) Net investment total	(6) Net fixed investment	(7) Net foreign investment	(8) Net domestic saving
A. Millions of 1913 rubles								
1885-89	8,478	76.0	7,078	690	686	409	23	709
1889-93	8,744	73.3	7,331	796	602	373	15	617
1893-97	11,215	90.4	9,200	977	1,220	619	-182	1,038
1897-1901	12,938	99.0	10,725	1,111	1,383	1,065	-281	1,102
1901-05	14,861	106.8	12,112	1,453	1,344	1,134	- 48	1,296
1905-09	14,959	99.8	12,203	1,602	1,301	1,014	-148	1,153
1909-13	18,228	111.0	14,502	1,765	2,215	1,567	-254	1,961
B. Percent of nat. income								
1885-89	100		83.5	8.1	8.1	4.8	.3	8.4
1881-93	100		83.8	9.1	6.9	4.3	.2	7.1
1893-97	100		82.0	8.7	10.9	5.5	-1.6	9.3
1897-1901	100		82.9	8.6	10.7	8.2	-2.2	8.5

1905-09	100	100	81.5	10.7	8.7	6.8	-1.0	7.7
1909-13	100	100	79.6	9.7	12.15	8.6	-1.4	10.75

C. Growth rates (% per annum)

1885-69 to 1889-93	0.7	-0.4	0.9	3.5	-3.3	-2.5		-3.5
1889-93 to 1893-97	6.4	5.3	5.7	5.1	18.9	13.3		13.8
1893-97 to 1897-1901	3.6	2.3	3.8	3.2	3.1	14.5		1.5
1897-1901 to 1901-05	3.4	2.0	2.9	7.0	-0.7	1.5		4.0
1901-05 to 1905-09	0.2	-1.7	0.2	2.4	-0.8	-2.6		-2.9
1905-09 to 1909-13	4.9	2.7	3.6	2.5	14.3	11.5		11.2
1885-89 to 1909-13	3.25 (3.3)[a]	1.7	3.05	4.05	5.0	5.8		7.3
1885-89 to 1897-1901	3.6 (3.5)[a]	2.3	3.5	4.05	6.0	8.3		3.7
1897-1901 to 1909-13	2.9 (3.1)[a]	0.95	2.55	3.9	4.0	3.3		4.9

Source: Table 3.1.
[a] Growth rates calculated from sector-of-origin index in Table 3.6. The early year period is for 1883-87 rather than 1885-89.

Composition of final expenditures

The changing composition of national expenditures is shown in panels B and C of Table 6.1. Over the entire period, the share of personal consumption expenditures declined by some 3 percentage points (from 83.5% to 79.6%), the share of government rose by approximately 1.5 percentage points (from 8.1% to 9.7%), and the share of net investment rose by 4 percentage points (from 8.1% to 12.15%). These share changes were by no means linear over the period: The investment rate rose to 11% during the rapid growth of the 1890s and then dropped between 1901 and 1909, and the government share peaked during the slow growth period 1901-5.

The rise in the share of net fixed investment (excluding inventory accumulation and livestock) was more substantial and steady than that of total net investment. The net fixed investment share rose from 4.8% to 8.6%. Fixed investment thus grew at a more rapid rate than inventory accumulation and livestock.

The manner of financing the increase in investment can be established by comparing the rise in net investment with that of net foreign investment (foreign savings) and net domestic saving. Before 1893, net foreign investment was virtually zero. In fact, the figures show a slight outflow of Russian savings abroad between 1885 and 1893 in preparation for convertibility. Thus, in the early period, investment was financed entirely out of domestic savings.

Immediately preceding and then following the introduction of the gold standard in Russia, investment came to be financed from both domestic and foreign saving. At its peak (1897-1901), some 20% of domestic investment was financed through foreign savings, and at the end of the period (1909-13), 12% was financed through foreign savings. Over the entire period, roughly one-half of the increase in the investment rate was the product of the increase in foreign savings, the remainder the consequence of increasing domestic saving. If one divides the entire period into pre-gold standard and gold standard eras, then some 6% of net investment was financed by foreign savings prior to convertibility in 1897 and 12% after attaining convertibility.[5] As foreign investment flowed almost exclusively into industry, it likely financed roughly 40% of all industrial investment (industrial plant and equipment, industrial inventory accumulation, and railroad construction) on the eve of World War I.[6]

Urban and rural consumption

Accurate calculations of shares and rates of growth of urban and rural
personal consumption expenditures cannot be made because retail sales
and services cannot be broken down into urban and rural components.[7]
However, if one crudely assumes that the rate of growth of peasant food
consumption was roughly equal to the growth rate of retained farm
products grown within the village and that peasant purchases of farm
and manufactured products in retail markets were small, then one has
proxies for trends in urban and rural consumption. The rural proxy is
the sum of retained farm products and rural housing payments, and the
urban proxy is the remainder of personal consumption expenditures
(retail sales, urban housing payments, personal service expenditures).

I must stress that these proxies are weak, primarily because
peasants did purchase manufactured goods in retail markets and because
peasants in grain-deficit provinces did indeed buy grain in retail
markets shipped from grain surplus areas. The weakness of the proxies
is evident from the fact that the urban proxy accounted for 46% of
personal consumption expenditures, whereas the urban population
accounted for, at best, 15% of total population. Thus, an unrealistically high urban-rural real income differential is suggested.

Nevertheless, even crude proxies like these may pick up substantial serial changes in urban-rural consumption shares, if such changes
did indeed occur. In this sense, they are worthy of investigation. In
Table 6.2 the urban and rural proxies are recorded, and they fail to
reveal dramatic differences in growth rates. Over the entire period,
the urban proxy grew at a slightly more rapid pace than the rural proxy
(3.2% versus 2.7%). Before the turn of the century, the urban proxy
grew more rapidly than the rural proxy. Thereafter, the growth rate
relationship was reversed. The important point is that these crude
proxies fail to indicate major shifts in the distribution of consumption expenditures between the city and countryside and fail to reveal
the disproportionate peasant burden predicted by Gerschenkron.[8]

In Table 6.2 information is provided on the relationship between
personal consumption expenditures as a whole and the other components
of national income (investment and government final expenditures). At

Table 6.2. *Personal consumption expenditures, "urban" and "rural" components, 1913 prices, 1885 to 1913, five-year averages*

	Personal consumption expenditures, "urban" proxy (retail sales, urban housing, services)		Personal consumption expenditures, "rural" proxy (retained farm consumption, rural housing)		Other final expenditures (government, investment)	
	(a) % National income	(b) Annual growth rate	(a) % National income	(b) Annual growth rate	(a) % National income	(b) Annual growth rate
1885–89	45.6		37.9		16.5	
1889–93	46.5	1.2	37.3	0.4	16.3	0.4
1893–97	45.3	5.7	36.2	5.9	18.5	11.9
1897–1901	49.0	5.7	33.9	1.6	17.1	3.4
1901–05	47.9	2.9	33.6	3.1	18.5	2.9
1905–09	47.8	0.1	33.8	0.3	18.4	1.0
1909–13	46.5	3.0	34.0	5.1	19.5	8.2
1885–89 to 1909–13		3.2		2.7		4.5
1885–89 to 1897–1901		4.2		2.6		5.0
1897–1901 to 1909–13		2.3		2.9		4.0

Source: Table 3.1.

issue is whether the rate of growth of consumption expenditures was extraordinarily depressed (the "Asian" model) in the Russian case relative to that of nonconsumption expenditures. As Table 6.2 reveals, personal consumption expenditures did indeed grow at a slower pace than the sum of government and investment expenditures, but this is a normal phenomenon in the course of modern economic growth.[9] Whether the growth differential between personal consumption and nonconsumption expenditures was unusual by standards of this period will be addressed in the following chapter on international comparisons.

Composition by sector of origin

As a final comparison, the composition of national income by sector of origin must be examined. Such information is given in Table 6.3 which breaks down national income among major producing sectors for three benchmark periods, 1883-7, 1897-1901, and 1909-13. These estimates have already been discussed in Chapter 3, where it was indicated that they likely do not adjust fully for depreciation and thus contain some gross product elements. This should not lead, however, to significant distortions in the share data.[10]

Table 6.3 yields the following results: the share of agriculture fell over the entire period from 57% to 51% but most of this decline occurred before the turn of the century. The share of industry rose from 23.5% to 32%, where industry is broadly defined to include construction, transportation, and communication as well as factory and handicraft industry. Again, most of the share increase occurred before the turn of the century. The shares of trade and services likely declined somewhat. These share changes are reflected in the differential sector growth rates, which show agriculture, trade, and services growing at rates below that of national income and industry (broadly defined) growing at a rate above that of national income. These share calculations appear to be close to those of S. N. Prokopovich for 1900 and 1913.[11]

The issue that these figures raise is whether the change in the composition of Russian output was in some way "unusual" relative to the experiences of other countries undergoing modern economic growth. In this respect, it is informative to examine as well changes in the sectoral composition of the labor force (and thus output per worker),

Table 6.3. Composition of national income, sector of origin, Russia, 1883-1913, 1913 prices

Period	(1) Agriculture		(2) Industry, construction, transportation, communication		(3) Trade and services		(4) National income	
	(a) % of national income	(b) Annual growth rate	(a) % of national income	(b) Annual growth rate	(a) % of national income	(b) Annual growth rate	(a) % of national income	(b) Annual growth rate
A. Sector output, structure, and annual growth rates								
1883-87	57.4		23.4		19.2		100.0	
1883-87 to 1897-1901		2.55		5.45		2.5		3.4
1897-1901	51.3		30.6		18.1		100.0	
1897-1901 to 1909-13		3.0		3.6		2.75		3.1
1909-13	50.7		32.3		17.1		100.0	
1883-87 to 1909-13		2.8		4.5		2.7		3.3
B. Sector labor force growth rates								
1883-87 to 1897-1901		1.1		3.4		1.4		1.4
1897-1901 to 1909-13		1.7		2.0		2.0		1.8
1883-97 to 1909-13		1.4		2.7		1.7		1.6

C. Sector growth rates:
   output per worker

1883-87 to 1897-1901	1.45	2.05	1.1	2.0
1897-1901 to 1909-13	1.3	1.6	0.75	1.3
1883-87 to 1909-13	1.4	1.8	1.0	1.7

Sources: Panel A: Table 3.6. Panel B: The growth rate of the Russian labor force is taken to be that of the able-bodied population (15-59 for males and 15-55 for females). The able-bodied population for the period 1883 to 1913 was calculated from the 1897 census of population (the Russian Empire excluding Finland). Forward and backward survival rates were calculated from sex-specific death-rate information and thirty-year survival rates of males and females in Frank Lorimer, *The Population of the Soviet Union: History and Prospect* (Geneva: League of Nations, 1946), p. 213. These survival rates were then applied to the 1897 population to reconstruct the able-bodied population of the Russian Empire. I am grateful to Robert Retherford of the East-West Population Institute for assistance in the preparation of the calculations. Industrial labor force growth rates are calculated from the following sources: For factory labor, Olga Crisp, "Labor and Industrialization in Russia," *Cambridge Economic History of Europe,* vol. 7 pt. 2 (Cambridge University Press, 1978), p. 349; transport workers, S. G. Strumilin, *Statistika i ekonomika* (Moscow: Nauka, 1963), p. 409; handicraft and construction, Paul Gregory, "Economic Growth and Structural Change in Tsarist Russia: A Case of Modern Economic Growth?" *Soviet Studies* 23, No. 3 (January 1972):433. Employment in trade is taken from Strumilin, *Statistika,* p. 436. Employment in domestic service is taken from Appendix C. Employment in government is assumed to grow at the same rate as government expenditures in constant prices; e.g., constant productivity is assumed for government employment. In all cases, the sector labor force growth rates are calculated from single benchmark years: 1886, 1900, 1913. This should not affect the outcome significantly. The rural labor force growth rates are calculated as residuals.

but data on agricultural and service labor inputs are inadequate to make accurate comparisons. Thus, only crude calculations can be provided (Table 6.3, panel B).

According to the Gerschenkron model, shifts in the composition of Russian output were unusually slow because of the significant restrictions placed on agricultural labor mobility by the 1861 emancipation. Thus the shift of labor resources out of agriculture and into urban sectors was impeded. If this thesis is correct, it should reflect itself in an abnormally slow decline in the share of the agricultural labor force and, to a lesser extent, in a slow decline in the product share of agriculture. Moreover, the freezing of rural labor in agriculture (coupled with labor-saving investment in industry) should lead to a rising labor productivity differential between industry and agriculture.

In panel B, Table 6.3, rough estimates of the growth rates of employment in agriculture, industry, and trade and services are supplied. The agricultural employment series assumes that the agricultural labor force grew at the same rate as the rural population. This is a rather tenuous assumption because of possible change in the age composition and female participation rates of the agricultural population and because part of the rural population was engaged in nonagricultural pursuits (at least part time). The other labor force series are based upon firmer data but are still of questionable quality.[12] These series are described in the notes to Table 6.3. I have not calculated labor force shares by sectors as the outcome depends upon arbitrary assumptions concerning labor force participation rates in agriculture.[13] I feel it is more realistic to compare growth rates of sector outputs and sector employment rather than output and labor force shares, given the vast uncertainties surrounding the measurement of the agricultural labor force.

Over the entire period, the agricultural labor force as measured grew at a rate slightly below that of the total labor force. Because of the uncertainties surrounding the agricultural labor force figures, one should not place too much emphasis on this result, but I think it is fair to assume that the decline in the labor force share between 1885 and 1913 was modest. If one accepts the panel B figures, then the agricultural labor force share would have declined by a factor of approximately 1.07 over the period. The trade and service labor force, according to panel B, grew at roughly the same rate as the total labor force; its share did not appear to change significantly over the period. The industrial labor force grew at a rate of slightly over 1% per annum greater than the total labor force; its share increased substantially (by a factor of approximately 1.25), but at a lower rate than its product share (which increased by a factor of almost 1.4).

Panel C provides data on sector growth rates of labor productivity (output per worker). The slowest productivity growth rates were recorded by the trade and service sector, but this may be due to the underlying assumption of constant real output per worker in the government sector and domestic service. Therefore, this result follows almost by assumption. Labor productivity in industry grew at a faster pace than that of agriculture. According to these calculations, industrial labor productivity grew at an annual rate 28% higher than that of agriculture. This differential was greater during the period 1883-7 to 1897-1901 (37%) than during the period after 1901 (23%).

What conclusions, if any, can be drawn from these statistics? The first is that the Russian economy did indeed experience shifts in the structure of output and labor force directionally consistent with those of other countries experiencing modern economic growth.[14] The product and labor force shares of industry rose and those of agriculture declined. The more important issue is whether there are substantive differences in magnitude between these structural changes and those that occurred in other countries during modern economic growth. This issue will be addressed in the next chapter.

Second, the rates of growth of industrial employment (broadly defined) were quite rapid, and this appears to contradict Gerschenkron's contention concerning the immobility of the agricultural population in the aftermath of the 1861 peasant emancipation. Third, the rates of growth of labor productivity in agriculture appear to be positive contrary to contentions in the literature.[15] In fact, they do not appear to diverge significantly from the economy-wide averages.

Fourth, it should be noted that the figures presented in panels B and C are subject to unknown margins of error. Agricultural labor was assumed to grow at the same rate as the rural population, relatively little is known about handicraft output and employment, and so on;

therefore, the reader should use these findings with great caution. Nevertheless, I believe that the major findings - relatively rapid growth of the industrial labor force, positive agricultural labor productivity growth not far from the economy-wide average, more substantial increases in industrial labor productivity than in agriculture - would stand up to a more sophisticated inquiry.

It remains to put these findings into international perspective by comparisons with other countries. This will be done in the following chapter. For now, several preliminary comments concerning the conventional Gerschenkron model of Russian industrialization can be made. The first is that Gerschenkron's periodization of Russian growth into a period of more rapid growth from the late 1880s to the turn of the century is basically correct, except that Gerschenkron apparently overstates the negative effect of the depression of 1900 upon Russian output. The major declines in output accompanied the civil unrest of 1905 and 1906, not the depression of 1900. Admittedly, Gerschenkron's periodization is based upon the behavior of Russian industrial output, and I have extended it to cover national income. Gerschenkron's periodization of the years after the Stolypin reforms (beginning in 1906) as a period of rapid growth appears to be valid as well.

Second, the emphasis of Gerschenkron and John McKay[16] upon the role of foreign capital in financing Russian development is supported by the data. Roughly one-half of the increase in the investment rate was financed by increases in foreign savings, and during the gold standard era roughly 40% of industrial investment was financed out of foreign investment. The critics of Russian monetary policy appear to have underestimated the positive impact of the introduction of the gold standard in Russia on the influx of foreign savings.[17]

Third, it remains to be established whether consumption standards, especially those of the peasant population, were indeed abnormally depressed and thus whether Russian development was "Asian" in Gerschenkron's sense of the term. The data do show a decline in the share of personal consumption and a rise in the investment rate, but this alone does not prove that the Russian experience was different from that of other countries. Crude proxies for the growth rates of peasant and city consumption, however, fail to reveal an unusual depression of peasant living standards relative to urban standards. If anything, the farm population appeared to participate in the economic growth of the economy much to the same extent as the urban population.

Fourth, Gerschenkron's hypothesis concerning the immobility of the Russian farm population is not supported by the data at hand. The rate of growth of the industrial labor force appeared to be quite rapid, indicating that labor supplies were being drawn rather freely from agriculture for industry. This transfer of labor is supported by other data as well.[18]

Fifth, labor productivity growth in agriculture was positive throughout the 1885 to 1913 period, and Gerschenkron's thesis of the stagnation of Russian agriculture is not supported by these data. In fact, the rate of growth of agricultural labor productivity was some two-thirds that of industry. It should be emphasized that these results are based upon rather weak data and cannot be fully trusted. However, I would doubt that the errors are sufficiently large to reverse any major findings. This description of Russian agriculture contrasts with the picture of stagnant productivity and growing immiserization painted by the past literature.

Sixth, government final expenditures did indeed grow at a more rapid pace than national income. Whether this rate was extraordinarily rapid by international standards remains to be investigated in the following chapter. It is unlikely, however, that a significant portion of such expenditures was devoted to promoting modernization. The share of defense spending (of imperial budget expenditures) rose from 50% to 56% between 1885 and 1913, and the bulk of the remainder was devoted to administrative expenditures, rather than to education and health expenditures. Moreover, the evidence on state subsidy activities fails to reveal a significant role except in the area of subsidizing private railroads. Thus the assertion of Arcadius Kahan,[19] arguing against the position of both Gerschenkron and Theodore von Laue,[20] that the Russian state did play an extraordinary role in promoting industrialization appears to be supported. One uncertainty is the fact that many crucial state activities - tariff policy, guaranteed purchases, police support against strikes, conservative monetary policy - although not reflected in the final expenditure figures, may have made an important contribution to Russian industrialization.

THE RUSSIAN ANNUAL SERIES AND BUSINESS CYCLES IN OTHER COUNTRIES
The subject of the correspondence of the Russian business cycle to
cycles in other countries cannot be explored in appropriate depth in
this study, but it has been subjected to a rather detailed analysis in
the Soviet literature. In fact, the Russian business cycle has
received more attention in the Soviet and tsarist literatures than in
the Western literature.[21] The impact of the world economic crisis at
the turn of the century does, however, play a prominent role in the
writings of some Western scholars, who regard it as an important turning point in Russian economic history.[22]

For the more modest purposes of this study, I have prepared three
diagrams (Figures 6.1 through 6.3) in which Russian annual indexes of
prices, output, and investment are compared with the corresponding
series of the world's major economic powers: England, France, Germany,
the United Kingdom, and the United States. Sweden is included as well.
Of this group, only Sweden and Russia were capital importers.[23] The
others were capital exporters with the United Kingdom and France serving as the most significant suppliers of portfolio capital to foreign
countries.

Price movements (Figure 6.1)
In Figure 6.1, indexes of Russian and world prices are plotted. In all
cases except France, the implicit national income deflator is used to
represent trends in prices in each country. It is evident from this
chart that the domestic price movements of each country were strongly
correlated, and this is the result one would expect in an open world
economy in which the major trading partners belong to a classic gold
standard. Russian prices tend to move closely with the prices of the
other countries: Russia participated in the world deflation of the
early 1890s and the world inflation of the late 1890s, experienced
rather stable prices during the early twentieth century like other
countries, and then shared in the experience of world inflation after
1905.

Slight distinguishing features can be discerned for the Russian
case: the increase in prices between 1890 and 1892 (the likely consequence of the disastrous grain harvest of this period), the generally
sharper decrease in prices between 1892 and 1895 than that experienced

by other countries (except the United States), and the generally sharper increase in prices between 1885 and 1888. Although Russian prices
were generally higher than world prices because of the imposition of
restrictive tariffs, this is not reflected serially in trends in
Russian and world market prices. During the late 1890s, for example,
when the restrictive Mendeleev tariff was put into effect,[24] Russian
and world market prices continued to move rather closely together.

The conclusion that one must draw from comparisons of Russian
prices and world market prices is that trends in the Russian price
level were largely dictated by the world market. Tariffs may indeed

---

Figure 6.1 (*page* 141). Russian and world prices, 1885 to 1913
(1913 = 100). *Sources:* Russia: calculated from Tables 3.1 and 3.2.
France: A. A. Mendel'son, *Teoriia i istoriia ekonomicheskikh krizisov i
tsiklov* (Moscow: Sotsekgiz, 1959), Vol. 1, Table 11, Vol. 2, Table 11
(Mendel'son cites official series from French publications on wholesale
prices). Germany: Walther Hoffmann, *Das Wachstum der Deutschen
Wirtschaft seit der Mitte des 19. Jahrhunderts* (Berlin: Springer,
1965), Tables 248 and 249. UK: Charles Feinstein, *National Income,
Expenditure and Output of the United Kingdom, 1855-1965* (Cambridge: At
the University Press), T-132. United States: Simon Kuznets, *Capital in
the American Economy* (Princeton: Princeton University Press, 1961),
Tables R-22 and R-23 (Variant 1). The U.S. price deflator is backcast
from 1889 to 1885 using the Warren-Pearson index of wholesale prices
cited in Mendel'son, *Teoriia*, Vol. II, p.596. Sweden: B. R. Mitchell,
European Historical Statistics 1750-1970 (New York: Columbia University
Press, 1976), Table K-1.

Figure 6.2: (*page* 142). Domestic investment in constant prices, Russia
and other Countries (1913 = 100). *Sources:* Table 3.1. France:
Maurice Levy-Leboyer, "Capital Investment and Economic Growth in
France," *Cambridge Economic History of Europe*, Vol. VII, Part 1
(Cambridge: Cambridge University Press, 1978), Table 60. German:
Hoffmann, *Wachstum*, Table 249. UK: Feinstein, *National Income,*
T14-T15. United States: Kuznets, *Capital*, Table R-22, variant 1.
Sweden: Mitchell, *European Historical Statistics*, Table K-1.

Figure 6.3 (*page* 143). Total output indexes in constant prices, Russia
and other Countries. (1913 = 100). *Sources:* Russia, Table 3.1.
France: Levy-Leboyer, "Capital Investment," Table 60. German:
Hoffmann, *Wachstum*, Table 249. UK: Feinstein, T14-T15. United States:
Kuznets, *Capital*, Table R-22, variant 1. Sweden: Mitchell, *European
Historical Statistics*, Table K-1.

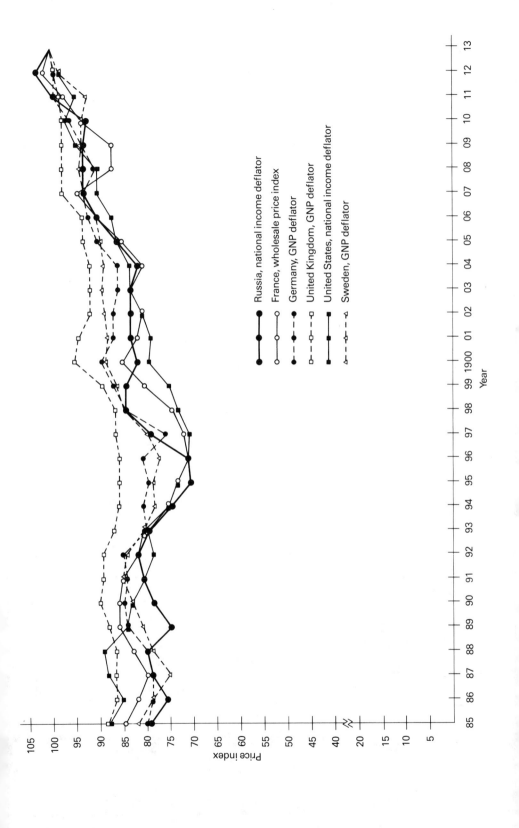

Price index

105
100
95
90
85
80
75
70
65
60
55
50
45
40
20
15
10
5

85 86 87 88 89 90 91 92 93 94 95 96 97 98 99 1900 01 02 03 04 05 06 07 08 09 10 11 12 13

Year

●——● Russia, national income deflator
○——○ France, wholesale price index
●——● Germany, GNP deflator
□----□ United Kingdom, GNP deflator
■——■ United States, national income deflator
△----△ Sweden, GNP deflator

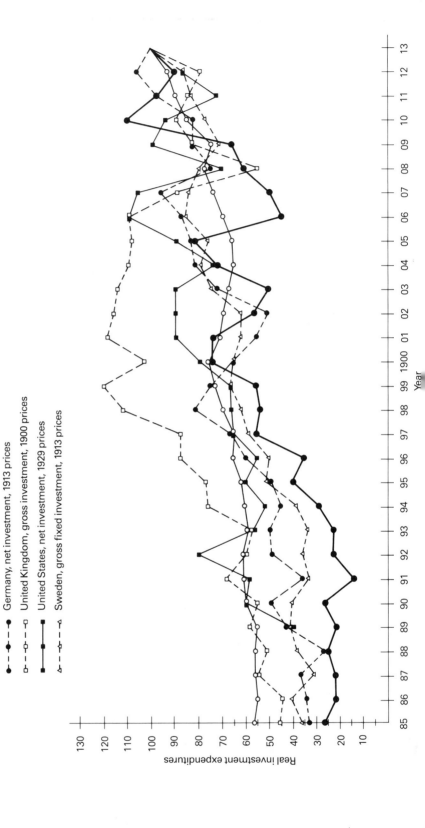

Russia, net fixed investment, 1913 prices

France, gross domestic fixed investment, 1910 prices

Germany, net investment, 1913 prices

United Kingdom, gross investment, 1900 prices

United States, net investment, 1929 prices

Sweden, gross fixed investment, 1913 prices

Real investment expenditures

Year

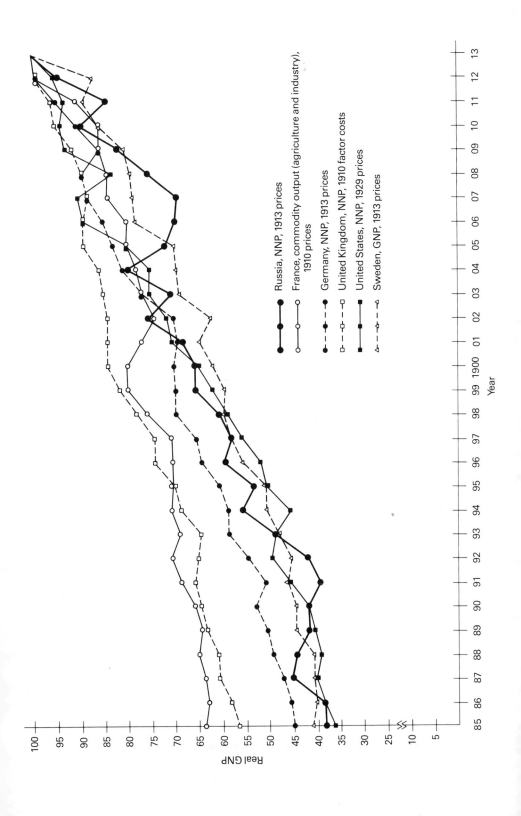

Real GNP

Year

Russia, NNP, 1913 prices

France, commodity output (agriculture and industry), 1910 prices

Germany, NNP, 1913 prices

United Kingdom, NNP, 1910 factor costs

United States, NNP, 1929 prices

Sweden, GNP, 1913 prices

have created differences in levels between Russian and world prices,
but as far as serial trends are concerned, Russian domestic prices were
strongly correlated with world market prices. The only evidence sug-
gestive of divergences of Russian prices from world prices is the
episode 1890-92, which was likely the consequence of crop failures in
Russia. Thus one would have to conclude that the Russian economy was
well integrated into the world economy in terms of price determination.

Investment cycles (Figure 6.2)
Investment cycles are more difficult to analyze visually, as relationships appear to be more complicated. In fact, the data presented in
Figure 6.2 could easily be the subject of a substantial scientific
investigation in its own right. The matter of leading and lagging
countries appears to be an especially interesting issue as the German
investment cycle generally appears to lead the Russian investment
cycle.

Several general statements can be made, however. The first is
that Russian investment cycles appear to be generally related to
investment cycles in other countries: Russia participated in the
general upswing in investment spending during the 1890s, in the general
decline near the turn of the century, and in the upswing in investment
spending between 1908 and 1913. It appears as if the Russian investment cycle is most closely related to the German and Swedish cycles.
The turning points appear to occur first in the larger economies (the
United Kingdom, France, and Germany) and then are transmitted to the
smaller economies like Sweden and Russia.

The major distinguishing feature of the Russian investment cycle
appears to be the impact of the civil unrest of 1905 upon Russian
investment. A significant decline in Russian investment spending
occurred in 1906 following the 1905 revolution, despite generally
rising investment expenditures in other countries. Russia was able,
therefore, to avoid the significant drop in investment spending experienced by other countries in 1908 and 1909 as it was recovering during
these years from the drop in investment spending in 1906. The decline
in investment spending that accompanied the crop failure of 1891 fails
to distinguish the Russian investment cycle significantly from that of
other countries as it appears to have been shared by other agricultural

countries (Germany, Sweden, and to some extent the United States).

The major conclusion is that the Russian investment cycle, like the Russian price level, was strongly linked to investment cycles in other countries. The exact nature of the linkage is difficult to establish because of the complex nature of leads and lags. The only strong distinguishing feature in the Russian case is the significant impact of the 1905 revolution on Russian investment spending, as this political event caused Russia to fall out of step with the world investment cycle.

Cycles in total output (Figure 6.3)
In Figure 6.3, indexes of total output for Russia and the five other industrialized countries are plotted. Again, as in the case of investment, the picture is a complicated one, and it is difficult to establish leads and lags among countries. A major independent inquiry would be required to untangle these relationships. As a general rule, however, one can say that prior to 1900 distinct similarities between the Russian business cycle and that of the United Kingdom, France, and Germany can be discerned. The Russian series, in general, appears to be subject to larger annual fluctuations, and these may be traceable to agricultural disturbances (e.g., the years 1890 and 1891). After 1900, the Russian business cycle appears to be more independent of the European business cycle. According to the calculated Russian national income series, the Russian economy did not turn down immediately in response to the slowdown in world economic activity around the turn of the century (except a short episode between 1902 and 1903) but did turn down in a significant manner in response to the civil unrest of 1905 and 1906, whereas the other European countries were generally recovering from the slow (and sometimes negative) growth of the turn of the century. The striking feature of the period 1905 to 1907 is the significant loss in output that accompanied the 1905 revolution and its aftermath (three years of negative growth). Without this three-year episode, the growth of Russian national income after 1900 would take on a quite different perspective. In fact, the slower growth recorded for the period 1900 to 1913 appears to be the sole consequence of the 1905 revolution and its aftermath.

THE DISTRIBUTION OF INCOME

It has been generally supposed that the income in Imperial Russia was unequally distributed by contemporaneous standards, although no formal calculation of the tsarist income distribution has been made. As a by-product of this study, some rather casual estimates can be presented for two years.

Calculations of the Russian income distribution are made possible by two studies conducted by the Ministry of Finance in 1905 and 1910 of income earners receiving more than 1000 rubles per year from land, capital, and labor income.[25] These studies were conducted to predict the impact of an income tax on upper income families, a tax that was never imposed. The methodology of these studies is described in some detail, and they appear to be competently done. Although not mentioned directly, one has the impression that the royal family and the church are not included, and this omission may understate considerably the degree of income inequality in Russia.

The Ministry of Finance studies give the total income received by individuals earning 1000 rubles or more annually and the number of such individuals both in 1905 and 1909-10. Five income categories (earnings from land, physical property, profits, money capital, and personal labor) are given, and it is possible that one individual could be counted in more than one category or that members of the same family (say, husband and wife) could be counted under different categories. Moreover, there is the important issue of the handling of the earnings of the royal family and the church, both of which would likely have been exempted from the proposed income tax. The income of the royal family cannot be gleaned from budgetary reports, which show them to receive rather modest annual stipends from the state.

In general, I believe the Ministry of Finance studies understate the income earned by the Russian upper class and may overstate the number of individuals (a result of double counting) earning 1000 rubles or more.

To calculate the distribution of income, one must know the percentage of families earning 1000 rubles or more and to do that one must know average family sizes for different income classes, information not provided by the Ministry of Finance. In the absence of family size information, I have chosen to estimate the Russian distribution of

Table 6.4. *Distribution of income in tsarist Russia, 1905 and 1909-10*

	% of families earning 1,000 rubles per year or more	% of total income
1905	1.0	15.0
1909-10	1.5	17.0

Sources: The earnings of individuals earning 1000 rubles or more annually are given in *Opyt priblizitel'nogo ischisleniia narodnogo dokhoda po razlichnym ego istochnikam i po razmeram v Rossii* (Petersburg: Ministerstvo finansov, 1906) and in A. L. Vainshtein, *Narodny dokhod Rossii i SSSR* (Moscow: Nauka, 1969), pp. 58-9. The labor force figures are from Paul Gregory, "Economic Growth and Structural Change in Tsarist Russia: A Case of Modern Economic Growth?" *Soviet Studies* 23, No. 3 (January 1972): p. 433. The proportion of families earning 1000 rubles or more is calculated by dividing the number of such individuals by the estimated labor force. The income proportion is calculated by dividing the earnings of those receiving 1000 rubles or more by national income. National income is calculated from NNP (Table 3.2) by taking the proportion of national income to NNP in Table 3.4.

income by taking the share of individuals earning 1000 rubles or more of the total labor force. This calculation is described in the notes to Table 6.4. In any case, the inexact nature of these calculations must be emphasized, and I would guess that they understate the degree of income inequality in Russia.

SUMMARY

In this chapter summary data on the growth of national income, and the changing structure of national income by final expenditure and by sector of origin were presented. It was noted that the tsarist economy grew at an annual rate of 3.25% between 1885-9 and 1909-13 and that growth was more rapid before the turn of the century than thereafter, primarily because of the loss of output during the civil unrest of 1905 and 1906. The growth of per capita income for the entire period was 1.7%, and per capita income growth was much more rapid before 1900 than thereafter because of the acceleration in population growth after 1900.

Economic growth was by no means steady over the five-year intervals studied. In fact, there were two episodes of negative per capita income growth (1885-9 to 1889-93 and 1901-5 to 1909-13), and peak growth was attained during the 1890s and after 1906.

The tsarist economy experienced structural changes that were directionally consistent with those of other countries undergoing modern economic growth. The share of personal consumption expenditures declined, and the shares of government and net investment expenditures rose, especially that of net fixed investment. It remains to be established in the next chapter whether the changes in the structure of final expenditures were unusual relative to those in the advanced industrialized countries. The share of industry in national output increased over the period as would be expected, and the share of agriculture declined. Again, it remains to be established whether these share changes were in any way unusual relative to the experiences of other countries. It should be noted as well that the major share changes occurred prior to the turn of the century.

The role of foreign capital was also investigated. Foreign savings came to finance a significant portion of domestic investment after 1893. Before 1893, domestic investment was financed entirely from domestic savings. At its peak, foreign savings financed one-fifth of all investment and at the end of the period likely accounted for 40% of industrial investment. The data on foreign capital inflows before and after the introduction of the gold standard in 1897 suggest that the gold standard made a significant contribution to the financing of Russian industrialization.

The assessment of the Gerschenkron model of Russian industrialization is reserved primarily for the following chapter on international comparisons, but a few comments can be made using the data presented in this chapter. First, Gerschenkron's periodization of the growth of Russian output appears to be basically correct (except for the overstatement of the negative effect of the 1900 depression) as is his emphasis (with McKay) on the important role of foreign capital in financing Russian industrialization. There is, however, little evidence to support his assertion that the Russian peasant paid for industrialization in terms of a depressed living standard, for the peasant population appeared to participate in the economic growth of the country to the same extent as the urban population. Gerschenkron's emphasis on the immobility of the Russian peasantry in the aftermath of the peasant emancipation is not supported by the data nor is his stagnation thesis for Russian agriculture during this period. Agricultural labor productivity grew at a positive rate, near the economy-wide average. The data on final government expenditures fail to reveal an extraordinary role for the Russian state in promoting industrialization, although it is admitted that important state activities may not be reflected in expenditure figures.

The major test of the Gerschenkron "Asian" model of Russian industrialization is undertaken in the following chapter on international comparisons, for only through comparisons with the experiences of other countries can it be established whether the Russian pattern of industrialization diverged significantly from that of other countries.

The Russian annual data on prices, investment spending, and national income were then compared with the annual data for other major countries over the period 1885 to 1913 to determine the extent to which the Russian economy was integrated into the world economy. These comparisons revealed a strong integration into the world economy. Russian prices, investment spending, and national income appeared to move strongly with business cycles in other countries. This is readily apparent from the price data. The relationship between Russian investment and output cycles and those of the major industrialized countries is more complex and is deserving of further analysis. One point is fairly clear: The political events of 1905 and 1906 caused Russia to diverge from the world investment and output cycle.

The traditional Marxist-Leninist interpretation of the Russian revolutionary process is not supported by these data. The 1905 revolution occurred during a period of rising prosperity both in the city and countryside. Thus the growing poverty of the industrial worker and the peasant farmer cannot be readily cited as the cause of the abortive revolution of 1905. The period immediately preceding World War I was one of rapidly rising per capita income both in Russia and abroad. To characterize World War I, therefore, as a struggle brought on by the declining economic fortunes of the major capitalist powers seems inaccurate.

NOTES TO CHAPTER 6

1   The Gerschenkron model of Russian industrialization is described in Alexander
     Gerschenkron, *Economic Backwardness in Historical Perspective* (Cambridge:
     Harvard University Press, 1962), essay 1; Alexander Gerschenkron "Agrarian
     Policies and Industrialization: Russia, 1861-1917," *Cambridge Economic History
     of Europe,* vol. 6, pt. 2 (Cambridge University Press, 1965); Alexander
     Gerschenkron "The Early Phases of Industrialization in Russia: Afterthoughts
     and Counter-thoughts," W. W. Rostow, ed., *The Economics of Takeoff into
     Sustained Growth* (New York: St. Martin's, 1963), pp. 151-169.

2   John McKay, *Pioneers for Profit: Foreign Entrepreneurship and Russian Indus-
     trialization* (Chicago: University of Chicago Press, 1972), has emphasized the
     role of foreign entrepreneurship as the distinguishing feature of Russian
     industrialization.

3   For a classic discussion of this controversy, see M. I. Tugan-Baranovsky,
     Statisticheskie itogi promyshlennago razvitiia Rossii (Petersburg: Tsepov,
     1898). In this report, read before the Imperial Free Economics Society,
     Tugan-Baranovsky attacks the agrarian socialist position represented by
     Nikolai-on. The crux of the debate was whether Russia was indeed progressing
     along a path of capitalist industrialization or was retrogressing in the
     industrial sector as argued by the agrarian socialists.

4   Gerschenkron's argument ("Agrarian Policies") that grain output per capita did
     not increase in the period following the emancipation depends strongly upon
     his use of a peak production year from the 1870s as a base year for his inves-
     tigation.

5   I have discussed the payoff of going on the gold standard in more detail in
     "The Russian Balance of Payments, the Gold Standard, and Monetary Policy: A
     Historical Example of Foreign Capital Movements," *Journal of Economic History*
     39, no. 2 (June 1979):379-400.

6   This figure is surprisingly close to that of Bonwetsch, calculated using quite
     different data. See Bernd Bonwetsch, "Das ausländische Kapital in Russland,"
     Jahrbücher für die Geschichte Osteuropas 22, no. 3 (1974):412-25.

7   I have attempted to calculate a crude breakdown for the year 1913 based upon
     the distribution of retail outlets between urban and rural areas. See Paul
     Gregory, "1913 Russian National Income: Some Insights into Russian Economic
     Development," *Quarterly Journal of Economics* 90, no. 3 (August 1976),
     statistical appendix.

8   Gerschenkron, "Agrarian Policies."

9   Simon Kuznets, *Modern Economic Growth* (New Haven: Yale University Press,
     1966), pp. 236-41.

10   The national income figure for 1913, which I have calculated from Falkus in
     table 3.6 is some 7% above the final expenditure figure. This difference is
     likely the consequence of inadequate allowance for depreciation. Such a small
     difference will not affect the distribution of output by sector in a signifi-
     cant manner.

11   S. N, Prokopovich, *Opyt ischisleniia narodnogo dokhoda 50 gubernii Evropeiskoi Rossii v 1900-1913 gg.* (Moscow: Sovet Vserossiiskikh Kooperativnykh Sezdov, 1918), p. 67.

12   The two major studies of the industrial labor force are: Olga Crisp, "Labor and Industrialization in Russia," *Cambridge Economic History of Europe,* vol. 7, pt. 2 (Cambridge University Press, 1978); L. E. Mints, "Ocherki razvitiia chislennosti i sostava promyshlennogo proletariata v Rossii," *Ocherki po istorii statistiki SSSR* (Moscow: Gosstatizdat, 1957), 2:171-267.

13   The author has attempted such calculations in an earlier paper but has since concluded that the labor force share data must be arbitrary until a major study of the rural labor force is undertaken. See Paul Gregory, "Economic Growth and Structural Change in Tsarist Russia: A Case of Modern Economic Growth?" *Soviet Studies* 23, no. 3 (January 1972):418-434.

14   Kuznets, *Modern Economic Growth,* Chaps. 3-5.

15   Gerschenkron, "Agrarian Policies," e.g., stresses the negative impact of growing rural population and rising land hunger upon agricultural output and argues that per capita grain output actually declined after the emancipation. Lazar Volin, *A Century of Russian Agriculture* (Cambridge: Harvard University Press, 1970), Chap. 1, makes a similar stagnationist argument about post-emancipation Russian agriculture.

16   McKay, *Pioneers for Profit,* Chap. 1.

17   The two most prominent critics of Russian monetary policy in the contemporary literature are Haim Barkai, "The Macro-Economics of Tsarist Russia in the Industrialization Era: Monetary Developments, the Balance of Payments, and the Gold Standard," *Journal of Economic History* 33 (June 1973):339-71, and Arcadius Kahan, "Government Policies and the Industrialization of Russia," *Journal of Economic History* 27, no. 4 (December 1967): 460-77. For a rebuttal, see Paul Gregory and Joel Sailors, "Russian Monetary Policy and Industrialization, 1861-1913," *Journal of Economic History* 36 (December 1976):836-51.

18   See the discussion of this matter in Appendix F.

19   Kahan, "Government Policies."

20   Theodore von Laue, *Sergei Witte and the Industrialization of Russia* (New York: Columbia University Press, 1963).

21   The standard Soviet works on the subject are: A. A. Mendel'son, *Teoriia i istoriia ekonomicheskikh kizisov i tsiklov,* 3 vols. (Moscow: Sotsekgiz, 1959), A. F. Iakovlev, *Ekonomicheskie krizisy v Rossii* (Moscow: Gosizpolit, 1955), and I. A. Trakhtenberg, *Denezhnye krizisy* (Moscow: Nauka, 1963).

22   Both Gerschenkron and McKay use 1900 as a dividing line in their models of Russian industrialization. According to Gerschenkron, Russian development after 1900 became more "European" in character. According to McKay, foreign participation in the Russian economy changed from direct to indirect investment after 1900.

23   Kuznets, *Modern Economic Growth,* pp. 236-9.

24   The most authoritative study of the Russian tariff system is by M. N. Sobolev,

Tamozhennaia politika Rossii vo vtoroi polovine XIX veka (Tomsk: Tipografiia Sibirskoe tovarichestvo pechatnago dela, 1911), who analyzes the impact of Russian tariffs upon Russian prices relative to domestic prices (Chap. 18).

25   *Opyt priblizitel'nogo ischisleniia narodnogo dokhoda po razlichnym ego istochnikam i po razmeram v Rossii* (Petersburg: Ministerstvo finansov, 1906). The results of the 1910 study are cited in A. L. Vainshtein, *Narodny dokhod Rossii i SSSR* (Moscow: Nauka, 1969), pp. 58-9.

CHAPTER 7

A COMPARATIVE APPRAISAL: RUSSIAN GROWTH BEFORE WORLD WAR I

The growth and structural change of the Russian economy during the late tsarist era must be viewed in appropriate historical perspective. Such perspective is provided by comparing the Russian data on economic growth and expenditure and output shares with those of other countries during the nineteenth and early twentieth centuries. Answers to some of the questions posed in the previous chapter should emerge from such international comparisons. The first question focused on the growth of the Russian economy. Was it slow, average, or rapid relative to the growth rates experienced by other countries over the same period? The second question was whether the Russian industrialization experience was different in some significant way (an "Asian" model) from the general Western pattern of economic development?

To make comparisons of this sort, a large mass of historical data must be available, calculated according to the same procedures as those used to assemble the Russian series. Several rich compilations of national historical series have been prepared and analyzed by Simon Kuznets, Angus Maddison, Paul Bairoch, and B. R. Mitchell,[1] and major studies of national income have been undertaken by Simon Kuznets and Robert Gallman (United States), Walther Hoffmann (Germany), Jan Marczewski and associates (France), Charles Feinstein, P. M. Dean, and W. A. Cole (Great Britain), O. J. Firestone (Canada), and Kazushi Ohkawa and Henry Rosovsky (Japan).[2]

My own examination of these studies suggests a similarity of methodology. Almost all (except Gallman for the United States) use price weights from the early twentieth century; almost all use material input prices to deflate capital goods (except Gallman); most use retail price deflators based upon the fixed weights of a "late" year from a major city; most do not adjust for the shift from home to market activities, and so on.

It is my opinion that the calculated Russian series are based upon a methodology and primary data much like those of the historical series of the other industrialized countries. In fact, in some countries whose level of economic development was far more advanced than that of Russia the statistical apparatus was much weaker (e.g., Great Britain). As domestic prices of traded goods were largely dictated by the world market during this period, and price weights are generally drawn from similar periods, it would appear unlikely that differences in relative prices will affect outcomes markedly.

SIZE AND LEVEL OF DEVELOPMENT: THE RUSSIAN ECONOMY
Russia on the eve of World War I was one of the world's major economic powers. General works typically rank Russia as the world's fourth or fifth largest industrial power behind the United States, the United Kingdom, France, Germany, and perhaps Austria-Hungary.[3] These rankings are based upon physical indicators of industrial outputs that show that the Russian Empire produced about as much industrial output as did the Austro-Hungarian Empire, but they fail to take into consideration the sheer size of Russian agricultural output.

To provide an overview, I have assembled data on population, national income, and various physical output indicators for Russia and other countries for two years: 1861 and 1913 (Table 7.1). The first year is taken as the year of Russia's entry into the "modern" era with the emancipation of the Russian serf, and 1913 represents the culmination of the economic achievements of the tsarist era.

The most striking feature of the data is the clear dichotomy between Russia's aggregate economic power, as dictated by the magnitude of the Russian Empire, and its relative poverty on a per capita basis. Russia began its modern era with a population twice that of the next most populous country in Europe and North America (France) and ended the era with a population almost three times as large as its largest European neighbor (Germany). In 1913 the only country rivaling the Russian Empire in size of population was the United States with slightly more than one-half the population of Russia.

Given Russia's large population, exceptionally low per capita levels would be required to prevent Russia from being one of the world's major economic powers. This fact is reflected in national income rankings in 1861 and 1913 (the early figures must be taken as

Table 7.1. *Selected economic and social indicators, Russia and other countries, 1861 and 1913*

	(1) Population (mil.)	(2) National income, 1913 rubles (mil.)	(3) Per capita national income	(4) Grain output		(5) Coal output		(6) Pig iron		(7) Crude steel		(8) Raw cotton		(9) Rail network 1000 km		(10) Infant mortality (per 1,000)
				a) Total, 100 metric tons	b) Per capita (metric tons)	a) Total mil. metric tons	b) Per capita (metric tons)	a) Total 1,000 metric tons	b) Per capita (kg)	a) Total[a] 1,000 metric tons	b) Per capita (kg)	a) Total 1,000 meters	b) Per capita (meters)	a) Total	b) Per capita	
Panel A: 1861																
Russia	74	5,269	71	41,500	.561	.38	.005	320	4.32	7	.095	43	.058	2.2	.029	239[b]
United Kingdom	20	6,469	323	--	--	85.0	4.25	3,772	188.6	334	16.70	457	22.85	14.6	.73	148
France	37	5,554	150	26,220	.708	9.4	2.541	967	26.1	84	2.27	110	2.97	9.6	.26	190
Germany	36	6,313	175	28,706	.797	18.7	5.194	592	16.4	143	3.97	74	2.05	11.5	.32	260
United States	32	14,405	450	39,318	1.229	13.3	.416	830	25.9	12	.38	213	(.65)	50.3	1.57	--
Sweden	4	449	112	1,265	.316	.03	.008	170	42.5	9	2.25	7.7	2.25	.57	.14	124
Italy	25	4,570	183	6,455	.258	.03	.001	27	1.08	0	0.0	12	.48	2.8	.11	232
Spain	16	--	--	--	--	.35	.022	67	4.2	--	--	27	1.68	2.9	.15	174
Austria-Hungary	35	--	--	20,745	.593	2.5	.071	315	9.0	22[c]	.63	44	1.26	3.2	.09	264

Panel B: 1913

Russia	171	20,266	119	123,000	.719	36.1	.211	4,641	27.1	4,918	28.8	424	2.48	70.2	.41	237
United Kingdom	36	20,869	580	8,948	.249	292.0	8.11	10,425	289.5	7,787	216.3	988	27.4	32.6	.91	108
France	39	11,816	303	30,870	.792	40.8	1.05	5,207	133.5	4,687	120.2	271	6.95	40.7	1.04	112
Germany	65	24,280	374	85,445	1.315	277.3	4.27	16,761	257.9	17,609	270.9	478	7.35	63.4	.98	151
United States	93	96,030	1,033	146,100	1.571	517.0	5.56	34,700	373.1	31,800	342.0	1,458	15.68	400.0	4.31	115
Netherlands	6	2,195	366	3,686	.614	1.9	.317	--	--	--	--	36	6.0	3.2	.55	91
Norway	2	918	659	1,076	.538	--	--	--	--	0	0	--	--	3.1	1.55	64
Sweden	6	2,040	340	4,979	.830	.36	.060	730	121.7	591	98.5	22	3.67	14.3	2.38	70
Italy	35	9,140	261	13,128	.375	.7	.020	427	12.2	934	26.7	202	5.77	18.9	.54	138
Spain	20	3,975	199	9,025	.451	3.9	.195	425	21.3	242	12.1	88	4.4	15.1	.76	155
Austria-Hungary	50	9,500	190	38,953	.779	54.2	1.084	2,381	47.6	2,611	52.2	210	4.2	23.0	.46	190
Belgium	7	2,440	330													
Denmark	3	1,119	440													
Switzerland	4	1,485	391													
Canada	7.5	3,548	473													
Japan	52	4,550	88													

Note: Dash indicates not available.   [a]1871.   [b]Average 1867-9.   [c]1870.

Table 7.1 (cont.)

Sources: The data in this table have been collected from a number of sources. Most of the figures are from B. R. Mitchell, *European Historical Statistics, 1750-1970* (London: Macmillan, 1975), tables B-1, D-2, E-2, E-8, E-9, E-16, G-1, K-1. The U.S., Canadian, and Japanese data are drawn from: Simon Kuznets, *Capital in the American Economy* (Princeton: Princeton University Press, 1961), table R-22; Robert Gallman, "Gross National Product in the United States, 1834-1909," in National Bureau of Economic Research, *Output, Employment and Productivity in the United States after 1800*, Vol. 30, *Studies in Income and Wealth* (New York: Columbia University Press, 1966), p. 26; A. A. Mendel'son, *Teoriia i istoriia ekonomicheskikh krizisov i tsiklov*, vol. 2 (Moscow: Sotseklit, 1964), statistical appendixes; Angus Maddison, *Economic Growth in the West* (New York: Norton, 1964), appendixes A and B; O. J. Firestone, *Canada's Economic Development, 1867-1953*, vol. 7, *Income and Wealth Series* (London: Bowes and Bowes, 1958), p. 74; Kazushi Ohkawa and Henry Rosovsky, *Japanese Economic Growth* (Stanford: Stanford University Press, 1973), table 3; U.S. Department of Commerce, *Historical Statistics of the United States from Colonial Times to the Present* (Washington, D.C.: U.S. Government Printing Office, 1975), Q284-312, Q321-8, B181-92, K502-16, K517-31, K532-7, P216-30.

The national income figures are calculated by applying 1913 exchange rates to the 1913 national income figures in current domestic prices. For those countries where only gross national product data are available, the United Kingdom 1913 ratio of net to gross product was applied. The exchange rates are given in P. A. Berlin et al., eds., *Entsiklopediia russkogo eksporta*, vol. 1 (Berlin: Torgovoe predstavitel'stvo SSSR v Germanii, 1924), p. 358. The Austria-Hungary national income figure is approximated (because of an apparent error in the Austrian figure) by assuming that per capita income in Austria was 20% above that of Hungary.

The 1860 national income figures are calculated by applying real growth indexes of national income and population to the 1913 figures. In the Russian case, a 1.8% annual growth rate is taken between 1860 and 1885 from Paul Gregory, "Economic Growth and Structural Change in Tsarist Russia: A Case of Modern Economic Growth?" *Soviet Studies* 23, No. 3 (January 1972): 433.

The Russian 1860 grain output figure is calculated by applying Goldsmith's index of grain output (including potatoes) for the 50 European provinces to the 1913 output figure. See Raymond Goldsmith, "The Economic Growth of Tsarist Russia, 1860-1913," *Economic Development and Cultural Change* 9, No. 3 (April 1961), table 1.

indicating rough orders of magnitude only). In 1861 Russian national
output was roughly one-half that of the United States, about 80% that
of the United Kingdom and Germany, and only slightly below that of
France. By 1913 Russia's national output was well above that of
France, roughly equal to that of the United Kingdom, about 80% that of
Germany, and was double that of Austria-Hungary. In relative terms,
the only decline over this period was vis-à-vis the United States, an
economy that grew rapidly in both population and per capita income
between 1861 and 1913.

   Russia's economic power was concentrated in the agricultural
sector. In 1861 Russia produced more grain than any other country and
only the United States produced more grain in 1913. Yet in 1861 Russia
was a minor producer of major industrial commodities (coal, pig iron,
steel) and had only a rudimentary transportation system, despite its
vast territory. By 1913 Russia's relative position had improved somewhat in regard to the outputs of major industrial commodities (especially relative to France and Austria-Hungary), but Russia still lagged
seriously behind the world's major industrial powers. It was only in
textiles that Russia occupied an aggregate position roughly equivalent
to that of Germany, the continent's largest industrial producer.

   The relative backwardness of the Russian economy is hidden by
such aggregate figures but is evident from the per capita figures.
Russia began its modern era with a per capita income roughly one-half
that of France and Germany, one-fifth that of the United Kingdom, and
15% that of the United States. By 1913 Russia's relative position had
deteriorated further, because of rapid population growth and slow
output growth until the 1880s.[4] Russia's 1913 per capita output was
less than 40% that of France and Germany, still one-fifth that of the
United Kingdom, and one-tenth that of the United States. Of the countries for which national income data are available, Russia's per capita
income in 1913 exceeded only that of Japan and was well below that of
Spain, Italy, and Austria-Hungary.

   The per capita figures reveal that Russia's imposing grain output
was not the consequence of high output per worker. Some three-quarters
of the labor force was engaged in agriculture,[5] yet per capita grain
output was well below that of France, Germany, and the United States in
1861 and below that of Germany and the United States in 1913. Yet it

is evident that Russia's per capita position was relatively more favorable in agriculture than in industry. For example, grain output per capita in Russia was roughly equal to that of Austria-Hungary in both 1861 and 1913; yet per capita output of industrial products in 1913 was typically one-half that of Austria-Hungary. That Russia's comparative advantage lay in agriculture is clearly demonstrated by Russia's emphasis on agricultural exports.

The most impressive relative improvement between 1861 and 1913 was the development of a rail network that was the largest on the European continent by 1913 (not unexpected given the vast territorial size of the Russian empire) and was comparable on a per capita basis to countries like Italy and Austria-Hungary.

One social indicator is provided in Table 7.1: infant mortality. Russian infant mortality in 1871 was not much different from that of Germany, Italy, and Austria-Hungary a decade earlier. Yet forty years later, Russian infant mortality was virtually unchanged, whereas in other countries it had declined significantly. The advances in public health services experienced in the other countries of Europe were not shared by the Russian masses in the villages.

By way of summary, one can say that Russia was obviously backward relative to its major European competitors both at the beginning of the "modern period" (1861) and at the end of the tsarist era. This conclusion emerges unambiguously from the per capita figures and from social indicators. On a per capita (and absolute) basis, Russia's relative strength was in agriculture where output per capita compared more favorably with other countries than in the industrial sphere. In industry, the most impressive per capita change was in textiles rather than in heavy industry.[6] On an absolute basis, Russia was indeed one of the world's major economic powers. In 1913 Russia's aggregate output was exceeded only by that of the United States, the United Kingdom, and Germany. This ranking was due, however, to the size of Russia's agricultural output. Russian grain output in 1913 was exceeded only by that of the United States. The most impressive achievement of the Russian Empire between 1861 and 1913 was the construction of a rail system that was the largest on the European continent by 1913. Moreover, on a per capita basis, Russia's rail network compared more favorably with those of Europe than almost any other per capita indicator.

A COMPARATIVE APPRAISAL OF RUSSIAN GROWTH SINCE 1885

The Russian real national income series presented in this book has taken 1885 as its starting point. This year was dictated not only by data considerations; it was also dictated by the evidence that economic growth prior to the mid 1880s was necessarily premodern in character. The most convincing support for this viewpoint is that the Russian rail network was not in place until the early 1880s, and modern growth in Russia prior to railroadization appears inconceivable.[7] The crude national income series that are available for the period prior to the 1880s do indeed show economic growth between 1861 and 1880 to be quite slow relative to that after 1880.[8]

We turn now to an assessment of Russian economic growth during the industrialization era (1885 to 1913). How did it compare with the growth rates of other countries during the course of their industrialization? I have assembled historical growth rate series for other countries for the purpose of comparison with the Russian series (Table 7.2). As noted already, the cited series are reasonably comparable. They employ a fairly common methodology, they use "late" year (postindustrialization) prices, and so on. It is, however, my suspicion that the more sophisticated series, such as those for the United States and Japan, avoid some of the systematic understatements of the other series.[9] However, as these biases apply primarily to the estimation of capital goods and capital goods represent a relatively small share of total output, I would not expect the differential biases to be large. On the other hand, there are likely a whole series of unsystematic biases in the various national series that have escaped attention; so one can only hope that these will be of a random character.

In comparisons of historical growth rates, one can never be assured of the comparability of the individual series or that divergences are real in some statistical sense. The point is, however, that one must make do with the available series and hope that major distortions in the individual series will eventually be discovered.

With these reservations, I turn to an analysis of the growth figures in Table 7.2. When available, series covering three periods are presented: "average period," "high period" (HP), and "early period" (EP) rates of growth. The average period rate represents the average long-term growth rate between 1850 and 1913 (if a series cover-

ing the entire time span is available). If such a long series is not
available, then the average period covers the longest available time
span prior to 1913.

The HP rates are those calculated by Simon Kuznets.[10] Kuznets
defines a "high period" as the "one period among several distinguished
(usually about 20 years in duration . . .) with the highest growth rate
in total product." The HP in two cases (Italy and Japan) comes after
1913, but in most cases, the HP falls within the desired 1850 to 1913
time span. I have calculated the HP rate for Russia from Table 3.1.
The generally higher growth rates after World War II are excluded from
Kuznets's HP calculations. The early period (EP) series represent the
earliest available series of the few countries for which long statistical records are available. For Russia, the EP is 1861 to 1883 and is
based upon Goldsmith's series.[11]

An examination of Table 7.2 reveals that the Russian growth rate
of total product compared quite favorably with the *average* long-term
rates of the industrialized countries between 1850 and 1914. In fact,
Russian growth was equaled or surpassed only by that of the United
States, Canada, Australia, and Sweden, and it equaled or exceeded the
growth of the two most important "follower" countries (Japan, Italy)
before to World War I. With the exception of Sweden and Denmark (with
above average rates for Europe), Russian growth was similar to that of
the European offshoots in North America and Australia, countries that
experienced rapid population growth through immigration and high rates
of natural increase. In the Russian case, however, rapid population
growth was entirely the consequence of high rates of natural increase
as Russia experienced a net out-migration during this period.

The conclusion that Russian growth was high by international
standards is supported by Angus Maddison's figures for the period 1870
to 1913.[12] Maddison calculates the average growth rate of "Western"
output (Europe and North America) at 2.7% per annum, as compared with
the Russian rate of 3.25%.

The high (by international standards) Russian growth of total
product was the consequence of rapid population (and thus labor force)
growth. However, on a per capita and per worker basis (columns D and
E), Russian growth is still respectable by the same international
standards. The "average period" Russian per capita growth rate (1.65%)

Table 7.2. *Average "high period" (HP) and "early period" (EP) growth rates of output, population, labor force, output per capita and per worker, incremental capital-output ratios, late 19th and early 20th centuries, Russia and industrialized countries (% per annum)*

		(A) Total product	(B) Population	(C) Labor force	(D) Per capita product	(E) Product per worker	(F) Incremental net capital-output ratios
1.	Russia (1883-87	3.25			1.65	1.6	
	to 1909-13)	(2.75)	1.6	1.65	(1.15)	(1.1)	3.1
	HP:1889-92 to 1901-04	4.7	1.3	-	3.4	-	-
	EP:1861-63 to 1881-83	1.8	1.1	-	0.7	-	-
2.	Great Britain (1855-64						
	to 1920-24)	2.1	1.0	0.8	1.1	1.6	3.3
	HP: 1870-74 to 1890-99	3.0	1.2	0.8	1.8	2.2	-
	EP: 1830-49	2.25	1.25	-	1.0	-	-
3.	France (1860-70 to						
	1900-1910)	1.5	0.2	0.7	1.3	0.8	-
	EP: 1781-90 to 1835-44	1.25	0.6	-	0.65	-	-
4.	Netherlands (1860-70						
	to 1900-10)	2.1	1.15	0.6	0.95	1.5	-
5.	Germany (1850-59						
	to 1910-13)	2.6	1.1	1.25	1.5	1.35	4.8
	HP:(1886-95 to 1911-13)	2.9	1.1	1.7	1.8	1.2	-
	EP: 1850-70	2.4	1.1	-	1.3	-	-
6.	United States (1880-89						
	to 1910-14)	3.5	1.9	1.7	1.6	1.9	3.1
	HP: 1869-78 to 1884-93	5.5	2.3	2.8	3.2	2.7	-
	EP: 1834-43 to 1869-78	4.1	-	-	-	-	-
7.	Canada (1870-74						
	to 1920-24)	3.3	1.7	1.9	1.6	1.4	3.0
	HP: 1891-1900 to						
	1911-20	4.0	1.6	2.4	2.4	1.6	-
8.	Australia (1861-69						
	to 1900-04)	3.4	2.85	-	0.55	-	2.9
	HP: 1861-65 to 1876-85	4.0	-	3.2	-	0.8	-
9.	Japan (1885-94						
	to 1905-14)	3.4	1.1	-	2.3	-	1.6
	HP: 1920-24 to 1938						
10.	Belgium (1970)						
	to 1913)	2.7	0.95	0.9	1.75	1.8	-
11.	Norway (1870						
	to 1913)	2.8	0.8	0.5	2.0	2.3	4.0
	HP: 1915-24 to 1939	3.2	0.7	1.2	2.5	2.0	-
12.	Sweden (1870						
	to 1913)	3.75	0.7	0.7	3.05	3.05	2.6
	HP: 1926-35 to 1948-52	4.2	0.7	0.3	3.5	3.9	-
13.	Italy (1870						
	to 1913)	1.45	0.65	0.35	0.8	1.1	-
	HP: 1920-23 to 1938-40	2.4	1.1	0.1	1.3	2.3	-
14.	Denmark (1870						
	to 1913)	3.2	1.1	0.9	2.1	2.3	2.4
	HP: 1890-99 to 1914	3.7	1.1	1.2	2.6	2.5	-
15.	Switzerland (1890						
	to 1913)	2.4	1.1	1.3	1.3	1.1	-

Note: Dash indicates not available. The Russian figures in parentheses are those of Raymond Goldsmith, "The Economic Growth of Tsarist Russia, 1860-1913," *Economic Developmer and Cultural Change* 9, No. 3 (April 1961).

Table 7.2 (*cont.*)

Sources: Simon Kuznets, *Economic Growth of Nations* (Cambridge: Harvard University Press, 1971), pp. 11-19; Angus Maddison, *Economic Growth in Japan and the USSR* (New York: Norton, 1969), Table B-1, Appendix C; Kuznets, "A Comparative Appraisal," in Abram Bergson and Simon Kuznets, eds., *Economic Trends in the Soviet Union* (Cambridge: Harvard University Press, 1963), pp. 338-9, Angus Maddison, *Economic Growth in the West* (New York: Norton, 1964), appendixes A-D; U.S. Bureau of the Census, *Historical Statistics of the United States, Colonial Times to 1970* (Washington, D.C.: U.S. Government Printing Office, 1975), P. 1, Chap. A and B; Kazushi Ohkawa and Henry Rosovsky, *Japanese Economic Growth* (Stanford: Stanford University Press, 1973), pp. 310-11.

The HP (High Period) figures are from the second Kuznets publication cited above. Kuznets defines (p. 339) the high period rate as the "one period among several distinguished (usually about 20 years in duration . . .) with the highest rate of growth in total product." Kuznets excludes the generally higher growth rates after World War II from this calculation. The approximate HP population growth rates (corresponding to the HP growth time periods) are from B. R. Mitchell, *European Historical Statistics, 1750-1970* (New York: Columbia University Press, 1976), Table B1. Labor force figures not supplied by Kuznets are taken from Mitchell, Table C1. Mitchell has taken his labor force statistics from Paul Bairoch, *The Working Population and Its Structure* (New York: Gordon and Breach, 1969). Often the periods do not coincide exactly with the product and population data, but resulting errors should be minor. The incremental capital output ratios are from Kuznets, "Comparative Appraisal," p. 354, and are calculated by dividing the average ratio of net investment to NNP by the growth rate of NNP. The Russian figures are calculated from Tables 3.1 and 3.2.

The EP (Early Period) figures are for Russia: Paul Gregory, "Economic Growth and Structural Change in Tsarist Russia: A Case of Modern Economic Growth?" *Soviet Studies* 23, No. 3 (January 1972): p. 433; United States: Robert Gallman, "Gross National Product in the United States, 1834-1909," in National Bureau of Economic Research, *Output, Employment and Productivity in the United States after 1800* (New York: Columbia University Press, 1966), p. 34. The EP figures for the other countries are cited in Mitchell, *European Historical Statistics*, Table K-1.

was surpassed or equaled only by Belgium, Norway, Sweden, the United States, and Denmark. According to Maddison,[13] the 1870 to 1913 average annual growth rate of per capita output in the West was 1.6%, that is, was equivalent to the Russian rate.

One must be cautious about the interpretation of the labor force growth figures (column C) and the resulting output per worker growth rates (column E) because of conceptual and statistical differences in the measurement of labor force among nations, particularly in the treatment of farm employment of females. No adjustment can be made for differences in hours worked per employed person, which likely fell during this time span but not at the same rate for all countries. The Russian figures are themselves crude, with agricultural employment assumed to grow at the same rate as agricultural population, and the data on employment in handicraft are grossly inadequate. Moveover, the part-time employment of agricultural workers in handicraft presents enormous difficulties. Similar weaknesses and ambiguities can be found in the labor force statistics of other countries.

Comparisons of the labor force and population growth rates fail to reveal a consistent pattern: In some countries, measured labor force growth exceeds measured population growth, in others it falls below, but only in the Italian and Dutch cases are population-labor force growth rate discrepancies substantial. From this I conclude (along with Kuznets)[14] that, as a general rule, population and labor force grew at roughly equivalent rates during this period and that the long-term growth rates of product per worker should, on the average, roughly equal those of product per capita, and this is what Table 7.2 reveals when the countries are averaged.

With these reservations, the data reveal the Russian growth rate of output per worker (1.6%) to be about average for the countries surveyed. Average hours worked per employed worker generally fell during this period, thus hours worked would rise at a slower rate than population. However, one cannot establish how average hours worked in Russia behaved relative to other countries. It is my guess that they declined less than in the more advanced European countries, but this is only a guess.

Incremental net capital-output ratios are provided in column F and are calculated by dividing the average ratio of net investment to NNP by the annual growth rate of NNP. International comparisons suggest that capital productivity (measured in marginal terms) in Russia was average at about 3 as judged by the experiences of the other countries in the sample. The exceptional cases appear to be Japan with an exceptionally low (1.6), and Germany with an exceptionally high (4.8), incremental capital-output ratio.

I shall not go through a detailed comparison of the Russian and the "high period" growth rates of the other countries (two of which date to the period after 1914), but the surprising finding from the "high period" comparison is that Russian growth performance (total output) remains about average when compared with the HP rates of the other countries. Russia still grows as fast or faster than the HP rates in Great Britain, Germany, Norway, and Italy, but notably slower than such countries as the United States, Canada, Australia, Japan, Sweden, and Denmark, which experienced short periods of exceptionally rapid growth. On a per capita (per worker) basis, the Russian average growth rate is below the HP rates of other countries. The "high period" growth rate of Russia covers a shorter time span than those of other countries (twelve years) and is not directly comparable to the Kuznets HP calculations. However, it may be noted that the Russian HP rate (covering primarily the 1890s) exceeds all other HP rates except that of the United States. On a per capita basis, the Russian HP rate compares favorably with the highest HP rates (United States, Japan, Sweden).

One cannot determine whether the growth rate differences noted in Table 7.2 are significant in a statistical sense. They use different total product concepts (NNP, national income, GNP, GDP), and the labor force statistics are especially unreliable. Nevertheless, I believe the conclusion is warranted that after 1883 the Russian Empire grew at total per capita and per worker rates which that *at least* "average" relative to those of other major industrialized and industrializing countries. Surprisingly, this statement would remain valid for total output even if the lower Goldsmith figure after 1883 was accepted. From this evidence alone, I would conclude that Russia had begun to experience modern economic growth after 1880, albeit this experience remained limited to less than thirty years. Accordingly, a long-term record is lacking in the Russian case, and I assume in the following chapter that the growth rates from the late tsarist era would have been representative of the long-term growth rate of a capitalist Russia after 1917.

STRUCTURAL CHANGE

Another means of establishing whether Russia was indeed undergoing the initial stages of modern economic growth after 1885 is to compare the course of structural change in Russia with that of the now industrial- ized countries during the first thirty years of their own modern econo-

Table 7.3. *Structural change at beginning of modern economic growth, first 30 years, Russia and other countries (% shares in national product)*

	Initial date of modern economic growth	National income, 1965 $ at initial date	(A) Agriculture			(B) Industry			(C) Services		
			1) Initial date	2) Initial date + 30 yrs.	(1-2)	1) Initial date	2) Initial date + 30 yrs	(1-2)	1) Initial date	2) Initial date + 30 yrs	(1-2)
1. Russia	1883-87	260	57	51	-6	24	32	+8	20	17	-3
2. United Kingdom	1786-85	227	45	32	-13	35	40	+5	20	28	+8
3. France	1831-40	242	50	45	-5	32	35	+3	18	20	+8
4. Germany	1850-59	302	32	23	-9	33	43	+10	35	24	-1
5. Netherlands	1865	492	25	20	-5	--	--	--	--	--	--
6. Denmark	1865-69	370	47	29	-18	--	--	--	--	--	--
7. Norway	1865-69	287	34	27	-7	32	35	+3	34	37	+3
8. Sweden	1861-69	215	39	36	-3	17	33	+16	44	31	-13
9. Italy	1895-99	271	47	36	-11	20	21	+1	25	28	+3
10. Japan	1874-79	74	63	39	-24	16	31	+15	21	31	+10
11. United States	1834-43	474	45	30	-14	24	39	+15	31	31	0
12. Canada	1870-74	508	50	36	-14	31	36	+5	19	28	+9
13. Australia	1861-69	760	18	21	+3	31	30	-1	51	48	-3

Source: Simon Kuznets, *Modern Economic Growth* (New Haven: Yale University Press, 1966) pp. 88-93, 131-2; Kuznets, *Economic Growth of Nations* (Cambridge: Harvard University Press, 1971, pp. 144-51, 24.
Note: Generally, the time spans covered by the Kuznets data exceed 30 years. In such cases the percentage changes are apportioned by the factor 30 ÷ number of years covered. Dash indicates data not available.

mic growth. Kuznets has attempted to estimate the approximate dates of the initiation of modern economic growth in these countries as well as per capita income at that date,[15] and these figures (which one must regard as only illustrative) are given in Table 7.3. From additional data supplied by Kuznets, I am able to calculate the approximate share changes of the major sectors (agriculture, industry, and services) during the first thirty years of modern economic growth, which are then compared with the Russian share changes between 1885 and 1913. I should emphasize the crude nature of these figures; some are in constant, others in current, prices; some are shares of GNP, others of national income, and so on. Moreover, rough adjustments have to be made to achieve comparable sector definitions. General conclusions can, however, be drawn despite these shortcomings.

Russia began modern economic growth with a relatively high share of agriculture and a low share of industry, much like Japan. Unlike other countries beginning modern economic growth with high agricultural and low industrial shares, such as Japan, the United Kingdom, Denmark, Italy, the United States, and Canada, the decline in the A share (the rise in the I share) was more gradual in the Russian case. In this respect, Russia parallels the French experience a half century earlier. Nevertheless, the amount of structural change, as measured by the changes in the Russian A and I shares between 1885 and 1913, was average or slightly below average when compared to that of the other countries surveyed. Russia, like the United Kingdom, France, Japan, and Canada, appeared to enter modern economic growth with a low share of services, but it is difficult to assess the reliability of this finding because of the varying coverage of services in the cited statistics.

Similar statistics could be cited for changes in the consumption, investment, and government shares of total product, but a casual examination of the available data suffices to indicate that the Russian 1885-1913 experience was generally similar to that of other countries during the early stages of modern economic growth.

RELATIVE AGRICULTURAL PRODUCTIVITY
In the preceding chapter, estimates of the relative growth rate of agricultural labor productivity vis-à-vis that of industry were made, and reservations were expressed concerning their reliability. The

question of the productivity performance of Russian agriculture is, however, of sufficient importance to pursue this matter further in spite of the rather weak underlying statistics. Substantial errors in the Russian estimates would be introduced only if the agricultural labor force grew at a rate substantially different from the rural population, and I would doubt that this occurred.

In Table 6.3 I estimated that agricultural labor productivity grew at an annual rate of approximately 1.35% between 1883-7 and 1909-13. The industry labor productivity growth rate was 1.8%, and the economy-wide rate was 1.5%. Thus in the Russian case, agricultural labor productivity failed to keep pace with that of industry and that of the economy as a whole. The relative agricultural labor productivity ratio (agriculture to industry) was approximately 3:4; that is, labor productivity in agriculture grew at three-quarters the pace of industry.

It is difficult to place these relative rates of growth in appropriate perspective for two reasons. First, one does not know how large the measurement errors are in the Russian case. Second, the relative rates of growth in the other countries during approximately the same period vary substantially.

According to Kuznets,[16] in the course of modern economic growth, agricultural labor productivity grows at a pace roughly equal to that of the economy as a whole (that is, the decline in agriculture's product share in constant prices is roughly equal to the decline in its labor force share), whereas industrial labor productivity grows more rapidly than the economy-wide average. The Russian experience is consistent with this pattern, but given the size of the agricultural sector both at the beginning and end of the period studied, it would not be expected for the rate of growth of agricultural labor productivity to diverge significantly from that of the economy as a whole.

Data on individual countries during the late nineteenth and early twentieth centuries are hard to come by as consistent product and labor force share data are required. In Table 7.4, I summarize the available evidence on relative rates of growth of agricultural and industrial labor productivity.

These figures must be handled with caution for several reasons. First, they are in most instances calculated from relative product and

Table 7.4. *The rate of growth of agricultural labor productivity ÷ rate of growth of industrial labor productivity, Russia and selected countries*

Country	Period	Relative growth rate
Russia	1883-1913	.75
Germany	1850-1909	.67
France	1870-1911	.99
United States	1870-1910	.87
Japan	1880-1920	.86
Norway	1875-1910	1.00
Canada	1880-1910	.77
United Kingdom	1801-1901	.74

Sources: The French and Norwegian figures are calculated from Simon Kuznets, *Modern Economic Growth* (New Haven: Yale University Press, 1966), Tables 3.1 and 3.2. The German data are calculated from Walther Hoffmann, *Das Wachstum der deutschen Wirtschaft seit der Mitte des 19. Jahrhunderts* (Berlin: Springer, 1965), pp. 33, 35. The Japanese figure is from Kuznets, "Notes on Japan's Economic Growth," L. Klein and K. Ohkawa, eds., *Economic Growth: The Japanese Experience since the Meiji Era* (Homewood, Ill.: Irwin, 1968), pp. 398-9. The Canadian, British, and American figures are from: O. J. Firestone, *Canada's Economic Development, 1867-1953,* Vol. 7, *Income and Wealth Series* (London: Bowes and Bowes, 1958), pp. 184-8; P. M. Deane and W. A. Cole, *British Economic Growth, 1688-1959* (Cambridge University Press, 1962), pp. 142, 166; Stanley Lebergott, "Labor Force and Employment, 1800-1960," *Output, Employment and Productivity in the United States after 1800,* Vol. 30, *Studies in Income and Wealth Series* (New York: Columbia University Press, 1966), pp. 118-20; U.S. Department of Commerce, *Historical Statistics of the United States from Colonial Times to the Present* (Washington, D.C.: U.S. Government Printing Office, 1975), F216-25.

labor force shares, the former often in current prices. Thus the ratios can be affected by changes in relative prices between agriculture and industry. Second, the resulting ratios are often dependent upon the period chosen. For example, the U.S. and Japanese ratios yield the typical pattern of agricultural productivity lagging behind that of industry, yet one can find subperiods where productivity grew at equal rates in the two major sectors.

The most reasonable conclusion to be drawn is that the Russian relative sector productivity ratio does not appear to be much different

from that of other countries. The Russian relative agricultural productivity ratio is indeed in the lower group of countries surveyed, but
it apparently does not diverge much from the ratios of Germany, Canada,
and the United Kingdom, countries that cannot be described as "dual
economies." I should reemphasize the suspect nature of these relative
productivity calculations, but I believe that they would be sensitive
enough to reveal substantive Russian deviations. Thus the Gerschenkronian (and Lenin) depiction of the Russian economy as a dual economy
comprised of a dynamic modern factory industry and a backward and
traditional peasant agricultural sector does not appear to be accurate,
at least as judged by the period 1885 to 1913.

DISTRIBUTION OF FINAL EXPENDITURES
The avowed objective of tsarist economic policy during the industrialization era was to raise the investment rate above rates that normally
would have prevailed in a low income country by attracting foreign
investment and increasing domestic savings. According to the Gerschenkron model of "Asian" development in Russia, the latter was to be
achieved largely by depressing rural living standards. The evidence
presented in the preceding chapter showed that the Russian investment
rate did indeed rise during the industrialization era, although it was
noted that its rate of increase was not unusual as judged by other
countries during the initial phases of modern economic growth. Moreover, the evidence does not support the Gerschenkron proposition that
the peasantry "paid for" this increase in the investment rate as
peasant living standards were likely rising at rates close to those of
urban standards (Chapter 6).

It remains to be established whether the distributions of final
expenditures in Russia among personal consumption, government, and
domestic investment show signs of a pattern of "Asian" development.
Insofar as these features cannot be detected in the serial developments
from 1885 and 1913, they would have had to be in place prior to 1885 if
they are to be found at all.

In Table 7.5, I have assembled data on the distribution of net
national product by final expenditure category in Russia and in other
countries for which data are available. These data are classified as
"early" - the 1850s to the 1890s - and "late" - typically from the turn

of the century to 1913. These figures allow one to detect deviations in the pattern of resource allocation in tsarist Russia from that of other countries.[17]

Definite signs of an "Asian" pattern are evident in both the early and late Russian figures. In 1885-9 the Russian net investment rate (7.8%) was exceeded only by Germany, the United States, and Australia - all countries with per capita incomes dwarfing that of tsarist Russia (Table 7.1). The other countries surveyed all have lower investment rates despite having much higher per capita income. The other country with an apparent "Asian" pattern is Japan with a net investment rate roughly equal to that of Russia despite lower per capita income. Yet in the Japanese case, a portion (15%) of net investment was financed out of foreign savings, whereas in Russia it was financed (during this early period) entirely from domestic savings.

The Russian national savings rate is accordingly quite high for a low income country, exceeded only by the United Kingdom (1870-4), Germany, France (1850-9), and the United States. Thus, the Russian personal consumption rate was exceptionally low for a low income country and also exhibits Asian characteristics. Whereas higher per capita income countries in this early period typically had consumption rates slightly below 90%, the Russian rate (83.7%) is more like those of the highest income countries (United Kingdom, Germany, and the United States).

Another distinguishing Asian feature of this early period is the large share of government final expenditures.[18] The Russian government share of final expenditures (8.2%) is the highest of the countries for which data are available. As Russian government expenditures were devoted primarily to defense and administration (and not to health and education), they reflect the heavy burden of engaging in military competition with the more advanced European countries and the relative size of the Russian bureaucracy.

Some of the Asian features noted for the early period became more pronounced on the eve of World War I. The Russian investment rate is now exceeded only by that of Germany and is roughly equal to that of the United States. The Russian domestic savings rate, however, is exceeded by several countries, as Russia had become, by this late period, a significant recipient of foreign savings. During the early

Table 7.5 *Distribution of NNP, Russia and other countries, current prices (% share of NNP)*

		1 Private consumption	2 Government consumption	3 Net domestic capital formation	4 Net foreign investment	5 Net national savings
A. Early Period						
Russia	1885-89	83.7	8.2	7.8	0.3	8.4
UK	1870-74	85.2	4.5	4.0	6.5	10.5
	1885-89	85.9	5.9	2.2	5.5	7.7
Germany	1870-74		90.3	11.8	2.1	13.9
	1885-89	78.4	6.8	12.1	2.7	14.8
France	1850-59			6.8	2.9	9.7
	1880-89		82.1	7.2	0.7	7.9
U.S.	1869-88	83.6	3.9	13.5 (13.9)	-1.0	12.5
Denmark	1870-89		96.8	5.1	-1.9	3.2
Norway	1865-74	87.9	4.0	6.9	1.3	8.2
	1875-94	89.4	5.1	7.0	-1.5	5.5
Sweden	1861-80	89.3	4.6	6.6	-0.5	6.1
	1881-90	89.2	5.7	6.8	-1.7	5.1
Italy	1861-80	92.4	4.4	4.6	-1.6	3.2
	1881-90	88.6	5.0	6.4	0.0	6.4
Canada	1870-90	94.0	6.1	7.6	-7.9	-0.3
Japan	1885-89	85.8	7.7	7.6	-1.0	6.6
Australia	1861-80		92.8	12.3	-5.1	7.2
B. Late Period						
Russia	1909-13	79.6	9.7	12.2	-1.4	10.8
U.K.	1909-13	82.7	7.9	2.6	8.2	10.8
Germany	1909-13	75.5	8.4	15.2	0.9	16.1
France	1910-13		87.8	8.9	3.3	12.2
U.S.	1889-1908	81.9	4.9	12.5	0.6	13.1
Denmark	1890-1909		93.9	8.6	-2.4	6.2
Norway	1885-1914	88.7	7.0	9.5	-5.2	4.3
Sweden	1901-20	86.4	6.1	8.0	-0.5	7.5
Italy	1901-10	84.3	4.5	9.6	1.5	11.1
Canada	1890, 1910, 1913	91.2	8.2	9.2	-8.8	0.4
Japan	1909-13	87.5	8.8	5.3	-1.6	3.7
Australia	1900/01- 1919/20		92.3	9.6	-1.9	7.7

Table 7.5 (*cont.*)

Sources: The Russian data are from Table 3.2. Most of the country figures are calculated from Simon Kuznets, *Modern Economic Growth* (New Haven: Yale University Press, 1966), pp. 236-50. The German and Japanese figures are from Walther Hoffmann, *Das Wachstum der Deitschen Wirtschaft seit der Mitte des 19. Jahrhunderts* (Berlin: Springer, 1965), pp. 450-80 and Kazushi Ohkawa and Henry Rosovsky, *Japanese Economic Growth* (Stanford: Stanford University Press, 1973), pp. 10, 278, 286. In the Japanese case, the 1887-1906 capital consumption ratio (from Kuznets, *Modern Economic Growth*, p. 250) is applied to the 1885-9 gross investment figure. The French figures are from Maurice Levy-Leboyer, "Capital Investment and Economic Growth in France, 1820-1930," *Cambridge Economic History of Europe*, vol. 7, pt. 1 (Cambridge University Press, 1978), p. 239. Insofar as inventory investment is excluded by Levy-Leboyer (p. 235), the UK ratios of total to fixed investment are used. These ratios are from Charles Feinstein, *National Income, Expenditure and Output in the United Kingdom, 1885-1965* (Cambridge: University Press, 1972). The French ratios are for gross investment. To convert them to ratios of net investment to net product, the average ratios of the share of net investment in net product to the share of gross investment in gross product from the other countries in this table are used. The UK data are calculated from Feinstein, Tables 1 and 2. The higher U.S. investment rate (for 1869-88) is from Lance Davis and Robert Gallman, "Capital Formation in the United States during the Nineteenth Century," *Cambridge Economic History*, vol. 7, pt. 2, pp. 2, 31. It is calculated by applying the gross investment share ratio in current to constant prices (p. 31) of .8 to the net share in 1860 prices (p. 2).

period (the period of preparation for the gold standard), Russia financed investment entirely out of domestic savings, by the end of the period, domestic investment came to be financed out of both domestic and foreign savings.

At the end of the tsarist era, the share of Russian government final expenditures remained the highest of the countries surveyed, but the differences between the Russian share and those of other countries had become smaller. Again, Japan exhibits Asian features much like that of Russia, namely, an exceptionally high share of government spending for a low income country. An examination of Russian government spending (Appendixes F and G) reveals that the bulk of such expenditures were devoted to defense and administration and not to human capital.

It is difficult to establish whether foreign capital played an exceptional role in Russian development,[19] as "normal" patterns of

Table 7.6. *Shares in national income of ordinal groups, Russia and selected countries*

	Top 1%	Top 5%
Russia		
1905	15	-
United Kingdom		
1880	-	48
1913	-	43
Prussia		
1854	-	21
1913	-	30
Denmark		
1870	-	37
1908	-	30
Norway		
1907	-	27-32
United States		
1913	14	24

Note: Dash indicates not available.
Source: Table 6.4; Simon Kuznets, *Modern Economic Growth* (New Haven: Yale University Press, 1966), pp. 208-11.

foreign capital inflows are not that well known.[20] As judged by the experiences of smaller capital-receiving countries (the Scandinavian countries, Canada, Australia, Japan, and the United States during its earlier period of debtor status),[21] the Russian experience (net foreign investment accounting for up to 20% of domestic investment) is not unusual. The main problem is that one lacks a notion of what a "normal" capital flow is, and the capital flow as a percentage of total output appears to be inversely correlated with size. I have already emphasized the large size of the Russian economy; so it may be that the flow of foreign investment into Russia was indeed exceptional. However, on the basis of these figures one must refrain from drawing conclusions.

In sum, resource allocation in tsarist Russia already at the beginning of the industrialization era exhibited "Asian" features in terms of relatively high domestic investment and domestic savings rates, high government spending shares, and low personal consumption shares for a low income country. In this regard, Russia resembles Japan. The puzzle is the mechanism by which Russia achieved its "Asian" distribution, for in Japan almost one-half of capital formation was from public investment,[22] whereas in Russia public investment (except in railroad construction) played a relatively minor role (Appendixes I-L).

THE PERSONAL DISTRIBUTION OF INCOME

That income was distributed unequally in Russia relative to the more advanced European countries is a proposition undisputed in the literature and is cited as a major cause of the revolutions of 1905 and 1917. It therefore comes as a major surprise (Table 7.6) that the Russian distribution of income calculated by the Ministry of Finance (Table 6.4) does not appear to be more unequal than that of the United States and is likely more equal than that of the United Kingdom.

In light of this unexpected result, one must question the validity of the Finance Ministry study. I would suggest that a reevaluation of the Finance Ministry study is necessary - a research effort beyond the scope of this work. A casual examination of the Finance Ministry study does reveal, however, a counter-intuitive finding, namely, that income from land accounted for only 17% of income over 1000 rubles.[23] In a country that was still largely agricultural with a highly unequal distribution of this land, such a low percentage seems implausible. Thus it appears that the calculated distribution well understates the degree of inequality in the Russian distribution of income. Until a major reevaluation of the Finance Ministry study is undertaken, I would suggest that the Russian figures be treated with skepticism.

SUMMARY

In this chapter the pattern of economic development in tsarist Russia between 1885 and World War I has been compared with that of other countries during the late nineteenth and early twentieth centuries. It was noted that tsarist Russia began and ended her "modern" era with an economy that was the world's fourth or fifth largest on an absolute basis but obviously backward on a relative per capita basis. Russia's comparative advantage lay in agriculture, and Russia's most impressive nonagricultural achievements relative to the other countries were the construction of a rail network and the development of a textile industry.

The Russian rate of growth of output was impressive as judged by the standards of other countries. The Russian growth rate was well above average long-term rates of other countries and was equaled or surpassed only by the United States, Canada, Australia, Sweden, and Japan. On a per capita (and per worker) basis, Russian growth performance was average vis-à-vis the other countries; thus the above average growth of total output was a consequence of the relatively rapid expansion of the Russian labor force. In general, the growth rate evidence suggests that the picture of a slow growing Russian economy on both an absolute and per capita basis painted by the past literature is not accurate.

The process of structural change in tsarist Russia during the industrialization era was then compared with other countries. It was concluded that the pattern of structural change (as measured by shares of producing sectors and final expenditure shares) in tsarist Russia was generally similar to that experienced by other countries during the first thirty years of modern economic growth. The one possible distinguishing feature in the Russian case was the relatively slow rate of relative decline of agriculture in a country entering modern economic growth with a relatively high share of agriculture.

Relative rates of growth of agricultural and industrial labor productivity were then examined, and it was concluded (despite weaknesses in the underlying data) that the lag in agricultural productivity growth behind that of industry in Russia was not significantly different from that of other countries that could not be described as "dual economics."

The "Asian" model of economic development described by Gerschenkron is not evident in the 1885 to 1913 serial data. There remains the question of whether Russia entered the industrialization era with an "Asian" allocation of resources. There is considerable evidence to support this proposition. Both at the beginning and end of the industrialization era, Russia had relatively high domestic investment and domestic savings rates, relatively high shares of final government expenditures, and relatively low shares of personal consumption expenditures for a low income country. It was not possible to establish whether foreign capital played an exceptional role in Russian economic development (as judged by its role in other countries), but it is true that at the beginning of the industrialization era, domestic investment was financed exclusively out of domestic savings, whereas at the end, foreign savings had come to play a significant role.

Data on the distribution of income prepared by the Russian Finance Ministry were then contrasted with the income distribution data of other countries. They failed to reveal the expected result - a more unequal distribution in Russia - and this result was viewed as casting considerable doubt on the reliability of the Finance Ministry study.

It remains to ask to what extent this evidence supports the classical Gerschenkronian depiction of Russian economic development after the peasant emancipation. The "Asian" features emphasized by Gerschenkron - the high investment and government shares for a low income country - are present at both the beginning and end of the industrialization era; yet it appears that Gerschenkron grossly over-estimated the rigidities placed upon Russian agriculture as a consequence of the peasant emancipation. The evidence on relative labor productivity and on peasant living standards fails to support Gerschenkron's view of a stagnant Russian agriculture. Whether Russia made a "substitution" of foreign savings for domestic savings that was significantly different from normal patterns cannot be established from the available data.

The mechanism by which Russia achieved its Asian allocation of resources remains to be established. The role of government investment was not substantial in the Russian case, and a definitive comparative study of relative tax burdens is still to be written.

NOTES TO CHAPTER 7

1   Simon Kuznets, *Modern Economic Growth* (New Haven: Yale University Press, 1966); Simon Kuznets, *Economic Growth of Nations* (Cambridge: Harvard University Press, 1971); Angus Maddison, *Economic Growth in the West* (New York: Norton, 1964); B. R. Mitchell, *European Historical Statistics, 1750-1970* (London: Macmillan, 1975); Paul Bairoch, *The Working Population and Its Structure* (New York: Gordon and Breach, 1969).

2   Simon Kuznets, *Capital in the American Economy* (Princeton: Princeton University Press, 1961); Robert Gallman, "Gross National Product in the United States, 1834-1909," in National Bureau of Economic Research, *Output, Employment and Productivity in the United States after 1800*, vol. 30, *Studies in Income and Wealth* (New York: Columbia University Press, 1966); Walther Hoffmann, *Das Wachstum der Deutschen Wirtschaft seit der Mitte des 19. Jahrhunderts* (Berlin: Springer, 1965); Jan Marczewski, "Le Produit physique de l'economie francais de 1789 a NB 1913 (comparaison avec le Grande-Bretagne)," *Histoire quantitative de l'economie francais, Cahiers de l' I.S.E.A.*, AF, 4, No. 163 (July 1965); Charles Feinstein, *National Income, Expenditure and Output of the United Kingdom, 1855-1965* (Cambridge: University Press, 1972); P. M. Deane and W. A. Cole, *British Economic Growth, 1688-1959* (Cambridge: University Press, 1962); O. J. Firestone, *Canada's Economic Development, 1867-1953*, vol. 7, *Income and Wealth Series* (London: Bowes and Bowes, 1958); and Kazushi Ohkawa and Henry Rosovsky, *Japanese Economic Growth* (Stanford: Stanford University Press, 1973).

3   M. E. Falkus, *The Industrialization of Russia, 1700-1914* (London and Basingstoke: Macmillan, 1972), pp.11-19; Olga Crisp, *Studies in the Russian Economy Before 1914* (London and Basingstoke: Macmillan, 1976), essay 1.

4   The 1860-80 output growth figures were calculated from Goldsmith and are given in Table 7.2.

5   Paul Gregory, "Economic Growth and Structural Change in Tsarist Russia: A Case of Modern Economic Growth?" *Soviet Studies* 23, no. 3 (January 1972):425.

6   This is contrary to Gerschenkron's conclusion that the pattern of Russian industrialization was biased in the direction of heavy industry. For a detailed study of this point, see Paul Gregory, "Some Empirical Comments on the Theory of Relative Backwardness: The Russian Case," *Economic Development and Cultural Change* 22, no. 4 (July 1974):657-61.

7   There is some controversy about this point based upon the concept of social saving. For a review of this controversy involving Alexander Gerschenkron, Theodore von Laue, Alexander Baykov, Jacob Metzer, and Colin White, see Paul Gregory, "Russian Industrialization and Economic Growth: Results and Perspectives of Western Research," *Jahrbücher für die Geschichte Osteuropas* 2, no. 25 (1977):213.

8   According to Raymond Goldsmith, "The Economic Growth of Tsarist Russia, 1860-1913," *Economic Development and Cultural Change* 9, no. 3 (April 1961):443, the growth rate from 1860 to the 1880s was about 2% per annum, about two-thirds the rate after 1880.

9   Both the U.S. and Japanese series use capital goods deflators that are more
    likely to reflect productivity improvements within the capital goods industry.

10 Simon Kuznets, "A Comparative Appraisal," in Abram Bergson and Simon Kuznets,
    eds., *Economic Trends in the Soviet Union* (Cambridge: Harvard University
    Press, 1963), pp. 338-9.

11 The figure cited has been recalculated from Goldsmith to add missing sectors
    and is from Gregory, "Economic Growth," statistical appendix.

12 Maddison, *Economic Growth in the West*, p. 28

13 Maddison, *Economic Growth in the West*, p. 30.

14 Kuznets, *Economic Growth of Nations*, pp. 52-61.

15 Kuznets, *Economic Growth of Nations*, p. 24.

16 Kuznets, *Modern Economic Growth*, pp. 86-126.

17 For an analysis of Russian national income in 1913 of this sort, see Paul
    Gregory, "1913 Russian National Income: Some Insights into Russian Economic
    Development," *Quarterly Journal of Economics*, 90, no. 3 (August 1976): 445-60.

18 Theodore von Laue, *Sergei Witte and the Industrialization of Russia* (New York:
    Columbia University Press, 1963), chap. 1.

19 It is the contention of John McKay, *Pioneers for Profit: Foreign Entrepre-
    neurship and Russian Industrialization* (Chicago: University of Chicago Press,
    1970), that the truly unique feature of Russian industrialization was its
    reliance on the combination of private enterprise and foreign capital and
    foreign entrepreneurship.

20 For a survey of the literature on the determinants of portfolio capital flows,
    see Erich Spitäller, "A Survey of Recent Quantitative Studies of Long-Term
    Capital Movements," International Monetary Fund, *Staff Papers*, 18 (March 1971),
    pp. 189-217.

21 This evidence is summarized in Kuznets, *Modern Economic Growth*, pp. 236-9.

22 Henry Rosovsky, *Capital Formation in Japan, 1868-1940* (New York: Free Press,
    1961), p. 14.

23 *Opyt priblizitel'nogo ischisleniia narodnogo dokhoda po razlichnym ego
    istochnikam i po razmeram v Rossii* (Petersburg: Ministerstvo finansov, 1906),
    p. xxxii.

CHAPTER 8

COMPARISONS WITH THE SOVIET PERIOD

The record of economic growth and structural change in the Soviet Union after 1928 is well established[1] and is not the topic of this chapter per se. Instead, the pattern of economic growth in the late tsarist era is to be compared with that of the Soviet Union during the era of central planning.

Especially for the early five-year-plan period (1928-40), index number effects complicate such a comparison, for the economic growth and structure of the Soviet economy are markedly affected by the choice of "early" or "late" year price weights. For example, the annual rate of growth between 1928 and 1937 (real GNP) was approximately 5.5% in 1937 and 1950 ("late") prices but was almost 12% in 1928 ("early") prices. The 1928 ratio of gross investment to GNP was 13%-14% in "late" prices but 25% in "early" prices.[2] Calculations of Soviet economic growth in "early" prices are not available for the period after 1937, but it is obvious that Soviet growth over the entire plan era would be much more rapid when valued in "early" prices. Thus the assessment of Soviet growth performance depends greatly upon the choice of price weights.

BIASES AND INDEX NUMBER EFFECTS

In Chapters 2 and 3, estimation biases in the tsarist period calculations and the effect of alternate price weights upon the tsarist period growth indexes were addressed. The major estimation bias in the tsarist figures, it was emphasized, was introduced by the reliance on material input price deflators for capital goods. Generous adjustment factors, imputed from Soviet ratios of material input prices to capital goods prices, were applied to the tsarist period series, and the potential impacts of these adjustments upon tsarist NNP were evaluated. It was concluded that the tsarist period annual growth rate (1885-1913) would have been raised by a maximum of 0.05% (from 3.25% to 3.3%) if the same procedures used to calculate Soviet national income had been applied to tsarist national income. This upward adjustment, however, must be regarded as on the high side, as it requires among other things a rate of real cost decline in the tsarist capital goods industry equivalent to that of the USSR between 1928 and 1940.

An asymmetry should be noted: If one reverses the calculation to measure what Soviet growth would have been had investment been deflated by material input price indexes (like the tsarist period series), the effect is larger because of the greater share of investment in the Soviet period. The 1928-55 GNP growth rate (in "late" prices) falls by 10% from 4.7% to under 4.5% per annum.[3] Nevertheless, the basic point remains valid that the higher growth of the Soviet period (to be discussed below) does not appear to be the consequence of the use of material input prices to deflate investment.

A more serious problem of comparability is that raised by the substantial discrepancies between the Soviet period series weighted in "early" and "late" year prices. In Chapter 2 I speculated about the effects of applying "early" and "late" prices of the tsarist period to calculate the Soviet period indexes and vice versa. Definitive answers could not be provided because not enough information is available to calculate Soviet real national income in tsarist period prices and vice versa. Using a stylized model of relative prices, I maintained that the use of "late" tsarist period prices would likely yield a result intermediate between the indexes in "early" and "late" Soviet period prices. This speculation, combined with the downward biases introduced by material input prices, caused me to argue for comparisons of tsarist period indexes in "late" prices (1913) with Soviet period indexes in "late" prices (1937 and later).

ECONOMIC GROWTH COMPARISONS

In Table 8.1 I have assembled data on the rates of growth of real NNP for the tsarist and Soviet periods. The tsarist growth rates are in 1913 prices ("late" tsarist prices), and the Soviet indexes are in the ruble factor costs of a "late" period, principally those of 1937.[4] The period 1940 to 1950 has been deliberately omitted to eliminate the impact of World War II and its aftermath on Soviet economic growth. The transitional 1913 to 1928 indexes are given, however, for reasons

Table 8.1. *Annual growth rates, tsarist and Soviet periods (%)*

	(1) Total product	(2) Product per capita	(3) Product per worker	(4) Incre- mental capital- output ratios (net)

A. Tsarist period,
   1885-89 to 1909-13
   (1913 prices)
	3.25	1.7	1.7	3.1

B. Transitional period, 1913-28 (1913 prices)	-0.5 to -0.7	-1.1 to -1.5	-	-

C. Soviet period,
   central planning era
   1928-40 "late" prices
	5.1	3.9	1.4	2.8

1928 prices	11.0[a]	9.8[a]	6.1[a]	-
1950-75 "late" prices	5.2	3.8	3.9	4.6
1950-60 "late" prices	5.9	4.3	4.8	3.7
1960-75 "late" prices	4.6	3.5	3.1	5.0

1928-75 (1940-50 omitted)
       "Late" prices
       Mixed index[b]
	
	5.15
	7.11
		
		3.86
		5.78
			
			3.07
			4.62
				
				4.0
				-

D. Transitional period plus
   Soviet period, central
   planning era (1913-75, period
   1940-50 omitted)
     Mixed index
     1913 prices
     and "late" Soviet
     prices
	
	3.43
		
		2.30
			
			-
				
				-

Note: Dash indicates not available.
[a] 1928-37 growth rate.
[b] 1928-40 index in 1928 prices, 1950-75 index in "late" prices averaged
by number of years.
Source: See Table 8.2.

that will be described immediately below. Three types of price weights are used: 1913 ("late" tsarist period) prices, 1928 ("early" Soviet period) prices, and "late" Soviet period prices. The "late" Soviet period prices are from the years 1937 (1928-40) and 1970 (1950-75). As Bergson has shown, the choice of price weights after 1937 has little impact on calculated growth rates.[5]

The growth rate figures cited in Table 8.1 illustrate the importance of index number relativity in assessing Soviet growth performance: The figures in both "late" and "early" prices indicate an acceleration in the rate of economic growth above the long-term tsarist rate after 1928. In late year prices, the pre-World War II and postwar growth rates are similar at slightly over 5% per annum where the postwar rate is a combination of high rates between 1950 and 1960 and relatively slower rates after 1960. In "early" prices, the 1928-40 growth rate is roughly double that in "late" prices.

I have argued above that it is more appropriate to use the "late" prices of each period in tsarist-Soviet period comparisons, and one can see that the magnitude of growth acceleration during the Soviet plan era hinges upon the choice of price weights. However, the existence of a growth acceleration is established by both sets of price weights.

This acceleration is even more prominent on a per capita basis because of the slower rate of growth of population after 1928 relative to the tsarist era. Even using the more conservative late year index, the growth rate of per capita product more than doubled between the tsarist and Soviet plan eras (from 1.7% to 3.8%-3.9% per annum).

On a per worker basis, the growth acceleration is also prominent, but only so after 1950. During the early five-year-plan era (1928-40), the growth rate of product per worker (expressed in "late" prices) was roughly equivalent to that of the tsarist era. This finding indicates that the initial growth acceleration during the early Soviet period was largely a consequence of the more rapid expansion of the labor force in the Soviet era.

Incremental capital-output ratios were generally higher in the Soviet era than in the tsarist era, although during the early five-year-plan era, incremental capital-output ratios were roughly comparable to those of the tsarist era. The trend in incremental capital-output ratios is consistent with trends in labor force growth: The

Soviet labor force expanded most rapidly between 1928-40[6] and this rapid growth would be expected to have a beneficial effect on incremental capital efficiency.[7]

The difference between the Soviet long-term growth rate (1928-75) in "late" prices (5.15%) and the tsarist long-term rate (1885-1913) in 1913 prices (3.25%) of 1.9% per annum provides one simple measure of the growth payoff of adopting the Soviet system of centralized allocation of resources. Cumulated over a fifty-year period, this growth acceleration factor yields a value of total Soviet output more than twice that which would have prevailed had the long-term tsarist rate held over the Soviet plan era. I need not emphasize that this calculation is highly speculative as it assumes that the tsarist long-term growth rate is indicative of the hypothetical rate of growth of a capitalist Russia after 1928. It is likely that a capitalist Russia would have participated in the world depression as well as the general acceleration in economic growth after World War II and the net balance is difficult to predict.

A quite different picture emerges if one assumes that the disruptions of the transition period (1913 to 1928) are a necessary concommitant of the transition from capitalism to socialist central planning. According to my estimates (Chapter 5), the growth of total product was slightly negative during the transition period and was substantially negative on a per capita basis. If one therefore includes the transition period in the computation of long-term Soviet growth, then the growth of total product in the Soviet era is only slightly higher than in the tsarist era. Such a comparison will understate the Soviet growth acceleration for two reasons. The first is that it includes the wartime destruction of the Russian economy, and this loss of output cannot be attributed to the transition from capitalism to planned socialism.[8] Second, it could be debated whether the disruptions that occurred after 1917 were indeed a necessary concommitant of the transition to planned socialism or whether they should be regarded as historical accidents.

COMPARISONS OF ECONOMIC STRUCTURE

In Table 8.2, I summarize the evidence on the economic structures of the tsarist and Soviet economies. The tsarist period figures are in

Table 8.2. *Relative shares of NNP, Russia and Soviet Union (%)*

	1885-89	1909-13
	1913 prices	1913 prices
A. Sector shares of NNP		
Agriculture (A)	57	51
Industry (I+) (broadly defined)	23	32
Services S-	20	17
B. End-use shares of NNP		
Personal consumption (PCE)	83.5	79.6
Government (G)	8.1	9.7
Net domestic investment (NDI)	8.1	12.2
Net foreign investment (NFI)	.3	-1.4
C. Foreign trade proportions (FTP) (exports & imports ÷ NNP)	17	15

[a]1958.

Sources: Table 8.2: The tsarist (and some Soviet) figures are from tables 5.3, 5.4, 6.1, 6.3. For the Soviet period, sector shares are calculated from data cited by Simon Kuznets in Abram Bergson and Simon Kuznets, eds., *Economic Trends in the Soviet Union* (Cambridge: Harvard University Press, 1963), table 8.5 (Bergson approximation, 1937 ruble factor cost), and from the sector growth indexes in Rush Greenslade, "The Real Gross National Product of the USSR, 1950-1975," Joint Economic Committee, *Soviet Economy in a New Perspective* (Washington, D.C.: U.S. Government Printing Office, 1976), p. 271. In using the Greenslade indexes, I assume that NNP and GNP grew at the same rate. The end-use shares are calculated from Abram Bergson, *The Real National Income of Soviet Russia Since 1928* (Cambridge: Harvard University Press, 1961), pp. 128-53 and from Bergson's paper in Bergson and Kuznets, eds., *Economic Trends,* pp. 36-7. The 1975 shares are approximated from Greenslade, "Real Gross National Product," pp. 275-7,

1928			1937		1955(58)	1975
1913 prices	1928 prices	1937 prices	1928 prices	1937 prices	1937 prices	1937 prices
-	-	49	-	31	22[a]	19
-	-	28	-	45	58[a]	62
-	-	23	-	24	20[a]	19
76.7-74.5	70.2	83.0	36.9	55.4	52	51
8.7	11.2	7.7	26.4	22.7	26	22
14.6-17.2	18.6	9.3	36.7	21.9	22	27
0	0	0	0	0	0	0
6	-	-	-	1	5	-

by applying one-half of capital repairs to depreciation and applying Abraham Becker's 1965 share of depreciation to GNP to 1975 GNP from Abraham Becker, *Soviet National Income, 1958-1964* (Berkeley and Los Angeles: University of California Press, 1969), table 5. The Russian foreign trade proportions are in current prices and are from appendix M. The other trade proportions are from Franklyn Holzman, "Foreign Trade," in Bergson and Kuznets, eds., *Economic Trends,* p. 290 (I assume exports balance imports).

Table 8.1: For the Soviet period, the growth figures are from Bergson in Bergson and Kuznets, eds., *Economic Trends,* pp. 36-37 and from Greenslade, "Real Gross National Product," p. 275. For the period 1950 to 1975, I assume equivalent rates of growth of NNP and GNP. This assumption likely causes a slight overstatement of NNP growth. The incremental capital-output ratios are calculated by dividing the average ratio of net investment to NNP by the growth rate of NNP.

1913 prices.[9] The Soviet period figures are primarily in 1937 factor
costs,[10] but for 1928, alternate figures are given in 1913 and 1928
prices. The figures in 1913 prices are from Chapter 5, and they are
given as ranges because of ambiguities in the choice of appropriate
price deflators. The foreign trade proportions (panel C) are in prices
of the current year.

In Chapter 7 it was noted that the tsarist economy began and
ended the modern era with an investment rate that was high and a consumption rate that was low by the international standards of the late
nineteenth century. In this sense, a general similarity to the classic
pattern of Soviet resource allocation was noted. It now remains to
contrast the tsarist and Soviet patterns of resource allocation, beginning with the year 1913.

Concentrating first on the net domestic investment rate (panel
B), we note that the transition period (1913 to 1928) witnessed an
increase in the investment rate. The most relevant figures are those
in constant 1913 prices, which indicate a rise from 12% in 1913 to a
low of 15% and a high of 17% in 1928. The high figure is not that much
different from that in prevailing prices (at 18.6%). In Chapter 5, I
expressed concern about the crude nature of the investment deflators
used to calculate these figures, for the expected substantial increase
in the relative price of capital goods was not indicated by the capital
goods deflators (Table 5.3).[11] Thus the 1928 investment proportion in
1913 prices must be used with great caution.

The contrast of the 1928 investment proportion in prevailing
prices and in 1937 prices underscores the dramatic decline in the
relative price of capital goods between 1928 and 1937, for the investment proportion in 1937 prices is one-half of the proportion in 1928
prices. A comparison of the 1928 investment proportion in 1913 and
1937 prices suggests that the 1937 relative price of capital was substantially below that of 1913 but less so than relative to 1928 prices.
This result conforms to the stylized version of relative prices
employed in Chapter 2. The relative price of capital rose between 1913
and 1928 and then fell between 1928 and 1937.

It was concluded in the preceding chapter that the 1913 tsarist
investment proportion was relatively high for a low income country. As
the Soviet investment proportion in 1928 was higher than in 1913 des-

pite a decline in per capita income and then doubled between 1928 and 1937, the Soviet investment proportion was exceptionally high relative to per capita income by the mid-1930s. The positive deviation of the tsarist investment rate from the "normal" proportion must be viewed as quite mild compared to the deviations of the Soviet plan era. The same can be said of the behavior of the consumption ratio and government spending ratio after 1928; namely, the deviations from "normal" patterns observed throughout the tsarist era were quite mild relative to the deviations of the Soviet plan era.

Long-term data on sector shares (panel A) are available only in the prices of 1913 for the tsarist era and in the prices of 1937 for the Soviet plan era; so the impact of changing price weights upon the structure of output by the producing sector cannot be investigated. My suspicion is that the switch from 1913 to 1937 prices would result in a lowering of the relative price of industrial goods and therefore in a lowering of the relative share of industry. Given the uncertainty surrounding these price effects, it is difficult to compare the structure of output during the tsarist and Soviet eras, especially the 1913 and 1928 structures.

In the preceding chapter it was noted that the change in output shares that occurred between 1885 and 1913 was generally consistent with the pattern typical of the early stages of modern economic growth, although the rate of decline of the agriculture share may have been slow for a country entering modern economic growth with a large share of agriculture. The Soviet Union began the five-year-plan era with an output structure much like that of the late tsarist period. Between 1928 and 1937, however, the Soviet planned economy experienced rapid change in the structure of output. Within one decade (1928-37), the decline in agriculture's and industry's product shares dwarfed (by at least a factor of two) the structural changes of the entire 1885 to 1913 period.

As these matters have been discussed in some detail elsewhere,[12] they need not detain us further. The basic point is that the deviations from "normal" patterns observed for the late tsarist period are inconsequential when contrasted with the structural changes that took place during the early plan era. One further point of contrast should be made, and that is the shift from fairly normal reliance upon world

product and capital markets during the tsarist era to minimal (or zero
reliance in the case of capital markets) reliance after 1928. The rise
in domestic investment proportions between 1885 and 1913 was financed
about 50% by the rise in net foreign investment, leaving the remainder
to be covered out of domestic savings. During the Soviet plan era, the
doubling of the investment rate within one decade was accomplished
without any influx of foreign savings. Thus, parallels between the
"Asian" pattern of development of the tsarist era and under Stalin
should not be overemphasized.

SOME COMMENTS ON FACTOR PRODUCTIVITY
This study has concentrated on the rate of growth of output during the
tsarist era; the growth of factor inputs has not been emphasized. The
principal reason for the neglect of factor inputs is the difficulty of
obtaining reliable estimates of labor inputs (either employment or
hours worked) in a relatively backward economy where employment is
concentrated in agriculture and handicraft. Estimates of capital stock
do emerge from the estimates of net investment. Some preliminary
comments can be made about tsarist period-Soviet period productivity
performance. Given the large discrepancies between the tsarist and
Soviet productivity experiences, the basic conclusions that follow are
likely valid (Table 8.1).

Between 1928 and 1975, output grew at an annual rate of 5.15%,
employment at a rate of 2%, and reproducible capital at a rate of 8%.
According to my capital stock figures (Appendixes I-L), reproducible
capital grew at approximately 3.5% per annum between 1885-1913, whereas
output grew at 3.25% per annum. Although satisfactory estimates of
labor force growth could not be obtained, my best guess was a growth of
aggregate employment of 1.6% per annum (this is the growth rate of the
able-bodied population) for the period 1885 to 1913. This last estimate is discussed in Table 6.3.

If one accepts these figures as portraying correct orders of
magnitude and makes simplifying assumptions concerning the Soviet
period and tsarist period aggregate production functions,[13] the following contrast is obtained: The aggregate rate of growth of factor
inputs for the tsarist era was 2.1% per annum; for the Soviet plan era
it was higher at 3.8% per annum. Thus, the principal force behind the
Soviet period growth acceleration is immediately apparent: the acceler-

ation of factor input growth after 1928. This acceleration "explains" almost the entire growth differential between the Soviet plan era and tsarist era. Subtracting the factor input growth rate from the output growth rate yields annual growth rates of output per unit of factor input of 1.15% for the tsarist period and 1.4% for the Soviet plan era, and it is not advisable (in light of the crude underlying data) to argue that the 0.25% differential is statistically significant.

It appears that both the tsarist and Soviet economies relied heavily upon a pattern of "extensive" growth, that is, growth based upon the expansion of factor inputs. In the tsarist case, some 70% of growth was accounted for by the expansion of factor inputs; in the Soviet case, some 75% was accounted for by the expansion of factor inputs.

SUMMARY

In this chapter the pattern of economic growth and structural change in tsarist Russia, 1885 to 1913, was compared with that of the Soviet Union during the plan era, 1928 to 1975.

The Soviet plan era did experience an acceleration in the rate of economic growth, and this acceleration may have led to a current day volume of total output more than two times what would have prevailed without this acceleration. If one includes the period of transition from capitalism to planned socialism, then the long-term growth rate of the Soviet economy is roughly equal to that of the long-term rate of the late tsarist era.

In the preceding chapter certain "Asian" features of tsarist economic development were noted, in particular, the high investment and government spending proportions and the low consumption proportion for a low income country. The shifts in the structure of output and final expenditures that occurred during the early five-year-plan era, however, dwarfed the deviations from "normal" patterns observed for the tsarist economy and established the Soviet experience as a unique and distinct development model.

An examination of probable trends in factor productivity revealed that the growth acceleration of the Soviet period was the consequence of an acceleration in the rate of growth of factor inputs and that both the tsarist and Soviet economies grew according to an extensive pattern of economic growth.

NOTES TO CHAPTER 8

1   For discussions of Soviet economic growth and a structural change during the
    plan era, see Abram Bergson, *The Real National Income of Soviet Russia Since
    1928* (Cambridge: Harvard University Press, 1961); Simon Kuznets, "A Comparative
    Appraisal," in Abram Bergson and Simon Kuznets, eds., *Economic Trends in the
    Soviet Union* (Cambridge: Harvard University Press, 1963), pp. 333-82; Gur Ofer,
    The Service Sector in Soviet Economic Growth (Cambridge: Harvard University
    Press, 1976); Paul Gregory, *Socialist and Nonsocialist Industrialization
    Patterns* (New York: Praeger, 1970); Paul Gregory and Robert Stuart, *Soviet
    Economic Structure and Performance* (New York: Harper and Row, 1974), chaps. 11
    and 12; and Rush Greenslade, "The Real Gross National Product of the USSR,
    1950-1975," in Joint Economic Committee, *Soviet Economy in a New Perspective*
    (Washington, D.C.: U.S. Government Printing Office, 1976), pp. 269-300.

2   Bergson, *Real National Income,* pp. 217, 237.

3   This is calculated from Bergson, *Real National Income,* p. 217, by applying the
    .8 adjustment factor (Chap. 2) to the annual growth rate of gross investment
    and then reaggregating according to the 1937 shares in final uses (Bergson,
    p. 237).

4   The Soviet indexes after 1958 are calculated by applying the Greenslade indexes
    of final expenditures and sector real output (valued in prices of 1970) to
    Bergson's series in 1937 factor costs. The details are given in the notes to
    Table 8.2.

5   Bergson, *Real National Income,* p. 217.

6   Kuznets, "A Comparative Appraisal," p. 337.

7   The relatively rapid growth of labor inputs would be expected to raise the
    marginal productivity of capital.

8   In fact, some major countries (Germany, the United Kingdom) also failed to
    experience substantial increases in real output between 1913 and 1928. On
    this, see B. R. Mitchell, *European Historical Statistics, 1750-1970* (New York:
    Columbia University Press, 1976), Chap. K.

9   The figure in Table 3.3 is for the year 1913. I convert this to the 1909-13
    average by taking the ratio of the 1913 and 1909-13 investment proportions.

10 See note 4.

11 In the stylized version of the NEP period (discussed in chapter 2), the late
    1920s witnessed a severe capital replacement crisis and a substantial increase
    in the relative price of capital.

12 See the references in note 1.

13 I apply fixed weights of .7 and .3 for labor and capital, respectively; thus I
    implicitly assume that the tsarist and Russian aggregate production functions
    were of the Cobb-Douglass type with a unitary elasticity of substitution
    between capital and labor. This assumption may not be accurate for the Soviet
    economy in the postwar period according to M. L. Weitzman, "Soviet Postwar
    Economic Growth and Capital-Labor Substitution," *American Economic Review,* 60,
    no. 4 (September 1970):676-92.

CHAPTER 9

CONCLUSIONS

Summaries have been provided at the end of each chapter, and an understanding of the major findings of this study is best gained by reread-
ing the chapter summaries in succession. In this final chapter I list
what I consider to be the most important conclusions of this work on
Russian national income.

FINDINGS

1.   The rate of growth of the tsarist economy has been understated by past studies of Russian national income. The annual growth
rate during Russia's "industrialization era" (1885 to 1913) was
approximately 3.25% (net national product) and 1.7% (net national
product per capita). This contrasts with Raymond Goldsmith's earlier
finding of rates of approximately 2.75% (GNP) and 1.25% (per capita
GNP) for the same period.

2.   The growth rate of the tsarist economy was relatively high by
the standards of the late nineteenth and early twentieth centuries.
Russia belonged to the group of more rapidly growing economies such as
the United States, Japan, and Sweden. On a per capita and per worker
basis, Russian growth was average when compared with the experiences of
the industrialized countries.

3.   Comparison of tsarist and Soviet growth rates reveals an
acceleration during the Soviet plan era, and this acceleration likely
raised the volume of real output of the contemporary Soviet economy (by
a factor of more than two) above that which would have prevailed under
a capitalist Russia. This judgment rests upon the crucial assumption
that the long-term growth rate of the tsarist economy would have been
indicative of the growth of a capitalist Russia after 1917. It also
omits the negative growth of the period of "transition" from capitalism
to planned socialism (1917-28). If the "transition" is included in the
computation of long-term Soviet growth, then the difference between the

long-term tsarist and the Soviet growth rate disappears.

4. The acceleration in the growth rate after 1928 was primarily
a consequence of the acceleration of the growth of factor inputs. If
factor inputs had continued to grow at the rates prevailing from 1885
to 1913, there would have been no Soviet period growth acceleration.

5. The economic growth and structural change of tsarist Russia
between 1885 and 1913 conforms to the pattern of modern economic growth
exhibited by the industrialized countries. I therefore have concluded
that Russia entered the era of modern economic growth during the period
1885 to 1913 - a process cut short by the outbreak of World War I in
1914.

6. Alexander Gerschenkron's depiction of tsarist economic
development as "Asian" in character is shown to be valid in some
respects and invalid in others. Tsarist Russia began and ended the
industrialization era with relatively high investment and government
spending proportions and low personal consumption proportions for a low
income country. These phenomena are in accord with Gerschenkron's
model of relative backwardness. However, the relatively high investment proportion cannot be explained by direct government action (as in
the case of Japan); therefore, the mechanism by which Russia achieved
such high investment proportions at an early stage of economic development remains to be established. Gerschenkron's view that the Russian
peasant was forced to "pay" for the high investment rate and his
emphasis on the poor performance of Russian agriculture are not supported by my results. The major disagreement between this study and
Gerschenkron centers on the performance of Russian agriculture. I
conclude that the performance of Russian agriculture (and of rural
living standards) was much better than that admitted by Gerschenkron.

7. The "Asian" features of the tsarist economy pale in contrast
to those of the Soviet economy after 1928. The Soviet investment rate
doubled between 1928 and 1937, after rising substantially between 1913
and 1928 despite declining per capita income. Similar conclusions can
be drawn from comparisons of government spending and personal consumption proportions in the tsarist and Soviet eras.

8. Foreign capital played a prominent role in tsarist economic
development and ameliorated some of its "Asian" features. One-half of
the increase in the investment rate between 1885 and 1913 was financed

out of rising foreign savings, thereby reducing pressure on domestic savings in a low income country. By contrast, the increase in the investment rate during the Soviet plan period was financed exclusively out of domestic savings.

9. The tsarist economy was well integrated into the world economy and fluctuations in prices and output levels were dictated largely by "external" forces. The domestic price level followed trends in world market prices, and fluctuations in investment spending and total output were coordinated (apparently on a lagging basis) with world investment and output cycles. The major distinguishing feature in the Russian case was the adverse impact of the revolution of 1905, which caused the Russian business cycle to fall out of step with the world business cycle.

10. The Marxist-Leninist interpretation of the economic causes of the revolutionary process in Russia is not supported by the evidence presented in this study. The period preceding the revolution of 1905 was one of rising per capita income, both in the city and countryside, and the period preceding World War I was, as well, one of rapidly rising per capita income in Russia and the other industrialized countries.

11. In 1913 the Russian economy was the world's fourth largest, almost equivalent in total output to the United Kingdom. Russia's high ranking is attributable to the large volume of agricultural output, and Russia's comparative advantage lay in agriculture. On a per capita basis, however, Russia belonged to the poorer countries of Europe with a per capita income one-third that of France, one-fourth that of Germany, one-fifth that of the United Kingdom, and 12% that of the United States.

12. Contrary to official Soviet claims, real per capita income likely declined between 1913 and 1928; 1928 per capita income was between 80% and 85% of the prewar level. Thus the recovery from the ravages of war, revolution, and civil war was completed sometime during the early five-year-plan era. The early years of the plan era should therefore be regarded as belonging to the recovery period.

AN AGENDA FOR RESEARCH

The weaknesses of this study provide an agenda for future research on

the quantitative history of the tsarist economy. I believe it would
not be productive to attempt to extend the national income series back
into the 1870s and 1860s. First, the available statistical material
appears too weak to support such an effort, and, second, such research
would likely only confirm Raymond Goldsmith's finding of slow growth
before the 1880s. Modern economic growth in tsarist Russia prior to
the development of the rail system appears to be unlikely.

I believe that future empirical research should focus upon
several research areas. First, the industrial production series cited
in this study (and used as well by Alexander Gerschenkron and Raymond
Goldsmith) date back to the work of N. D. Kondratiev published in the
mid-1920s.[1] The number of industrial commodities included in the
Kondratiev index is limited, and the Kondratiev study does not appear
to have been a major research effort. It would thus be worthwhile to
reexamine industrial production in Russia and attempt to improve upon
the Kondratiev study.

Second, the whole matter of factor inputs has not been dealt with
satisfactorily in this study, and, admittedly, the investigation of
factor inputs was not a major goal of this research. Yet recent publications on the Russian labor force by Olga Crisp and L. E. Mints suggest that an exhaustive reexamination of the Russian nonagricultural
labor force could be undertaken.[2] It remains to be seen whether reliable estimates of the agricultural labor force can be obtained, and
this is a major stumbling block in the way of study of Russian labor
inputs. In view of the rather substantial disagreement between my
capital stock series and that of Arcadius Kahan, it would be fruitful
to a reexamine of the capital stock issue.

Third, the relative price structures of 1913 and the late 1920s
could bear intensive investigation. My own examination of this question failed to reveal the substantial increase in the relative price of
capital between 1913 and 1928 predicted by the literature. For this
reason, I was doubtful of the accuracy of my deflation of 1928 Soviet
national income. A large mass of information on the prices of the
period 1913 to 1928 is available, and a careful analysis of this
evidence may shed light on this issue.

Fourth, much work remains to be done on linking 1928 and 1913.
The real national income comparisons of 1928 and 1913 presented in this

work must eventually be tested against independently derived physical production series.

Finally, I would suggest an extensive investigation of the sources (causes) of the relatively high investment proportions of the late tsarist era. These proportions are not to be explained (as Gerschenkron has argued) by direct state activity and remain a puzzle. A comparative study of the tsarist tax system, the sources of savings, and other factors should be undertaken to explain why the investment rate was so high in a country so poor on a per capita basis.

NOTES TO CHAPTER 9

1   *Ekonomicheski Biulleten Koniunkturnogo Instituta*, no. 2 (February 1926):17-20.

2   Olga Crisp, "Labor and Industrialization in Russia," *Cambridge Economic History of Europe*, vol. 7, pt. 2 (Cambridge University Press, 1978), pp. 308-415; L. E. Mints, *Trudovye resursy SSSR* (Moscow: Nauka, 1975).

APPENDIXES

PERSONAL CONSUMPTION EXPENDITURES IN RETAIL OUTLETS

RETAIL SALES IN CURRENT PRICES

Personal consumption expenditures in retail outlets are supplied in Table A.1. For the period 1889 to 1913, I use Dikhtiar's[1] estimates of total retail sales in current prices. Dikhtiar's own estimates are based upon Strumilin's[2] reporting of total wholesale and retail trade turnover for the entire 1885 to 1913 period; so a word on the Strumilin data is in order. The Strumilin trade series is based upon trade turnover data reported to tax authorities. In this period, trade and industrial establishments were subject to two types of taxation; first, patents (*svidetel'stva*) for the privilege of conducting trade were required, and the magnitude of the patent tax depended upon the particular order (*razriad*) to which the enterprise belonged. Trade establishments were ordered in five *razriady*, according to size and type of establishment. For example, large wholesalers, major agricultural brokers, large credit establishments, grain elevators, and expeditors belonged to the first *razriad*; large retailers, small agricultural brokers, spirits wholesalers, and wholesalers of imported tobacco belonged to the second *razriad*; small retailers, kiosk establishments, and so on belonged to the third, and so on. A fairly complete description of the various *razriady* is supplied by Dikhtiar, and summary statistics of tax revenues broken down by *razriady* are to be found in the *Ezhegodnik ministerstva finansov* series for the period after 1900 and in special publications for the 1880s and 1890s.[3] In 1908 patent revenues from trade establishments yielded over 25 million rubles to the state treasury.

A supplementary tax (*dopol'nitel'ny promyslovy nalog*) was levied along with the basic "patent" tax starting in 1885 and varied with the annual turnover and profits of the establishment. The tax averaged between 1.5% and 2% of profits during the 1880s and 1890s. In the case of the first three *razriady*, trade turnover had to be reported to the tax authorities.[4] Reported trade turnover figures form the basis of Strumilin's trade estimates, which he calculates by netting out non-trade establishments (primarily credit institutions). The supplementary tax was levied on the first three *razriady*; small or nonprofitable establishments were, in certain cases, exempted, as were other establishments already subject to an excise tax. A 3% tax on enterprise profits was levied on trade corporations subject to public disclosure; thus the sales of corporate trade establishments have to be estimated using coefficients of profits to turnover. The major exemption from indirect taxes was the state spirits monopoly, but direct data on spirits sales are available. The system of supplementary taxation was extremely complicated, varying by region, type of establishment, and other characteristics. Some fifty pages of text are required in the official Ministry of Finance publication to describe the system.[5]

Using Strumilin's figures on total (retail and wholesale) trade volume, Dikhtiar estimates retail trade volume by excluding wholesale trade establishments from the overall sum of trade turnover. This he accomplishes by analyzing each *razriad* to omit the sales of wholesale establishments. The raw tax data are not detailed enough to segregate wholesale and retail trade with great precision, but Dikhtiar maintains that his estimates will be reasonably accurate. State sales of spirits (*kazennaia prodazha pitei*) need not be estimated from tax data, as such data were supplied regularly and in great detail by the Ministry of Finance.[6] Total retail sales are then the sum of sales of retail establishments (estimated from tax data) and of spirits sales by the state monopoly.

Dikhtiar's figures cover only the period 1899 to 1913. I backcast them to 1885 by duplicating the process by which Dikhtiar derived retail trade from total trade turnover for the 1899 to 1913 period. Specifically, I construct an index of retail trade from Strumilin's total trade volume data by applying fixed weights of .58 to *razriad* I + II sales and .84 to *razriad* III sales. State spirits sales are then added to these figures to form a pre-1899 index of retail sales. Comparing this constructed index with the Dikhtiar estimates for 1899 to 1913, I find a close correspondence between the two indexes (a 2% discrepancy for the 1900 to 1907 period and a 1% discrepancy for the 1907 to 1913 period). From this exercise, I conclude that my constructed pre-1899 index provides a reasonable duplication of the Dikhtiar methodology. The Dikhtiar figures plus the backcast figures are given in Table A.1, column 1.

In view of the importance of retail trade expenditures (38% of 1913 national income[7]), it is important to have some evaluation of the accuracy of the Dikhtiar-Strumilin estimates used in this study. Strumilin himself writes that his own figures must be regarded as "approximative."[8] Two major sources of measurement errors must be considered: significant tax evasion would result in an underreporting of sales, and all wholesale sales may not be netted out from trade turnover. In the former case, two countervailing forces should be present: the enterprise's desire to avoid paying the tax versus the desire of the state to collect it. Fines for violations of these tax regulations were not inconsequential, and this should have provided an incentive to report all sales. In 1890 trade enterprises paid almost 750,000 rubles in fines - a figure that equals almost 10% of supplementary tax collections and 2% of total tax collections from trade establishments.[9] One cannot argue a priori that one force outweighs the other, but I believe that official tax data should provide a reasonable approximation of trade turnover, especially as an index over time. This is also the conclusion reached by B. V. Avilov, the compiler of the statistical appendix of the *Granat* encyclopedia.[10] My own suspicion is that underreporting would be most serious in remote areas, where markets operated on a more informal basis, for example, intrapeasant markets in villages. In Appendix D, I consider whether such sales will be captured by the farm consumption-in-kind figures.

The accuracy of Dikhtiar's delineation of wholesale from retail trade also cannot be established a priori. One can only say that the assumptions Dikhtiar was forced to make in the absence of concrete data appear to be reasonable and should not lead to systematic bias, especially if the ratio of wholesale to retail trade remained relatively stable. The most convincing evidence in support of the Dikhtiar estimates is the relatively close correspondence between estimates of 1913 NNP by sector of origin and by end use,[11] for a major error in the retail trade figure would show up as a major discrepancy between the two.

This author attempted to construct an independent index of retail sales prior to 1899 from detailed tax information of the Finance Ministry (*Istoricheski ocherk*, statistical appendixes), but I quickly discovered that the available data are not detailed enough to improve upon the extrapolation of the Dikhtiar-Strumilin estimates. Although this tax information is broken down in considerable detail, one cannot use it readily to separate wholesale from retail sales, except in quite obvious instances. In any case, rough calculations from this data appear to support the extrapolations of the Dikhtiar figures.[12]

RETAIL SALES IN 1913 PRICES

For the deflation of retail expenditures, three alternate price indexes are available.[13] Two *retail* price indexes, the Petersburg index of the Institute of Economic Research (Institut ekonomicheskikh issledovanii) and the retail price index for Petersburg and Moscow prepared by M. E. Kokhna, were compiled during the period under investigation. In both cases the underlying weights were based upon the structure of average budget expenditures of industrial workers in the two cities. Comparisons of the two indexes show that the Petersburg portion of the combined Kokhna index coincides closely with the Institute of Economic Research index. There are discrepancies, however, between the two Petersburg price indexes and the Moscow price index. These discrepancies may be due to regional price variation, which was especially prominent for agricultural products.[14] The indexes vary in product coverage as well: The Institute of Economic Research index encompasses 27 products, whereas the Kokhna Petersburg (Moscow) indexes encompass 24 (15) products. Thus the differences between the Moscow and Petersburg indexes could be either the product of divergent regional prices or the consequence of different product coverage.

A third price index is the Podtiagin index. The Podtiagin index is a pseudo-retail price index as its weights are based on average worker budgets, but it uses wholesale prices taken from the annual publication of the Ministry of Trade and Industry, *Survey of Commodity Prices in Major Russian and Foreign Markets*, annual editions, 1897-1915 (*Svod tovarnykh tsen*).[15] The Podtiagin index covers 66 commodities and uses annual averages of monthly prices from various regional markets, often including Petersburg or Moscow markets. It is thus better suited to capture national price trends. On the other hand, it does employ wholesale prices, and in some instances even includes world market prices, both of which could diverge significantly from retail prices because of variations in wholesale and retail margins, changes in indirect taxes, and differential tariffs.

Each of the three indexes has its advantages and shortcomings. The Petersburg and Moscow-Petersburg indexes are constructed from observed retail prices and do

represent price trends from a uniform market over time. Their drawback is that
major city indexes may fail to reflect national price trends when regional price
variation is significant. The Podtiagin index should better capture national price
movements, but it suffers from the drawback of being based upon wholesale price
quotations.

In Table A.1 I supply the three alternate retail price indexes for the 1885 to
1913 period: the Institute of Economic Research Petersburg index (2a), the M. P.
Kokhna combined Moscow-Petersburg index (2b), and the M. E. Podtiagin pseudo-retail
price index (2c). Comparisons of the three indexes reveal some major discrepancies
during specific subperiods: The Petersburg and combined Moscow-Petersburg indexes
fail to show the upward discontinuity in prices between 1906 and 1907 that the
Podtiagin index indicates. However, the three indexes are in more general agreement
concerning trends over the full 1900 to 1913 period. During the industrialization
decade of the 1890s, the Podtiagin index reveals a steeper drop in the price level
during the first five years and a steeper rise thereafter than the two major city
indexes. Again, however, the three indexes are in more general agreement concerning
overall price trends over the full 1885 to 1900 period. In general, the Podtiagin
index, based as it is on wholesale price quotations, appears to fluctuate more than
the two major city indexes, which use retail price observations. This is especially
true of the bulge in agricultural prices after 1905, which show up more dramatically
in the Podtiagin index than in the other two indexes.[16] The greater sensitivity of
the Podtiagin index to fluctuations in agricultural prices (which can be observed
directly from *Svod tovarnykh tsen*) suggests either a greater weight for agricultural
products in the Podtiagin index or a lesser sensitivity of the Petersburg and Moscow
retail markets to fluctuations in wholesale agricultural prices.

Fortunately, the choice of the appropriate price index is not as crucial as it
might appear, especially if one is interested in long-term trends. Again assuming
that relatively small differences in annual growth rates are not statistically
significant, I find that, according to all three price indexes, the annual rate of
growth of real retail sales for the entire 1885 to 1913 period was slightly over
3.5%, that is, all three round to 4% per annum. For the subperiods 1885 to 1900 and
1900 to 1913, the annual growth rate varies from 4% to 5% for the earlier period and
rounds in all three cases to 2% in the later period. For the industrialization
decade (1891-1900), the growth rate rounds to 7% in the case of the major city
indexes and to 8% for the Podtiagin index. The greatest discrepancy among the
indexes is for the period 1900 to 1907 and 1907 to 1913. The Podtiagin index
reveals a substantial (14%) decline between 1900 and 1907 and then a dramatic
increase (47%) from 1907 to 1913. The major city indexes, on the other hand, reveal
a stagnant level of real retail sales between 1900 and 1907 and a less substantial
increase between 1907 and 1913.

In the course of this research, the author contemplated constructing independently a fourth retail price index for the deflation of retail sales but rejected
the idea because it appeared doubtful that such an index would result in an
improvement over the existing indexes. First of all, the major source of price

quotations available to the author (*Svod tovarnykh tsen*) consists of wholesale price quotations, which are theoretically inferior to the retail prices of the Petersburg and Moscow indexes.   Second, it is questionable whether the author could have constructed a superior set of weights from the available budgetary data for families of industrial workers and farm families.[17]

Table A.1. *Retail trades, consumer prices, retail sales in 1913 prices (million rubles)*

	(1) Retail sales current prices	(2) a) Petersburg (Institute of Economic Research, Petersburg)	b) Moscow-Petersburg (M. P. Kokhna)	c) Average prices, various regional markets (Podtiagin)	1÷2a	Index 1913=100	1÷2b	Index 1913=100	1÷2c	Index 1913=100
1885	2052	78.0	80.2	75.4	2631	37	2559	36	2722	38
1886	2096	73.9	75.1	73.1	2836	40	2791	39	2867	40
1887	2409	67.7	75.2	74.1	3558	50	3203	45	3251	46
1888	2364	70.2	76.5	75.4	3368	47	3090	43	3135	44
1889	2319	74.5	78.1	72.8	3113	44	2969	42	3185	45
1890	2364	69.6	75.4	70.4	3397	48	3135	44	3358	47
1891	2365	74.7	78.1	85.6	3166	44	3028	42	2763	39
1892	2409	79.1	81.4	88.2	3046	43	2960	42	2731	38
1893	2587	78.3	80.2	78.8	3304	46	3226	45	3283	46
1894	2810	72.8	76.2	66.4	3560	50	3688	52	4232	59
1895	3034	72.1	72.7	62.3	4214	59	4173	58	4870	68
1896	3123	71.2	71.4	62.2	4386	61	4374	61	5021	70
1897	3257	70.3	72.8	72.2	4633	65	4473	63	4511	63
1898	3524	77.6	77.3	79.2	4541	64	4559	64	4450	62
1899	4461	78.7	78.0	78.3	5668	79	5719	80	5697	80
1900	4292	75.0	78.7	76.0	5723	80	5454	76	5647	79
1901	4397	76.5	78.9	77.9	5748	81	5573	78	5644	79
1902	4441	78.1	79.7	79.0	5686	80	5573	78	5622	79
1903	4630	78.6	79.0	77.8	5891	83	5861	82	5951	83
1904	4725	76.9	80.9	80.1	6144	86	5841	82	5899	83
1905	4975	78.2	83.3	84.6	6362	89	5973	84	5881	82
1906	4906	81.1	88.2	91.0	6049	85	5562	78	5391	76
1907	4982	86.5	93.1	102.7	5760	81	5351	75	4851	68
1908	5167	93.8	97.7	103.3	5509	77	5289	74	5002	70
1909	5415	93.4	96.3	98.6	5798	81	5623	79	5492	77
1910	5861	90.0	94.3	94.4	6512	91	6215	87	6209	87
1911	6221	90.9	94.1	94.6	6844	96	6611	93	6576	92
1912	6665	98.2	99.4	101.5	6787	95	6705	94	6567	92
1913	7141	100.0	100.0	100.0	7141	100	7141	100	7141	100

Sources: Retail sales current prices: G. A. Dikhtiar, *Vnutrenniaia torgovli v dorevoliutsionnoi Rossii* (Moscow: Nauka, 1960), p. 73. For a discussion of the Dikhtiar estimates and the backcasting 1899 to 1885, see text. Retail price indices: S. G. Strumilin, *Ocherki ekonomicheskoi istorii Rossii i SSSR* (Moscow: Nauka, 1966), p. 89, and Strumilin, *Istoriia chernoi metallurgii v SSSR* (Moscow: Nauka, 1966) pp. 431-2. The Petersburg index encompasses 27 commodities, the combined Moscow-Petersburg index encompasses 39, and the Podtiagin index encompasses 66. We cite the Petersburg index net of the rental price index. In all instances, the weights are based upon worker budgetary expenditure data, presumably from the period 1900 to 1913. The exact dating of the underlying budget weights does not appear to be crucial because expenditure patterns did not appear to change radically during this period. On this see Dikhtiar, pp. 47-58.

NOTES TO APPENDIX A

1 G. A. Dikhtiar, *Vnutrenniaia torgovlia v dorevoliutsionnoi Rossii* (Moscow: Nauka, 1960), p. 73.

2 S. G. Strumilin, *Statistiko-ekonomicheskie ocherki* (Moscow: Gosstatizdat, 1958), p. 680.

3 E. g., *Ezhegodnik ministerstva finansov, vypusk 1909 goda* (Petersburg: Izdania Ministerstva finansov, 1909), pp. 654-77, and Ministerstvo finansov, *Istoricheski ocherk oblozheniia torgovli i promyslov v Rossii* (Petersburg: Kirschbaum, 1893).

4 The original trade turnover figures are reported in *Entsiklopedicheski slovar' Granat*, 7th ed. vol. 36, pt. 4, statistical appendix.

5 *Istoricheski ocherk*.

6 The annual publication *Ezhegodnik ministerstva finansov* published an entire section on state sales and production of spirits (*kazennaia prodazha pitei*).

7 Paul Gregory, "1913 Russian National Income: Some Insights into Russian Economic Development," *Quarterly Journal of Economics* 90, no. 3 (August 1976): 458-9.

8 S. G. Strumilin, *Statistika i ekonomika* (Moscow: Nauka, 1963), p. 437.

9 *Istoricheski ocherk*, p. 360 and appendix, p. 77.

10 B. V. Avilov, ed., "Statisticheski obzor razvitiia narodnogo khoziaistva v dorevoliutsionnoi Rossii," *Entsiklopedicheski slovar' Granat*, 7th ed., vol. 36, pt. 4, p. 56.

11 Gregory, "1913 Russian National Income," p. 456.

12 For 1890, e.g., I take the sum of second guild turnover from *Istoricheski ocherk*, statistical appendix (3041 million rubles), and I assume that the ratio of retail trade to total guild 1 and 2 turnover applies to guild 2 (37%). This yields a guild 2 retail trade turnover of 1135 million rubles. To this figure, I add non-guild retail trade turnover (588 million rubles) and 90% of guild 3 trade turnover (from Strumilin, *Statistiko-ekonomicheski ocherki*, p. 680), or 526 million rubles, to obtain a total retail trade figure of 2249 million rubles. The extrapolated figure is 2364 million rubles.

13 The three price indexes discussed in this section are duplicated in S. G. Strumilin, *Ocherki ekonomicheskoi istorii Rossii i SSSR* (Moscow: Nauka, 1966), p. 89.

14 For a statistical analysis of regional price variation in agricultural prices, see I. D. Koval'chenko and L. V. Milov, *Vserossiisky agrarny rynok, XVIII - nachalo XX veka* (Moscow: Nauka, 1974).

15 Summary price data for the 1899 to 1913 period are given in *Svod tovernykh tsen na russkikh i inostrannykh rynkakh za 1913 god*, Ministerstvo torgovli i promyshelnnosti (Petersburg: N.P., 1915), table 2-7.

16 See, e.g., the various argicultural price series in *Svod tovernykh tsen*, between 1906 and 1907.

17 Dikhtiar, *Vnutrenniaia torgovlia*, Chap. 2, gives a good survey of the available

budgetary studies of workers and peasants for the late tsarist period. For a
more detailed study of peasant budgets, see F. A. Shchebrina, "Krestianskie
biudzhety i zavisimost' ikh ot urozhaev i tsen na khleba," in A. I. Chuprov and
A. S. Posnikov, eds., *Vliiani urozhaev i khlebnykh tsen na nekotoryia storony
ruskkago narodnogo khoziaistva*, Tom II (Petersburg: Kirschbaum, 1897), 2:1-79.

CONSUMER EXPENDITURES ON HOUSING RENTS (URBAN AND RURAL AREAS)

URBAN RENTS

Estimates of urban and rural housing rental payments are summarized in this appendix. I begin by estimating 1913 urban housing rents, which I then use as a benchmark for the time series figures. The estimate for 1913 is taken from an earlier paper,[1] but I summarize its derivation briefly here. S. G. Strumilin,[2] working with survey data from 87 Russian provinces prepared by the Ministry of Finance in 1914, estimated that the number of two-room equivalent apartments in the Russian Empire in 1913 was 3.92 million. According to Strumilin (from a 1910 study by the Central Statistical Committee), the average annual urban rental rate in 1910 was 224 rubles, which I convert into 1913 prices by applying the rental price index from Petersburg to yield an average 1913 rental rate of 264 rubles.[3] This I multiply by 3.92 million apartments to yield a total rental figure of 1035 million rubles in 1913.

A rough check against budget studies of factory workers in Baku, Petersburg, and Kiev reveals that this estimate of urban rental payments is not unreasonable. The average Petersburg worker in 1912, for example, had a ratio of rental to retail expenditures of around 27%. For families of Moscow workers, the ratio was 19% in 1918. According to my figures, the overall ratio of urban rental payments to urban retail expeditures was between 21% and 26% in 1913,[4] and this range is consistent with budget data.

The estimation of the index of real urban housing rental payments for the period 1885-1913 is based upon Arcadius Kahan's index of the urban housing stock in 1913 constant prices.[5] By employing this index, I assume that the ratio of real rental payments to the value of the real urban housing stock remained constant throughout the period. I should note a major discrepancy between urban rents imputed from Kahan's estimate of the stock of urban dwellings in 1913 (about 500 million rubles) and the 1913 estimate used in this study (1035 million rubles). I reject the lower Kahan figure because it suggests a ratio of urban rental to urban retail expenditures of only 10% to 13%. Nevertheless, I assume Kahan's index over time to be correct for lack of adequate data. To convert the 1885 to 1912 figures into current prices, a rental price index for Petersburg is used. These calculations are shown in Table B.1. Of course, the use of a single city index to inflate constant price expenditures is risky because the Petersburg housing market may have differed from other urban rental markets, but this is the only index available.

RURAL RENTS

To estimate the imputed rental value of the rural house stock (Table B.2), I rely on a 1928 study by E. M. Tarasov, the results of which are summarized by Strumilin.

Tarasov estimated the 1913 capitalized value of the 19 million peasant homesteads (including only living space and not garden plots, tool sheds, etc.) at 4350 million rubles.[6] To this value, I apply the rental capitalization rate of 7% used commonly during this period, according to the Ministry of Finance, to obtain a 1913 imputed rental value of 305 million rubles for rural peasant housing.[7] The Tarasov estimate is broadly consistent with that of Vainshtein,[8] who estimates the value of peasant dwellings ("nonproductive" structures) in 1913 at 3995 million rubles. To the Tarasov figure for peasant households, I add Vainshtein's estimate of the value of "capitalist" (landlord) dwellings in 1913 of 1790 million rubles, for a 1913 rental value (again imputed at 7%) of 125 million rubles. Therefore, the total of peasant and landlord rental payments for 1913 is 430 rubles. This figure is below, but broadly compatible with, Kahan's estimate of farm dwellings in 1913,[9] which yields (at 7%) a rental value of 490 million rubles.

The calculation of rural rents for the other years proceeds by applying indexes in prevailing and constant prices of the value of the stock of rural structures to the 1913 value. These indexes are described in Appendix J and are estimated from fire insurance data. During the period 1885-1913, the insurance of peasant property for fire losses was comprehensive, having been introduced on a compulsory basis in the 1870s. The system of insurance of peasant structures was a complicated one, and the reader is referred to several sources in the accompanying note that seek to explain the system.[10]

Two potential sources of measurement error should be mentioned, which could affect the reliability of this calculation. The most important is the possibility that the growth in the insured value of rural structures could be the consequence of increased insurance coverage rather than growth in the value of the stock. This issue is discussed in considerable detail by Vainshtein,[11] who also used insured value in his capital stock estimates, but for a much shorter period than that covered here. In support of the use of insurance data, I can cite the long tradition of compulsory insurance, a likely product of the *obshchina* with its collective liability system, and the reliance of the state on tax collection from the peasantry, all of which would have interested the state in fostering insurance protection among the peasantry. Vainshtein's discussion of this problem appears also valid for our usage of insurance data, and I refer the interested reader to Vainshtein. In any case, I would find it difficult to imagine a decline in insurance coverage during the period under investigation; so the bias, if any, would be in the direction of overstatement of the growth of rural housing rents.

A second source of potential measurement error is that an index of the total stock of rural structures - including barns, sheds, and so on - is being used. In the case of farm structures, however, it would be virtually impossible to distinguish dwelling space from other types of structures because of their close intertwining, even if more detailed insurance data were available. The underlying assumption, therefore, is that the stock of rural dwelling space grew at the same rate as the stock of structures employed for productive purposes. This is the only assumption one can make under the circumstances, and its impact should be minimal anyway.

Table B.1. *Urban housing rental payments (million rubles)*

	(1) In constant 1913 prices	(2) Petersburg rental price index (1913 = 100)	(3) in current prices
1885	466	67.1	313
1886	475	65.7	312
1887	484	63.9	309
1888	494	64.3	318
1889	504	64.7	326
1890	513	63.8	328
1891	522	64.4	336
1892	528	66.3	351
1893	524	68.7	360
1894	518	69.1	358
1895	534	71.3	381
1896	550	72.7	400
1897	560	74.4	417
1898	583	88.7	517
1899	593	81.3	482
1900	591	82.1	485
1901	610	82.0	500
1902	660	81.9	541
1903	702	83.5	586
1904	722	81.8	591
1905	761	81.5	620
1906	800	83.4	667
1907	808	84.3	681
1908	818	84.8	694
1909	832	84.6	704
1910	876	85.1	746
1911	931	89.6	834
1912	983	96.6	950
1913	1035	100.0	1035

Sources: Column 1: See text. Column 2: The Petersburg index of rental prices was compiled by the Petersburg Institute for Economic Research and is cited by S. G. Strumilin, *Istoriia chernoi metallurgii v SSSR* (Moscow: Nauka, 1967), 431-32.

Table B.2. *Rural rental payments, 1884-1913, current and constant 1913 prices*

	(1) Index of rural housing stock, current prices	(2) Rural rental payments, current prices	(3) Index of rural housing stock, 1913 prices	(4) Rural rental payments, 1913 prices
1884	31.6	136	38.0	163
1885	33.3	143	40.2	173
1886	33.5	144	40.4	174
1887	30.2	130	36.8	158
1888	35.9	154	42.3	182
1889	36.4	157	45.0	194
1890	38.0	163	48.1	207
1891	39.0	168	47.0	202
1892	40.1	172	48.3	208
1893	40.0	172	48.3	208
1894	41.2	177	48.4	208
1895	42.7	184	52.6	226
1896	43.0	185	52.5	226
1897	43.4	187	49.3	212
1898	45.6	196	51.1	220
1899	48.7	209	51.4	221
1900	51.6	222	55.5	239
1901	54.7	235	60.8	258
1902	57.8	249	64.9	279
1903	61.1	263	65.0	280
1904	61.1	263	66.5	286
1905	68.4	294	74.3	320
1906	71.6	308	76.1	327
1907	74.8	322	80.5	346
1908	78.4	337	85.3	367
1909	82.1	353	90.3	388
1910	89.3	384	95.0	409
1911	92.5	398	98.4	423
1912	95.7	412	99.8	429
1913	100.0	430	100.0	430

Sources: See text.

NOTES TO APPENDIX B

1   Paul Gregory, "1913 Russian National Income: Some Insights into Russian
     Economic Development," *Quarterly Journal of Economics* 90, no. 3 (August 1976):
     p. 458.
2   S. G. Strumilin, *Statistika i ekonomika* (Moscow: Nauka, 1963), pp. 301-24.
     Strumilin's study relies heavily upon A. Nikitsky, "Tsennost' gorodskikh
     nedvizhimykh imushchestv," *Statisticheskoe obozrenie*, no. 10 (1928). One can
     find a fairly lengthy discussion of Strumilin's study in A. L. Vainshtein,
     *Narodnoe bogatstvo i narodnokhoziaistvennoe nakoplenie predrevoliutsionnoi
     Rossii* (Moscow: Gosstatizdat, 1960), Chap. 11.
3   The index is duplicated in S. G. Strumilin, *Istoriia chernoi metallurgii v
     SSSR* (Moscow: Nauka, 1966), pp. 431-2.
4   These calculations are made from Prokopovich's study of Petersburg worker
     budgets summarized in G. A. Dikhtiar, *Vnutrenniaia torgovlia v dorevoliutsion-
     noi Rossii* (Moscow: Nauka, 1960), p. 49, and from S. G. Strumilin's analysis
     of Moscow budgets in S. G. Strumilin, *Problemy ekonomiki truda, Izbrannye
     proizvideniia* (Moscow: Nauka, 1964), 3:162-3. I assume that two-thirds of
     the workers surveyed were married and the remaining one-third unmarried. I
     also assume that heating costs are included in the rental figures. To calcu-
     late the overall ratio of urban rental payments to urban retail expenditures,
     I add 1913 urban rental payments plus utility expenditure and divide by the
     upper and lower urban retail sales figures in Gregory, "1913 Russian National
     Income," statistical appendix.
5   Arcadius Kahan, "Capital Formation During the Period of Early Industrializa-
     tion in Russia, 1890-1913," *Cambridge Economic History of Europe*, vol. 7, pt.
     2 (Cambridge University Press, 1978).
6   S. G. Strumilin, *Statistiko-ekonomicheskie ocherki* (Moscow: Gosstatizdat,
     1958), pp. 482-514.
7   *Opyt priblizitel'nogo ischisleniia narodnogo dokhoda po razlichnym ego
     istochnikam i po razmeram v Rossii* (Petersburg: Ministerstvo finansov, 1906),
     p. xiv.
8   Vainshtein, *Narodnoe bogatstvo*, pp. 154-66.
9   Kahan, "Capital Formation," p. 299.
10   The most complete discussion of peasant insurance is found in V. V.
     Veselovski, *Istoriia zemstva za sorok let*, 4 vols. (Petersburg: Popov,
     1909), 2:449-637. Other discussions are given in the encyclopedias:
     Brokgauz-Efron, 27, and *Granat*, 41, under the subject *Strakhovania*
     (insurance). For a brief discussion of the entire insurance system, see V. I.
     Kovalevski, ed., *Rossii v Kontse XIX veka* (Petersburg: Ministerstvo finansov,
     1900), chapter by M. A. Danilovski on insurance, pp. 622-755.
11   Vainshtein, *Narodnoe bogatstvo*, Chap. 1.

HOUSEHOLD SERVICE EXPENDITURES (TRANSPORTATION, COMMUNICATION, UTILITIES, PERSONAL MEDICAL CARE, AND DOMESTIC SERVICE)

SERVICE EXPENDITURES IN CURRENT PRICES

I describe in this appendix the estimation of five types of service expenditures not included either in retail sales or in rental payments, namely, payments for transportation, communication, domestic service, personal medical care, and utilities. Some of these categories (transportation, medical care) can be estimated with a good degree of accuracy; others (communications, domestic service, utilities) can only be approximated. Nevertheless, I would doubt that large intertemporal errors are involved.

Railroad travel

Data on passenger expenditures for rail travel are available in considerable detail thanks to the excellent system of data reporting for the Russian railroad system. The figures cited in Table C.1 are for gross sales of rail tickets to passengers for the Russian Empire and are drawn from various sources cited at the bottom of the table.

This calculation of consumer transportation expenditures is likely biased in two opposing directions. A portion of passenger rail expenditures is intermediate in nature (business trips) and should be netted out, but I would imagine such intermediate expenditures to be a relatively small fraction of the total. On the other hand, transportation expenditures on other forms of transport (horse-drawn coach, water, etc.) are not included, but these should be small as well. In the absence of better information, I assume that these two items offset each other.

Communication (telephone, telegraph, post)

Personal (as opposed to business) expenditures for communication services cannot be estimated with precision because of the difficulty of differentiating private from business expenditures. My procedure is to make rough estimates of the ratio of private to total postal expenditures by eliminating obvious business mail (advertising, mass shipment of newspapers, etc.) from total mail deliveries and then assuming (subjectively) that 75% of the remainder (largely packages and first-class mail) is for private purposes. These communication services were all state owned; as a consequence, detailed information on telephone, telegraph, and postal revenues is provided in the various official statistical publications. I acknowledge that this procedure is arbitrary and will likely lead to measurement errors; nevertheless, communications expenditures are not large, and this procedure should not seriously distort trends over time. My results are recorded in Table C.1, column 2; the sources and calculation methods are described in the table, source note 1.

Utility expenditures

Utility expenditures also cannot be estimated with precision. Instead, circuitous procedures are required to obtain consumer expenditures for utilities. Two difficulties must be dealt with in estimating private utility expenditures: The first is the distribution of total utility expenditures among private and business uses; the second is the estimation of total revenues from the sale of utility services to both private and business users. To approximate the private-business distribution I use the 1912 ratio of the value of the urban housing stock to the total stock of urban structures including commercial and industrial establishments (83%),[1] which I subjectively lower to 75% to adjust for greater industrial energy usage by industrial and commercial consumers.[2] I then apply this 75% ratio to the entire 1885 to 1913 period as my estimate of the ratio of private to total utility expenditures. This procedure has been described by this author in an earlier study.[3] It then remains to estimate total utility revenues over the period. Direct data on utility receipts are not available, with the exception of some information on municipally owned utilities.[4] On the other hand, the capital stock of utility corporations (water, sewerage, gas and electricity, and local transportation) is known.[5] Therefore, to determine the annual revenues of corporately owned utilities, I first calculate the approximate capital-output ratio of municipally owned utilities (4.0)[6] and apply this ratio to the capital stock of corporate utilities (at original value) to estimate their annual revenues. Because of the lack of further data, I assume the capital-output ratio to be constant over the entire period.

In effect, what I am doing is backcasting 1913 utility expenditures by an index of municipal and corporate utility capital stock. For this procedure to result in large intertemporal distortions, substantial changes either in the utility capital-output ratio or in the private-business mix of utility expenditures would be required. I uncover no strong evidence of such changes, although admittedly such evidence would be extremely difficult to find. It is surprising that so little data on utility receipts are available for Russia, a likely consequence of the tax system and the paucity of data on local government. With this estimation procedure, I believe that major errors would be more likely to be found in levels rather than in trends over time.

A rough check on the reasonableness of the utility expenditure figures is to calculate the ratio of utility to rental expenditures (from Tables B.1 and C.2). I find that the ratio was around 12% in 1913 and 11% in 1900. Such ratios do not appear unreasonable upon first glance but are well below the 1928 USSR ratio of 40%.[7] In fact, the 40% ratio was used in my earlier study of 1913 national income to estimate 1913 private utility expenditures. I now believe this procedure to be in error because of the subsidization of housing rents in 1928 versus the market pricing mechanism of 1913.

One further potential source of downward bias in my estimates is the fact that much heating was done by wood furnaces and stoves, and it is not known whether such purchases would be included in the retail sales figures (Table A.1). To get some rough notion of the potential bias, I note that gas and electricity payments, according to my figures, accounted for approximately 35% of total utility payments in 1913. If one liberally assumes that wood fuels were equally as important as gas and electricity (with coal purchases likely already included in consumer retail expenditures), then the utility expenditure estimate would have to be raised by 40 million rubles (for 1913), that is, from 12% to 15% of rental payments. In my subsequent discussion, I adhere to the original estimates; however the possibility that they are understated by as much as 40 million rubles should be noted.

Domestic service

The estimation of total expenditures on domestic services is more straightforward: I take annual employment in domestic service and multiply it by the average annual wage of domestic servants. The latter is known only for 1904 (an average of 132 rubles for male and female servants),[8] and this wage is extrapolated over time using the nominal wage index of Russian factory workers.[9] The product of the average annual wage and the average employment in domestic service then serves as my estimate of expenditures for domestic service in Table C.1 (column 4). The index of average annual employment in domestic service is calculated from the ratio of domestic servants in Moscow and Petersburg to the total population of these cities (see the notes to column 11 in Table C.1). These cities accounted for over 20% of the urban population of the 50 European provinces (1917), and the Moscow-Petersburg ratios for selected benchmark years are applied to the urban population figures (50 European provinces) to obtain an index of domestic service employment. This index uses the assumption that the Moscow-Petersburg ratios are typical for other cities. The 1913 figure on domestic servants in the Russian Empire is taken from Rashin.[10]

Medical care

Expenditures for medical care are calculated as the sum of expenditures on physicians and paramedical personnel and on prescription drugs. A detailed description of this calculation is found in the notes to Table C.1. These figures should be reasonably reliable as medical personnel in the civilian sector were reported in some detail in the various statistical yearbooks published during this period.

SERVICE EXPENDITURES IN CONSTANT PRICES

Price indexes for the deflation of service expenditures are supplied in columns 5 through 8 of Table C.1. Much of my price information was gathered from contemporary Baedeker travel handbooks for Russia along with various issues of the *Petersburger Kalendar*.[11] The railroad price deflator is the series on revenues per passenger-verst of state and private railroads taken directly from the annual yearbook of the Transportation Ministry (*Statisticheski sbornik Ministerstva putei soobshcheniia*).

The postage price deflator is the cost of a closed letter within the Russian Empire, and the telegram price deflator is the cost of a ten-word telegram sent within the Russian Empire. The telegram tariff system was changed slightly after

1885, after which it was vastly simplified; so my calculation of a comparable rate for 1885 is somewhat complex but should be reasonably accurate. Postage rates remained unchanged over the entire 1885 to 1913 period. Telegram rates remained fixed from 1885 to 1913.

The utility price deflator is an input price index compiled from the major material inputs into energy production: coal, wood fuels, oil products, and labor.

The estimation of domestic service expenditures in 1913 prices is done by multiplying service employment in the various years by the 1913 annual wage of domestic servants. The deflated service categories are supplied in columns 9 through 12 of Table C.1.

Table C.1. *Consumer expenditures on services – transportation, communication, utilities, domestic service, and medical care (million rubles)*

| | Expenditures in current prices | | | | | Price indices, 1913 = 100 | | | |
| | (1) Passenger railway expenditures | (2) Personal communications expenditures (postage, telephone, telegraph) | (3) Personal utility expenditures including local transportation | (4) Domestic service expenditures | (5) Medical care | (6) Average passenger price per verst, Russian railroads | (7) Communications price index | | |
							(a) Sealed letter, mailed within	(b) 10-word telegram within empire	(c) combined (.7a + .3b)
1885	42	12	37	140	35	158	100	95	99
1888	47	14	45	147	44	144	100	100	100
1891	51	16	51	155	53	136	100	100	100
1894	57	17	53	153	56	128	100	100	100
1896	66	19	60	151	57	106	100	100	100
1900	102	25	66	158	63	107	100	100	100
1903	122	29	76	200	59	109	100	100	100
1907	146	38	97	222	90	98	100	100	100
1910	186	52	111	240	108	99	100	100	100
1913	222	65	118	268	126	100	100	100	100

Table C.1 (cont.)

Expenditures in 1913 prices

	(8) Utility price index	(9) Passenger railway expenditures	(10) Communication expenditures	(11) Utility expenditures	(12) Domestic service a) Employment (million)	b) Expenditure (employment × 1913 average annual wage)	(13) Medical expenditures	Total 9 + 10 + 11 + 12b + 13
1885	51	27	12	72	1.21	209	44	364
1888	56	33	14	80	1.26	218	59	404
1891	59	38	16	86	1.33	230	65	425
1894	60	45	17	88	1.30	225	69	444
1896	62	62	19	96	1.32	228	76	478
1900	80	95	25	83	1.26	218	83	504
1903	81	112	29	94	1.30	225	89	549
1907	82	149	38	118	1.41	244	101	650
1910	94	188	52	125	1.47	254	117	736
1913	100	222	65	118	1.55	268	126	799

Sources: (1) V. I. Kovalevski (ed.), *Rossiia v kontse XIX veka* (Petersburg: Brokgauz-Efron, 1900), 702; *Entsiklopedicheski slovar'* Brokgauz-Efron, Vol. 22, 789; Paul Gregory, "1913 Russian National Income – Some Insights into Russian Economic Development," *Quarterly Journal of Economics* 90,3 (August 1976), 458.

(2) Data on postal, telegraph and telephone revenues (the latter is negligible over the period) are from *Ezhegodnik ministerstva finansov*, selected years under the section: *pochta, telegraf i telefon; Statisticheski sbornik za 1913-1917 gg*, 238; *Statisticheski sbornik Rossii*, 1910, 149; *Statistika rossiiskoi imperii 1884-85*, 245-247. I calculate the following ratios of private to business mail on the basis of the distribution of total mail deliveries: 1885: .46, 1891: .47, 1896: .48, 1900: .50, 1907: .50, 1913: .54. Intermediate years are interpolated using an index of post-telegraph revenues.

(3) First, the capital stock of corporately owned utilities is calculated (the sum of property and inventories) from the *svodny balans* of corporations given in the annual publication *Ezhegodnik ministerstva finansov*. Water, garbage, gas, electricity, local transporation, and local telephone companies are included in these capital stock figures. From A. L. Vainshtein, *Narodnoe bogatstvo i narodnokhoziaistvennoe nakoplenie predrevoliutsionnoi Rossii* (Moscow: Gosstatizdat, 1960), 288, I compare the total capital stock of utilities to that of corporately owned utilities to obtain the capital stock of municipal utilities as a residual. For 1913 (the year for which the Vainshtein estimate is available), I calculate the capital-output ratio of municipal utilities as the ratio of municipal revenues from municipal utilities to municipal utility capital stock and obtain a capital output ratio of 4.0. The 1910 figure is obtained by applying an annual growth rate of 1.5 percent to the 1913 figure (Vainshtein, 281-82). The data on municipal utility revenues are from Paul Gronsky and Nicholas Astrov, *The War and the Russian Government* (New Haven: Yale University Press, 1929), 145. I then apply this capital-output ratio to the corporate utilities to obtain their annual revenues in 1913. In this manner, I calculate the annual revenues of corporate and municipal utilities in 1913 to be 157 million rubles. This figure multiplied by .75 (the assumed ratio of private to total utility revenues) yields 188 million rubles as the 1913 estimate of private utility expenditure. I extrapolate this over time using the index of corporate utility revenues (assuming a constant capital-output ratio) and the index of municipal utility revenues. In the latter case, there is no further direct information of municipal revenues, only on municipal utility expenditures. I therefore must use the index of municipal utility expenditures to extrapolate municipal utility revenues, but I think that this will not result in large measurement errors. The 1885-1894 values are calculated assuming a constant 20 percent share of services.

(4) Domestic service expenditures are calculated as the product of employment in domestic service and the average annual wage of domestic servants. The wage series is constructed by applying the index of average annual wages of industrial factory workers duplicated in S. G. Strumilin, *Ocherki ekonomicheskoi istorii Rossii i SSSR* (Moscow: Nauka, 1966), 91-94 to the 1904 annual wage of domestic servants (132 rubles) calculated from Tsentral'ny Statisticheski Komitet, *Goroda Rossii v 1904 g.* (Petersburg, 1906). (Page numbers cannot be given as the average was calculated from material scattered throughout the book.) This 132 ruble figure is an unweighted average of male (180) and female (84) servant wages and assumes an equal distribution of employment between male and female domestic servants. Domestic service employment is calculated by applying the combined Moscow-Petersburg ratios of domestic servants to population to the urban population of the 50 European provinces to obtain an index of service employment. Annual service employment is calculated by applying this index to Rashin's figure on service employment in 1913 (1.55 million), cited in Gregory, statistical appendix. The figures on Moscow-Petersburg service employment are from A. G. Rashin, *Naselenie Rossii za 100 let*, (Moscow: Gostatizdat, 1956), 114, 115, 323-25. The urban population series is from V. Zaitsev and V. G. Groman (eds.), *Vliianie neurozhaev na narodnoe khoziaistva Rossii*, 1927, Part II, 65. The approximate ratios of domestic servants to urban population are: 1885-1890: 11%; 1894 and 1896: 10%; 1900: 8.5%; 1903: 8.3%; 1907: 8%; 1910: 7.9%; 1913: 7.7%. These ratios are rough and involve interpolations between benchmarks, but one would imagine that changes in the ratios would be relatively slow and orderly.

(5) Medical care in current prices is calculated as the sum of expenditures on drugs, physicians, feldshers, and midwives. Data on drug expenditures are found in *Statisticheski ezhegodnik Rossii*, annual series, 1904-1914 under the section *organizatsia vrachebnoi pomoshchi* and

Table C.1 (cont.)

in *Sbornik svedenii po Rossii*, 1884-85, 1890, and 1896 editions under the same title. Figures are available for only a limited number of benchmarks prior to 1904. The missing years had to be interpolated, but the errors should be small as annual fluctuations were small. I estimate expenditures on physician and paramedical services by multiplying the number of physicians, feldshers, and midwives by their assumed average annual wages. Data on the number of physicians and paramedical personnel are found in the same sources mentioned above, but interpolations prior to 1906 are also required. I calculate average annual earnings of physicians in 1905 at 2254 rubles. This figure is based upon the fact that roughly one half of Russian physicians earned more than 1000 rubles in 1905, for an average (of those over 1000 rubles) of 3758 rubles. This is from *Opyt priblizitel'nago ischisleniia narodnago dokhada po razlichnym ego istochnikam*, Ministerstvo Finansov, 1905, Table 22. I then assume that the remaining 50 percent (under 1000 rubles) earned 750 rubles per year, yielding an overall average of 2254 rubles. I then inflate this figure using the index of average annual earnings of telegraph workers. I further assume that paramedical personnel earned 1/4 that of physicians. To calculate real drug expenditures, I assume that real expenditures maintained the same ratio to outlays on medical personnel as money expenditures.

(667) The price index of passenger rail tariffs is calculated by dividing passenger rail revenues by the number of passenger-versts. This data is from *Statisticheski sbornik Ministerstva putei soobshcheniia*, Table VII, selected years. The cost of a ten-word telegram sent within the Russian empire and the cost of a closed letter sent within the Russian empire is from the following sources: *St. Petersburg kalender 1886*, 167, 118, 289, and from *Baedeker's Russland*, 4th, 7th, and 1914 English edition and *Baedeker's St. Petersburg*, all published by the Baedeker Verlag in Leipzig. For more information on rail tariffs, see J. N. Westwood, *Geschichte der russischen Eisenbahnen* (Zurich: Füssli Verlag, 1964, 78-82). Further sources, unavailable to the author, on this question are "Zur Geschichte des Eisenbahntarifwesens in Russland," *Archiv für Eisenbahnwesen*, 1915 and "Die Einführung des neuen Personentarifs auf den Eisenbahnen Russlands," *Archiv für Eisenbahnwesen*, 1908. The weights for combining the postal and telegraph price indexes are .7 and .3 respectively and are taken from the distribution of capital stock.

(8) Direct price information on utility prices paid by consumers is available only in scattered form; there are, for example, isolated quotations in *Ocherki istorii Leningrada*, Vol. II (Moscow-Leningrad: Akademia nauk, 1957), section on *Gorodskoe khoziaistvo* as well as in *Istoriia Moskvy*, Vols. III and IV (Moscow: Akademiia nauk, 1954), same section. I must therefore construct a proxy for utility prices which I accomplish by constructing an input price index. This input price index takes the major material inputs into energy production (coal, 50 percent, and oil products, 50 percent) and assigns (arbitrarily) a weight of .75 and then assigns a weight of .25 to labor inputs. The wage index is the index of nominal average annual wages of industrial workers cited above. For the internal weighting of the material inputs, I assign (again arbitrarily) weights of .3 to coal, .3 to wood fuels, .3 to kerosine, and .1 to fuel oil. Input prices are taken from *Svod tovarnykh tsen*, Table A.2 (h), column 26, and from V. I. Pokrovsky (ed.), *Sbornik svedenii po istorii i statistike vneshnei torgovli Rossii* (Petersburg: Departament tamozhennykh sborov, 1902), 215-222.

NOTES TO APPENDIX C

1   The estimate of the ratio of the value of housing to industrial and commercial
    structures is from S. G. Strumilin, *Statistika i ekonomika* (Moscow: Nauka,
    1963), p. 307, and derives from a 1912 survey.

2   This assumption does not appear to be too far off, at least as far as the
    industrial consumption of electricity in Moscow and Petersburg in 1908 was
    concerned. This was slightly under 35% according to L. G. Davydova,
    Ispol'zovanie elektricheskoi energii v promyshlennosti Rossii (Moscow: Nauka,
    1966), p. 65.

3   Paul Gregory, "1913 Russian National Income: Some Insights into Russian
    Economic Development," *Quarterly Journal of Economics*, 90, no. 3 (August
    1976), statistical appendix. I revise estimates of utility expenditures
    considerably downward in this study, as is explained in the text.

4   These data are described in Appendix F on government expenditures, under the
    section on local government.

5   The capital stock data on utilities is found in the *svodny balans* section of
    the *Ezhegodnik ministerstva finansov* (annual editions).

6   For 1913, I calculate the capital-output ratio of municipally owned utilities
    by subtracting corporate utility capital stock (from *Ezhegodnik ministerstva
    finansov, vypusk 1915*, p. 399) from total utility capital stock (from A. L.
    Vainshtein, *Narodnoe bogatstvo i narodnokhoziaistvennoe nakoplenie
    predrevoliutsionni Rossii* [Moscow: Gosstatizdat, 1960], p. 288) to obtain the
    capital stock of municipal utilities (365 million rubles). Municipal revenues
    from utilities were 90 million rubles, yielding a municipal capital-output
    ratio of approximately 4. This capital-output ratio is surprisingly close to
    later Soviet period relationships, when the 1964 capital-output ratio was 3.5,
    according to *Narodnoe khoziaistvo SSSR v 1964 g.*, p. 153.

7   Abram Bergson, *The Real National Income of Soviet Russia Since 1928*
    (Cambridge: Harvard University Press, 1961), pp. 316-18.

8   The average has been calculated from Tsentral'ny Statisticheski Komitet,
    Goroda Rossii v 1904 g. (Petersburg: Ts.S.K., 1906), p. 453.

9   This wage index is cited by S. G. Strumilin in *Ocherki ekonomicheskoi istorii
    Rossii i SSSR* (Moscow: Nauka, 1966), pp. 91-4.

10 A. G. Rashin, *Formirovanie rabochego klassa Rossii* (Moscow: Sotsekizdat,
    1958), p. 171.

11 Karl Baedeker, *Russland, Handbuch für Reisende,* 4th, 7th, and 1st English
    eds. (Leipzig: Baedeker, 1897, 1912, 1914); Baedeker, *St. Petersburg und
    Umgebungen* (Leipzig: Baedeker, 1901); *St. Petersburg Kalender 1886*
    (Petersburg: Schmissdorf, N.d.).

ESTIMATION OF MARKETING AND FARM CONSUMPTION IN KIND

Conceptually, farm consumption in kind is the value of farm products retained by the grower for his own consumption. Farm products retained for production purposes (for seed and animal fodder) are excluded. A great deal of data on gross and net output of grains, supplied by a number of agencies, the most important being the Central Statistical Committee of the Ministry of Interior, the Ministry of Agriculture, and the *zemstvo* statistical committees, make the estimation of grain marketings and consumption in kind possible with (I believe) a reasonable degree of accuracy. Considerable controversy still surrounds tsarist agricultural statistics, and a vast literature (prerevolutionary, early Soviet period, and contemporary) exists on this subject.[1] The most important issue raised by this literature is whether a substantial upward adjustment of the official Central Statistical Committee figures is needed. The accumulation of vast data on grain output, transport, and consumption is explained by the importance of agricultural marketings as a major instrument of tax collections, international payments policy,[2] and by the persistent threat of famine.[3]

Farm consumption in kind can be estimated according to two alternate methods: The first, used by Prokopovich[4] for his 1900 and 1913 estimates and by Bergson[5] for the later Soviet period, is the residual method, whereby agricultural marketings other than intravillage sales are subtracted from net agricultural output (gross output minus seed and feed for own animals). The residual represents farm consumption in kind. The drawback of this first approach in the Russian case is that it is difficult to obtain accurate information on the marketings, which must be subtracted from net agricultural production. Complete data on agricultural exports are available, but information on domestic marketings is highly deficient. Liashchenko,[6] in his authoritative 1908 study, supplies a detailed account of available marketing data, which he shows to be limited to rail and water shipments of agricultural products, deliveries to selected major urban markets, and estimates of urban and rural consumption from family budgetary data. Liashchenko concludes that the most reliable and useful intertemporal data are those on rail and water shipments of agricultural products of the Ministry of Transportation, a conclusion I share in this study. The reader is also referred to Karcz's survey of marketing data already referenced.

The use of transport data is not without problems: Prokopovich, in his noted national income study, used data on rail and water shipments to calculate the marketed portion (*tovarnost'*) of net agricultural output but was troubled by the problems of doublecounting and intravillage marketings. A further difficulty is that shipments data do not capture short hauls by carts to nearby markets. In some cases, such as deliveries to southern Russian ports, road deliveries, according to the one available study, were substantial, but in general road shipments were usually transshipped farther by water or rail.[7] A final problem is that transportation statistics were not collected for a wide variety of less important agricultural deliveries, such as minor grains, fruits, vegetables, and potatoes. This accounts for my emphasis on major grains in this study.

Despite these drawbacks, I have determined that shipments data provide the most reliable means for estimating grain marketings over time. Data on shipments of major grain products are quite detailed,[8] and these major grains dominate both marketings and retained agricultural output. Thus, if one can correctly estimate major grain marketings and major grains retained for own consumption, one has then captured the major portion of agricultural marketings.

The only alternative to the residual method is the use of survey data on peasant budgets. Under the aegis of *zemstvo* statistical committees, numerous budget surveys were conducted in a large number of provinces. These budgetary surveys are summarized in Svavitski and Svavitski and by Maress and form the basis for most reported estimates of net (extra-rural) marketings.[9] One problem, which such survey data raise, is the question of representativeness, although the broad territorial coverage of these surveys makes this a less serious problem than one might expect. That all peasant families were not self-sufficient in farm products is another problem, for this means that a portion of peasant food consumption (in food deficit provinces) had to be purchased in retail outlets and must be netted out of peasant food consumption to obtain in-kind consumption.

The major difficulty has to do with intertemporal trends: Budget information is available for isolated years,[10] and it is impossible to obtain comparable data over an extended time period. One can obtain estimates of per capita peasant consumption of various farm products for one or two benchmark years,[11] but this would not solve the problem at hand. The major issue is what happens to these consumption norms when agricultural output fluctuates. To determine this, one would require budgetary data for a large number of years, and this is simply not available. As a consequence, budgetary data can be used intertemporally as a rough check at best on farm consumption estimated by the transport data method. Budget data are more useful for establishing independent benchmarks, and I do use an estimate for 1913 marketings (the Nemchinov-Kondratiev estimate) as a benchmark against which my grain marketing estimates are compared.

In sum, it is my objective to employ data on net production and transport (by rail and water) to estimate a time series of marketings and retained consumption of major food grains for the period 1885 to 1913. Budgetary data are used as a check on the reasonableness of these estimates.

GRAIN FARM CONSUMPTION IN KIND ESTIMATED FROM TRANSPORTATION DATA

The first step in estimating marketings and farm consumption of food grains between 1885 and 1913 is to obtain data on net agricultural output. We limit ourselves initially to the three major food grains used primarily for human consumption (*prodovol'stvennye khleba*), namely, wheat (*pshenitsa*), rye (*rozh*), and barley (*iachmen'*). Potatoes (*kartofel'*) are also included as a fourth major food staple. Other grains, most notably oats (*oves*) and maize (*kukuruza*), are excluded, as they were used primarily as animal fodder.

Gross and net production of grains

The estimation process begins with the Ministry of Interior estimates of gross and net production of wheat, rye, barley, and potatoes. Data are drawn from three principal sources, all of which cite the official Central Statistical Committee of the Ministry of Interior figures: *Bulletin Russe de Statistique financiere et de Legislation*, 5th ed. (which cites unpublished figures compiled for the Ministry of Interior by M. E. Kuhn); *Ezhegodnik Ministerstva finansov*, 1905 edition; and *Ezhegodnik Rossii*, annual editions, 1904 to 1914, section 7. The Central Statistical Committee figures are discussed in considerable detail in a number of sources, and there is no general agreement as to their reliability.[12] There is some consensus that they capture intertemporal trends reasonably well; the major controversy is over the necessary degree of upward correction required for a given base year, and the reader is referred to the discussions in note 1. My basic assumption is that the official series capture intertemporal movements with reasonable accuracy, and I use them to compile indexes of net output for the period 1885 to 1913. For the 1913 benchmark, I accept the approximate 7% upward adjustment coefficient suggested and eventually used by the Central Statistical Committee in the 1920s (likely using a study by A. F. Fortunatov). In this, I accept Wheatcroft's argument that the substantial "Ivantsov" correction used by Gosplan (and later dropped by Gosplan) is without firm basis and that the more modest Fortunatov correction is more appropriate.[13] The 7% coefficient is slightly below the 10% coefficient used by Falkus.[14]

A minor difficulty with the official output figures is territorial coverage. There are consistent series for the 50 European provinces plus the Polish provinces for the entire 1885 to 1913 period, thanks to the M. E. Kuhn figures.[15] Data for the western Caucasian provinces and for the Asian and Siberian provinces are available only for 1896 to 1913. In Table D.1, I report two territorially consistent series, one for the *63 European provinces* and one for the *Russian Empire*. The former series requires only adjustment to include the western Caucasian provinces prior to 1896 (some 10% to 15% of the 63-province total at the turn of the century) and should be reasonably accurate. The second requires an additional adjustment for the Asian and Siberian provinces, which came to represent a substantial share of wheat production after 1906. But for the period before 1896 (when the data were first collected), their share of output was small (approximately 5%); so my territorial adjustments (which assume a rise of from 4% to 5% for wheat between 1885 and 1896) should be reasonably accurate.

The gross and net production figures for wheat, rye, barley, and potatoes are given in Table D.1. References and explanatory notes are located in the notes to the table. As one can see, the ratio of net to gross production varied considerably during this period but averaged around 82% for most crops. As one might expect, the ratio fell during bad harvest years, when the peasants had to set seed aside to ensure the next year's harvest. Net production is defined as gross production minus production retained for seed and for livestock feeding (which is negligible in the case of these grains). I believe that there is also provision for harvesting losses, as these ratios appear to be too high for seed purposes alone.[16] As one can see from Table D.1, the ratios of net to gross output rose substantially from averages of .78 (.78) for wheat (rye) in 1885-90 to .86 (.84), respectively, in 1909-13.

Transportation data

Remarkably detailed data on shipments of major grains by rail and water were published by the Ministry of Transportation in its annual publication *Statisticheski sbornik Ministerstva putei soobshcheniia* and special publications on *dvizhenie tovarov* (movement of goods). Shipments of major grains are detailed for every rail line and, indeed, for every station. Similar detail is provided for shipments by water. An important point for this study is that transshipments from water to rail and rail to water are reported, and one can net them out to avoid serious double counting. Double counting will occur, however, if grain was shipped to one point, say, for storage and then later shipped (in unprocessed form) to another point. Data on shipments of wheat, rye, and barley are reported in Table D.1.

Some major problems remain: The first is that there is no information on shipments of grains by roads. One would imagine that such shipments would be principally to nearby intravillage markets. Because of the absence of data, I must ignore such shipments completely. This is not a problem if grains transported by road are eventually transshipped farther by rail or water, as they would be captured in the rail and water transport statistics at that point. It is a problem if the grain was to reach the urban consumer directly via road transport, and I have no means for adjusting for this eventuality, except to assume its share of the total remained fairly stable over the period. I believe that the failure to include road transport will introduce an unknown degree of measurement error into the analysis, but if such deliveries to the final consumer were largely for local peasant markets, then the error will likely be small. To have a large intertemporal error would require both a large initial share and a major shift away from road transport during the 1885 to 1913 period. One reason for comparing these estimates of marketings with budgetary evidence is to gauge the seriousness of the omission of road transport.

The second problem with the transportation data is the possibility of grain shipments in the form of flour from the original grower to the final consumer. Thus, if grain was milled into flour prior to entering the rail and water transportation network, then this grain would be missed, as I am counting only shipments of raw grain. Although I do have data on both unprocessed grain and flour shipments, I decided that flour shipments should not be counted. The principal reason for this conclusion is that shipments in unprocessed form were much safer and

economical (the flour had to be sacked, and spoiled easily, etc.), and this conclusion appears to be borne out by the small share of flour shipments abroad.[17]
This point is ignored by many prewar studies of gross marketings based on transport
data, which included flour shipments as well as raw grain and thus overstate grain
marketings.[18]

The third problem relates to sales lagging behind production. Casual inspection of net output and transportation data (Table D.1) indicates that not all grain
eventually marketed from a particular grain harvest entered the transportation
system during the calendar year in which it was produced. Instead, grain shipments
in one year would typically represent the sum of shipments from the harvest of the
previous calendar year and of the current calendar year. This phenomenon is quite
obvious for poor harvest years (1891, e.g. see Table D.1). During these years,
shipments were affected over a two-year period, often more seriously in the second
year than in the first. This is because a portion of the previous year's harvest
was typically withheld for sale in the next year. Numerous studies of the pattern
of grain sales and deliveries have been made,[19] and they all point to a pattern of
early sales by small producers at the time of the harvest (summer and early fall) at
which time the price of grain would be seasonably depressed. The larger producers
and wholesalers with storage facilities on the spot would withhold their grain until
the next year, at which time it would enter the transportation network.

Because of these timing difficulties, Russian statistical authorities frequently employed the concept of the "agricultural year" (*sel'skokhoziastvenny god*)
in which the timing of production and sales better coincided. I, however, am unable
to utilize this type of data as my other data refer to calendar years. To correct
for this problem, I have made adjustments to account for the seasonal pattern of
agricultural deliveries by econometric estimation of the lag structure of sales. I
assume a simple lag structure in which the shipment of grain in year t is a function
of the net output in years t and $t-1$ (and even $t-2$). Once the lag structure is
known, one can then estimate sales attributable to a particular harvest year.
Further elaboration of this adjustment is given in the discussion of Table D.2.

The final problem concerns the intertemporal consistency of the transport data
during the 1885 to 1913 period. My own impression is that the railroad transport
data tended to be quite accurate, and the presence of large biases in the "early"
figures mentioned by Karcz[20] seems unlikely to this author. My survey of the literature on transportation data has failed to uncover any evidence of bias in the
early figures. Given the frequent contemporaneous use of these statistics, one
would imagine that such evidence would be available if it existed.

Grain prices and the value of grain output
To determine aggregate marketings, retained production, and net production of food
grains, average annual prices must be known. There was substantial regional
variation in grain prices as well as marked seasonal variation throughout the 1885
to 1913 period;[21] so the determination of which prices to use is not as obvious as
one might think. I report in Table D.1 price series for wheat, rye, barley, and

potatoes and calculate the value of their net outputs.[22] Two value series are given: net output in constant 1913 prices and in current prices. Finally, an aggregate production series is reported, again in 1913 prices and in current prices and from these an implicit food grains price deflator is formed. The sources of this price information are given in considerable detail in the notes to Table D.1.

Calculation of grain marketings and retained product
In Table D.1, I have supplied data on net agricultural output in physical and value terms and on rail and water transport in physical terms for major food grains.

COMPARISON OF GRAIN MARKETINGS AND RETAINED GRAINS WITH OTHER ESTIMATES
Alternate intertemporal estimates of grain marketings and retained grain production are not available; therefore, my 1885-1913 series cannot be compared with the estimates of others. I have already noted the major sources of potential bias in my figures: errors in the intertemporal net production figures and grain transport series. On the first error source, I have found no substantial study of the intertemporal consistency of the official production series. Instead, most researchers (prerevolutionary and contemporary) assume that the official series are reasonably accurate over time but understate production by an unknown (but assumed fixed) percentage in each year. My use of grain transport data could introduce errors into my analysis in several ways. The first is the possibility, mentioned by Karcz without any reference to the source of his information, that the rail and water grain transport data are understated for the "early" years by as much as 15% to 20%.[23] As I stated in the text, I know of no corroborative evidence to support Karcz's contention, but the important point is that such an error would tend to *understate* true early-year marketings and thus *understate* the growth rate of retained grains. Such a correction would thus intensify my surprising finding of rapid growth rates of retained food grains.

I mentioned three other potential problems with the grain transport series. The first, which worried Prokopovich, is that there will be some double counting of shipments, despite my efforts to eliminate them. The major source of double counting would be to count both processed and unprocessed grain shipments, and this I have not done. However, if raw grain was shipped by rail or water to, say, a storage facility, stored, and then later shipped to another destination, there would be double counting. Double counting would, of course, overstate marketings and understate retained grains, but I see no reason for marked changes in the degree of double counting over the years. Thus I doubt that double counting would cause serious intertemporal errors, and this study emphasizes intertemporal trends, not levels. The second problem is the possibility of flour shipments going directly from the grower to the final consumer, for I count only unprocessed grain shipments. According to Liashchenko,[24] this omission would understate the growth of wheat marketings, especially during the latter part of the period investigated. I have made alternate calculations, including 50% of flour shipments in the sales estimate. This inclusion lowers the growth rate of retained food grains by less than 10%.

The third problem is the matter of grain shipments by cart. As one might expect, there are no series on grain shipments by cart. There are only some "theoretical" calculations of the Ministry of Transportation on shipments of grains by carts (*guzhem*) between 1900 and 1904 to border and port cities.[25] These "theoretical" figures reveal such shipments to be quite substantial: 40% of the volume of shipments of wheat, rye, and barley by rail and water. If cart shipments were indeed as substantial as this, then serious intertemporal bias could be introduced into my marketing estimates by changes in the distribution of total grain shipments between rail and water and carts. Liashchenko gives no reference to the Ministry of Transportation study, and it may well come from unpublished sources.

I am very skeptical of this result. The major problem is that cart shipments of this volume require wheat and barley marketing ratios of 50% or more, and such ratios appear to be fully inconsistent with the independent data on grain marketings cited below. My suspicion is that the Transport Ministry calculated cart shipments as a residual between grain exported and grain sold in the border and port cities (Petersburg and Odessa, e.g.) and grain arriving by rail and water, and such calculations would be subject to a wide margin of error. For example, I have found the transport ministry's figures on grain stocks in port and border cities (reported regularly in *Vestnik finansov*) to be quite unreliable.

But even if one were to accept cart shipments from producer to final consumer of this magnitude, the bias introduced into the intertemporal series again would be in the direction of *understating* the growth rate of peasant consumption. The most likely hypothesis is that the share of cart transport would have declined between 1885 and 1913 with the growth of the rail network. Thus 1885 marketings are *understated* relative to 1913 marketings, and correction for this relative understatement would yield even more rapid growth of peasant grain consumption.

One way to check the magnitude of the biases introduced by double counting and the omission of flour shipments and cart shipments is to compare the estimated marketing figures with figures derived independently from consumption (budget studies) and export data. Several independent estimates have been made for the period 1909-1913 and are summarized by Karcz and Wheatcroft.[25] They are all in physical rather than value terms; so we must compare our *physical* marketing figures in Table A.4b with these alternate estimates.

In my opinion, the most reliable estimate of marketings for this period is the so-called Nemchinov estimate, which is really based upon a 1921 study by Kondratiev. The Kondratiev-Nemchinov figure is derived by adding together grain exports, urban and army consumption, industrial grain usage, and shipments of grain to peasants in grain-deficit provinces. Thus intravillage marketings are not counted, and the Kondratiev-Nemchinov estimate is conceptually quite close to my own. For the four major grains (wheat, rye, oats, and barley), the Kondratiev-Nemchinov estimate of average 1909-13 marketings is 1099 million puds. Adding oats to my marketing figures in Table D.2 yields my own estimate of 982 million puds, a figure 90% of the Kondratiev-Nemchinov estimate. Thus the understatement resulting from omission of cart transport and flour is nowhere as serious as the Liashchenko figures suggest (assuming the Kondratiev-Nemchinov estimate to be correct). If one applies the 40% cart transport figure, my marketing estimate would rise to 1375 million puds, 25% above the Kondratiev-Nemchinov figure.

The other estimate for the 1909 to 1913 period, comparable conceptually to my estimate, was made by Gosplan in 1921. Gosplan estimated that the marketings of all grains including potato equivalents varied from a low of 1000 million puds to a high of 1312 million puds between 1909 and 1913. If I adjust my own marketing estimate to include omitted grains (principally oats, buckwheat, and maize),[27] I obtain a 1909-1913 low of 925 and a high of 1357 million puds. Thus my marketing estimates are generally consistent with the Gosplan figures.

Finally, a word on the ratio of marketings (retained grains) to net production: One of my principal findings is that these ratios remained remarkably stable between 1885 and 1913 despite substantial annual fluctuations. The ratios reported in Table D.2 do not involve corrections of the net output figures or the marketing figures. As I have noted, there has been considerable controversy over the upward corrections necessary in the net production figures, with suggested corrections ranging from zero to 19%. I refer the reader to Wheatcroft's discussion of this debate.[28] After reading Wheatcroft, I find his arguments in favor of the Fortunatov correction (about 7%) convincing. Thus the net product figures should be raised, I believe, by some 7%. If one accepts the Kondratiev-Nemchinov marketing estimate as being correct, then my marketing figures should be raised by approximately 10%. For 1913, for example, these corrections would yield a net product of 3725 million rubles, marketings of 957 million rubles, and retained product of 2768 million rubles. Thus the ratio of marketed output would be 26% and that of retained product would be 74%, that is, the correction of marketings and net output roughly cancel each other. The average 1909-1913 marketing ratio, given these corrections, would be roughly 30% and would be close to the marketing ratios estimated by Kondratiev-Nemchinov and Gosplan (31%-32% of net output).

OTHER RETAINED AGRICULTURAL PRODUCTS

According to my calculations for 1913, retained food grains accounted for 50% of all retained agricultural fishing and forestry products.[29] It is thus important to estimate the rates of growth of other retained products, such as meat and dairy products, technical crops, gardening and viticulture, forestry and fishing, to obtain a complete coverage of retained products of agriculture, fishing, and forestry (Table D.3). Unfortunately, it is not possible to make direct estimates of retained products in the case of these other products, for, although data on output may be available, there simply is no information on marketings, except for the single benchmark of 1913. In some instances (such as milk, forestry products, fishing, and gardening) time series on outputs are not even available.

To estimate other retained farm, fishing, and forestry products, I employ the following methodology: For those products where production series are available (or capital stock series as in the case of livestock), I assume constant ratios of marketings to net output. As the case of grains suggests, this assumption may not be a bad one, but I have no evidence to justify this assumption. This assumption is applied to estimate retained meat and dairy products and retained technical crops, all of which grew (in output terms) at slower rates than grains. If the output indexes are correct, it is unlikely that large errors are introduced by the assumption of constant retention ratios. For technical crops, for example, the retention ratio was 52% in 1913. A substantial decline in this ratio from 75% to 52% would lower the calculated growth rate from 3% to 2% per annum (rounded) between 1885 and 1913. For those products for which even production series are lacking, I must assume that they grew, in the aggregate, at the same rate as included retained farm products. These latter products (forestry, fishing, gardening) accounted for 8% of personal consumption expenditures in 1913; so they are not inconsequential. To provide some feel for the possible magnitude of error introduced by this assumption, I calculate that if these omitted categories grew in aggregate at an annual rate ± 1 percentage point of the rate of included retained farm products, the annual growth rate of retained farm products would change by 0.2 of 1%. Thus I doubt that a large error is introduced by the assumption of rates of growth of these omitted products equal to included retained farm products.

Retained meat products

Prokopovich's estimates of 1913 retained meat products (adjusted for territorial coverage) yield the 1913 benchmark value of 720 million rubles.[30] No data are available to estimate either the output of meat or its distribution between market sales and retained product over time; therefore I assume a constant marketed share and a constant capital-output ratio and extrapolate retained food products back to 1885 using the index of the stock of livestock valued in 1913 constant prices from Appendix H. This is obviously a less than satisfactory method of calculating retained meat products, but I would doubt that large errors are introduced as a result.

Retained technical agricultural products

Prokopovich's estimates of 1913 retained technical products (fibers, sunflower oil, sugar beets, etc.) adjusted for territorial coverage provide the 1913 benchmark value of 256 million rubles. I extrapolate this figure backward with Goldsmith's index of the output of technical crops.[31] This means that I am assuming a constant share of marketings. This method is also far from satisfactory, but again I doubt that large errors in growth rates are introduced.

Retained dairy products

There is no direct information on the outputs and marketings of dairy products beyond Prokopovich's estimate of 1913 marketings (1126 million rubles after adjustment for territorial coverage). I therefore backcast this 1913 benchmark using the index of the stock of "large horned animals" in 1913 prices from Appendix H. This category is not broken down to show the growth of the number of cows; so I must assume their proportion remained relatively fixed.

Omitted products (forestry, fishing, gardening, viticulture)
The 1913 value of other retained products (forestry, fishing, gardening, viticulture) is estimated from Prokopovich to be 1396 million rubles. This figure is
backcast by assuming that this category grew at the same rate as all included
retained farm products.

Retained agricultural products, current prices
In Table 3.2 of the text, retained farm products in current prices are given. These
figures have been calculated using the same procedures employed for the 1913 price
figures except that the available current price indexes were used. Retained grains
in current prices are given in Table D.2. Meat and dairy products in current prices
are calculated using the appropriate livestock series in current prices from
Appendix H. Technical crops are inflated using a price index calculated from cotton
and flax prices. Omitted products are assumed to grow at the same rate as included
products in current prices.

Table D.1. Gross and net agricultural output of grains for human consumption and transport by rail and water, prices, and value of output 1885-1913, Russian empire (million puds)

| | A. Wheat (pshenitsa) | | | | | B. Rye (rozh) | | | | |
| | (1) 63 Provinces | | (2) Empire | | (3) Net shipments by rail and water, empire | (4) 63 Provinces | | (5) Empire | | (6) Net shipments by rail and water, empire |
	a) Gross production	b) Net production	a) Gross production	b) Net production		a) Gross production	b) Net production	a) Gross production	b) Net production	
1885	327	240	340	249	191	1087	865	1108	880	99
1886	303	215	315	224	115	1023	802	1043	818	99
1887	493	410	513	426	175	1148	925	1171	943	110
1888	508	426	528	444	235	1079	859	1101	876	126
1889	309	225	321	234	184	842	623	860	634	94
1890	370	278	386	289	181	1029	799	1050	815	76
1891	298	205	313	215	193	774	542	789	553	98
1892	436	341	458	358	138	927	712	946	726	66
1893	644	553	676	581	185	1127	915	1150	934	73
1894	626	532	664	565	219	1310	1088	1336	1110	110
1895	586	486	621	515	244	1204	982	1228	1002	134
1896	604	497	640	527	251	1188	961	1221	990	120
1897	474	361	507	386	222	970	742	989	757	97
1898	677	563	718	597	242	1098	880	1120	898	135
1899	654	530	693	562	190	1366	1133	1393	1155	113
1900	656	526	702	563	196	1402	1162	1427	1183	154
1901	668	528	721	570	240	1145	905	1171	925	142
1902	933	793	1008	857	280	1387	1151	1425	1183	158
1903	917	770	1036	870	363	1365	1119	1414	1160	150
1904	1034	879	1106	940	384	1517	1290	1564	1329	131
1905	943	783	1056	877	362	1099	890	1143	926	149
1906	748	590	845	668	352	990	782	1034	817	183
1907	727	603	851	706	279	1200	960	1253	1002	161
1908	812	682	950	798	265	1177	954	1214	983	121
1909	1183	1041	1301	1145	472	1360	1129	1370	1137	139
1910	1162	999	1383	1189	510	1308	1099	1358	1141	122
1911	743	602	936	758	398	1151	921	1191	953	135
1912	1035	890	1335	1148	340	1568	1333	1622	1379	119
1913	1391	1210	1711	1489	431	1508	1282	1568	1333	134

C. Barley (*Iamchen'*)   D. Potatoes (*kartofel'*)

	Barley 63 Provinces		Barley Empire		Net shipments by rail and water empire	Potatoes 63 Provinces		Potatoes Empire	
	a) Gross production	b) Net production	a) Gross production	b) Net production		a) Gross production	b) Net production	a) Gross production	b) Net production
1885	185	133	190	137	27	541	419	552	427
1886	238	187	246	192	28	584	462	595	471
1887	290	238	299	246	43	619	496	631	506
1888	263	213	271	220	64	589	449	601	458
1889	192	142	198	147	41	608	470	620	479
1890	273	218	282	225	40	662	509	675	579
1891	235	182	242	187	43	538	386	459	394
1892	291	228	300	235	46	899	702	917	716
1893	483	423	497	436	89	1031	832	1052	849
1894	397	338	409	348	102	936	735	955	750
1895	328	273	338	281	72	1291	1040	1317	1061
1896	326	268	338	276	58	1418	1128	1446	1151
1897	318	259	331	289	54	1338	1053	1365	1074
1898	398	338	414	352	64	1422	1123	1450	1146
1899	290	230	302	240	61	1453	1148	1482	1170
1900	299	248	315	261	42	1545	1282	1591	1320
1901	304	240	319	252	58	972	768	1458	1152
1902	432	372	450	387	89	1680	1344	1730	1384
1903	450	387	475	409	120	1445	1156	1503	1202
1904	448	381	460	391	113	1470	1176	1514	1211
1905	450	378	461	387	100	1716	1390	1750	1418
1906	404	323	415	332	124	1561	1233	1592	1258
1907	457	384	470	395	111	1719	1375	1753	1402
1908	488	415	502	427	132	1761	1409	1796	1437
1909	618	556	629	566	173	1950	1599	1989	1631
1910	597	525	630	554	198	2183	1791	2227	1826
1911	537	446	581	482	203	1869	1500	1937	1530
1912	607	528	660	574	146	2254	1803	2322	1858
1913	741	667	798	718	159	2117	1651	2181	1701

Table D.1. (cont.)

E. Wholesale agricultural prices, selected internal markets (*svod tovarnykh tsen*) rubles/pud

	(1) Wheat	(2) Rye	(3) Barley	(4) Potatoes
1885	.90	.72	.74	.20
1886	.81	.62	.75	.20
1887	1.01	.54	.72	.16
1888	1.07	.66	.79	.21
1889	.98	.70	.75	.20
1890	.83	.65	.67	.18
1891	1.12	1.04	.82	.26
1892	1.08	.99	.70	.19
1893	1.84	.65	.57	.15
1894	.63	.46	.42	.11
1895	.55	.37	.45	.12
1896	.56	.34	.57	.12
1897	.79	.46	.69	.16
1898	1.01	.63	.75	.22
1899	.92	.62	.74	.22
1900	.79	.49	.64	.17
1901	.86	.55	.61	.16
1902	.85	.62	.62	.16
1903	.80	.58	.57	.15
1904	.80	.60	.55	.15
1905	.87	.73	.65	.17
1906	.97	.79	.67	.18
1907	1.22	.99	.84	.22
1908	1.33	.98	.82	.28
1909	1.13	.86	.76	.28
1910	.99	.70	.66	.18
1911	1.12	.79	.88	.24
1912	1.24	.90	.86	.21
1913	1.09	.76	.75	.18

F. Value of net grain output, empire (million rubles)

	(1) Wheat		(2) Rye		(3) Barley		(4) Potatoes	
	(a) Current prices	(b) 1913 prices	(a) Current prices	(b) 1913 prices	(a) Current prices	(b) 1913 prices	(a) Current prices	(b) 1913 prices
1885	224	271	641	676	102	104	85	77
1886	181	244	513	629	146	142	94	85
1887	431	465	515	725	179	187	81	91
1888	475	484	585	672	176	167	96	82
1889	230	255	448	487	111	111	96	86
1890	240	315	536	626	152	170	93	93
1891	242	235	581	425	155	142	102	71
1892	387	390	726	558	166	178	136	129
1893	488	634	613	718	327	331	127	153
1894	356	615	516	852	147	263	83	135
1895	283	561	371	762	127	213	127	191
1896	295	574	337	752	157	207	138	207
1897	305	421	348	575	199	217	172	193
1898	603	651	566	682	264	264	252	206
1899	517	613	716	878	178	180	257	211
1900	445	614	580	899	167	196	224	238
1901	490	621	509	703	154	189	184	207
1902	729	934	733	899	240	290	221	249
1903	696	948	673	882	233	307	180	216
1904	752	1025	797	1010	215	293	182	218
1905	762	956	676	704	252	290	241	255
1906	648	728	645	621	222	249	226	226
1907	861	770	992	762	332	296	308	252
1908	1061	870	963	747	350	320	402	259
1909	1294	1248	978	864	430	425	457	294
1910	1177	1296	799	867	366	416	329	329
1911	849	826	753	724	424	362	367	275
1912	1424	1251	1241	1048	494	431	390	334
1913	1623	1623	1013	1013	539	1013	306	306

G. Total value net grain output for human consumption

	(1)		(2)		H. Implicit price deflator grain products (G1a ÷ 2a) (1913 = 100)
	(a) Current prices	(b) Index 1913 = 100	(a) 1913 Prices	(b) Index 1913 = 100	
1885	1052	30	1128	32	93
1886	934	27	1104	32	85
1887	1206	35	1468	42	82
1888	1332	38	1405	40	95
1889	885	25	939	27	94
1890	1021	29	1204	35	85
1891	1080	31	873	25	124
1892	1415	41	1255	36	113
1893	1555	45	1836	53	84
1894	1102	32	1865	54	59
1895	908	26	1727	50	53
1896	927	27	1740	50	53
1897	1024	29	1406	40	73
1898	1685	48	1803	52	94
1899	1668	48	1882	54	89
1900	1416	41	1947	56	73
1901	1337	38	1720	49	78
1902	1923	55	2372	68	81
1903	1782	51	2353	68	76
1904	1946	56	2546	73	76
1905	1931	56	2205	63	88
1906	1741	50	1824	52	96
1907	2493	72	2080	60	120
1908	2776	80	2196	63	126
1909	3159	91	2831	81	112
1910	2671	77	2908	84	92
1911	2393	69	2187	63	109
1912	3549	102	3064	88	116
1913	3481	100	3481	100	100

Table D.1 (*cont.*)

Sources: *Production   Statistics*:   1884-1897:   *Bulletin   Russe   de   statistique
financiere   et   de   legislation*, 5th edition, 1898, 222-31.   Based upon unpublished
data from the Ministry of Interior compiled by M. E. Kuhn.   1897-1903:   *Ezhegodnik
Ministerstva finansov*, 1905 edition, 494-7.   1903-13:   *Statisticheski ezhegodnik
Rossii*, annual editions 1904 to 1913.

   Territorial adjustments: Production data are available for the 50 European
provinces   and   the   Polish   provinces   for   the   entire   1885   to   1913   period   (60
provinces).   To obtain series for the 63 European provinces, an adjustment is made to
include the 3 West Caucasian provinces for the period prior to 1896.   I simply
assume a constant share for these provinces between 1885 and 1897.   The three West
Caucasian provinces accounted for relatively small shares of wheat (14 percent) and
rye (6 percent); so this territorial adjustment is a minor one.   Production figures
for the entire empire are available from 1897 onwards.   For wheat, I assume a
decline in the ratio of empire to 63 province wheat production from 1.07 in 1897 to
1.04 in 1885.   For rye, I assume a decline in the ratio from 1.03 to 1.02.   As the
reader can see these adjustments are relatively minor, as the Siberian and Asian
provinces became major wheat producers only after 1906.

   Estimation of ratios of net to gross production: For the period 1885 to 1897,
detailed data on the ratios of net to gross production for specific crops are
available.   For the period after 1897, less specific information is supplied by the
Ministry of Interior.   Liashchenko cites net production figures for the period 1901
to 1905 for the 50 European provinces.   On this, see P. I. Liashchenko, *Ocherki
agrarnoi evoliutsii Rossii* (Petersburg: no publisher given, 1908), 437; so I take
the net to gross ratios for the 50 provinces to be representative of the 63
province and empire figures.   The net to gross ratios for the period 1897 to 1900
are   also   calculated   from   net   figures   cited   by   Liashchenko,   p.   430.   The
Statisticheski ezhegodnik Rossii series gives net to gross production ratios for
summer (*iarovye*) and winter (*ozimye*) grains.   As rye was almost exclusively an
ozimye grain, I use these ratios to calculate net rye output, and as wheat was
primarily a summer grain, I use these ratios to calculate net wheat output.   The net
to gross ratios are quite similar anyway; so this choice is not all that crucial.
For potatoes, I have direct data on net to gross ratios only for the period 1885 to
1897, and for 1900 and 1913.   The latter two observations are from Prokopovich (see
reference below), p. 8, and from M. E. Falkus, "Russia's National Income, 1913; A
Re-evaluation," *Economica*, NS, 137 (February 1968), 64 (1907/13 average).   The
missing year ratios are interpolated using an estimated regression equation of the
net   to   gross   ratio   regressed   against   gross   output   for   years   for   which   such
information is available (1885 to 1897, 1900, 1913).

   Transportation data: The data on transport of grain by rail and water are
taken   from   the   following   sources: *Statisticheski   sbornik   ministerstva   putei
soobshcheniia*, annual editions on transport of goods (*dvizhenie tovarov*); and
"Statisticheski obzor razvitiia narodnogo khoziaistva v dorevoliutsionnoi Rossii,
Prilozhenie", in *Entsiklopedicheski slovar' Granat*, 7th edition, Vol. 36, Part IV,
Tables 42 and 43.   These series net out transfers among the various railroads and
trans-shipments from rail to water and from water to rail.

   Agricultural wholesale prices: Two basic data sources are available for
agricultural wholesale prices: average annual wholesale price quotations from
selected internal and port markets, and average agricultural wholesale prices for
the 63 European provinces.   The former series is given in Column E and is taken
principally from the Ministry of Trade and Industry publication *Svod tovarnykh tsen
na glavnykh russkikh i innostrannykh rynkakh*, annual editions, 1890/95 to 1913.   The
Svod series gives average annual wholesale prices of wheat and rye for the period
1890 to 1913 from selected internal and port markets.   I report here only the
internal prices, which for wheat are from Moscow, Samara, and Saratov and for rye
for Elets, Samara, and Saratov.   For the period 1885 to 1890, I construct my own
series using the same markets from price quotations supplied in N. V. Grigor'ev,
"Vliianie urozhaev i khlebnykh tsen na gorodskoe naselenie Rossii," in A. I. Chuprov
and A. S. Posnikov (ed.), *Vliianie urozhaev i khlebnykh tsen na nekotorye storony
russkago narodnago khoziaistva* (Petersburg: Kirshbaum, 1897), 164, 168.

   Barley prices cited in *Svod* are for the South Russian port markets only.   In
their place, I decided to use the unweighted average prices for the 63 European
provinces.   These price quotations are found in GUZ i Z, Otdel sel'skoi ekonomiki,
*Sbornik   statistiko-ekonomicheskikh   svedenii   po   sel'skomu   khoziaistvu   Rossii   i
innostrannykh gosudarstv*, Petrograd 1915, Vol. VII, 468; *Statisticheski ezhegodnik
Rossii*, 1905 and 1910 editions (section: *srednye godovye tseny* . . . .).   The pre-1900

Table D.1 (*cont.*)

figures are drawn from the following sources: *Sbornik svedenii po Rossii*, 1896 edition, 47 (index of average prices from Petersburg, Riga, Libau, Odessa, Nikolaev, Novorossisk, Rostov, Moscow, Saratov, and Warsaw), Leo Jurowsky, *Der Russische Getreideeexport* (Stuttgart: Union Deutsche Verlaggesellschaft, 1910), 38 (index of Petersburg, Libau, North Russian, Elets, and South Russian prices) and I. I. Kaufman, *Svedeniia o mezhdunarodnoi knlebnoi torgovle, Vremmennik tsentral'nogo statisticheskago komiteta*, No. 5, 1889, 3.

Relatively little information is available on potato prices. For the period, 1905 to 1913, the cited prices are unweighted averages from Voronezh, Simbirsk, Samarsk, Kharkov, and Poland and are taken from the GUZ publication cited above, 1916 edition, 471 and 1912 edition, 384-5. I also have scattered price quotations for the years 1887, 1891, and 1900 from F. A. Shcherbina, "Krestianskie biudzhety i zavisimost ikh ot urozhaev i tsen na khleba," in Chuprov and Posnikov (eds.), Vol. 2, 91 and 96, and from S. N. Prokopovich, *Opyt ischislenia narodnogo dokhoda 50 gubernii Evropeiskoi Rossii v 1900-1913 gg.* (Moscow: SVKS, 1918), 8. The missing price quotations are filled in by assuming constant relative prices between potatoes and barley. For the years for which we have price quotations for the two products, this assumption holds quite well.

Change from volume to weight measure: Care must be exercised in converting the pre- 1895 crop data expressed in volume measures into weight measures. The official series cited after 1895 are not explicit about the conversion coefficients used, and the conversion is not all that obvious as the relationship between weight and volume differed by grain type and region. Apparently a conversion factor for all grain of approximately 7.5 pud per chetvert was used, according to data in V. I. Pokrovsky, *Sbornik svedenii po istorii i statistiki vneshnei torgovli Rossii* (Moscow: Departament tamozhennykh sborov, 1902), p. 8, and in Liashchenko, *Ocherki*, p. 430. These conversion ratios appear close to the French system. I have chosen to use the official conversion rates (deduced from the 50 province data), although there is some controversy about the appropriate conversion. It is my opinion that the official conversion factors may cause an overstatement of the decline in grain production between 1894 and 1895.

Table D.2. Calculation of grain marketings using lagged production data - wheat, rye, barley, potatoes (million puds, million rubles)

A. Wheat

	(1) Net production	(2) Sales	(3) Ratio of sales to production 2/1	(4) Retained product	(5) Value of 4 1913 prices
1885	249	162	.65	87	95
1886	224	110	.49	114	124
1887	426	215	.51	211	230
1888	444	239	.54	205	223
1889	234	143	.61	91	99
1890	289	192	.66	97	106
1891	215	178	.83	37	40
1892	358	166	.46	192	209
1893	581	229	.39	352	384
1894	565	216	.38	349	380
1895	515	244	.47	271	295
1896	527	253	.48	274	299
1897	386	194	.50	192	209
1898	597	283	.47	314	342
1899	562	183	.33	379	413
1900	563	196	.35	367	400
1901	570	241	.42	329	359
1902	857	336	.39	521	568
1903	870	369	.42	501	546
1904	940	398	.42	542	591
1905	877	350	.40	527	594
1906	668	311	.47	357	389
1907	706	287	.41	419	457
1908	798	283	.36	515	561
1909	1145	540	.47	605	660
1910	1189	519	.44	670	730
1911	758	313	.41	445	485
1912	1148	416	.36	732	780
1913	1489	498	.33	991	1080

B. Rye

	(1) Net production	(2) Sales	(3) Ratio of sales to production 2/1	(4) Retained product	(5) Value of 4 1913 prices
1885	880	101	.12	779	592
1886	818	98	.12	720	547
1887	943	111	.12	832	632
1888	876	133	.15	743	565
1889	634	80	.13	554	421
1890	815	65	.08	750	570
1891	553	101	.18	452	344
1892	726	54	.07	672	511
1893	934	93	.10	841	639
1894	1110	130	.12	980	745
1895	1002	143	.14	859	653
1896	990	117	.12	873	663
1897	757	72	.10	685	521
1898	898	134	.15	764	581
1899	1155	150	.13	1005	764
1900	1183	175	.15	1008	766
1901	925	117	.13	808	614
1902	1183	167	.14	1016	772
1903	1160	165	.14	995	756
1904	1329	147	.11	1182	898
1905	926	118	.13	808	614
1906	817	144	.18	673	511
1907	1002	173	.17	829	630
1908	983	131	.13	852	648
1909	1137	154	.14	983	747
1910	1141	133	.12	1008	766
1911	953	115	.12	838	637
1912	1378	150	.11	1228	933
1913	1333	158	.12	1175	893

C. Barley

	(1) Net production	(2) Sales	(3) Ratio of sales to production 2/1	(4) Retained product	(5) Value of 4 1913 prices
1885	137	14	.10	123	92
1886	192	41	.21	151	113
1887	246	56	.23	190	143
1888	220	58	.26	162	122
1889	147	23	.16	124	93
1890	225	59	.26	166	125
1891	187	34	.18	153	115
1892	235	58	.25	177	133
1893	436	137	.31	299	224
1894	348	81	.23	267	200
1895	281	63	.22	218	164
1896	276	57	.21	219	164
1897	289	57	.20	232	174
1898	352	79	.22	273	205
1899	240	34	.14	206	155
1900	261	47	.18	214	161
1901	252	56	.22	196	147
1902	387	121	.31	266	200
1903	409	125	.31	284	213
1904	391	109	.28	282	212
1905	387	99	.26	288	216
1906	332	111	.33	221	166
1907	395	126	.32	269	202
1908	427	140	.33	287	215
1909	566	206	.36	360	270
1910	554	195	.35	359	269
1911	482	186	.39	296	222
1912	574	168	.29	406	305
1913	718	194	.27	524	393

D. Potatoes

	(1) Net production	(2) Sales	(3) Ratio of sales to production 2/1	(4) Retained product	(5) Value of 4 1913 prices
1885	427	107	.25	320	58
1886	471	104	.22	367	66
1887	506	116	.23	390	70
1888	458	115	.25	343	62
1889	479	120	.25	359	65
1890	519	130	.25	389	70
1891	394	126	.32	268	48
1892	716	136	.19	580	104
1893	849	170	.20	679	122
1894	750	143	.19	607	109
1895	1061	244	.23	817	147
1896	1151	242	.21	909	164
1897	1074	215	.20	859	155
1898	1146	275	.24	871	157
1899	1170	164	.14	1006	181
1900	1320	224	.17	1096	197
1901	1152	242	.21	910	164
1902	1384	304	.22	1080	194
1903	1202	288	.24	914	165
1904	1211	218	.18	993	179
1905	1418	326	.23	1092	197
1906	1258	365	.29	893	161
1907	1402	336	.24	1066	192
1908	1437	302	.21	1135	204
1909	1631	489	.30	1142	206
1910	1826	493	.27	1333	240
1911	1530	197	.26	1132	204
1912	1858	390	.21	1468	264
1913	1701	340	.20	1361	245

Table D.2 (cont.)

| | E. Total: Food grains | | | | F. Total: All grains | |
	(1) Value of net product (1913 prices)	(2) Value of retained product (1913 prices)	(3) Nonmarketed Net (1913 prices)	(4) Index of ratio 2/1	(1) 1913 Prices retained	(2) Current prices products (1913 = 100)
1885	1128	868	.76	33.2	1183	1100
1886	1104	850	.77	32.6	1058	899
1887	1468	1075	.73	41.1	1322	1084
1888	1405	972	.69	37.2	1198	1138
1889	939	678	.72	25.9	840	790
1890	1204	871	.72	33.3	1074	913
1891	873	547	.63	20.9	669	829
1892	1255	957	.76	36.6	1183	1336
1893	1836	1369	.75	52.4	1680	1411
1894	1865	1434	.77	54.9	1758	1037
1895	1727	1259	.73	48.2	1556	825
1896	1740	1290	.74	49.3	1591	843
1897	1406	1059	.75	40.5	1307	954
1898	1803	1285	.71	49.2	1588	1525
1899	1882	1513	.80	57.9	1869	1663
1900	1947	1524	.78	58.4	1885	1376
1901	1720	1284	.75	49.2	1588	1239
1902	2372	1734	.73	66.4	2143	1736
1903	2353	1680	.71	64.4	2079	1580
1904	2546	1971	.77	75.5	2437	1852
1905	2205	1601	.73	61.3	1979	1742
1906	1824	1227	.67	47.0	1517	1456
1907	2080	1481	.71	56.7	1830	2196
1908	2196	1628	.74	62.4	2014	2538
1909	2831	1883	.67	72.1	2327	2606
1910	2908	2005	.69	76.8	2479	2281
1911	2187	1548	.71	59.3	1914	2086
1912	3064	2282	.75	87.4	2821	3272
1913	3481	2611	.75	100.0	3228	3228

Note: Regression results: Wheat $b = .196$, rye $b = .036$, $c = .069$ (2-year lag), barley $c = .240$.

I also noted that the transport data could not be employed directly as estimates of marketings from the calendar year harvest because of delivery lags. Thus adjustments must be made in order to calculate the marketed portion of a particular calendar year harvest. Adjustment requires the econometric estimation of the general lag structure of sales.

The postulated simple adjustment model is:

$$s_t = a + bNP_t + cNP_{t-1}$$

where s_t equals rail and water shipments of grain j in year t and NP refers to the net production of grain j in years t and $t - 1$. Once a, b and c are estimated, shipments attributable to net production in year t (denoted by S_t) can be established as follows:

$$S_t = (s_t - cNP_{t-1}) + cNP_t$$

$$= s_t + c(NP_t - NP_{t-1})$$

The estimated coefficients are given at the bottom of Table D.2.

Sales attributable to corresponding calendar year harvests are reported in Table D.2 along with the net production figures from Table D.1. From this information, the ratios of sales to net output and retained product are calculated for wheat, rye, barley, and potatoes. The value of retained product in 1913 prices is also reported. The aggregate values in 1913 prices of net product and retained product of the four grains are given in column E along with the ratio of retained product to net output.

The series for the four major grains is expanded by a constant factor of 1.23 to include omitted grains (other than feed grains) and peas, lentils, and beans (column F). The adjustment factor is calculated from Falkus's data on net agricultural production in 1913. I assume that these omitted categories grew at the same rate as the four major food grains.

Table D.3. *Retained farm products, summary table, 1913 prices (million rubles)*

	(1) Retained grains	(2) Retained meat products	(3) Retained technical crops	(4) Dairy products	(5) Omitted products	Total
1885	1183	437	108	673	624	3024
1886	1058	438	100	677	591	2864
1887	1322	439	125	732	681	3300
1888	1198	479	149	732	665	3222
1889	840	480	138	744	573	2777
1890	1074	487	133	738	632	3063
1891	669	471	110	717	511	2476
1892	1183	459	131	721	648	3140
1893	1680	462	172	729	791	3833
1894	1758	467	179	746	819	3969
1895	1556	490	195	859	812	3912
1896	1591	545	223	887	850	4096
1897	1307	555	187	885	768	3702
1898	1588	555	213	905	854	4115
1899	1869	569	164	928	924	4454
1900	1885	576	169	891	923	4444
1901	1588	567	149	912	842	4058
1902	2143	579	215	912	1008	4857
1903	2079	578	195	876	976	4704
1904	2437	569	192	968	1092	5258
1905	1979	603	192	931	970	4675
1906	1517	587	230	912	850	4096
1907	1830	572	251	908	933	4494
1908	2014	570	238	1046	1013	4881
1909	2327	657	184	1105	1119	5392
1910	2479	688	202	1115	1174	5658
1911	1914	701	215	1059	1019	4908
1912	2821	679	246	1174	1289	6209
1913	3228	720	256	1126	1396	6726

NOTES TO APPENDIX D

1   For detailed discussions of tsarist agricultural statistics by Soviet and
     Russian authors, see V. I. Smirnsky, "Iz istorii zemskoi statistiki," in
     Akademiia nauk, *Ocherki po istorii statistiki SSSR, Sbornik tretii* (Moscow:
     Gosstatizdat Ts.S.U., 1960), pp. 130-45; A. I. Gozulov, *Istoriia
     otechestvennoi statistiki* (Moscow: Gosstatizdat, 1957), pp. 1-81. See also,
     P. I. Liashchenko, *Ocherki agrarnoi evolutsii Rossii* (Petersburg: N.P., 1908),
     pp. 278-301. Detailed accounts of the various estimates of prerevolutionary
     agricultural output and marketings with analyses of their strengths and
     shortcomings are found in: Jerzy Karcz, "Back on the Grain Front," *Soviet
     Studies* 22, no. 2 (October 1970): 262-94; S. G. Wheatcroft, "The Reliability
     of Russian Prewar Grain Output Statistics," *Soviet Studies* 36, no. 2 (April
     1974):157-80; R. W. Davies, "A Note on Grain Statistics," *Soviet Studies* 21,
     no. 3 (January 1970):314-30. The central issue concerns the so-called
     Ivantsov correction, which *Gosplan* used in the mid-1920s to adjust the Central
     Statistical Committee figures upward by 19%. As one can imagine, an
     adjustment of this magnitude makes a considerable difference in estimates of
     output and marketings. We discuss this in more detail below.

2   E.g., the annual budget report of the Ministry of Finance during this period
     would generally contain a discussion of agricultural exports and world
     agricultural prices as would innumerable special reports and monographs. On
     this, see *Entwurf des Reichsbudgets für das Jahr* (various years). Detailed
     records of external and internal prices of farm products were maintained by
     the Ministry of Interior, and frequent detailed analyses of the world grain
     market were undertaken by various government agencies such as the tariff
     office. Reports on the grain market were published monthly in the Finance
     Ministry's official journal, *Vestnik finansov*. For a bibliography of official
     publications on the grain market, see P. A. Zaionchkovski, *Spravochnik po
     istorii dorevoliutsionnoi Rossii* (Moscow: Kniga, 1971), pp. 75-93.

3   Because of the famine threat, the government required peasant communities to
     accumulate prescribed reserves of grain and capital to be utilized during
     famine years. For a discussion of this reserve system, see *Khlebnye zapasy v
     obshchestvennykh magazinakh i mestnye prodovol'stvennye kapitaly*, Tsentral'ny
     Statistichiski Komitet, *Vremmenik*, no. 24 (1892).

4   S. N. Prokopovich, *Opyt ischisleniia narodnogo dokhoda 50 gubernii Evropeiskoi
     Rossii v 1900-1913 gg.* (Moscow: Sovet Vserossiiskikh Kooperativnykh Sezdov,
     1918).

5   Abram Bergson, *The Real National Income of Soviet Russia since 1928*
     (Cambridge: Harvard University Press, 1961).

6   P. I. Liashchenko, *Ocherki*, pp. 278-301.

7   Liashchenko, *Ocherki*, p. 293; L. N. Maress, "Proizvodstvo i potreblenie khleba
     v krestianskom khoziaistve," in A. I. Chuprov and A. S. Posnikov, eds.,
     Vliianie urozhaev i khlebnykh tsen na nekotoryia storony ruskkago narodnogo

khoziaistva (Petersburg: Kirshbaum, 1897), p. 53.

8   *Statisticheski sbornik ministerstva putei soobshcheniia, Dvizhenie Tovarov,*
    selected years. Karcz, "Back on the Grain Front," p. 283, suggests that the
    "early" shipments data may be understated by 15% to 20% but fails to supply a
    reference or to indicate what is meant by "early."

9   Z. M. Svavitski and N. A. Svavitski, *Zemskie podvornye perepisi 1880-1913*
    (Moscow: Izdanie Ts.S.U., 1926); L. N. Maress, "Proizvodstvo," p. 53; Karcz,
    "Back on the Grain Front," pp. 280-6.

10 The most complete study of this sort is by F. A. Shcherbina, "Krestianskie
    biudzhety i zavisimost' ikh ot urozhaev i tsen na khleba," in A. I. Chuprov
    and A. S. Posnikov, eds., *Vliianie urozhaev i khlebnykh tsen na nekotorye
    storony ruskkago narodnogo khoziaistva* (Petersburg: Kirshbaum, 1897), 1-79.

11 These budgetary studies are summarized in G. A. Dikhtiar, *Vnutrenniaia
    torgovlia v dorevoliutsionnoi Rossii* (Moscow: Nauka, 1960), Chap. 2.

12 On this point, the reader is referred to the references in note 1, in
    particular to the Karcz and Wheatcroft studies. The most widely cited
    evaluation of prewar agricultural statistics is the study by D. N. Ivantsov, *K
    kritike russkoi urozhainnoi statistiki* (Petersburg: N.P., 1915). During the
    course of this study, I was not able to obtain a copy of the Ivantsov book.
    Its contents, however, are summarized by S. G. Strumilin in *Statistiko-
    ekonomicheskie ocherki* (Moscow: Gosstatizdat, 1958), pp. 328-9. Various
    studies of the necessary adjustment coefficient to be applied to the official
    harvest figures are also discussed by Maress, "Proizvodstvo," p. 7. For
    samples of the actual survey questionnaires used by the Ministry of Interior,
    see *Urozhai khlebov po ukazaniiam krest'ian-starozhilov iz obsledovaniia 1893
    g. 46 gub. Evropeiskoi Rossii,* Vremmenik Tsentral'nogo Statisticheskago
    Komiteta, no. 30 (1893).

13 On this, see Wheatcroft, "Reliability of Russian Prewar Grain Output
    Statistics," pp. 157-80.

14 M. E. Falkus, "Russia's National Income, 1913: A Revaluation," *Economica,* N.S.
    35, no. 137 (February 1968):65.

15 The Kuhn (unpublished) figures are cited in *Bulletin Russe de statistique
    financiere et de legislation,* 5th ed. (1898), pp. 222-31.

16 According to Strumilin, citing a study by the Department of Agriculture for 42
    provinces, the ratio of seed to total output was 12% for the period 1912-14
    for all grains, S. G. Strumilin, *Ocherki ekonomicheskoi istorii Rossii i SSSR*
    (Moscow: Nauka, 1966), pp. 207-8.

17 V. I. Pokrovsky, ed., *Sbornik svedenii po istorii i statistiki vneshnei
    torgovli Rossii* (Petersburg: Departament tamozhennykh sborov, 1902), p. 31.
    In the late nineteenth century, shipments of flour abroad accounted for about
    2% of the value of foreign grain sales.

18 Karcz, "Back on the Grain Front," p. 283.

19 The most notable of these are by Liashchenko, *Ocherki,* pp. 314-28, and Leo
    Jurowsky, *Der Russische Getreideexport* (Stuttgart: Druck der Union Deutsche

Verlaggesellschaft, 1910). For the pattern of deliveries for shipment abroad, see Pokrovsky, *Sbornik svedenii,* pp. 40-3.

20   Karcz, "Back on the Grain Front," p. 283.

21   For a specialized study of price variation, see I. D. Koval'chenko and L. V. Milov, *Vserossiisky agrarny rynok XVIII-nachalo XX veka* (Moscow: Nauka, 1974).

22   There is no information on the shipment of potatoes. We infer the potatoes marketing index from the index of marketings of wheat, rye, and barley, applied to Prokopovich's *(Opyt ischisleniia, p. 72)* estimate of 19% for the ratio of potato marketings to net output.

23   Karcz, "Back on the Grain Front," p. 283.

24   Liashchenko, *Ocherki,* p. 322.

25   Liashchenko, *Ocherki,* p. 322.

26   Karcz, "Back on the Grain Front," pp. 262-94, and Wheatcroft, "Reliability of Russian Prewar Grain Output Statistics," statistical appendix.

27   I use marketing ratios from Prokopovich, *Opyt ischisleniia,* p. 71.

28   Wheatcroft, "Reliability of Russian Prewar Grain Output Statistics," pp. 157-180.

29   Paul Gregory, "1913 Russian National Income: Some Insights into Russian Economic Development," *Quarterly Journal of Economics* 90, no. 3 (August 1976), statistical appendix.

30   Prokopovich, *Opyt ischisleniia,* p. 78.

31   Raymond Goldsmith, "The Economic Growth of Tsarist Russia, 1860-1913," *Economic Development and Cultural Change* 9, no. 3(April 1961):450, 458.

MILITARY SUBSISTENCE

MILITARY SUBSISTENCE IN CURRENT PRICES

Relatively good information is available for the estimation of the in-kind consumption of military personnel. On the one hand, the detailed budgetary reports
prepared by the Ministry of Finance[1] supply a mass of detail on the breakdown of
military expenditures by department. From these reports, I am able to estimate
expenditures for military consumption in kind by the war and marine ministries as
the sum of expenditures for provisions and uniforms (including accessories). My
figures on military consumption in kind in current prices are given in Table E.1,
column 1.

MILITARY SUBSISTENCE IN 1913 PRICES

Detailed information for the deflation of military consumption in kind is also
available. Weights of food versus uniform expenditures in 1913 can be gleaned
directly from the budgets of the War and Marine ministries, which are broken down
into these two categories. The distribution of expenditures among major food
products for the armed forces is supplied by Beskrovny[2] for the turn of the century.
Insofar as such things tend to change slowly, one can readily take this food product
distribution as representative of 1913.

The price weights thus established, it remains to collect the necessary price
information. My index of uniform prices is an unweighted index of wool and cotton
cloth prices, where the wholesale prices are taken from *Svod tovarnykh tsen* and
Sobol'ev.[3] The prices of foodstuffs consumed by the military are taken from *Svod
tovarnykh tsen* and from other sources for the pre-1900 period.[4] The calculated food
and uniform price indexes are given in Table E.1, column 2. These indexes are then
applied to the current price figures to obtain military consumption in kind in
constant 1913 prices (column 3).

Table E.1. *Military subsistence, 1885-1913, current and constant 1913 prices (million rubles)*

	(1) Military subsistence, current prices	(2) Size of armed forces (1000s)	(3) Per capita military subsistence (rubles)	(4) Price index for deflation of military subsistence, prices	(4a) Foodstuffs prices	(4b) Uniforms and accessories	(5) Real military subsistence in 1913 prices (1 ÷ 4)
1885	65	856	72	88	93	76	74
1888	60			89	95	76	67
1891	57	886	64	110	124	75	52
1894	62	976	64	65	59	77	95
1896	64	1010	63	60	53	78	107
1900	76	1040	73	78	78	80	97
1903	82			78	76	83	105
1907	147			114	120	99	129
1910	169			106	109	99	159
1913	175	1400	125	100	100	100	175

Sources: (1) The military consumption in-kind figures are taken directly from the *Entwurf des Reichsbudgets* series, the *Bericht des Finanzministers* series, *Les Finances de la Russe*, *D'Apres les Documents Officiels* 1892, and "Allgemeines Reichsbudget der Einnahmen und Ausgaben für das Jahr 1886," *Russische Revue*, Band XXVI, 1886, 1-21. The figures cited are for provisions and uniforms of the intendatur departments of the war and marine ministries.
(2) Data on the size of the armed forces are from P. A. Zaionchkovsky, *Samoderzhavie i russkaia armiia na rubezhe XIX-XX stoletii* (Moscow: Mysl', 1973), 114-67; L. G. Beskrovny, *Russkaia armiia i flot v XIX veke* (Moscow: Nauka, 1973), 42-44, 548; Paul Gregory, *Appendices to Russian National Income in 1913*, mimeographed, 8.
(3) Column 1 / Column 3.
(4) 1913 weights for foodstuffs versus uniforms and accessories are taken directly from their 1913 share in expenditures from *Entwurf des Reichsbudgets* 1913, 111. The weights are .72 and .28 respectively. Beskrovny, 474-75, gives 1900 weights for the distribution of food expenditures, which are taken to be representative (due to the slow change in consumption patterns) of 1913 weights. Food price data are from Table 4a, Column H (appendix 4). The Petersburg retail price index of clothing and footwear from S. G. Strumilin, *Istoriia chernoi metallurgii v SSSR* (Moscow: Nauka, 1967), 431-32 is used as the index of uniform prices.

NOTES TO APPENDIX E

1   The most detailed budgetary reports are *Entwurf des Reichsbudgets für das Jahr* (annual editions for the period 1907-14), Ministry of Finance, Petersburg, Buchdruckerei der kaiserlichen Akademie der Wissenschaften, and *Bericht des Finanzministers über das Reichsbudgets für das Jahr* (annual editions for the period 1897 to 1906), Petersburg, Buchdruckerei der kaiserlichen Akademie der Wissenschaften.

2   L. G. Beskrovny, *Russkaia armiia i flot v XIX veke* (Moscow: Nauka, 1973), pp. 474-6.

3   *Svod tovarnykh tsen na glavnykh russkikh i inostrannykh rynakakh za 1913 g.* (Petersburg, Ministerstvo torgovli i promyshlennosti, 1915); M. N. Sobolev, *Tamozhennaia politika Rossii vo vtoroi polovine XIX veka*, pt. 2 (Tomsk: Tipografiia sibierskoe tovarichestvo pechatnago dela, 1911), appendixes 1-18.

4   Sobolev *Tamozhennaia politika*, and V. I. Pokrovsky, ed., *Sbornik svedenii po istorii i statistike vneshnei torgovli Rossii*, vol. 1 (Petersburg: Departament tamozhennykh sborov, 1902).

EXPENDITURES OF THE IMPERIAL GOVERNMENT

In Table F.1 I supply data on the distribution of imperial budget expenditures. For national income estimates, it is necessary to separate expenditures for goods and services (administration, health and welfare, and defense) from other types of expenditures, namely, interest and principal payments on government debt, subsidies and transfer payments, and expenditures on government enterprises. Moreover, if possible, one would also like to determine the distribution of government expenditures between current and capital expenditures.

EXPENDITURES IN CURRENT PRICES

I have analyzed the budgetary data provided in the various reports of the Ministry of Finance[1] for the purpose of determining the magnitude and distributions of government expenditures. Budgetary data vary in the amount of detail for various years, ranging from approximately 600 expenditure categories (the 1913 budget) to 150 positions (the 1900 budget). The accounting system was fairly uniform throughout the 1885 to 1913 period, a fact that greatly assisted my analysis. The capital expenditure data suffer especially from the varying detail, as such capital expenditures are likely to be lost in the aggregation of budget positions. By the use of assumptions derived from distributions in nearby years for which more detailed information is available, I sought to avoid downward bias in the capital expenditure figures in the years for which less detailed data are available, but I must caution that the capital expenditure figures are approximate and are not to be regarded as reliable.

During the period under investigation, intermediate government expenditures were substantial, with the state-owned railroads and the state spirits monopoly accounting for almost 90% of such intermediate expenditures.[2] The remainder was accounted for by the state telephone company, metallurgy enterprises, and state-operated agricultural enterprises. Subsidy and transfer payments can be differentiated fairly well from other expenditures with the available budgetary data. I should mention that the bulk of subsidies and pensions were paid by the Ministry of Finance. For example, in 1907 almost 90% of all transfers and subsidies (a total of 147 million rubles) were distributed through the budget of the finance minister. It should also be noted that these subsidies and pensions were granted for a wide variety of purposes, ranging from grants to the imperial family and nobility to industrial subsidies, and it would be difficult to make the case that such payments were important in the support of industrialization.[3] The most important subsidy in support of industrialization was the annual payment to meet state profit guarantees to the private railroads. To provide some feel for the magnitude of these profit guarantees, I note that they were some 11 million in 1913, 38 million in 1907, and 13 million in 1885. In 1900 they were exceptionally large (6 million under "normal" expenditures and 85 million under "extraordinary" expenditures).[4] Yet even in 1900, such subsidies accounted for only 6% of all government expenditures.

On the distribution of state expenditures between defense and administrative outlays, I was careful to include certain types of expenditures not included in the budgets of the War and Marine ministries in the category of defense outlays. Such expenditures as the maintenance of local militia, the costs of quartering troops, and so on are not substantial and do not materially alter the distribution of expenditures between defense and administration. For example, in 1913 such hidden defense expenditures accounted for 12 million rubles, approximately 1% of total defense expenditures. There is a further source of potential hidden defense outlays, namely, railroad and port construction, where it is difficult to distinguish pure military outlays from other nondefense expenditures. In these instances, I have not included such expenditures in the defense outlay category.

Detailed information on interest and principal payments on state debt is available for all the years under investigation. For 1885, it is necessary to differentiate debt service in gold rubles from those in credit rubles for the conversion into a credit ruble figure. The 1885 budget is broken down into gold and credit ruble obligations with gold ruble obligations accounting for 63% of the total.[5] These gold ruble obligations are converted into credit rubles using the prevailing gold ruble-credit ruble exchange rate. Expenditures for health and education were scattered among three ministries: Education, Interior, and the Holy Synod. The Ministry of Finance operated some schools during this period, but the overall expenditure was insignificant. The War and Marine ministries also operated military schools and hospitals (an expenditure of 14 million rubles in 1896), but such outlays are left in the military budget. The major expenditures in health and education were made by the Education Ministry and the Holy Synod for schools (24 million and 6 million, respectively, in 1896) and by the Interior Ministry for public health (3 million in 1896).

A more complete explanation of my derivation of Table F.1 is not possible as this would require a detailed discussion of each budgetary position. Some detail is given in Table F.2 on the derivation of government capital expenditure figures. As a final point, I should note that my analysis of the detailed budgetary reports yields conclusions quite similar to those of Shebalin (for 1900 and 1913) on the distribution between expenditures for goods and services and other expenditures.[6]

EXPENDITURES IN CONSTANT PRICES

Virtually no information is available on the average earnings of civil servants employed by the imperial government and local government organizations. This is true even though state salaries were nominally determined by schedules for various ranks, and these schedules were published periodically in the *Complete Collection of Laws (Polnoe sobranie zakonov)*.[7] Inspection of these schedules, however, indicates that they remained stable over a century of time and that supplements and exceptions to these schedules were the principal determinants of earnings in the bureaucracy.

Although I made numerous efforts to calculate salaries of civil servants by indirect means, namely, from employment and personnel expenditure data, sufficient data simply were not available, either for civil servants or for public-school teachers. In the latter case, one can obtain isolated examples of salaries, generally in publications designed to stress the economic misery of teachers,[8] but one cannot derive a time series of earnings over this period from this information. Apparently the only way to obtain reasonable direct information on the earnings of civil servants and teachers would be to engage in archival research on the subject.[9]

For the deflation of personnel expenditures by the imperial government, I have selected two wage series, which I believe provide the closest approximations of such earnings: (a) average earnings of workers and employees of the telegraph service of the state railroads, (b) average earnings of factory workers. The rationale for using the first series is that employees of the railroads occupied semi-civil service positions, and of the wage series supplied by the Ministry of Transportation,[10] employment in telegraph offices comes the closest to approximating working conditions in the bureaucracy. Moreover, an added advantage is that the earnings series published by the Ministry of Transportation are likely reasonably accurate, and I might further note that the number of employees (approximately 20,000 in 1910) in the telegraph service was not so small as to make the series volatile, as it was, for example, for those employed in administration of the state railways.[11] The wage series of industrial factory workers[12] is used as a second deflator on the grounds that it should capture wage trends for the lower ranks of the bureaucracy (maintenance personnel, lower clerks, etc.) for whom industrial employment was a likely alternative.

The deflation of nonpersonnel expenditures is based upon Bobrov's wholesale price index (see Appendix I) for material expenditures and upon my construction price deflator (Appendix J).

From these wage and price series, aggregate price deflators for the three categories of government expenditures are calculated, where the weights are based upon the distribution of 1913 expenditures.[13] According to my calculations, the overall ratio of personnel to nonpersonnel expenditures for administration was 50%, with capital expenditures accounting for 15% and materials for 35% of the total. These are the weights underlying the administration deflator series, where I arbitrarily assign weights of .25 and .25 to the two wage series. For health and education expenditures the weights are .6 for personnel (A1), .1 for construction, and the remainder for materials (.3). For defense, the distribution is .4 for personnel, .25 for equipment and construction, and .35 for materials. These calculations are shown in Table F.3. The deflated expenditure categories are summarized in Table F.4.

Table F.1. *Expenditures of imperial government, 1885-1913, current prices (million rubles)*

	(1) Administrative expenditures	(2) Expenditures for education and health	(3) Defense expenditures	(4) Expenditures on final goods and services	(5) Interest and principal payments on government debt	(6) Expenditures on government enterprises, including state railroads	(7) Subsidies and transfer payments including subsidies to private railroads	Total (1-7)
1885	194	23	240	457	310	49	50	866
1888	207	21	249	477	288	64	59	888
1891	247	26	296	569	257	101	56	962
1894	250	30	331	611	264	150	59	1084
1896	295	31	347	673	269	361	58	1361
1900	326	46	483	855	317	570	147	1889
1903	391	52	436	879	287	818	98	2072
1907	443	57	570	1070	449	827	147	2496
1910	536	101	558	1195	412	899	86	2592
1913	583	154	970	1707	424	1064	188	3383

Sources: *Entwurf des Reichsbudgets für das Jahr...*, 1907, 1908, 1911, 1913, 1914 editions; *Bericht des Finanzministers über das Reichs-budget für das Jahr...*, 1894, 1897, 1900, 1904 editions; *Russische Revue*, Band XXVI, 1886, 1-24; Iu. Shebalin, "Gosudarstvenny biudzhet tsarskoi Rossii," *Istoricheskie zapiski*, T65, 1959; *Les Finances de la Russe, D'Apres les Documents officiels* (Paris: Imprimerie et Libraire centrales des Chemins de Fer, 1892). See text for a discussion of the derivation of these figures. For 1900, the distribution of expenditures between (5) and (6) is from the preliminary budgetary data in *Bericht*, 1900. The remaining figures are from Shebalin, 190.

Table F.2. Capital expenditures of imperial government, 1885-1913, current prices (million rubles)

	A. Capital expenditures				B. Capital expenditures on government				
	(1) Administration	(2) Education and health	(3) Defense	Total ΣA1-3	(1) Telephone, telegraph, and post	(2) Publicly owned railroads	(3) Spirits monopoly	(4) Other	Total ΣB1-4
1885	15	1	29	45	2	25	—	1	28
1888	18	1	43	62	nc	nc	nc	nc	nc
1891	23	1	44	68	2	35	—	1	38
1894	25	1	53	79	nc	nc	nc	nc	nc
1896	29	2	41	72	3	150	2	1	156
1900	47	5	62	114	4	149	2	2	157
1903	44	4	80	128	nc	nc	nc	nc	nc
1907	35	3	51	89	4	51	3	4	62
1910	52	8	77	141	6	63	4	10	83
1913	92	8	225	325	13	133	5	13	164

Note: Nc denotes not calculated. — denotes insignificant.

Sources: 1896, 1894, 1891, and 1888: These capital expenditure figures are from Bericht des Finanzministers für das Jahr 1897 and 1895, and from Les Finances de la Russe, D'Apres les Documents officiels, 1889 and 1892 editions. Ratios of capital to operating expenditures prevailing in later years are applied to forestry operations and to 1896 spirits monopoly expenditures. "Other" capital expenditures are assumed to equal one million rubles in both years. 1900: The capital expenditure data for 1900 are taken directly from the preliminary budget data in Bericht des Finanzministers für das Jahr 1900. Capital expenditures for the spirits monopoly are approximated by applying the 1907 ratio of capital to total expenditures for the spirits monopoly to 1900 expenditures (.025). A ratio of 10% is applied to the construction and current operating expenditures of the Ministry of Agriculture and State Property to approximate capital expenditures. The major capital expenditure for 1900 was, as the figures show, the enormous investment in the Trans-Siberian railroad, which alone occasioned an extraordinary expenditure of 59 million rubles (Bericht, 47). 1907: Calculated in same manner as 1913 from Entwurf des Reichsbudgets für das Jahr, 1907. Again, capital expenditures in column B4 are calculated as 10% of total "other" expenditures. 1910: Same as for 1913 from Entwurf, 1911. 1913: The capital expenditure data are taken directly from Entwurf, 1913 and 1914, and encompass the obvious capital expenditure positions of the budget. Only total expenditure data are given for forestry, metallurgy, and mining operations (labeled "other" in column B4), and a 10% capital to total expenditure ratio is used to approximate "other" capital expenditures.

Table F.3. *Deflation of government spending, imperial budget*

A. Wage and price series (1913 = 100)

	(1) Average annual earnings, telegraph employees, full-time	(2) Nominal wages, factory workers, by factory inspections	(3) Wholesale price index, (Bobrov)	(4) Construction price index	(5) Equipment price index
1885	80	66	82	83	93
1886	82	66	79	83	104
1887	77	66	81	82	98
1888	76	69	86	85	100
1889	78	64	83	81	101
1890	78	63	74	79	105
1891	82	64	75	83	106
1892	82	64	73	83	104
1893	78	67	76	83	100
1894	80	64	69	85	106
1895	79	63	71	81	100
1896	78	63	72	82	102
1897	74	64	74	88	96
1898	74	68	78	90	94

B. Deflators for:

	(1) Administration (.25A1 + .25A2 + .35A3 + .15A4)	(2) Health, education (.6A1 + .3A3 + .1A4)	(3) Defense (.4A1 + .35A3 + .13A4 + .12A5)
1885	78	81	83
1886	77	81	84
1887	76	78	82
1888	79	81	83
1889	77	80	83
1890	78	77	80
1891	75	80	83
1892	75	79	82
1893	76	78	81
1894	73	78	80
1895	73	76	80
1896	74	77	80
1897	74	75	79
1898	76	76	80

Year								
1899	74	69	81	94	94	78	77	81
1900	75	73	84	93	95	80	79	82
1901	75	76	80	91	96	80	78	82
1902	75	77	76	89	95	78	77	80
1903	65	79	77	94	97	77	71	77
1904	78	81	80	92	94	82	80	82
1905	79	77	82	92	94	82	81	84
1906	88	87	89	94	94	89	89	89
1907	89	91	97	93	105	93	91	95
1908	87	92	93	92	97	92	88	92
1909	92	89	91	91	101	91	91	93
1910	92	90	92	94	99	92	92	93
1911	98	94	95	94	99	96	97	96
1912	101	96	98	96	101	97	100	98
1913	100	100	100	100	100	100	100	100

Sources: *Column A1*: *Statisticheski sbornik ministerstva putei soobshcheniia*, annual series. Figures for 1911 to 1913 estimated using average annual earnings of all railway workers from S. G. Strumilin, *Statistiko-ekonomicheskie ocherki* (Moscow: Gosstatizdat, 1958), p. 642. *Column A2*: Series cited by S. G. Strumilin, *Ocherki ekonomicheskoi istorii Rossii i SSSR* (Moscow: Nauka, 1966), pp. 91-4. *Column A3*: Index compiled by C. P. Bobrov from 62 commodities cited in *Svod tovarnykh tsen na glavnykh russkikh i inostrannykh rynkakh za 1913 g.* (Petersburg: Ministerstvo torgovli i promyshelnnosti, 1915). Weights are based upon rail and water shipments. Series is cited in Strumilin, *Ocherki*, p. 89. *Column A4*: See table J.2, column F. *Column A5*: Appendix I.

Table F.4. *Expenditures of imperial government, 1913 prices (millions of rubles)*

	(1) Administration expenditures	(2) Expenditures for education and health	(3) Defense expenditures	Total
1885	249	28	289	566
1888	262	26	300	588
1891	329	33	357	719
1894	342	39	414	795
1896	399	40	434	873
1900	408	58	525	991
1903	508	73	566	1147
1907	476	63	600	1139
1910	583	110	600	1293
1913	583	154	970	1707

NOTES TO APPENDIX F

1   *Otchety Gosudarstvennogo kontrolia po ispol'neniiu gosudarstvennoi i finansovykh smet; Entwurf des Reichsbudgets für das Jahr; Bericht des Finanzministers über das Reichsbudgets für das Jahr.*

2   These figures are calculated for the year 1913 from *Entwurf des Reichsbudgets für das Jahr 1914.* Before the introduction of the state spirits monopoly in 1894 such expenditures represented a much smaller proportion of the total as Table F.1 indicates.

3   This supports the findings of Arcadius Kahan, "Government Policies and the Industrialization of Russia," *Journal of Economic History* 27, no. 4 (December 1967):460-77, who argues that expenditures in support of industrialization were not exceptionally large in the Russian case.

4   These figures are from *Bericht des Finanzministers über das Reichsbudgets für das Jahr 1900,* pp. 41, 47.

5   *Russische Revue,* 26 (1886):3-5.

6   In fact, the 1900 figures (part A) are taken directly from Iu. Shebalin, "Gosudarstvenny biudzhet tsarskoi Rossii," *Istoricheskie zapiski,* 62 (1959):190.

7   The salary information for the various ranks is contained in A. M. Niurenberg, ed., *Svod zakonov rossiiskoi imperii* (Moscow: Levinson, various years).

8   See, e.g., N. V. Chekhov, *Narodnoe obrazovanie v Rossii* (Moscow: Levenson, 1912), and W. H. E. Johnson, *Russia's Educational Heritage* (Pittsburgh: Carnegie Press, 1950), Chap. 10.

9   Such research would have to be based on the various directories of ministerial officials (*spisok lits* . . .) published annually by the various ministries and upon the salary schedules and exceptions published by the ministries. For listings of such publications, see P. A. Zaionchkovski, *Spravochnik po istorii dorevoliutsionnoi Rossii* (Moscow: Kniga, 1971), under the heading *gosudarstvennye organy.*

10 This series comes directly from *Statisticheski sbornik ministerstva putei soobshcheniia,* annual edition, section 12 and is for full-time employees of the telegraph service of the state railroads.

11 Originally, I had thought that the wage series on the earnings of employees administering the state railroads would be the best series. This series, however, proved to be unacceptable, as the numbers of those classified as administrative personnel (*po upravleniiu*) increased remarkably after 1890, and the average earnings of such employees dropped at roughly the same rate. This suggests a reclassification of lesser employees into administrative positions during this period, which make the series a distorted one.

12 This series is compiled from wage series cited by S. G. Strumilin, *Ocherki ekonomicheskoi istorii Rossii i SSSR* (Moscow: Nauka, 1966), pp. 91-4. For the period 1885 to 1897, the series is one constructed by Gosplan under the direction of M. E. Podtiagin from correlations with various price and wage

indexes (of agricultural and railroad workers). This series, according to Strumilin, coincides closely to the isolated evidence on average earnings during this period. For the period 1897 to 1913, the series is for average earnings of workers in factories subject to factory inspection and, according to Strumilin, is a reasonably reliable index.

13   The weights are based upon an analysis of detailed budetary data in *Entwurf des Reichsbudgets für das Jahr 1914*, which supplied the greatest detail concerning the implementation of the 1913 budget.

EXPENDITURES IN CURRENT PRICES

Local government in the Russian Empire consisted of a confusing interweaving of organizations, which makes the analysis of local governmental expenditures a complicated matter. For a summary description of the organization of local government, the reader is referred to the works of Yaney and Gribowski.[1] The highest level of local government, the *guberniia*, was administered by the *gubernator*. A parallel representative governmental body, the *zemstvo*, existed in 34 *guberniia*, but this representative body was lacking in 40 *guberniia* (Siberia, Caucasus, the Baltic).[2] The Polish territories were administered separately by a governor-general. Moreover, the Don Cossack, Turkestan, and two Siberian provinces were under the direct administration of the War Ministry.

At the local level, there were the municipal governments of towns and cities and the local administration of agricultural collective organizations. In the latter case, individual *mirs* belonged to *volosti*, and the expenditures of tax revenues collected from the *mir* organizations were subdivided into *volost'* expenditures if expended for all *volost'* activities or *mir* expenditures if expended for the benefit of a particular *mir*.[3]

Local government expenditures are not too difficult to estimate as rather substantial information on *zemstvo* and non-*zemstvo* expenditures and on municipal government expenditures is available. Less information is available on the *volost'* and *mir* expenditures, especially for the period after 1905. The greater difficulty involves the netting out of intermediate expenditures of municipal and *mir* and *volost'* expenditures. In some cases these were substantial, as the cities operated numerous industrial and commercial enterprises (utilities, local transport, slaughterhouses, etc.) as did the *volost'* and *mir* administrations (marketing of products, operating retail stores, etc.).

In Table G.1, I supply my estimates of local government expenditures broken down into the four administrative levels: *zemstvo guberniia, non-zemstvo guberniia,* municipal, and *volost'* and *mir* expenditures. These are subdivided into administrative expenditures (Table G.1), health and education expenditures (Table G.2), and local military expenditures (Table G.3). In all cases, I have sought to net out intermediate expenditures on enterprises operated by local government and intergovernmental transfer payments (in this case, flowing primarily from the central government to local governments). The details of my calculations are provided in the notes to Table G.1. I feel that these figures are reasonably accurate. In most cases, data on the distribution of municipal and *mir* and *volost'* expenditures are available only for 1885, 1895, and 1913 (only for 1895 in the case of the distribution of the latter expenditures). Thus, the distributions for other years had to be assumed from these benchmarks, and this represents the major source of possible measurement error in my calculations. A great deal of data are available on the distribution of *zemstvo* and non-*zemstvo* governmental expenditures, and these calculations should be accurate. Apparently, data on *volost'* and *mir* expenditures were not gathered after 1905; therefore, I calculated these expenditures by using an index of *mir* and *volost'* revenues. This index should provide a reasonably accurate approximation of expenditures as I have found no information on substantial changes in indebtedness or substantial subsidies from other governmental units during this period.

I have also sought to estimate capital expenditures of local government on the basis of the distribution data at my disposal. For the *guberniia* and *mir* and *volosti*, the major single capital expenditure item was for road construction, and these expenditures are itemized separately. For municipal government, capital expenditures encompass both construction (municipal buildings, prisons, etc.) and road construction. Capital expenditures of municipal and *mir* and *volost'* organizations had to be estimated for isolated years for which distribution data are available. On the other hand, the capital expenditure data of the *guberniia* are reasonably complete.

Finally, I should note that local government incurred certain military expenditures as well, which should be incorporated into the overall military budget. Such expenditures fell primarily on the municipalities in the form of quartering troops, supplying horses, and so on and accounted for almost 10% of municipal expenditures. According to the information at my disposal, *guberniia* military expenditures (*raskhody po voinskoi povinosti*) were minimal.[4] The *mirs* had certain obligations as well, especially the obligation to supply horses to the military, but I have no data on the magnitude of this obligation.

EXPENDITURES IN CONSTANT PRICES

The administration, health and education, and defense deflators used to deflate imperial expenditures are applied to the current price figures to obtain local government expenditures in constant 1913 prices (table G.4).

Table G.1. *Administrative expenditures, local government, 1885-1913, current prices (million rubles)*

	(1) 34 zemstvo guberniia	(2) Non-zemstvo guberniia	(3) Municipal expenditures, excluding military outlays	(4) Expenditures of *volost'* and *mir* organiza- tions	(5) Total
1885	29 (3)	3 (0)	30 (10)	26 (4)	85 (16)
1888	21 (3)	4 (0)	33 (11)	29 (5)	87 (19)
1891	23 (3)	6 (1)	36 (12)	32 (6)	97 (22)
1894	32 (3)	8 (2)	41 (15)	36 (6)	117 (26)
1896	38 (8)	11 (4)	42 (16)	40 (6)	128 (32)
1900	38 (8)	14 (5)	59 (22)	43 (7)	154 (42)
1903	46 (10)	14 (4)	72 (26)	45 (7)	177 (47)
1907	60 (13)	14 (4)	85 (31)	47 (8)	206 (56)
1910	68 (16)	14 (5)	120 (45)	51 (8)	253 (74)
1913	128 (20)	14 (4)	162 (62)	53 (9)	357 (95)

Note: Capital outlays in parentheses.
Sources: *(1)* V. I. Kovalevski, *Rossiia v kontse XIX veka* (Petersburg: Ministerstvo Finansov, 1900), pp. 776-7; V. V. Veselovski, *Istoriia zemstva za sorok let* (Petersburg: Popov, 1909), 1:253 (figures read from chart), 4:4; *Entsiklopedicheski slovar' Brokgauz-Efron*, 24:522; *Statistika rossiiskoi Imperii, sbornik svedenii*, 1890, p. 30, and 1896, pp. 310-14, *Granat*, vol. 21, p. 7, of supplement "zemskoe khoziaistvo." The Veselovsky chart (p. 253) fails to show the drop in *zemstvo* expenditures between 1890 and 1895 indicated by *Sbornik svedenii*, 1896, but we believe the *Sbornik* figures to be more accurate.
     (2) *Ezhegodnik ministerstva finansov*, selected years; Kovalevski, *Rossiia v kontse* . . . , p. 781; *Brokgauz*, 24:520-2. The distribution of health and education expenditures in 1885 is taken to be the same as in 1890. The 1894 and 1896 figures are interpolated from the 1890 and 1900 figures, and the 1888 figure is interpolated from the 1885 and 1890 figures.
     (3) *Statistika Rossiiskoi Imperii, sbornik svedenii*, 1884-5, pp. 212-18; 1890, p. 242; and 1896, p. 325; Kovalevski, *Rossiia v kontse*. . . . pp. 784-6; Paul Gronsky and Nicholas Astrov, *The War and the Russian Government* (New Haven: Yale University Press, 1929), p. 161; Albrecht Martiny, "Der Einfluss der Duma auf die Finanz- und Haushaltspolitik (1907-1914)," (Ph.D. diss., Freiburg, 1974), p. 253; Margaret Miller, *The Economic Development of Russia, 1905-1914*, 2nd ed. (London: Cass, 1967), p. 170. The above data include Polish municipal expenditures. Data on the distribution of municipal expenditures among administration, health and education, utilities, and defense are available only for the period 1888 to 1895 and 1913. The other distributions are approximated from this information.

Table G.1 (*cont.*)

(4)   Kovalevski, *Rossiia v kontse* . . ., pp. 785-9; Martiny, "Einfluss der Duma,"
p. 256; *Statistika Rossiiskoi Imperii, sbornik svedenii*, 1884-5, pp. 230-1, and
1896, pp. 302-9. The expenditure distribution is available only for 1894 and 1895
and is used to net out intermediate expenditures on *mir* stores and on other
intermediate expenditures (21% of the total). Because of the lack of distribution
data for other years, the 1895 ratio of intermediate to final expenditures was
assumed to obtain for the whole period.   The 1910 and 1913 expenditures are
estimated by applying an index of peasant *mir* payments (*mirskie platezhi*) for the
period 1907 to 1913 to the 1907 figure. The index is calculated from A. M. Anfimov,
"Nalogi i zemel'nye platezhi krestian Evropeiskoi Rossii v nachale XX veka," in
Akademiia Nauk SSSR, *Ezhegodnik po agrarnoi istorii Vostochnoi Evropy, 1962 g.*
(Minsk: Nauka i tekhnika, 1964), p. 502.   The 1888 and 1903 figures are simply
interpolations between intervening years. The resulting errors should be small.

Table G.2. *Health and education expenditures, local government, 1885-1913,
current prices (million rubles)*

	(1) 34 zemstvo guberniia	(2) Non-zemstvo guberniia	(3) Municipal expenditures	(4) Volost and mir organizations	(5) Total
1885	12	2	6	5	25
1888	16	2	10	5	33
1891	17	3	11	6	36
1894	19	3	12	6	40
1896	28	4	14	7	53
1900	36	5	23	8	72
1903	51	7	28	8	94
1907	71	10	34	8	123
1910	91	13	52	9	165
1913	163	10	74	9	256

Sources: See notes to Table G.1.

Table G.3. *Military expenditures,*
municipal government, 1885-1913,
current prices (million rubles)

1885	4
1888	5
1891	5
1894	5
1896	6
1900	8
1903	10
1907	12
1910	19
1913	30

Sources: See notes to table G.1.

Table G.4. *Local government expenditures, 1885-1913, 1913 prices (million rubles)*

	(1) Administrative expenditures	(2) Health and education	(3) Defense	(4) Total
1885	109	31	5	145
1888	110	41	6	157
1891	129	45	6	180
1894	160	51	6	217
1896	173	69	8	250
1900	193	91	10	294
1903	230	132	13	375
1907	222	135	13	370
1910	275	179	21	475
1913	357	256	30	643

NOTES TO APPENDIX G

1   George Yaney, *The Systematization of Russian Government* (Urbana: University of
     Illinois Press, 1973), Chap. 9: Wiatscheslaw Gribowski, *Das Staatsrecht des
     Russischen Reiches* (Tübingen: Mohr, 1913), Chap. 7.

2   For a listing of the non-*zemstvo guberniia*, see *Ezhegodnik ministerstva
     finansov*, section *zemskoe khoziaistvo*.

3   V. I. Kovalevski, ed., *Rossiia v Kontse XIX veka* (Petersburg: Ministerstvo
     finansov, 1900), p. 785.

4   See, e.g., the expenditure figures in the non-*zemstvo guberniia* in *Ezhegodnik
     ministerstva finansov (zemskoe khoziaistvo)*.

INVESTMENT AND CAPITAL STOCK IN LIVESTOCK

LIVESTOCK HERDS

Detailed information about livestock herds is available for the period 1885 to 1914. Data on livestock and animals in agriculture are to be found in various publications, the most important being the *Statisticheski ezhegodnik Rossii*, annual editions 1904 to 1914, section *kolichestvo sel'skikh domashniykh zhivotnykh* and *Sbornik statistiko-ekonomicheskikh svedenii po sel'skomu khoziaistvu Rossii i inostrannykh gosudarstv*, (Petrograd, 1915), vol. 7, same section title. Moreover, Vainshtein[1] has published a major study of prewar livestock statistics with an evaluation of their reliability and has made estimates of total livestock herds, including animals owned by urban dwellers, for the period 1911 to January 1, 1914.[2]

My estimates of the value of the stock of livestock herds in current and constant prices are calculated in the following manner: I begin by taking Vainshtein's estimate of the 1913 value of livestock herds including animals owned by city dwellers (some 2% of the total in 1913).[3] This figure is based upon Vainshtein's recalculation of the official Central Statistical Committee's figures for 1913 on the basis of comparisons with the detailed agricultural census of 1916.[4] In this manner, Vainshtein adjusts the official 1913 figures upward to obtain more complete coverage.

In his evaluation of prewar livestock statistics, Vainshtein concludes that, the official figures (gathered by veterinary authorities and by the Ministry of Interior) although they understate the total, are fairly reliable in capturing movements over time. Vainshtein does suggest that coverage may have improved after 1896, but the increase in herds recorded for 1896 does not appear to be seriously out of line, so no attempt at adjustment is made. Following Vainshtein, therefore, I proceed to calculate value indexes of livestock herds from the official Central Statistical Committee's figures. I do so by applying the average annual prices of horses, beef animals, swine, and sheep and goats to the corresponding number of such animals in each year. My price data on livestock are drawn from *Svod tovarnykh tsen* series, which reports prices for "large horned" animals (*krupny rogaty skot*) and for swine. Prices of horses are drawn from the *Sbornik svedenii po sel'skomu khoziaistvu* series. For the period 1885 to 1890, which the *Svod* series does not cover, indexes of average prices of Russian livestock exports from V. I. Pokrovsky, ed., *Sbornik svedenii po istorii i statistike vneshnei torgovli Rossii* (Table 3), are used to backcast each price series to 1885.

To obtain a consistent series for empire territory, important territorial adjustments are required for the period prior to 1900 and for the Asian provinces after 1900. From 1900 on, livestock herds for the entire empire are given, but prior to 1900, data are only available for the 50 European provinces and for the Polish provinces. In 1900, for example, the 50 European and Polish provinces accounted together for approximately 80% of all livestock holdings. What I have done is to use an index of the population share of Siberian and Asian provinces to Russian and Polish provinces to backcast Siberian and Asian province livestock holdings. Thus I assume that the share of the non-European provinces of livestock grew at the same rate as its population share. To provide some frame of reference for the magnitude of errors introduced by this assumption, I note that if one makes the extreme (and unrealistic) assumption that there were no livestock holdings in the Asian and Siberian provinces in 1885, then the annual growth in the stock (in constant prices) would have been higher by one-half of 1% per annum. At the other extreme, if one assumes that Siberian and Asian livestock herds grew at the same rate as in the European provinces, then the growth rate is reduced by about one-half of 1%. As this example demonstrates, it would be difficult to imagine an error of more than one-half of 1% per annum resulting from our territorial adjustment prior to 1900.

According to Asalkhanov's specialized study of Siberian livestock statistics,[5] the official figures for Siberia were grossly understated after 1900 because of changes in the taxation and reporting system. In fact, Asalkhanov concludes that the Asian livestock figures are not credible. Therefore, to estimate Asian stocks after 1900, I assume that the per capita livestock endowments of new settlers reported by Asalkhanov (horses: 63/100; large horned animals: 64/100; sheep and goats: 23/100) remained constant after 1900, and I apply these ratios to population growth to estimate the growth of Asian herds after 1900.

My figures are supplied in Table H-1. In part A I supply the adjusted figures on numbers of livestock and prices. In part B I supply calculated indexes of live-stock holdings in current and constant 1913 prices (columns 1 and 2). I then apply these indexes to Vainshtein's estimate of 1913 (end of year) livestock holdings, including nonagricultural animals, to obtain value series in current and constant 1913 prices (columns 3 and 4). I then divide column 3 by column 4 to obtain the implicit livestock price deflator, and in columns 6 and 7 I calculate livestock investment in current and constant prices by taking the annual increment (decrement) in the stock.

An alternate series for the value of livestock herds in constant 1913 prices has been estimated by Kahan for the period 1890 to 1913,[6] and the Kahan series is in marked disagreement with my own. According to my series (part B, column 4), the stock grew by a factor of 1.45 between 1890 and 1913; Kahan shows it to grow by a factor of 1.07. One of the difficulties in evaluating the merits of the two series is that Kahan does not describe his data sources and methodology, although he apparently rejects the veterinary department and Ministry of Interior figures as "extremely inaccurate,"[7] an opinion apparently not shared by Vainshtein. In the absence of information concerning the Kahan series, I am not in a position to comment on the likely sources of the discrepancies between his and my series.

There is, however, in my opinion evidence to suggest that Kahan's finding of virtually no growth of livestock is implausible. The first is that a zero growth of livestock over a twenty-three-year period suggests a decline in per capita livestock holdings in agriculture of over 40%. If a decline of such magnitude had indeed taken place, it is likely that it would have been noted by the contemporary literature. My own series suggests roughly constant per capita livestock holdings in agriculture, a finding that appears more plausible to me. The second piece of evidence is that feed grains grew between 1890 and 1913 by a factor of 1.6,[8] namely, at a faster rate than my livestock series. A static livestock herd therefore would suggest an increase in per annual consumption of almost 50% over the period 1890 to 1913, another implausible result in my opinion. Third, as Kahan indicates, the output of animal products was increasing between 1890 and 1913, another apparent contradiction to his finding of static livestock herds.

Table H.1. *Livestock herds, constant 1913 and current prices (middle of year), Russian Empire*

	A. Numbers of animals (millions)				B. Value in 1913 prices (million rubles)					
	(1) Horses	(2) Large horned animals	(3) Sheep and goats	(4) Swine	(1) Horses (78R)	(2) Large horned animals (138R)	(3) Sheep and goats (7R)	(4) Swine (30R)	Total	Index (1913 = 100)
1885	22.8	31.8	60.9	11.3	1778	4388	426	339	6931	63.0
1886	22.5	32.1	61.8	11.2	1755	4430	433	336	6954	63.2
1887	22.2	32.3	63.1	11.1	1732	4457	441	333	6963	63.3
1888	26.1	34.4	65.8	11.6	2036	4747	461	348	7592	69.0
1889	26.3	34.9	63.0	11.6	2051	4816	441	348	7656	69.6
1890	26.4	35.5	60.4	11.6	2059	4899	423	348	7727	70.2
1891	23.9	35.2	60.6	10.7	1864	4858	424	321	7467	67.9
1892	23.4	34.2	57.3	10.7	1825	4720	401	321	7267	66.1
1893	23.6	34.4	58.4	10.9	1841	4747	409	327	7324	66.6
1894	23.7	34.8	59.2	11.1	1849	4802	414	333	7398	67.2
1895	24.2	35.6	69.6	16.1	1888	4913	487	483	7771	70.6
1896	26.2	41.0	67.0	15.6	2044	5658	469	468	8639	78.5
1897	26.3	42.3	68.3	14.5	2051	5837	478	435	8801	80.0
1898	26.7	42.2	67.5	14.0	2083	5824	473	420	8800	80.0
1899	27.5	43.2	69.5	14.3	2145	5962	487	429	9023	82.0
1900	27.7	44.3	62.0	14.6	2161	6113	434	438	9146	83.1
1901	28.1	42.5	71.0	14.2	2192	5865	497	426	8980	81.6
1902	28.9	43.5	72.3	13.8	2254	6003	506	414	9177	83.4
1903	29.0	43.5	70.0	13.7	2262	6003	490	411	9166	83.3
1904	30.5	41.8	65.4	13.7	2379	5768	458	411	9016	81.9
1905	30.0	46.2	65.7	13.0	2340	6376	460	390	9566	86.9
1906	30.3	44.4	62.6	12.7	2363	6127	438	381	9309	84.6
1907	29.3	43.5	59.5	12.3	2285	6003	417	369	9074	82.5
1908	29.1	43.3	58.5	12.4	2270	5975	410	372	9027	82.0
1909	33.2	49.9	78.7	12.7	2590	6886	551	381	10408	94.6
1910	34.3	52.7	80.2	13.4	2675	7273	561	402	10911	99.2
1911	35.8	53.2	79.3	14.1	2792	7342	555	423	11112	101.0
1912	34.4	50.5	75.1	13.5	2683	6969	526	405	10763	97.8
1913	35.1	53.0	75.0	14.2	2738	7314	525	426	11003	100.0
1914	36.2	53.7	73.3	14.2	2824	7411	513	426	11174	101.6

C. Value in current prices (million rubles)

	(1) Horses	(2) Large horned animals	(3) Sheep and goats	(4) Swine	Total	Index (1913 = 100)	D. Value of stock Vainshtein base (1) Current prices	(2) 1913 prices	E. Livestock investment (ΔI) (1)[a] Current prices	(2) 1913 prices
1885	752	2926	244	113	4035	36.7	2568	4408	8	14
1886	945	2664	247	134	3990	36.3	2540	4422	4	7
1887	1066	2649	252	122	4089	37.2	2603	4429	235	399
1888	1148	2821	263	151	4383	39.8	2785	4828	24	42
1889	1210	3211	252	197	4870	44.3	3099	4870	27	42
1890	1003	3266	242	186	4697	42.7	2988	4912	-98	-161
1891	813	2746	182	161	3902	35.5	2844	4751	-76	-126
1892	796	2804	172	182	3954	35.9	2512	4625	19	35
1893	850	3130	234	218	4432	40.3	2820	4660	26	42
1894	877	3097	236	233	4443	40.4	2827	4702	143	238
1895	910	3133	278	306	4627	42.1	2946	4940	331	553
1896	996	3444	268	281	4989	45.3	3170	5493	61	105
1897	1052	3469	273	247	5041	45.8	3205	5598	0	0
1898	1068	3587	270	294	5219	47.4	3317	5598	83	140
1899	1320	3672	278	329	5599	50.9	3561	5738	43	70
1900	1302	3943	248	350	5843	53.1	3715	5808	-63	-98
1901	1265	3868	284	327	5744	52.2	3652	5710	81	126
1902	1416	4046	289	345	6096	55.4	3876	5836	-5	-7
1903	1508	3959	280	356	6103	55.5	3883	5829	-66	-98
1904	1586	3929	262	343	6120	55.6	3890	5731	237	349
1905	1590	4666	263	351	6870	62.4	4366	6080	-116	-161
1906	1636	4351	250	381	6618	60.2	4212	5919	-104	-147
1907	1612	4829	298	406	7145	64.9	4541	5772	-27	-34
1908	1601	5326	351	422	7700	70.0	4898	5738	749	881
1909	1826	6337	394	445	9002	81.8	5724	6619	280	322
1910	2024	6535	481	457	9497	86.3	6038	6941	109	125
1911	2041	6384	476	409	9310	84.6	5920	7066	-187	-223
1912	2442	6717	451	378	9988	90.8	6353	6843	143	154
1913	2738	7728	525	426	11003	100.0	6997	6997	112	112
1914	2824	7411	513	426	11174	101.6	7109	7109	112	112

[a] Calculated by inflating E2 with implicit livestock price index calculated from D.

NOTES TO APPENDIX H

1 A. L. Vainshtein, "Iz istorii predrevoliutsionnoi statistiki zhivotnovodstva," *Ocherki po istorii statistiki SSSR*, (Moscow: Gosstatizdat, 1960), 3:86-115.

2 A. L. Vainshtein, *Narodnoe bogatstvo i narodnokhoziaistvennoe nakoplenie predrevoliutsionnoi Rossii* (Moscow: Gosstatizdat, 1960), pp. 185-9.

3 Vainshtein, *Narodnoe bogatstvo*, p. 187.

4 *Balans narodnogo khoziaistva Soiuza SSSR, 1923-24* (Moscow: N.P. 1926), p. 38. Cited by Vainshtein, *Narodnoe bogatstvo*, p. 185.

5 I. A. Asalkhanov, *Sel'skoe khoziaistvo Sibiri kontsa XIX de nachala XX v.* (Novosibirsk: Nauka, Sibirskoe otdelenie, 1975), pp. 190-5.

6 Arcadius Kahan, "Capital Formation During the Period of Early Industrialization in Russia, 1890-1913," *Cambridge Economic History of Europe*, vol. 7 pt. 2 (Cambridge University Press), p. 300.

7 Kahan, "Capital Formation," p. 281.

8 Production figures on feed grains are drawn from the sources given in Table D.1.

INVESTMENT IN AGRICULTURAL AND INDUSTRIAL EQUIPMENT

EQUIPMENT INVESTMENT IN CURRENT PRICES

In this appendix I discuss my estimation of investment in agricultural and non-agricultural equipment. I begin by calculating the sum of domestic machinery production and machinery imports in current prices, which, assuming this equipment does not go into inventories or as an intermediate input into final machinery, will yield the sum of gross annual investment in durable equipment. I then break this figure down into agricultural and nonagricultural equipment using independent studies of agricultural investment. From this information on agricultural and nonagricultural investment in equipment, I compile indexes in current and constant 1913 prices using agricultural and nonagricultural equipment price deflators. These indexes are applied to Vainshtein's estimates of 1913 investment in agricultural and nonagricultural equipment to obtain value series of net equipment investment in current and constant 1913 prices. These calculations are shown in Table I.1. The equipment estimates in constant 1913 prices are then contrasted with Kahan's estimates of net equipment investment for the period 1890 to 1913, derived from his net capital stock series.

It is difficult to evaluate the reliability of the current price investment series (panel A) as this will depend upon the reliability of the series on domestic equipment production and imports. The data on machinery imports should be reasonably reliable. The data on domestic machinery production, however, should be less trustworthy, primarily because reliable industrial production statistics were not available before the Varzar studies for 1900 and 1908.[1] The production series are those cited by Strumilin[2] and are based primarily on the V. E. Varzar and L. B. Kafengauz studies of factory production in Russia.[3] There is the further problem that the cited series are principally for factory production and likely omit some machinery produced in small handicraft shops. Although such production was not large as a percent of the total,[4] its omission nevertheless could distort the series. Moreover, the cited series likely include some intermediate production in addition to final capital equipment. The series to 1897 is for machinery and foundry production; the 1898 to 1913 series is for metalworking. Later comparison with Vainshtein's figures for 1913 suggests substantial double counting (about 32%) in the production series, but if the ratio of intermediate to final equipment production remained fairly steady, the intertemporal index would still be reasonably accurate. Moreover, the intertemporal index will approximate an index of *gross* investment in equipment. As the ratio of net to gross investment likely fell during this period, a gross series should slightly overstate the rise of the net series. Finally, the series prior to 1897 are for the 50 European provinces; thus one must

271

assume that the production indexes for these provinces are indicative of the empire as a whole. This last assumption should not introduce large errors into the analysis as machinery production was concentrated in European Russia. The equipment series in current prices is supplied in Table I.1, panel A. Sources are described in the notes to the table.

EQUIPMENT PRICE DEFLATORS

As one might expect, it is difficult to obtain sufficient information on equipment prices to construct reliable equipment price deflators. However, this is a problem that all historical investment series must face. The equipment price deflators used in this study represent a pragmatic blend of equipment prices and material inputs into equipment, aggregated using rough weights. The raw equipment price and input price data are supplied in panel B of Table I.1 along with other price series needed for the other appendixes. The aggregate nonagricultural and agricultural equipment price deflators are given in panel C; and the constant 1913 price investment indexes are calculated in panel D.

Unfortunately, the choice of weights has an important effect on the equipment price deflators. The wage series and most individual equipment series (locomotives, sickles and scythes, steam engines) exhibit a slight rising (but cyclical) trend over the period, but the material input prices, such as iron and steel, exhibit a declining trend. This is also true of tractor (locomobile) prices, an important ingredient in the agricultural equipment deflator. The net result is that both agricultural and industrial equipment deflators fail to reveal substantive long-term price increases with the assigned weights. The industrial price weights are constructed by first calculating the proportion of railroad equipment in the total from Vainshtein[5] (25% in 1909-13) and then assigning for railroad equipment internal weights of .5 for locomotives, .25 for steel rails, and .25 for the wage index of railroad mechanics. For the remaining 75%, the unweighted average of the railroad mechanics and heavy industry wage indexes are assigned an internal weight of .5. Foreign trade weights[6] are then used to assign internal weights to iron, steam engines, and locomobiles for the remaining 50%.

Although there is more information concerning the value distribution of agricultural investment,[7] there is less long-term information on agricultural equipment prices. Two types of equipment for which price information is available (sickles and scythes, locomobiles) were used exclusively or extensively in agriculture. Information on plough prices (available only back to 1898) reveals quite erratic price movements, which caused me to doubt the reliability of the plough price series, and I rejected it for use in the deflators despite the importance of ploughs in the agricultural equipment series. I had to assign relatively arbitrary weights to the usable price series. They are .3 for the heavy industry wage index, .2 for iron prices, .2 for sickles and scythes, .2 for locomobiles, and .1 for steam engines. The results of this weighting scheme are given in column 2 of panel C.

I must admit that a large margin of error may be incorporated in these equipment price deflators, but I should also note that the margin of error is large in

most historical investment studies. Capital equipment is, by its nature, a hetero-
geneous product, more subject to technological improvements than other commodities.
Prices per unit of weight such as used here will likely fail to capture quality
improvements; few prices are available anyway, and input prices will also fail to
capture price movements adjusted for quality. Nevertheless, these equipment
deflators are likely as reliable as those used for the historical series of other
countries,[8] and my finding that equipment prices grew more slowly than the general
price level is what one would expect for this historical period.[9]

EQUIPMENT IN CURRENT AND CONSTANT PRICES, VAINSHTEIN BASE
In panel D, equipment investment in constant 1913 prices and current prices is
given. These series are calculated by applying the indexes from panel A, columns 4
and 5, to Vainshtein's[10] estimates of 1913 equipment investment. As a comparison of
panel D and panel A shows, Vainshtein's 1913 estimate (454 million rubles) is well
below the Strumilin-Varzar-Kafengauz production (plus imports) figure (601 million
rubles). This discrepancy is most likely due to the inclusion of intermediate
production in the later figures. As I noted above, this will cause intertemporal
distortions only if the intermediate-final equipment mix changed dramatically over
time.

COMPARISON WITH KAHAN'S ESTIMATES OF NET INVESTMENT IN EQUIPMENT
Arcadius Kahan has estimated the net capital stock in agricultural and industrial
(excluding railroads) equipment for the period 1890 to 1913, and one can calculate
annual net investment in equipment from his series. The Kahan capital stock and
implied net investment series are supplied in Table I.2, and they are stated in
constant 1913 prices as is my series in Table I.1.

       Kahan's series differs from my own in the following respects: First, it is
derived from net capital stock series, and thus should better approximate the growth
of net investment than my own, which theoretically should reflect the movement of
gross investment. Second, the Kahan series for industry does not include railroad
equipment, whereas my series does. Third, I have no information on the equipment
price deflators used by Kahan, only his end results in 1913 prices; so differences
between the two series could easily be the consequence of differences in price
deflators.

       It is difficult to evaluate the Kahan series as Kahan's discussion of his
estimates is quite terse, and little information is supplied on methodology and
sources. I believe that the industrial equipment series is based upon insured
values of industrial equipment deflated by relevant price indexes. I have no
information on how the agricultural equipment series is derived.

       In comparing my series with those of Kahan, several prominent differences can
be observed. The first is that his industrial equipment series is subject to
greater annual fluctuations than my own, which shows (perhaps unrealistically) a
smooth growth of equipment investment. On the other hand, Kahan's series reveals
enormous annual fluctuations and six years of net disinvestment. In 1903 and 1906,

according to Kahan, net disinvestment in industrial equipment was 12% and 13% of net
industrial equipment capital stock. Insofar as gross investment was positive during
these two years (judging from my data on domestic production and machinery imports),
this result implies unrealistically high annual depreciation well above 13% of net
capital stock, likely in the range of one-fourth of net capital. Such depreciation
rates appear too high to me; so I would argue that the Kahan estimates overstate the
degree of annual fluctuation of the net industrial equipment capital stock. My own
series may understate the true degree of annual fluctuations, but it would seem that
at least the machinery import data should reflect cyclical fluctuations. The second
major discrepancy is the substantial net disinvestment indicated by the Kahan series
between 1903 and 1907 (in industry), whereas my series shows only modest slowdowns
in the rate of annual investment during this period. Third, Kahan's absolute values
of investment in agricultural equipment fall well below those used in this study,
which are adapted directly from the 1913 Vainshtein estimate. One cannot make
direct comparisons of the absolute values of the Kahan and Vainshtein industrial
equipment investment figures, as the Kahan figures omit railroad equipment.
Nevertheless, there is evidence that the two are at least broadly compatible.[11]

    The disagreement between my industrial investment series between 1903 and 1907
and that of Kahan is so substantial that it does not merit further comment. The
most crucial question, however, is whether the long-term growth rates of equipment
investment calculated by Kahan support or contradict the growth rates suggested in
Table I.1. The best way to establish this (in view of the substantial annual
fluctuations in the Kahan data) is to compare three-year moving averages calculated
from the two series. If this is done, the derived annual growth rates for the
period 1891-93 to 1911-13 are as follows:

Annual growth rates of investment (%)

	Industrial equipment	Agricultural equipment
Kahan	11%	13%
Gregory	8%	9%

    As I noted above, the industrial equipment series are not directly comparable
because of Kahan's omission of railroad equipment. As I show in Appendix L, the
annual growth of investment in railroad equipment during this period was in the
neighborhood of 8% per annum, and its inclusion would reduce Kahan's growth figure
to 9%-10% per annum. Thus there is broad agreement between my series and that of
Kahan on the matter of industrial equipment, namely, industrial investment in
equipment grew at a rapid rate (between 8% and 10% per annum). The remaining
discrepancy between my figure and that of Kahan is most likely traceable to different industrial equipment price deflators.

    There is regrettably less agreement between my series on investment in agricultural equipment and that of Kahan. The Kahan series indicates an annual rate of growth 44% above my own. As I know little about Kahan's methodology and sources, I cannot evaluate these discrepancies, nor can I argue that one series is "better" than another. I have chosen to use my own series in this study for two reasons: The first is that I am familiar with the strengths and weaknesses of my series. The second is that the Kahan growth rate strikes me as being too high, given the rate of growth of agricultural production. In any case, the choice of the Kahan or Gregory series for agriculture is not all that crucial insofar as we are talking about one-half of 1% of the national income.

Table I.1. Investment in equipment, selected prices and equipment deflators, Russian empire (million rubles)

A. Investment in equipment, current prices

	(1) Domestic production of machinery, factory and handicraft	(2) Imports of machinery	(3) Total	(4) Agricultural equipment a) Million rubles	(4) b) 1913 = 100	(5) Nonagricultural equipment a) Million rubles	(5) b) 1913 = 100
1885	47	16	63	9	7.6	54	11.2
1886	54	18	72	10	8.5	62	12.8
1887	55	17	72	10	8.5	62	12.8
1888	60	23	83	12	10.2	72	14.9
1889	63	27	90	9	7.6	81	16.8
1890	59	25	84	10	8.5	75	15.5
1891	57	26	83	9	7.6	75	15.5
1892	56	28	84	11	9.3	74	15.3
1893	83	33	116	13	11.0	103	21.3
1894	92	52	144	19	16.1	125	25.9
1895	98	59	157	20	17.0	137	28.4
1896	148	72	220	21	17.8	199	41.2
1897	174	61	235	19	16.0	216	44.7
1898	202	86	288	23	19.5	265	54.9
1899	198	105	303	26	22.0	277	57.3
1900	191	83	274	28	23.7	246	50.9
1901	218	63	281	43	36.4	238	49.3
1902	202	58	260	37	31.4	223	46.2
1903	219	70	289	54	45.8	235	48.9
1904	230	69	299	22	44.1	247	51.1
1905	249	66	315	62	52.5	253	52.3
1906	231	72	303	52	44.1	251	52.0
1907	233	80	313	56	47.5	257	53.2
1908	214	92	306	68	57.6	238	49.3
1909	225	108	333	87	73.7	246	50.9
1910	252	126	378	97	82.2	281	58.2
1911	271	160	431	117	99.2	314	65.0
1912	317	163	480	124	105.1	356	73.7
1913	418	183	601	118	100.0	483	100.0

B. Price index for deflation of equipment and other prices (1913 = 100)

	(1) Wage index: mechanic and maintenance personnel railroad	(2) Locomotives, cost/ton	(3) Price of iron	(4) Price of sickles and scythes/pud	(6) Price of locomotives/pud	(7) Portland cement
1885	77	85	131	75	116	117
1886	83	85	134	78	143	118
1887	85	86	136	86	126	118
1888	85	105	141	87	113	122
1889	85	105	142	94	113	122
1890	82	118	147	94	95	119
1891	85	118	147	88	105	121
1892	84	112	147	90	117	125
1893	84	107	147	84	110	122
1894	90	108	147	80	109	124
1895	87	108	139	81	121	109
1896	85	109	137	85	135	108
1897	86	107	141	76	117	120
1898	84	107	140	78	106	124
1899	85	107	139	75	97	132
1900	86	104	139	81	97	116
1901	87	105	133	94	81	116
1902	91	106	136	81	89	128
1903	91	107	126	83	101	169
1904	93	105	118	77	92	123
1905	87	103	114	77	96	145
1906	98	104	93	82	95	119
1907	98	105	113	89	126	121
1908	92	104	100	95	112	112
1909	98	104	96	92	120	102
1910	97	101	91	101	116	100
1911	98	108	92	93	110	100
1912	101	113	95	79	103	100
1913	100	100	100	100	100	100

Table I.1 (cont.)

B. Cont.

	(8) Steam engines/ pud	(9) Hard coal	(10) Oil	(11) Anthracite	(12) Wholesale price index (Bobrov)	(13) Wage index, heavy industry (Varzar)	(14) Steel rails/ pud
1885	69	80	45	86	69	75.8	126
1886	83	80	40	86	67	75.8	206
1887	73	73	37	86	68	75.8	152
1888	90	73	34	100	77	79.2	120
1889	91	73	34	107	83	73.6	148
1890	102	73	40	93	80	72.3	212
1891	101	67	40	71	75	73.6	190
1892	111	67	34	64	69	73.2	136
1893	92	67	32	64	74	76.6	120
1894	85	73	32	71	69	73.2	226
1895	87	67	42	71	71	71.9	130
1896	83	60	34	71	72	71.9	140
1897	72	60	42	71	74	71.9	99
1898	81	60	45	71	78	74.0	82
1899	83	73	50	71	81	74.5	89
1900	84	87	58	64	84	76.6	101
1901	115	93	61	64	80	77.9	85
1902	86	80	53	64	76	78.3	89
1903	92	73	45	64	77	82.1	91
1904	81	73	45	71	80	81.3	91
1905	98	80	58	79	82	77.9	90
1906	95	87	76	79	89	79.6	91
1907	98	87	82	93	97	99.2	107
1908	99	87	87	79	93	93.2	78
1909	102	87	76	79	91	89.4	110
1910	103	87	71	100	92	90.2	95
1911	108	80	63	100	95	94.9	82
1912	105	100	97	100	98	96.6	82
1913	100	100	100	100	100	100.0	100

C. Equipment price deflators   D. Equipment in current and 1913 prices, Vainshtein 1913 base

	C. Equipment price deflators		D. (1) Agricultural equipment		(2) Nonagricultural equipment		(3) Total	
	(1) Nonagricultural	(2) Agricultural	a) Current prices	b) 1913 prices	a) Current prices	b) 1913 prices	a) Current prices	b) 1913 prices
1885	934.4	93.9	6	6	43	46	49	52
1886	103.7	102.1	6	6	49	47	55	53
1887	97.8	99.7	6	6	49	50	55	56
1888	99.8	100.9	9	9	57	57	64	66
1889	100.9	101.1	6	6	64	63	70	69
1890	105.2	99.0	6	6	59	56	65	62
1891	106.0	100.3	5	5	59	56	64	61
1892	104.3	103.8	7	7	58	56	64	63
1893	100.1	100.5	8	8	81	81	89	89
1894	106.4	97.6	12	12	99	93	111	105
1895	100.3	98.5	12	12	108	108	120	120
1896	101.5	101.3	13	13	157	155	170	183
1897	95.8	95.6	12	13	170	178	182	191
1898	94.3	95.1	14	15	209	222	223	237
1899	94.3	93.0	16	17	218	231	234	248
1900	95.3	94.9	17	18	194	204	213	222
1901	96.0	96.5	27	28	188	196	215	224
1902	95.2	93.0	23	25	176	185	199	210
1903	97.2	95.8	33	35	186	191	219	226
1904	93.7	89.8	32	36	195	208	227	244
1905	93.6	90.6	38	42	199	213	237	255
1906	93.6	87.5	32	37	198	211	230	248
1907	105.1	105.1	35	33	203	193	238	226
1908	97.3	99.2	42	42	188	193	230	235
1909	100.9	98.5	54	55	194	192	248	247
1910	98.5	98.9	60	61	222	225	282	286
1911	99.8	98.3	72	73	248	248	320	321
1912	100.6	95.0	77	81	281	279	358	360
1913	100.0	100.0	73	73	381	381	454	454

Table I.1 (cont.)

Sources: Panel A, column 1: Domestic production of machinery in millions of credit
rubles. This data is taken directly from S. G. Strumilin, *Ocherki ekonomicheskoi
istorii Rossii i SSSR* (Moscow: Nauka, 1966), pp. 442, 445, 449, 453. The pre-1897
figures are for the 50 European provinces only; so the 1913 ratio of heavy
industrial output of the 50 provinces to empire production from M. E. Falkus,
"Russia's National Income, 1913: A Revaluation," *Economica*, 62 N.S. 35, No. 137
(February 1968):62, was used to convert to empire territory.
     Column 2: Imports of machinery in millions of credit rubles: These figures
are drawn from V. I. Pokrovsky, *Sbornik svedenii po istorii i statistike vneshnei
torgovli Rossii*, Tom I (Petersburg: Departament tamozhennykh sborov, 1902), p. 133;
Statisticheski ezhegodnik Rossii, annual editions 1904 to 1914, section *vneshniaia
torgovlia po gruppam i vazhnym predmetam privozam, Ezhegodnik Ministerstva finansov*
1905, section *vneshniaia torgovlia;* and *Bulletin Russe de statistique financiere et
de legislation*, 1904, vol. 1, p. 76.
     Columns 4 and 5: Domestic production of agricultural machinery, handicraft
and factory production: Estimates for the period prior to 1900 are from Arnold
Bonwetsch, *Der Handel mit Landwirtschaftlichen Maschinen und Geräten in Russland*
(Berlin: Ebering, 1921), pp. 18, 21, 28, 31, 50, and from L. B. Kafengauz, *Razvitie
russkago sel'skokhoziaistvennago mashinostroeniia* (Kharkov: Berkman, 1910), p. 29;
and Ia. Ia. Polferov, *Sel'skokhoziaistvennyia mashiny i orudiia, ikh proizvodstvo i
vvoz v Rossii* (Petrograd: Ministerstvo Finansov, 1914), p. 5.
     These production figures must be regarded as approximative and involve
interpolations between benchmark observations for the years 1885 and 1887. Also,
the figures on handicraft production of agricultural equipment are quite rough. The
period 1900 to 1906 must also be interpolated, as Bonwetsch does not provide figures
for this period. This is done by using the aggregate index of machinery production.
The import data are more exact and are taken from Pokrovsky, *Sbornik*, p. 97A;
Departament zemledeliia, *Sel'skokhoziaistvenny promysel v Rossii* (Petrograd:
Golike, 1914), p. 13; and *Entwurf des Reichsbudgets für das Jahr 1913* (Petersburg:
Kaiserliche Akademie der Wissenschaften, 1913), 2:43.
     Panel B, Column 1: Wage index, annual earnings of mechanics and maintenance
personnel, full-time employees, state and private railroads. This series is from
the annual editions of *Statisticheski sbornik Ministerstva putei soobshcheniia*,
section 12.
     Column 2: This index is taken directly from the *Statisticheski sbornik
Ministerstva putei soobshcheniia* series for the period 1896 to 1913 from section 3
poddvizhny sostav. This figure is the annual inventory value of the stock of
locomotives owned by the state and private railroads divided by their weight in
tons. Although the locomotives are valued at acquisition cost (*pervonachal'naia
stoimost'*), the index will be a fairly close approximation of the intertemporal
movements in price per ton as the following formula indicates:

$$\frac{Pi}{Po} = \frac{Vi}{Vo} + \frac{\Delta P \Delta Q^2}{P(Q_o^2 + Q_o\Delta Q)}$$

where *Pi* denotes the price per ton in year *i*, *ΔP* denotes the change in price between
year *i* and year *o*, *Vi* denotes the inventory value (acquisition cost) per ton in year
i, *Qo* denotes the total weight in the base year, and *ΔQ* denotes the change in weight
between year *i* and year *o*.
     The second term denotes the distortion resulting from the use of acquisition
costs, which will be small if the change in the stock is small relative to the total
stock and if price changes were small, which is what one would expect. For the
period prior to 1896, the price per ton of imported locomotives including the tariff
per ton (from Pokrovsky, *Sbornik*, pp. 97, 268) is used.
     Column 3: The price of iron (rubles per pud) is taken from the *Svod tovarnykh
tsen* series for the period 1895 to 1913 (Petersburg prices). For the period 1885 to
1895, the price series is taken from M. N. Sobolev, *Tamozhennaia politika Rossii vo
vtoroi polovine XIX veka*, Vol. 2 (Tomsk: Tipografiia sibirskoe tovarichestvo
pechatnago dela, 1911), statistical appendix.
     Column 4: The price series for scythes and sickles (per pud) is the average
price per pud paid for imported sickles and scythes plus the import tariff per pud.
This information is from Pokrovsky, *Sbornik*, p. 96b, Table 45, where the portion of
the tariff due in gold rubles is converted into credit rubles at the prevailing rate

of exchange. The post-1900 figures are from *Ezhegodnik ministerstva finansov*, annual editions 1905 to 1911, section *vneshniaia torgovlia* and from *Sbornik statistiko-ekonomicheskikh svedenii po sel'skomu khoziaistvu Rossii i inostrannykh gosudarstv*, vol. 7 (Petrograd: Ministerstvo zemledeliia, 1915), section *vneshniaia torgovlia*; and from Kafengauz, *Razvitie*, p. 44, insert. Tariff data for this period is from Ministerstvo torgovli i promyshlennost', *Tamozhennye tarify po evropeiskoi torgovle* (Petersburg: Kirshbaum, 1913), section 160, and from Kafengauz, *Razvitie*, p. 35.

   Column 5: Same sources as column 4. Prices per pud plus tariff per pud.
   Column 6: Foreign trade price per pud of *lokomobili* for pulling harvesters and mechanized ploughs plus tariff per pud. For the period 1885 to 1892, an index of general *lokomobili* prices is used. All data are from *Obzor vneshnei torgovli Rossii po evropeiskoi i aziatskoi granitzam za g.* (Petersburg: Departament tamozhennykh sborov, 1885 to 1914, annual editions.
   Column 7: Price of Portland cement per ton: This series is drawn from several sources as the *Svod tovarnykh tsen* series reports cement prices only for the period 1890 to 1898. For the period 1885 to 1890, I use Sobolev's (*Tamozhenniaia*, statistical appendix) series on cement prices. For the period 1899 to 1913, I construct a series of average prices paid per ton plus import tariffs per ton on Portland cement. These prices come from *Obzor vneshnei torgovli Rossii po evropeiskoi i aziatskoi granitzam* series.
   Column 8: Price of imported steam engines per pud plus average tariff per pud from *Obzor vneshnei torgovli* series.
   Columns 9-11: Prices of fuels paid by the state and private railroads: These prices are given in the *Statisticheski sbornik ministerstva putei soobshcheniia* series, annual edition, Table 5.
   Column 12: Wholesale price index: This is the wholesale price index compiled by C. P. Bobrov from 62 commodities cited in the *Svod tovarnykh tsen* series. Weights are constructed by Bobrov from shipments data by rail and water. The Bobrov index is cited in S. G. Strumilin, *Ocherki ekonomicheskoi istorii Rossii i SSSR* (Moscow: Nauka, 1966), p. 89.
   Column 13: Average annual wages, workers in heavy industry. This series is cited for the years 1887, 1892, 1897, 1902-9 by A. F. Iakovlev, *Ekonomicheskie krizisy v Rossii* (Moscow: Gosizpolit., 1955), p. 326. The series, compiled by V. E. Varzar, was unpublished but preserved in the archives of the Academy of Sciences, USSR. The missing years are interpolated using Strumilin's index of average annual earnings of factory workers, cited in Appendix F.
   Column 14: Average price of imported steel rails per pud plus average tariff per pud from *Obzor vneshnei torgovli* series.
   Panel C: See text for sources.

Table I.2. *Equipment capital stock and investment, Russian Empire, 1890-1913, Kahan estimates, 1913 prices, end of year (million rubles)*

	(1) Industry			(2) Agriculture		
	a) Net capital stock	b) Net investment	c) Net investment 3-year moving average	a) Net capital stock	b) Net investment	c) Net investment 3-year moving average
1890	598			1430		
1891	648	50		1460	30	
1892	676	28	18	1465	5	17
1893	653	-23	41	1482	17	16
1894	772	119	64	1508	26	26
1895	869	97	78	1542	34	31
1896	886	17	69	1575	33	33
1897	979	93	52	1606	31	30
1898	1026	47	57	1633	27	30
1899	1058	32	37	1666	33	31
1900	1091	33	78	1700	34	34
1901	1259	168	120	1734	34	36
1902	1417	158	58	1775	41	41
1903	1265	-152	-16	1822	47	49
1904	1210	-55	-34	1882	60	51
1905	1314	104	-33	1927	45	48
1906	1166	-148	-21	1966	39	40
1907	1138	-28	-10	2003	37	40
1908	1283	145	73	2047	44	51
1909	1385	102	70	2118	71	65
1910	1348	-37	67	2199	81	84
1911	1504	156	97	2298	99	92
1912	1675	171	146	2395	97	100
1913	1785	110		2498	103	

Source: Arcadius Kahan, "Capital Formation During the Period of Early Industrialization in Russia, 1890-1913," *Cambridge Economic History of Europe,* Vol. VII (Cambridge: Cambridge University Press, 1978), 300, 302.

NOTES TO APPENDIX I

1   L. Rosovsky, "Perepisi russkoi promyshlennosti 1900 i 1908," Akademiia nauk
     SSSR, *Ocherki po istorii statistiki SSSR, Sbornik III* (Moscow: Gosstatizdat,
     1960), pp. 58-85.

2   S. G. Strumilin, *Ocherki ekonomicheskoi istorii Rossii i SSSR* (Moscow: Nauka,
     1966), pp. 442-53.

3   Strumilin cites the Varzar-Kafengauz index of industrial production in
     Ocherki, appendix 2.

4   Value added of non-census industries of total machinery production was
     approximately 6% in 1912.   On this, see Paul Gregory, "Socialist
     Industrialization Patterns," Ph.D. diss., Harvard University, 1969, appendix
     2.A.

5   A. L. Vainshtein, *Narodnoe bogatstvo i narodnokhoziaistvennoe nakoplenie
     predrevoliutsionnoi Rossii* (Moscow: Gosstatizdat, 1960).

6   From *Obzor vneshnei torgovli* series.

7   L. B. Kafengauz, *Razvitie russkago sel'skokhoziaistvennago mashinostroeniia*
     (Kharkov: Berkman, 1910); Ia. Ia. Polferov, *Sel'skokhoziaistvennyia mashiny i
     orudiia, ikh proizvodstvo i vvoz v Rossii* (Petrograd: Ministerstvo finansov,
     1914).

8   See, e.g., Lance Davis, Richard Easterlin, and William Parker, *American
     Economic Growth* (New York: Harper and Row, 1972), Chap. 2.

9   The phenomenon of index number relativity suggests that the prices of high
     technology (rapidly growing) products *decline* relative to the economy-wide
     average in the course of economic growth.   This is exactly what is being
     observed here.   For a discussion of index number relativity, see Alexander
     Gerschenkron, "The Soviet Indices of Industrial Production," *Review of
     Economics and Statistics* 29, no. 4 (November 1947):217-26.

10   Vainshtein, *Narodnoe bogatstvo*, pp. 368-9.

11   Vainshtein, *Narodnoe bogatstvo*, pp. 368-9, 420, shows the railroad share of
     total equipment investment to be 25% for the period 1911-13.

NET CAPITAL STOCK AND NET INVESTMENT IN INDUSTRIAL, AGRICULTURAL,
AND RESIDENTIAL URBAN STRUCTURES

METHODOLOGICAL PROBLEMS AND DATA SOURCES

My estimates of net capital and net investment in structures are based upon three
separate studies; Kahan's estimates of capital stock in structures for the period
1890-1913, upon Vainshtein's estimates of industrial, urban residential, and rural
structures for the period 1911 to January 1914, and our independent study of
agricultural structures between 1883 and 1914.[1] The point of departure for these
estimates of capital in structures is the insured values of agricultural and
industrial structures (adjusted for coverage). The use of insured values should
yield a net stock series (or an approximation thereof), as, at least in the long
run, the insured value should reflect the market value of the existing net stock.
The net stock series in current market prices are then deflated by a construction
cost price index to yield series in constant prices. Net investment is then
calculated by taking first differences.

Kahan's study does provide real net capital stock estimates of the three
relevant series (industry, agriculture, and urban residential structures) from 1890
to 1913; so it would seem that it would only be necessary to extend his series back
to 1885 to obtain net stock and investment figures for the entire period. In this
study, I employ the Kahan estimates only in specific instances. I do use his index
of the net stock of industrial structures without alteration, but I apply this index
to Vainshtein's ruble estimate of 1914 net stock in industrial structures, which is
higher than Kahan's own (end of 1913) figure by a factor of 1.6. According to
Kahan's own description of his work, the industrial structures series is based upon
insurance data, and Kahan appears to have more confidence in his industry series
than in his other series.[2] There is serious disagreement between Kahan and
Vainshtein concerning the net increment to the stock of industrial structures in
1913 and between 1911 and 1913 (Vainshtein estimates the former at 248 million
rubles, Kahan at 129 million rubles); so I present the net investment series in two
variants, one using the higher Vainshtein, the other the lower Kahan 1913 net
investment figure. Both series use Kahan's net investment index to backcast to
1885. It follows that the "Vainshtein base" net investment series will not be
consistent with the net capital stock series.[3]

Kahan's series on net capital stock in urban residential structures and the
net increments thereof are used in this study for the period 1890 to 1910. As
Kahan's net stock series coincides closely with urban population growth up to 1900,
I use the rate of growth of urban population[4] to backcast the Kahan net stock index
back to 1885. Kahan's and Vainshtein's figures are close for 1910, but for the
period 1910 to the beginning of 1914, Kahan's estimates are in serious disagreement

with those of Vainshtein: Vainshtein estimates an increase in the net stock of approximately 25%, whereas Kahan obtains a decline in the stock of 6%. I accept the Vainshtein figures for 1910 to 1914 as more realistic, for I see no evidence pointing to a decline in the real stock of urban housing during this period - a time of rising urban population and rising real income.[5] In fact, a 6% decline in the stock suggests a decline in the per capita stock of urban housing of 14%, and I find such a decline implausible.

I do not use Kahan's estimates of the net stock of rural structures, for his series is apparently based upon the assumption that this stock grows at the same rate the number of peasant households. Kahan's reasoning is that household formation was a function of rural population growth and real income growth.[6] Using this assumption, he obtains a real growth of rural structures from 1890 to 1913 (1.3% per annum) below that of rural population growth. I chose not to use the Kahan series because our independent study of insurance data on rural structures indicates a rising real stock of structures per capita (and per household) in agriculture - an expected consequence of rising real income in agriculture, especially after 1905. According to our investigation of cross-section peasant budget data, the demand for rural housing was income elastic, and such evidence supports our series over the slower growing Kahan series.[7] Later in this appendix I discuss our estimates of the net stock of rural structures in some detail.

The availability of alternate series and alternate data sources has complicated this study. One of the most serious complications is that Kahan's capital stock estimates are presented with little discussion of their derivation. Thus one must assume certain points about their estimation in order to make comparisons and evaluations. Vainshtein, on the other hand, provides a detailed discussion of this methodology and sources, but his study is limited to the period 1910 to the beginning of 1914. In general, I have decided to rely where possible more on the Vainshtein figures than those of Kahan, primarily because I know more about the former and, moreover, they appear more realistic in certain instances (such as the case of urban housing). From Kahan's own limited discussion of his series, I conclude that his estimates of the stock of industrial structures are the most reliable of his various series; thus they play a prominent role in my estimates. Kahan does concede that his series on agricultural structures should only be regarded as a first approximation; therefore, I would imagine that he would welcome a new series based upon insurance data.[8]

INSURANCE DATA AND CAPITAL STOCK
The use of data on the insured values of industrial and agricultural structures to estimate net capital stock in structures requires further discussion. Methodologically, the most thorny problem presented by such data is that of inferring market values from data on insured values. Much of Vainshtein's monograph is devoted to discussing his own manipulations of insured values to obtain market values,[9] and it is unfortunate that Kahan does not discuss how he deals with this difficult issue in his own calculations. In the presentation of my series on the

net stock of agricultural structures, I discuss in some detail the matter of adjustment for coverage and indicate that my series rests principally upon trends in the value of peasant structures insured under compulsory insurance programs, for I believe that coverage rates remained fairly steady over the period investigated.

One cannot expect to obtain sufficient information to calculate from series on the insured values of structures annual changes in the ratios of insured to market values. First, structures were typically insured at less than 100% of value. Foundations were not insured and peasant structures, for example, were typically insured at only half their market value. Thus adjustments must be made to calculate the value of the structure from its insured value. Above and beyond this problem, there is uncertainty concerning insurance behavior.

Two polar models of insurance behavior can be postulated, and one does not know a priori which one in fact held in tsarist Russia. The first model assumes that the insured value of the structure will be adjusted in each year to reflect its current market value. If this model holds, the insured value in each year will equal the net capital stock in current prices. A real net stock series can then be calculated by deflating the series in current prices by an appropriate price deflator. In notational form, the first model assumes that:

$$(1) \qquad I_1 = P_1 \, [\Delta K + (1 - d)K_0]$$

where I_1 equals the insured value in year 1

P_1 is the market price of the structure in year 1

d is the annual depreciation rate

K_0 is the real net capital stock in year 0

The point to emphasize is that if the first model holds, the appropriate procedure for calculating real net investment (say, in prices of year 0) is to deflate the net stock and then take first differences in the stock:

$$(2) \qquad (P_0/P_1) \, I_1 - I_0 = P_0\Delta K - P_0 dK_0$$

The second model of insurance behavior assumes that net additions to the stock of structures will be valued at current market prices, but the initial stock will remain valued at original cost. It should be noted that this model reduces to the second if there is no price inflation of structures. Notationally, this second model assumes that:

$$(3) \qquad I_1 = P_1 \, (\Delta K - dK_0) + P_0 K_0$$

To calculate real net investment using this second assumption, it is necessary to calculate first net investment in current prices by taking first differences in the insured values and then to deflate this series by an appropriate price deflator:

$$(4) \qquad P_0/P_1 \, (I_1 - I_0) = P_0\Delta K - P_0 dK_0$$

One can, without great difficulty, establish the direction of error if the first model procedure is applied when the second model behavior actually holds. In this case, estimated real investment (in base-year prices) will equal:

$$\text{Estimated net investment} = P_0\Delta K - dP_0K_0 + (P_0/r - P_0)K_0$$

where r equals P_1/P_0. Thus during periods of inflation, estimated net investment will understate true net investment. Conversely, if the second model procedure is applied when the first model behavior actually holds, then the estimated net investment figures will overstate true net investment during periods of inflation:

$$\text{Estimated net investment} = P_0\Delta K - dP_0K_0 + (P_0 - P_0/r)K_0$$

There is no way to know which model of insurance behavior is correct, and the results yielded by applying the two sets of assumptions can differ if significant annual price changes are involved. In fact, if the first model procedure of deflating the insured values first and then taking first differences is applied, substantial annual fluctuations in the net investment series can result as can unrealistically high net disinvestment rates. Application of the second model procedure of taking first differences in the insured values and then deflating the current price investment series yields a more stable net investment series, but, as noted above, may tend to overstate net investment if insurers constantly updated their insurance coverage to reflect changing market values.

Likely, the "correct" model of insurance behavior is some mixture of the two polar models, where insurers periodically revalued their structures (but not annually) to reflect changing market values. If this were so, these periodic revaluations would create discontinuities in the net investment as that would further complicate the estimation of net investment. When such discontinuities appear, I have averaged them out using three-year moving averages.

The period 1885 to 1913 witnessed a fairly gradual increase in construction prices (and I assume market values rose with construction prices in this study), according to the construction price indexes used in this appendix. The annual rate of price increase was nearly 1%; thus the depreciation rate likely exceeded the inflation rate. There were also episodes of price deflation, and these episodes further complicate the estimation of real net investment from insurance data.

I attempt to assess these problems by investigating different variants based upon alternate assumptions concerning insurance behavior. Although I cannot be certain of this, the difference between the Kahan and Vainshtein 1913 net investment figure for industrial structures may be the consequence of a different handling of these assumptions. However, I know little about how Kahan's estimates were derived; so the following explanation may be incorrect. Vainshtein is explicit about the fact that he begins with an assumption of model 2 investment behavior. He argues that such behavior was not irrational for the period he investigated (1911-January 1914) because the rates of depreciation and inflation were virtually equal and thus canceled each other. According to my figures, there is merit to this argument: The construction price inflator grew at approximately 2% during this short interval, and this rate would not differ much from the depreciation rate. If so, the Vainshtein estimate would contain only minimal bias. If, as I suspect, Kahan assumed model 1 behavior, then his net investment figure would understate net investment in industrial structures if prompt adjustments for inflation were not made. This is the outcome one observes in Table J.1, columns 4a and 4b, with Kahan's estimates for 1913 and 1911-1913 about one-half those of Vainshtein. In Table J.1, I supply two net investment series in industrial structures (4a, 4b). Each series uses Kahan's intertemporal index of net investment, but this index is applied to different 1913 bases. The higher figure is that of Vainshtein; the lower is from Kahan. In my results, I use the higher Vainshtein figures for the reasons given above.

I have also calculated two variants for net investment in agricultural structures from the series on the insured values of agricultural structures (panel B, columns 2 and 4). The column 2 series assumes model 2 insurance behavior (deflates increments in insured values), and the column 4 series deflates the net stock and then takes increments (assumes model 1 insurance behavior). The column 2 net investment series does not exhibit the extreme variability of the column 4 series (which is what one would expect from the polar insurance assumptions), and the column 2 series yields average investment figures 5% higher for the period 1885-1895 and 23% higher for the period 1904-1913. Thus the model 2 insurance assumption appears to yield generally higher net investment estimates than the model 1 assumption in the case of agricultural structures. I use the model 2 series for agricultural structures in Table 3.1 because it yields what appear to be more realistic results. Extreme annual fluctuations in net investment are avoided as are certain obviously unrealistic results (net disinvestment equal to 6% of the net capital stock in 1896, net disinvestment in 1912, etc.).

My series on the net capital stock and net investment in industrial, agricultural, and urban residential structures are presented in Table J.1. The derivation of each series is described in the notes to this table, and some general comments have already been supplied in the above discussion. I should emphasize that it is very difficult to ascertain the degree of potential measurement error in each series. The industry and agriculture structures series are based upon insurance data, and, as I have pointed out, there are significant problems in interpreting and adjusting such data. The urban residential structures series are taken from Kahan and Vainshtein (for the end of the period), and Kahan gives little information concerning his estimates; because I am not in a position to evaluate his series, I must accept it on face value.

In Table J.1, I have used the variant I series because I find these results more plausible. First, I know more about the Vainshtein study upon which the variant I industrial structures series is based. Second, I have argued that the variant I agricultural structures series appears to be more realistic. The choice of variant I or II is not crucial, as the long-term growth rates indicated by the two series are not that different (5.1% versus 6.1%, 1885-88 to 1910-1913).

Because of the general problem of erratic changes in coverage (with lagged adjustments to changes in market values), the safest way to deal with such data is to calculate averages to smooth out discontinuities. However, as the above discussion suggests, if underlying assumptions concerning insurance behavior do not hold, such averaging will not remove biases, which appear to be in a downward direction in a period of generally rising prices. Another source of measurement error lies in the choice of an appropriate construction price deflator. Because I do not know what type of deflator(s) is used by Kahan I cannot rule out the possibility that disagreements between his estimates and those of Vainshtein are not the result of using different price deflators.

AGRICULTURAL STRUCTURES

The series on industrial and urban residential structures cited in Table J.1 are taken from the Kahan and Vainshtein studies and, accordingly, require little explanation. The series on agricultural structures is, however, based upon an independent study for the period 1885 to 1910, after which the Vainshtein estimates are used and thus require more comment.[10] In general terms, I have attempted to duplicate the methodology used by Vainshtein in his estimates of the stock of agricultural structures (1911-1914) from data on insured values. This methodology is then applied to the earlier period.

Specifically, I begin by accepting Vainshtein's net stock estimates for 1910 to the end of 1913, and the reader is referred to Vainshtein's lengthy discussion of his calculation of the value of farm structures.[11] We then gathered and prepared a series on the insured values of farm structures from official data sources,[12] which we determined to be consistent with Vainshtein's series for 1910-1914. The key assumption employed to calculate our series on the value of farm structures is that the growth of the value of farm structures is best captured by the growth of the value of farm structures insured under governmental compulsory insurance programs. This assumption is supported by the finding that the relationship between the percentage of the value of structures insured under the compulsory insurance program to market value (*otsennochnaia stoimost'*) remained virtually unchanged between 1889 and 1911-13;[13] so that the growth of compulsorily insured property appears not to be a consequence of the growth of coverage of structures but of the growth of the value of structures.

It is necessary to provide some background information on why one would expect the growth of insured values under compulsory insurance programs to be a reasonably accurate indicator of the growth of the aggregate market values of farm structures.[14] Beginning in 1864, the tsarist government enacted legislation for the compulsory insurance of peasant farm structures. This compulsory program was handled by the *zemstvos* in those provinces (*zemskie gubernii*) where *zemstvos* existed and by *gubernskoe* insurance in the non-*zemstvo* provinces. In addition to compulsory insurance, the requirements of which were dictated by legislation, additional "voluntary" (*dobrovol'noe*) insurance was made available to insure farm property not covered by compulsory insurance. The property of the gentry and large landowners (called "capitalist" structures by Vainshtein) was typically insured using voluntary insurance programs or private insurance corporations.

The owner of peasant farm structures was obligated by law to insure his property for no lower than a specified percentage of its market value (the percentage varied by type of structure). Although the peasant owner had the right to insure his structures with private companies for the amount prescribed by law, he typically chose to insure under the zemstvo or gubernskoe program. It is important to note that the zemstvos were financially responsible for the loss of structures (for the amount specified under the compulsory program) whether or not insurance premiums had been paid by the peasant.

These matters are of extreme importance to our estimates because the natural hypothesis to make for an agrarian society (such as Russia with its low literacy rates) would be that the percentage of insured peasant structures would rise over time. The fact that the Russian government, through national legislation, made local government in the countryside responsible for the compulsory insurance of farm structures makes our hypothesis of coverage of all peasant structures at the compulsory rates more palatable. The reason for governmental interest in the insurance of peasant property, in my opinion, was the state's interest in the financial solvency of the peasant and the village commune, as state revenues were directly related to this. If one couples this interest with the great incidence of fire damage to peasant property in Russia,[15] one can understand why the government introduced compulsory fire insurance at such an early date in Russia.

On the basis of these considerations, I have opted to accept the index of the insured value of peasant structures under compulsory insurance programs as the indicator of the growth of the market values of peasant structures between 1885 and 1913. Although the compulsory insurance program was implemented differently in the various provinces, there is no evidence that the rates of compulsory coverage were changed during this period, and evidence supports the fact that coverage rates remained stable over the period investigated.

There remains the problem of dealing with the value of capitalist (nonpeasant) structures not covered by compulsory insurance. According to Vainshtein, structures covered by voluntary insurance programs (principally "capitalist" structures) accounted for 28% of the value of agricultural structures of January 1, 1914.[16]

According to the available data on zemstvo and gubernskoe insurance programs,[17] the value of agricultural structures insured under voluntary programs as a percent of compulsory programs rose between 1889 and 1913 from 20% to 36%. Over this period, the value of peasant property insured under the compulsory program rose by a factor of 2.9, whereas property insured under voluntary programs increased by a factor of 5.4. If one combines zemstvo and gubernskoe insurance, the insured value of agricultural properties rose by a factor of 3.0 when voluntary insurance is included and by a factor of 2.7 when excluded. The question is whether the value of non-capitalist structures did indeed grow at the more rapid rate indicated by the development of voluntary insurance programs. If so, using the growth of compulsory insurance alone would tend to understate slightly the growth of agricultural structures.

My decision is to continue to use the growth of compulsory insurance as the indicator of the growth of agricultural structures, for example, I assume that nonpeasant structures grew at the same rates as peasant structures. First, the growth rate differences are not that great anyway, whether voluntary insurance is included or not (an 11% difference in annual growth rates). Second, it is our perception that the differential growth of voluntary over compulsory insurance reflects primarily the later development of voluntary insurance programs in agriculture under the sponsorship of local government. Thus capitalist property, which was earlier insured by private companies or not insured at all, came to be insured by *zemstvo* insurance, once such programs were offered by local government. Third, it is my desire to avoid overstating the growth of agricultural structures; so I would prefer to err in the direction of understatement. As it stands, with the assumption of equivalent growth rates of peasant and capitalist property, my net capital stock series for agricultural structures grows at an annual rate of 3.5% as opposed to Kahan's estimate of 1.3% per annum.

PRICE DEFLATOR: CONSTRUCTION

In Table J.2, the index used for the deflation of structures is described. I employ one index and do not differentiate between urban and rural construction, primarily because of insufficient information for such an undertaking. In addition, in column E I supply an index for deflating construction in transportation (railroad construction), which is used in Appendix L. The sources and derivation of the construction price deflator used in Table J.2 (column F) are described in some detail in the notes to the table.

Table J.1. *Net capital stock and net investment, industrial, agricultural, and*
urban residential structures, beginning of year (million rubles)

A. Industry, 1913 prices

	(1) Industrial structures, net stock index (Kahan index) 1913 = 100	(2) Industrial structures, net investment (Kahan index) 1913 = 100	(3) Industrial structures, net stock, Vainshtein base	(4) Industrial structures, net investment (a) Vainshtein base	(b) Kahan base	(5) Net investment current prices (a) Vainshtein base	(b) Ka... ba...
1885	29.4	30	642	74	40	61	
1886	31.2	33	682	82	41	68	
1887	33.1	33	723	82	42	67	
1888	35.0	36	765	89	48	76	
1889	37.2	38	813	94	48	76	
1890	39.4	40	861	99	52	78	
1891	41.8	-3	913	-7	-4	-6	
1892	41.6	24	909	60	31	50	
1893	43.0	34	940	84	43	70	
1894	45.0	10	983	25	13	21	
1895	45.6	48	996	119	62	96	
1896	48.4	31	1058	77	39	63	
1897	50.2	80	1097	198	103	174	
1898	54.9	35	1200	87	46	78	
1899	57.0	73	1246	181	93	168	
1900	61.3	85	1339	211	110	196	1
1901	66.3	38	1449	94	48	86	
1902	68.5	-31	1497	-77	-40	-69	-
1903	66.7	-8	1457	-20	-8	-19	
1904	66.3	36	1449	89	46	82	
1905	68.4	91	1495	226	118	208	1
1906	73.8	-61	1613	-151	-79	-142	-
1907	70.2	15	1534	37	19	34	
1908	71.1	45	1553	112	57	103	
1909	73.7	35	1610	87	46	79	
1910	75.8	56	1656	139	72	131	
1911	79.1	121	1728	300	180	282	1
1912	87.3	115	1908	285	148	273	1
1913	94.1	100	2056	248	129	248	1
1914	100.0		2185				

Table J.1 (*cont.*)

B. Agriculture				C. Urban residential structures		
(1) Net investment current year prices	(2) Net investment, 1913 prices, variant I	(3) Net capital stock, 1913 prices	(4) Net investment, variant II	(1) Net capital, Vainshtein base, 1913 prices	(2) Net investment, 1913 prices	(3) Net investment, current prices
164	198	3504	197	3425	72	60
68[a]	89[a]	3701	128[a]	3497	64	53
68[a]	89[a]	3765	128[a]	3561	71	58
68[a]	89[a]	3276	128[a]	3632	78	66
47	58	4085	163	3710	65	53
148	187	4248	-26	3775	67	53
87	105	4222	105	3842	45	37
100	121	4327	120	2887	-34	-28
0	0	4447	-105	3853	-43	-36
102	120	4342	120	3810	120	102
139	172	4462	333	3930	112	91
33	40	4795	-289	4042	80	66
32	36	4506	-65	4122	166	146
239	266	4441	65	4288	77	69
212	226	4506	277	4365	17	16
308	331	4783	443	4348	140	130
284	312	5226	437	4488	365	332
289	325	5663	6	4853	308	274
324[a]	350[a]	5669	344[a]	5161	153	144
324[a]	350[a]	6125	344[a]	5314	280	258
324[a]	350[a]	6120	344[a]	5594	289	266
296	315	6702	390	5883	61	57
299	322	7092	403	5944	70	65
335	364	7495	450	6014	104	96
339	372	7945	107	6118	327	298
663	705	8052	705	6445	402	378
296	315	8757	126	6847	383	360
296	308	8883	-59	7230	383	368
392	392	8824	392	7613	403	403
		9216		8016		

Table J.1 (*cont.*)

D.   Totals

	Net capital, 1913 prices (A3 + B3 + C1)	Net investment in structures, 1913 prices		Net investment, current prices (A5a + B1 + C3)
		Variant I (A4a + B2 + C2)	Variant II (A4b + B4 + C2)	
1885	7571	344	309	285
1886	7880	235	233	189
1887	8049	242	241	193
1888	7673	256	254	210
1889	8608	217	276	176
1890	8884	353	93	279
1891	8977	143	146	118
1892	9123	147	117	122
1893	9240	41	-105	34
1894	9135	265	253	225
1895	9368	403	507	326
1896	9895	197	-170	162
1897	9725	400	204	352
1898	9929	430	188	386
1899	10117	424	387	396
1900	10470	682	693	634
1901	11163	771	850	702
1902	12013	556	274	494
1903	12287	483	489	449
1904	12888	719	670	664
1905	13209	865	751	798
1906	14198	225	372	211
1907	14570	429	492	398
1908	15062	580	611	534
1909	15673	786	480	716
1910	16153	1246	1179	1172
1911	17332	998	689	938
1912	18021	976	472	937
1913	18493	1043	924	1043
1914	19417			

[a]Denotes 3-year average figure.

Table J.1 (cont.)

Sources: Panel A, columns 1 and 2: The series on investment and net capital stock in industrial structures are derived in the following manner: From Kahan's net capital stock series in industrial structures in 1913 prices, I prepare two indexes with base year 1913; namely, an index of net capital stock and, by taking increments, an index of net investment. The Kahan series are cited in Arcadius Kahan, "Capital Formation During the Period of Early Industrialization in Russia," *Cambridge Economic History of Europe*, vol. 7, Pt. 2 (Cambridge University Press, 1978), p. 302. The Kahan figures are backcast from 1890 to 1885 using the deflated value of the Strumilin index of industrial capital stock from S. G. Strumilin, *Statistika i ekonomika* (Moscow: Nauka, 1963), p. 334. The extrapolation is described by Anna Kuniansky in a technical working paper entitled "Industrial Capital in Russia, 1885-1913" (mimeographed 1978) which compares the deflated Strumilin series with that of Kahan. The comparison of the Strumilin and Kahan figures shows that they are in general agreement except for the period 1896-1900, and for the period 1891-96, Kahan shows an 8% annual growth rate, whereas Strumilin indicates a 9% rate. From this I conclude that the Kahan series can be backcast from 1890 to 1885 without introducing major distortions using the Strumilin index.

Column 3: Column 3 is calculated by applying the column 1 index from Kahan to Vainshtein's estimate of the net stock of industrial structures on January 1, 1914. Vainshtein's estimate is from A. L. Vainshtein, *Narodnoe bogatstvo i narodnokhoziaistvennoe nakoplenia predrevoliutsionnoi Rossii* (Moscow: Gosstatizdat, 1960), p. 369, and includes the categories *stroeniia i sooruzheniia*. The Vainshtein figure is 61% higher than Kahan's estimate for the end of 1913.

Column 4: Vainshtein base: This column is calculated by applying the net investment index in column 2 to Vainshtein's (p. 420) estimate of 1913 net investment in industrial structures. Kahan base: This column is calculated by applying the column 2 index to the 1913 increment in column 3 (or equivalently, taking increments from column 3).

Column 5: Column 5 is calculated by inflating the two variants in column 4 by the construction price deflator in Table J.2.

Panel B: These series are described in general terms in the text. They are described in more detail by Paul Gregory and Anna Kuniansky in a technical paper entitled "The Value of Agricultural Structures in Russia, 1885-1913" (mimeographed, 1978).

Column 1: This series is calculated by taking increments in the insured value of peasant and "capitalist" structures covered under compulsory and voluntary programs after upward adjustment to capture the value of the foundation and that portion of the value of the structure not covered by insurance. As noted in the text, the growth rate of capitalist structures is assumed to be the same as that of peasant structures.

Column 2: This series is calculated by deflating column 1 by the construction cost index of Table J.2.

Column 3: This series is the deflated value of the insured value of peasant and capitalist structures (described under column 1).

Column 4: This series is calculated by taking increments in the net stock series in column 3.

Panel C, column 1: For the period 1910-13, the deflated values are taken from Vainshtein, pp. 368, 417, 420, and include some trade establishments as well as urban residential structures. This series is backcast from 1910 to 1890 using Kahan's index of net capital stock in urban dwellings from Kahan, p. 297. The series is backcast from 1890 to 1885 using the growth of the urban population.

Column 2: This series is calculated by taking increments from column 1.

Column 3: This series is calculated by inflating column 2 by the construction cost deflator.

Table J.2. *Deflation of investment in structures*

	(A) Average annual earnings, rail- road full-time construction workers, 1913 = 100	(B) Lumber prices, railroad ties, 1913 = 100	(C) Lumber, pine, 1 amst. ft. 1913 = 100	(D) Other con- struction materials 1913=100	(E) Transpor- tation con- struction	(F) Construc- tion price deflator (.33A + .33B + .33D)
1885	76	55	77	95	74	83
1886	77	55	77	96	74	83
1887	76	53	74	96	74	82
1888	82	53	74	100	78	85
1889	78	47	65	99	73	81
1890	77	46	64	97	73	79
1891	80	46	69	99	74	83
1892	78	45	69	102	73	83
1893	79	45	69	100	73	83
1894	79	48	75	101	73	85
1895	81	55	72	89	74	81
1896	79	58	80	88	74	82
1897	81	57	85	98	77	88
1898	82	62	88	101	80	90
1899	82	52	93	108	80	94
1900	85	56	100	95	79	93
1901	83	53	98	91	75	91
1902	86	70	94	86	79	89
1903	88	52	103	91	75	94
1904	86	49	94	95	75	92
1905	89	51	88	100	79	92
1906	94	54	88	101	82	94
1907	95	50	88	95	80	93
1908	96	43	88	91	76	92
1909	96	45	93	85	75	91
1910	98	54	100	83	78	94
1911	98	49	100	85	78	94
1912	101	94	100	88	94	96
1913	100	100	100	100	100	100

Sources: Column A: This series is taken directly from the *Statisticheski sbornik ministerstva putei soobshcheniia* annual series (average annual earnings of full-time employees employed on construction and maintenance of the rail beds).
       Column B: Price series, prices of construction lumber, pine, one amst. foot. This series is based upon the series reported in *Svod tovarnykh tsen* and is for a uniform grade of lumber over the period covered by the *Svod* series (1890 to 1913). The series is extrapolated back to 1885 using the average prices paid by the state railroads for wood fuel (*drov'*). Although this is likely not a good assumption, as this is for wood used for fuel not construction, one would not expect major distortions from the use of this assumption.
       Column C: Price series, railroad ties (*shpaly*). This series is again from the *Svod tovarnykh tsen* series (Riga prices) and the extrapolation from 1885 to 1890 is again with the price series for wood fuels.
       Column D: Other construction materials: The *Svod tovarnykh tsen* series does not report a consistent series on other construction materials, exclusive of iron and steel. I have constructed therefore a series from cement, plaster, and brick price quotations. The cement price series (Portland cement) forms the basis of the series with a series for the period 1885 to 1908 available. This series is from *Svod tovarnykh tsen*, supplemented by the average price paid for imported cement plus tariffs for the years that the *Svod* series does not report. The latter data are from V. I. Pokrovsky, ed., *Sbornik svedenii po istorii i statistike vneshnei*

Table J.2 (*cont.*)

torgovli Rossii (Petersburg: Departament tamozhennykh sborov, 1902), 1:88, and from
the *Ezhegodnik ministerstva finansov* series, section *vneshniaia torgovlia*. For the
period 1908 to 1913, the series is constructed from a weighted average of brick and
plaster prices (weights in foreign trade volume), as additional price information on
cement prices is not available. Again, these prices are prices paid per pud for
imported bricks and plaster plus tariffs per pud. This information is obtained from
table 7 of GUZ i Z, Otdel sel'skoi ekonomiki, *Sbornik statistiko-ekonomicheskikh
svedenii po sel'skomu khoziaistvu Rossii i inostrannykh gosudarstv* (Petrograd:
Ministerstvo zemledeliia, 1915), vol. 7. I would have preferred to have a
consistent series on bricks, plaster, and cement for the entire period, but price
data on construction materials is quite deficient.

    Column E: Deflator for construction: I have no information on the cost
shares of labor, capital, and intermediate materials; so I have assigned rather
arbitrary weights to the various cost components. First, I assume that the wage
series for railroad construction workers is the appropriate one for the inflation of
industrial construction and that the railroad ties series is the appropriate lumber
price index. I then assign the following weights: .3 for labor, lumber, and other
construction materials and .1 for metallurgy and fuel prices.

    Column F: Here I assume that the wage series for railroad construction
workers is the appropriate one for the deflation of residential construction and
also that the pine lumber price series is appropriate for this series as well.
Moreover, I assume a zero weight for metallurgy and fuels. Then I assign labor,
lumber, and other construction materials equal weights of .33.

NOTES TO APPENDIX J

1   Arcadius Kahan, "Capital Formation During the Early Years of Industrialization
     in Russia 1890-1913," *Cambridge Economic History of Europe*, vol. 7, pt. 2
     (Cambridge University Press, 1978), pp. 265-307; A. L. Vainshtein, *Narodnoe
     bogatstvo i narodnokhoziaistvennoe nakoplenia predrevoliutsionnoi Rossii*
     (Moscow: Gosstatizdat, 1960); Paul Gregory and Anna Kuniansky, "The Value of
     Agricultural Structures in Russia, 1885-1913," mimeographed, 1978.

2   Kahan, "Capital Formation," pp. 286-288.

3   They are not consistent because I have applied the Kahan net investment index
     to Vainshtein's estimate of 1913 net investment. As Vainshtein's net
     investment figure is twice as large as Kahan's, it follows that the
     "Vainshtein base" investment figures will not be consistent with the net
     capital stock series.

4   The urban population series is for the 50 European provinces

5   Between 1910 and 1913, the urban population of European Russia rose from 17.2
     to 18.6 million. These figures are from V. Zaitsev and V. G. Groman, ed.,
     Vliianie neurozhaev na narodnoe khoziaistvo Rossii (Moscow:N.P. 1927), pt. 2,
     p. 65. Real retail sales increased by a minimum of 10% (from Appendix A).
     Thus it seems implausible to expect a decline in the real stock of urban
     housing between 1910 and the end of 1913.

6   Kahan, "Capital Formation," p. 278.

7   In S. N. Prokopovich, *Krestianskoe khoziaistvo po dannym biudzhetnykh
     isledovannii i dinamicheskikh perepisei* (Berlin: Kooperativnaia mysl', 1924),
     pp. 106, 107, cross-section data on peasant income, family expenditures and
     family size are provided (from the Tambov and Novgorod provinces). From this
     information, I have calculated income elasticities of peasant expenditures on
     housing using a double log regression equation. The combined-province income
     elasticity is 1.34 (higher than I expected), and an examination of the data
     suggests that the elasticity rises with income (a higher elasticity at high
     income levels). In any case, these cross-section data strongly suggest that
     the peasant housing income elasticity was at least unity and that housing
     expenditures should rise at about the same rate as income. Of course, one
     cannot directly apply such cross-section elasticities to time series behavior,
     but this is at least partial evidence that peasant expenditures on housing
     were indeed responsive to income changes.

8   Kahan, "Capital Formation," p. 278.

9   Vainshtein, *Narodnoe bogatstvo*, chap. 3, pt. 2.

10   Gregory and Kuniansky, "Value of Agricultural Structures."

11   Vainshtein, *Narodnoe bogatstvo*, pp. 177-84.

12   The most important sources of data on farm insurance are: S. Rybnikov,
     Ocherki sovremennogo polozheniia v Rossii strakhovaniia ot ognia (Petersburg:
     N.P., 1912); *Entsiklopedicheski slovar' Brokgauz-Efron*, vol. 27, pp. 373-8;
     Tsentral'noe Statisticheskoe Upravlenie, *Statisticheski sbornik za 1913-1917*

gg., Vypusk vtoroi, section *strakhovanie; Sbornik statiticheskikh svedenii po gubernskomu i zemskomu strakhovaniu, 1866-1895* (Petersburg, 1900); *Vzaimnoe strakhovanie ot ognia, gubernskoe i gorodskoe, 1889-1892,* Vremenik Tsentral'nogo Statisticheskago Komiteta, 1893; *Sbornik svedenii po Rossii,* 1884-5, 1890 editions.

13   From Vainshtein, we calculate a ratio of approximately .5 for the ratio of insured to market value (*otsenochnaia stoimost'*) for the period 1911-13. From *Vzaimnoe strakhovanie,* we find that the ratios for 1889-92 (*gubernskoe* compulsory insurance) were approximately 44% for the 50 European provinces and 77% for Siberia. They were much higher (90% for Poland), but the Polish figures contain urban structures in Polish urban centers. Applying reasonable weights to these regional percentages results in an average of approximately 50% for the early 1890s.

14   For descriptions of the Russian system of rural fire insurance, see V. V. Veselovski, *Istoriia zemstva za sorok let,* 4 vols. (Petersburg: Popov, 1909).

15   The Ministry of Interior, e.g., would issue periodic reports in its publication *Vremenik tsentral'nago statisticheskago komiteta* on "fires in Russia."

16   Vainshtein, *Narodnoe bogatstvo,* p. 182.

17   These figures are taken from the sources in note 12.

INVENTORY STOCKS AND INVESTMENT

INVENTORY INVESTMENT IN CURRENT PRICES

Information on inventory stocks of industry, trade, and agricultural producers is available from several sources. In this appendix I describe my estimates of inventories and inventory investment during the period 1885 to 1913. Inventory stocks of railroads are included in the railroad capital stock and investment series in Appendix L.

A major source of data on inventories is that supplied by the balance sheets of corporations and mutual associations (*aktsionernye i paevye organizatsii*). In their annual reports, the aggregates of which were recorded in *Ezhegodnik ministerstva finansov* (section *Aktsionernye obshchestva*), corporate assets and liabilities were listed. Major assets were broken down into property (*imushchestvo*), meaning the value of buildings, land, and equipment, and stocks of materials (*tovary i zapasy*). The latter form the basis for my figures on industry and trade inventories.

The major obstacle to the use of these inventory figures is that they apply only to corporations, and in trade and agriculture corporations accounted for small shares of output. As relatively little information is available on the inventory holdings of noncorporate businesses, their stock-building behavior must be inferred from that of corporate producers. For this, I accept the methodology of S. G. Strumilin,[1] who utilizes noncorporate output and profit data to infer noncorporate property and inventory values for industry and trade.

Basically, Strumilin's method for calculating inventories is to assume equivalent capital-output ratios and similar capital stock distributions between corporate and noncorporate producers. In some cases, the inclusion of noncorporate enterprises requires relatively modest modifications. In industry in 1913, according to Strumilin's figures, corporations accounted for 70% of total industrial capital stock. In the case of trade, corporations accounted for only 5% of total profits. Thus, the estimation of total inventories of trade organizations from those of trade corporations is likely a risky undertaking.

In Table K.1, I supply my figures on industrial and trade inventories. The estimation procedures are described in detail in the notes to Table K.1.

Industrial inventories

These figures are calculated directly from Strumilin's estimates of industrial capital stock (including handicraft), including corporations, private proprietorships and partnerships. I calculate inventories held by handicraft industry by assuming that the ratios of inventory stocks to total capital of factory industry (calculated from Strumilin) also hold for handicraft. The deflated series (panel C, column 1) is close to Kahan's estimates for 1890-1913.[2] For 1890, I obtain a figure of 551 million rubles; Kahan's figure is 545 million rubles. For 1913, the two figures are 2558 and 2274, respectively. For the entire period, the annual growth rate differential is less than one-half of 1%.

Inventories of trade organizations
These figures are subject to substantial margins of error if two underlying assumptions are not met. These assumptions are: (a) that equal profit capitalization factors hold for both corporate and noncorporate trade, and (b) that inventory to total capital stock ratios are equal in the corporate and noncorporate trade sectors. That these assumptions be understood by the reader is important because, as noted above, I am using relationships that prevail in 5% of the trade sector to estimate relationships for the whole sector. The first assumption is the more important, and the most important point in its favor is that one would expect, at least over time, an equalization of rates of return on invested capital between corporate and noncorporate enterprises.

My method of calculating trade inventories is: From the Ministry of Finance data cited by Strumilin, I calculate the annual ratios of profits to total capital stock in the corporate trade sector. These ratios varied from 9% to 10% throughout the period. I then use these ratios to capitalize the total profits of the trade sector (corporate and noncorporate) to obtain estimates of the capital stock of trade organizations. Such profit data are available because of the tax levy on the profits of trade corporations, a matter discussed in Appendix A. I then apply the corporate ratios of inventory stocks to total capital to the total capital stock figures to obtain estimates of inventory stocks held by both corporate and noncorporate trade organizations. A similar investigation indicated that stocks held by utilities were insignificant; thus utility inventories are ignored.[3]

Inventories held by farm producers
The Department of Excise Tax Collections of the Ministry of Finance gathered annual data on stocks of grain products held by producers and by dealers on July 15. These figures include grain held by producers, in storage and in transit by rail and water. Data on grain held by dealers were published monthly in the *Vestnik finansov* periodical, but figures on grain held by producers were never officially published by the Ministry of Finance. Nevertheless, such figures are cited for various years for the period 1897 to 1913 by Liashchenko and Antsiferov et al.[4] Data on grain held by dealers are broken down by that in ports, internal markets, and elevators and warehouses of the railroads and are available for the period 1892 to 1913.

Insofar as grain held by dealers would be automatically (if imperfectly) included in the trade inventory figures of Table K.1, only the inventories of farm products held by the producers themselves remain to be included in the estimates of inventories. For this, I have the Ministry of Finance estimates for 1897-1906 and for 1909-1912. I have no information about the Ministry of Finance figures, and my

Table K.1. *Inventories in current and constant 1913 prices, beginning of year,*
(million rubles)

| | A. Inventory stocks in current prices | | B. Price indexes | |
	(1) Industrial stocks, factory and handicraft	(2) Trade organi- zations, corporate and noncorporate	(1) Industry	(2) Trade, Bobrov price index
1885	382	965	94	82
1886	390	1065	97	79
1887	428	1074	94	81
1888	505	1137	102	86
1889	563	1126	101	83
1890	540	1223	98	74
1891	537	1181	94	75
1892	557	1159	92	73
1893	644	1342	94	76
1894	748	1529	95	69
1895	823	2207	91	70
1896	787	1661	89	72
1897	868	2038	89	74
1898	986	2417	89	78
1899	1095	2637	93	81
1900	1155	2663	97	84
1901	1174	2419	97	80
1902	1145	2496	93	76
1903	1282	3128	92	77
1904	1377	3154	91	80
1905	1263	3426	91	82
1906	1351	2721	91	89
1907	1547	3047	103	97
1908	1602	3149	97	93
1909	1633	3165	94	91
1910	1747	3366	94	92
1911	1941	3779	91	95
1912	2184	4062	98	98
1913	2406	4346	100	100
1914	2558	4565	100	107

Sources: Panel A, column 1: Industrial stocks: My estimates of industrial
inventories come almost directly from S. G. Strumilin, *Statistika i ekonomika*
(Moscow: Nauka, 1963), p. 334. To estimate noncorporate capital stock, Strumilin
used imputed capital output ratios, which he allowed to vary with the size of the
enterprise. For his estimates of handicraft capital stock, Strumilin relied on the
work of Gukhman. I assume that the ratios of inventories to total capital stock of
factory industry, calculated by Strumilin, apply for the handicraft sector as well.
Strumilin's study is based upon the aggregate balances of corporate organizations
published regularly in the *Ezhegodnik ministerstva finansov* series under the section
svodny balans aktsionernykh predpriiatii.
     Column 2: My procedure for estimating the stocks of trade organizations,
wholesale and retail, is described in the text. I first calculate the ratios of
profits to capital stock of corporate trade organizations and then apply these
capitalization factors to total profits of all trade organizations, corporate and
noncorporate, to obtain estimates of the total capital stock of trade organizations.
I then take the ratios of inventory stocks to total capital stock of trade
corporations and apply them to the total capital stock figures to obtain estimates

C. Inventory stocks in constant 1913 prices

D. Inventory investment

1) Industry	2) Trade	Total	1) Industry		2) Trade	
			(a) Current prices	(b) 1913 prices	(a) Current prices	(b) 1913 prices
406	1177	1583	8	-4	100	171
402	1348	1750	38	53	9	-22
455	1326	1781	77	40	63	-4
495	1322	1817	58	62	-11	35
557	1357	1914	-23	-6	97	295
551	1652	2203	-3	20	-42	-77
571	1575	2146	20	34	-22	13
605	1588	2193	87	80	183	177
685	1765	2450	104	102	187	451
787	2216	3003	75	117	678	936
904	3152	4056	-36	-20	-546	-845
884	2307	3191	81	91	377	447
975	2754	3729	118	133	379	345
1108	3099	4207	109	69	220	157
1177	3256	4433	60	14	26	-86
1191	3170	4361	19	19	-244	-146
1210	3024	4234	-29	21	77	260
1231	3284	4515	137	162	632	778
1393	4062	5455	95	120	26	-119
1513	3943	5456	-114	-125	272	235
1388	4178	5566	88	130	-705	-1121
1518	3057	4575	196	77	326	187
1595	3244	4839	55	57	102	142
1652	3386	5038	31	85	16	92
1737	3478	5215	114	122	201	273
1859	3659	5518	194	274	413	319
2133	3978	6111	243	96	283	167
2229	4145	6374	222	177	284	201
2406	4346	6752	152	152	219	219
2558	4565	7123				

of stocks. My basic data is the *svodny balans* data published in *Ezhegodnik ministerstva finansov* and the profits data reported in Strumilin, *Statistika i ekonomika*, p. 439. Inventory stocks for the period 1885 to 1894 are extrapolated using the total capital stock index, as distributions between inventories and total capital stock are not available. The same is done for the period 1909 to 1914.

Panel B, column 1: The price deflator, industrial stocks series consists of five price series (iron, coal, oil, cotton textiles, nonagricultural machinery) weighted by their value added shares. These series are from Appendix I except for cotton textiles, which is taken from the *Svod tovarnykh tsen*. The *Svod* cotton textiles series is backcast from 1890 to 1885 using the price quotations in M. N. Sobolev, *Tamozhennaia politika Rossii vo vtoroi polovine XX veka*, Pt. 2 (Tomsk: Tipographiia Sibirskoe tovarichestvo pechatnogo dela, 1911), statistical appendix. The value added weights are from Raymond Goldsmith, "The Economic Growth of Tsarist Russia, 1860-1913," *Economic Development and Cultural Change* 9, No. 3 (April 1961), mimeographed appendix, table 13-2.

Column 2: For the price deflator, stocks of trade organizations, I use the Bobrov wholesale price index cited in Appendix I.1.

guess is that they are very rough. I attempted to extrapolate the Finance Ministry
figures by calculating correlations with the grain-held-by-dealers series and with
net grain production series, but I could not uncover any systematic relationships,
even after averaging out for price variation. This absence of systematic relationships suggests to me that the data are highly inaccurate, and that they should not
be taken too seriously.

In the face of such evidence, I have decided to assume that inventories of
farm products held by producers did not change during the period investigated.
According to the evidence assembled in Table K.2, there may have been a slight
decline between the 1890s and the period 1909-1912, despite the significant rise in
net grain output. However, it would be speculative to attach real significance to
this statistical decline because of the crudeness of the underlying data. Thus I
believe the best assumption to make is one of constant stocks held by producers. I
believe that the declining ratio of farm inventories to farm output was real and is
likely explained by improvements in the supply and transportation network. A com-
plicating factor was the state's role in requiring prescribed inventory levels to be
accumulated by local rural government.[5]

Table K.2. *Stocks of grain products held by producers and dealers,*
July (million puds)

	(1) Grain held at ports	(2) Grain held by dealers, internal market	(3) Grain held in warehouses and elevators of railroads	(4) Total (1 + 2 + 3)	(5) Grain held by producers	(6) Grain harvest, all grains
1893	24.0	9.7	5.2	38.9	108	
1894	29.3	18.8	5.2	53.3	110	
1895	43.6	28.0	8.7	80.3	98	
1896	33.8	28.3	7.0	69.1	100	
1897	24.8	27.9	8.7	61.4	483	84
1898	15.7	32.1	5.5	53.3	293	98
1899	28.7	8.6	5.3	42.6	340	111
1900	13.9	17.5	4.2	35.6	416	106
1901	11.6	14.0	4.3	29.9	439	94
1902	7.8	7.2	2.8	17.8	293	127
1903	14.1	11.1	2.2	27.4	346	122
1904	20.1	11.0	2.2	33.3	355	136
1905	18.2	20.5	3.4	42.1	438	118
1906	19.7	30.7	2.6	53.0	315	101
1907	6.2	6.4	.9	13.5	-	114
1908	7.8	7.7	3.0	18.5	-	118
1909	6.9	7.5	1.3	15.7	219	146
1910	21.3	23.1	7.6	52.0	389	143
1911	24.6	23.4	3.2	51.2	412	113
1912	11.9	7.1	1.4	20.4	244	149
1913	11.2	14.9	1.5	27.6	-	169

Note: Dash indicates not available.
[a] Four major grains: wheat, rye, oats, barley.
Sources: Columns 1-3: *Vestnik finansov*, 1893-1914, section *Vidimye zapasy khlebov*.
Column 5: P. I. Liashchenko, *Ocherki agrarnoi evolutsii Rossii* (Petersburg: n.p.
1908), pp. 287-91; A. N. Antsiferov, *Russian Agriculture During the War* (New Haven:
Yale University Press, 1930), p. 181.

NOTES TO APPENDIX K

1   S. G. Strumilin, *Statistika i ekonomika* (Moscow: Nauka, 1963), p. 334.

2   Arcadius Kahan, "Capital Formation During the Period of Early Industrialization in Russia, 1890-1913," *Cambridge Economic History of Europe*, vol. 7, pt. 2 (Cambridge University Press, 1978), p. 302.

3   I came to this conclusion after examining the inventories of utility companies reported in the *Ezhegodnik ministerstva finansov* series, section *aktsionernye obshchestva*.

4   See the notes to table K.2.

5   For example, *Sbornik svedenii po Rossii*, 1896 edition, reports stocks of grain held in public stores (*obshchestvennye magaziny*). These stocks were maintained under a government program designed to prevent famine in the countryside.

NET CAPITAL STOCK AND NET INVESTMENT IN RAILROADS, TRANSPORTATION AND COMMUNICATION,
AND GOVERNMENT INVESTMENT

NET CAPITAL STOCK AND NET INVESTMENT: RUSSIAN RAILROADS

My figures on net capital stock and net investment in Russian railroads are based
upon data published by the Ministry of Transportation in its annual yearbook
Statisticheski sbornik Ministerstva putei soobshcheniia, section "expenditures of
capital on the construction of the rail network" (*zatrata kapitalov na ustroivstvo
seti zh. dorog*). S. G. Strumilin has published gross and net capital stock series
using the Ministry of Transportation data,[1] but the widely cited Strumilin figures
are not suitable for compiling series on net investment and net capital stock.
Prior to 1897, loans for railroad construction and equipment acquisition were
floated both in gold (primarily abroad) and in credit rubles. The Ministry of
Transportation reported two series for this early period, one for capital expenditures in metallic rubles and the other for expenditures in credit rubles. The
exchange rate between the two currencies fluctuated, at times quite widely, but a
par value of 1 metallic ruble equal to 1.5 credit rubles was employed to combine the
two series. Upon conversion to the gold standard in 1897, the new gold ruble was
introduced at a rate 33% below the old metallic ruble, and a stable rate of 1:1 was
then maintained between the gold and credit ruble.[2]

To estimate a consistent net capital and net investment series in credit
rubles, I had to adjust the official capital expenditure series (with flotation
costs netted out) for annual fluctuations in the credit ruble-metallic ruble
exchange rate prior to 1897. Strumilin simply converted *cumulated* metallic ruble
capital expenditures as reported by the Ministry of Transportation into credit
rubles using the prevailing exchange rate of that year. Strumilin recognized that
this represented an approximation of cumulated capital expenditures in credit
rubles, and the Strumilin series shows negative net investment in three years (1887,
1892, 1893), although the rail network continued to expand in those years.[3] My
method is different and should yield a more consistent credit ruble series: I take
the stock of cumulated capital expenditures in 1885 and convert the metallic ruble
portion into credit rubles using the 1885 exchange rate. Incremental capital
expenditures denominated in metallic rubles in the years between 1885 and 1897 are
then translated into credit rubles using the average exchange rate of each year.
From 1897 on, I use the annual increments in capital expenditures reported in the
official data, as the exchange rate was stabilized from this point on.

The calculated series on cumulated capital expenditures in Russian railroads,
both state and private, represents a series of gross capital stock with assets
valued at acquisition costs. The gross figures are converted into a net series
(excluding land) by using Strumilin's calculation that annual depreciation amounted

to 1.25% of the gross capital stock throughout the period. This depreciation rate suggests an average service life of eighty years for track and rolling stock, and appears to be fairly realistic. Land is omitted by assuming that land accounted for 7% of the gross stock throughout the period. The 1913 end-of-year value is calcu- lated by applying the 3% growth rate of transportation capital stock reported by Vainshtein for the period January 1, 1913, to January 1, 1914.[4] The net capital stock series (in acquisition costs) is reported in column 1 of Table L.1.

Net investment in current year prices is calculated directly from the net capital stock figure by taking annual increments in the stock. This series is reported in column 2.

NET INVESTMENT AND NET CAPITAL STOCK, 1913 PRICES: RAILROADS
To deflate the net investment series in column 2, I compile a price deflator from four price series. The four price series are: The average annual wage of railroad construction workers (Appendix K), the average annual prices of railway ties (Appendix K), an index of the prices of "other construction materials" (Appendix K), and an index of the price of locomotives per ton (Appendix I). These are combined using weights of .34, .16, .17, and .33, respectively. This constructed priced deflator (column 3) is then applied to the net investment series in current prices (column 2) to obtain a net investment series in 1913 prices (column 4).[5] This net investment series is then used to compile a net capital stock series (column 5).

CAPITAL EXPENDITURES: TRANSPORTATION AND COMMUNICATION
I use the railroad net investment data to approximate net investment in transpor- tation and communication. Insofar as equipment expenditures are already included in Appendix I, I must eliminate equipment expenditures and deal only with inventory and construction investment. According to Vainshtein,[6] net investment in structures and inventories in transportation and communication equaled 208 million rubles in 1913, the overwhelming portion of which was invested by the railroads. I thus use the net railroad investment indexes in Table L.1 to extrapolate to the total transportation and communication net investment index. The major assumption underlying this constructed index is that railroad equipment investment grew at the same rate as total investment in railroads. The resulting net investment series are given in Table L.2.

CAPITAL EXPENDITURES: IMPERIAL AND LOCAL GOVERNMENT
Capital expenditures of the imperial government and local government have already been estimated in Appendixes F and G. The current price figures are provided in Table L.3 along with the figures in 1913 prices. The reader is referred back to Appendixes F and G for discussions of these estimates.

Table L.1. *Net capital stock and net investment, state and private railroads, beginning of year (million rubles)*

	(1) Net capital stock, acquisition costs	(2) Net investment, current prices	(3) Price deflator, railroad capital stock, 1913 = 100	(4) Net Investment, 1913 prices	(5) Net capital stock, 1913 prices
1885	1998	51	79	65	1440
1886	2049	69	79	87	1505
1887	2118	80	79	92	1592
1888	2198	81	87	94	1684
1889	2279	80	86	90	1778
1890	2359	41	89	46	1868
1891	2400	30	90	34	1914
1892	2430	149	88	173	1949
1893	2579	208	86	239	2121
1894	2787	100	87	115	2360
1895	2887	132	87	152	2475
1896	3019	174	87	220	2627
1897	3193	291	89	327	2827
1898	3484	220	90	244	3154
1899	3704	220	90	244	3398
1900	3924	297	88	338	3642
1901	4221	218	87	251	3980
1902	4439	162	90	180	4231
1903	4601	115	89	129	4411
1904	4716	215	88	244	4540
1905	4931	217	90	241	4784
1906	5148	226	92	246	5025
1907	5374	151	91	166	5271
1908	5525	174	89	196	5437
1909	5699	56	89	63	5633
1910	5755	281	89	316	5696
1911	6036	273	91	300	6012
1912	6309	176	102	173	6312
1913	6485	195	100	195	6485
1914	6680				6680

Table L.2. *Net investment in transportation and communication (excluding equipment)*

	(1) Net investment, current prices	(2) Net investment, 1913 prices
1885	54	69
1886	74	93
1887	85	98
1888	86	100
1889	85	96
1890	44	49
1891	32	36
1892	159	185
1893	222	255
1894	107	123
1895	141	162
1896	186	213
1897	311	349
1898	235	260
1899	235	260
1900	317	361
1901	233	268
1902	173	192
1903	123	138
1904	229	260
1905	232	257
1906	241	262
1907	161	177
1908	186	209
1909	60	67
1910	300	337
1911	291	320
1912	188	185
1913	208	208

Table L.3. *Capital expenditures, imperial and local government (million rubles)*

	A. Capital expenditures, current prices		B. Price deflator	C. Capital expenditures, 1913 prices	
	1) Including defense	2) Excluding defense		1) Including defense	2) Excluding defense
1885	66	37	79	84	47
1888	88	45	84	105	54
1891	97	53	83	117	64
1894	109	56	82	133	68
1896	113	72	82	138	88
1900	168	104	83	202	125
1903	185	105	80	231	131
1907	156	105	86	188	122
1910	221	144	84	263	171
1913	451	126	100	451	126

Sources: Column A: Table F.2, sum of columns 1-3, panel A, columns 1, 3, and 4, panel B, and table G.1, column 5 (bracketed figures). Column B: Nonagricultural equipment price deflator, appendix I (weight .25) and construction price deflator, appendix J (weight .75).

NOTES TO APPENDIX L

1   S. G. Strumilin, *Statistiika i ekonomika* (Moscow: Nauka, 1963), p. 406.

2   For discussions of the Russian monetary reforms in the 1890s, see Olga Crisp, *Studies in the Russian Economy Before 1914* (London and Basingstoke: Macmillan, 1976), essay 4; P. P. Migulin, *Reforma denezhnago obrashcheniia v Rossii i promyshlenny krizis* (Kharkóv: Pechatnoe delo, 1902); Karl Elster, *Vom Rubel zum Tscherwonjez* (Jena: Fischer, 1930), Chap. 1.

3   Strumilin, *Statistika i ekonomika*, p. 399.

4   A. L. Vainshtein, *Narodnoe bogatstvo i narodnokhoziaistvennoe nakoplenie predrevoliutsionnoi Rossii* (Moscow: Gosstatizdat, 1960), pp. 368, 420.

5   The 1885 investment figure is calculated from data on kilometers of track opened between 1884 and 1888.

6   Vainshtein, *Narodnoe bogatstvo*, p. 420.

In this appendix I describe the estimation of net foreign investment, that is, the balance of trade plus invisibles, such as dividend and interest payments to foreigners and net tourist expenditures abroad. The balance of trade plus invisibles is called in the Russian and later Soviet literature the *raschetny balans*, whereas in the early Soviet literature the compilation of the *raschetny balans* generally followed the procedures of the League of Nations for calculating net foreign investment.[1]

The subject of net foreign investment was one of considerable concern preceding and following the introduction of the gold standard in 1897. Much discussion was devoted to the issue: Was the Russian *raschetny* balance positive or negative? The debate was summarized by Migulin, writing in 1902, and by Engeev, writing in 1928.[2] Various attempts have been made to estimate net foreign investment, the first being Ol's estimates (1897) for 1881 to 1895, followed by Vyshnegradsky's estimates for 1888 to 1895.[3] Khrulev, writing in 1916, estimated net foreign investment for 1908 to 1913.[4] In the late 1920s, estimates were made by Engeev for 1881 to 1913 and Pasvolsky and Moulton for 1894 to 1914.[5] Later Soviet reference works typically cite Engeev's estimates, although in some instances those of Khrulev are used.[6] Bukovetsky apparently compiled independent estimates for 1911 to 1913, but he supplies no explanatory notes to his figures.[7] Finally, this author has prepared estimates of 1913 net foreign investment.[8]

In estimating net foreign investment, I follow the League of Nations methodology,[9] which calls for the estimation of three balances, namely, the merchandise balance, the interest and dividend balance, and the services balance. In the merchandise balance, exports are valued f.o.b. and imports c.i.f., and net silver imports are included. The dividend and interest balance consists of net interest and dividend payments abroad, both public and private, and repatriated profits of foreign-owned nonincorporated enterprises. The service account consists first of shipping services, where own-country receipts from international shipping for both imports and exports are included in net of payments to foreign shippers for inter-port shipping within the country. These items are included to adjust for the c.i.f. valuation of imports. Second, the service account includes net payments to foreigners for commissions, insurance, and so on. Third, it includes the sum of net transfers from abroad by emigrants and net expenditures abroad by tourists.

THE MERCHANDISE ACCOUNT

In Table M.1 I supply the official figures on Russian imports (c.i.f.) and exports (f.o.b.) from the official *Obzor vneshnei torgovli* (Survey of Foreign Trade) series

Table M.1. *Russian exports and imports, including silver and net merchandise balance, 1885 to 1913 (million credit rubles)*

	(1) Exports, excluding silver	(2) Silver exports	(3) Total exports	(4) Imports excluding silver	(5) Silver imports	(6) Total imports	(7) Merchandise balance (6 - 3)
1885	538	3	541	435	4	439	+102
1886	484	2	486	427	5	432	+54
1887	617	3	620	400	4	404	+216
1888	784	4	792	386	11	397	+395
1889	751	3	754	432	9	441	+313
1890	692	4	696	407	7	414	+282
1891	707	5	712	372	11	383	+329
1892	476	4	480	400	9	409	+71
1893	599	7	606	450	18	468	+138
1894	669	7	676	554	22	576	+100
1895	689	1	690	526	14	540	+150
1896	689	2	691	590	29	619	+72
1897	727	5	732	560	47	607	+125
1898	733	3	736	618	31	649	+87
1899	627	2	629	651	34	685	-56
1900	716	18	734	626	29	654	+71
1901	762	4	766	593	9	602	+164
1902	860	6	866	599	6	605	+261
1903	1001	2	1003	682	7	689	+314
1904	1006	35	1041	651	19	670	+371
1905	1077	40	1117	635	57	692	+425
1906	1095	7	1102	801	16	817	+285
1907	1053	1	1054	847	9	856	+198
1908	998	4	1002	913	12[a]	925	+77
1909	1428	-[a]	1428	906	12[a]	918	+510
1910	1449	-[a]	1449	1084	12[a]	1096	+353
1911	1591	-[a]	1591	1162	13[a]	1175	+416
1912	1519	-[a]	1519	1172	18[a]	1190	+329
1913	1520	-[a]	1520	1374	18[a]	1392	+128

[a] Net figures are given only.

Sources: *Obzor vneshnei torgovli Rossii po evropeiskoi i aziatskoi granitsam za . . . .* (Petersburg: Departament tamozhennykh sbory, various years); V. I. Pokrovsky, ed., *Sbornik svedenii po istorii i statistike vneshnei torgovli Rossii*, vol. 1 (Petersburg: Departament tamozhennykh sborov, 1902). The silver (net) import figures are taken for the period 1911-13 from A. I. Bukovetsky, "'Svobodnaia nalichnost' i zolotoi zapas tsarskogo pravitel' stva v kontse XIX nachale XX v.," in M. P. Viatkin, ed., *Monopolii i inostrany kapital v Rossii* (Moscow: Nauka, 1962), p. 274.

published by the Department of Tariff Collections (Departament tamozhennykh sborov).[10] Controversy surrounds the *Obzor* figures, for some observers claim that they overstate the value of imports and understate the value of exports and thus render the merchandise balance less positive than it actually was. Such criticism of the *Obzor* figures is based upon two types of evidence: The first is evidence that the Russian customs evaluation system led directly to the understatement of exports and the overstatement of imports. This position has been advanced by Miller and by Sonntag.[11] On the import side, Miller supplies some anecdotal evidence regarding the overstatement of the value of imported steel rails (p. 43) and explains this phenomenon as an attempt by the importer to justify higher steel prices in the Russian market. I find this argument to be generally unconvincing, for the customs declaration would have had little to do with the eventual market price of the imported commodity, and I see little to be gained by a high customs declaration. The exception may have been instances where the importer sold directly to the state (such as the cited instance of steel rails), but even here the state was well aware of the market price of steel rails abroad and would be in a position to evaluate the reliability of the customs evaluation. On the export side, Miller cites the 1902 work of V. I. Pokrovsky, the long time director of the statistical department of the customs office, concerning comparisons of customs prices and market prices of cereal exports.[12] Pokrovsky finds the correspondence between customs prices, domestic market prices, and foreign market prices imperfect. In fact, in some years, the deviations appear to be substantial. In defense of the customs prices, one should note that for the period investigated by Pokrovsky (1851 to 1897, where the period 1885 to 1897 is of primary concern to us) there is no uniform tendency for customs prices to understate the domestic market price: in some years it exceeded, in other years it was less than, the market price. Thus the Pokrovsky study does not support the understatement argument. It does show that *foreign* cereal prices (London and Germany) were above both domestic market prices and customs prices in Russia, but this is more likely the consequence of adding on freight and insurance charges to the price of imported cereals in these markets. Miller's own explanation of the understatement argument is that exporters had to pay for the customs price and thus attempted to understate the values of the exported product. I find this argument also unconvincing, first because the cost of the customs evaluation was minimal anyway and second because customs officials had easy access to current market prices of cereal products and raw materials, most of which were quoted on local exchanges and were published regularly in trade journals.

The more likely explanation for the divergence between customs prices and market prices was the nonintegration of the Russian wheat market and the considerable seasonal fluctuations in market prices, especially of cereals. Odessa market prices and average prices of several markets are used by Pokrovsky for his comparisons; yet one can find considerable deviations between Odessa market prices, internal prices, and other port market prices.[13] In fact, if one uses Odessa prices alone, one finds (using Pokrovsky's data) that the customs prices (weighted by value in exports) of major grains were about 4% below Odessa prices. When one uses average market prices, one finds that customs prices were 3% above market prices in the 1880s and 1890s. Moreover, the customs prices were levied at the moment of export and would thus reflect seasonal fluctuations in cereal prices, whereas the market prices are simply unweighted averages of monthly price quotations. This point was not overlooked by Pokrovsky, who noted that this alone could lead to considerable deviations between customs and "market" evaluations. In sum, comparisons of customs prices and market prices fail to reveal substantive differences in the case of cereal grains. One cannot generalize from this experiment to all exports, but this seems to provide powerful support for customs prices because of the importance of cereal exports (about one-half the total value of exports).

The second source of evidence against the use of the *Obzor* figures is that they deviate from totals compiled by adding up exports to and from Russia cited by foreign statistical authorities.[14] The Department of Customs Collections was itself cognizant of these differences and published comparisons of its own statistics with aggregates of Russian exports and imports compiled from the foreign trade statistics of other countries.[15] Such comparisons show that the value of imports reported as being received *from* Russia by foreign countries exceeded the value of Russian exports reported by the *Obzor* series. On the other hand, the value of exports reported by foreign countries as being sent to Russia fell short of the Russian import figure cited by the *Obzor* series. For 1908, for example, the value of imports received by twenty countries *from* Russia was 1408 million rubles, as compared to the Russian export figure of 930 million rubles, whereas the value of exports *to* Russia reported by these countries was 738 million rubles, as compared with the official Russian import figure of 873 million rubles.[16] From this evidence, after adjustment for transport costs, Sonntag concludes that Russian exports were grossly undervalued and that the positive merchandise trade balance was grossly underestimated.[17]

I find Sonntag's arguments less than convincing. First, as the Russian authorities and much later Bonwetsch[18] have pointed out, one cannot rely upon aggregations of the foreign trade statistics of other countries because there will be considerable double counting of imports from Russia. For example, some countries counted goods received directly from Russia but later transshipped to other countries as imports from Russia and then these same goods entered the import statistics of the third country. Only the exporting country can unambiguously avoid this double counting. Second, it should be noted that the *Obzor* series does indeed net out goods transshipped to third countries by counting only commodities released for domestic consumption, whereas the import statistics of other countries likely include double counting. Moreover, as the above figures for 1908 indicate, the difference between foreign aggregate and *Obzor* import valuations is fairly small and is likely accounted for by transport costs (the foreign figures are f.o.b. and the Russian import figures are c.i.f.) plus some double counting. Thus, in my view, the foreign import aggregates generally *support* the accuracy of the *Obzor* import series. The major discrepancy is in the Russian export series. Here it should be noted that a freight cost adjustment (approximately 25%) would eliminate approximately one-half of the discrepancy, and in my view double counting could easily account for the remainder. In general, I would argue that, given the wide knowledge of prices of raw materials and food products within Russia, customs officials would be quite unlikely to deliver a downward-biased estimate of Russian exports. In fact, the Ministry of Finance, of which the customs office was a part, was at the time making every effort to present an image of financial stability to the rest of the world. It is therefore unlikely that the Ministry of Finance would tolerate biased esti- mates of Russian imports and exports that would damage this image. In fact, if anything, the temptation would be to reverse the bias and overstate (understate) the value of exports (imports). The figures on customs and market prices of Russian exports suggest that Russian statistical authorities were able to resist this temptation.

My conclusion thus is that the official *Obzor* series are the most reliable estimates of Russian exports and imports and are sufficiently reliable for use in this study. I share this judgment with B. V. Avilov,[19] the authoritative editor of the statistical appendix on Russian economic development for the *Granat* encyclo- pedia, who argues that tsarist foreign trade statistics were reliable, an enthusiasm Avilov failed to hold for other official statistical series. This judgment is also shared by E. V. Dvoretski in his doctoral dissertation on Russian historical foreign trade statistics conducted for the Institute of History of the USSR Academy of Sciences.[20]

Turning to the *Obzor* figures for the period 1885 to 1913 (Table M.1), one can see that the merchandise balance was positive throughout the period with the exception of one year (1889). If one breaks this period into three subperiods, pre-gold standard (1885-1897), gold standard to the conclusion of the civil unrest in 1905 (1897-1906), and then the immediate prewar period (1906-1913), then once can note a steady increase in the positive merchandise balance from an annual average of about 200 million rubles (1885-1897), to 225 million rubles (1897-1906), and to 290 million rubles (1906-1913). One should also note the considerable annual fluctuations in the merchandise balance, ranging from a low of -56 million rubles in 1899 to a high of 510 million rubles in 1909.

INTEREST AND DIVIDEND PAYMENTS ABROAD

Tsarist financial officials, Soviet authors, and Western government authorities have shared an interest in Russia's foreign indebtedness. Tsarist authorities were concerned about the magnitude of foreign indebtedness, its impact on the balance of payments, and the possibility that continued dependence upon foreign capital would lead to a loss of economic and political independence.[21] On the other hand, foreign capital was viewed as a means to accelerate Russia's economic development by sub- stituting for inadequate domestic savings and technological know-how.[22] At the same time, there was fear that a chronic balance of payments deficit would force per- sistent borrowing abroad and would thus occasion a loss of political independence.[23] The later Soviet literature, stimulated by Lenin's noted studies of Russian economic development and imperialism, also recognized the advantages and disadvantages of foreign capital.[24]   Lenin himself noted that foreign capital could accelerate the economic development of backward countries and lead to a position of semi-colonial dependence.   During the Stalin era, where the avoidance of foreign capital was a matter of basic policy, the negative aspects of foreign capital were emphasized, and tsarist Russia was depicted as a "semi-colony" of the capitalist West.[25]   More recent Soviet literature has come to emphasize again the positive aspects of foreign capital, making the point that tsarist Russia was able to attract foreign capital without the loss of political and economic independence.[26]

The interest of Western authorities in Russian foreign indebtedness dates back to the period when Western investors were making substantial direct and indirect investments in Russia.[27]   In the early Soviet period, this interest was translated into efforts to reconstruct balances of Russian foreign indebtedness in the hope that the Bolshevik regime would eventually assume responsibility for tsarist debts.[28]

Because of this interest in foreign indebtedness from various sides, a rather substantial literature exists on Russian external debts, both public and private. In this study, I employ this literature, first, to estimate Russian foreign debt and then to establish interest and dividend yields for calculating annual debt service obligations abroad.   I begin first with the foreign indebtedness of the imperial government and of quasi-governmental banks (the Noble Land Bank and the Peasant Land Bank).

External debt of the imperial government

I employ two types of information to calculate annual interest payments to foreigners by the imperial government.   The first is the published budgetary data on annual interest payments on public debt; the second is data on the percentage of such payments (or the percentage of debt) received by foreigners.   Information on interest payments is readily available in the annual reports of the Ministry of Finance on the execution of the imperial budget in which a special account for "payments of state debt" was reported.[29]   More problematic is the estimation of the percentage of such interest payments going to foreigners.

For the estimation of the percentage of public interest payments abroad several types of data are available, upon which the numerous official Russian and later Soviet studies are based.   The first is information reported annually by the Ministry of Finance on the "presence" (nalichnost') of public debt instruments on deposit in Russian banks.[30]   Such data were reported for the period 1893 to 1914. By subtracting the value of public debt instruments held within the country from the total in circulation, the residual serves as a rough indicator of public debt held abroad.   These nalichnost' figures are typically regarded as overstating[31] the percentage of public debt held by foreigners, as many Russian bondholders did not keep them in banks where they would enter the nalichnost' statistics.

The second source of information on the distribution of public debt between domestic and foreign holders is limited to the period 1904 to 1914.[32]   This is data gathered by the Ministry of Finance on actual bank payments on public debt made abroad (*oplata russkikh gosudarstvennykh zaimov v Imperii i zagranitsei*). The total of such foreign payments is typically regarded as an *understatement* of actual interest payments to foreigners, as many foreign debt holders received interest payments through accounts in Russian commercial banks. For the period prior to 1893, the only sources of information on the distribution of public debt between internal and external owners was that on location of issue (was the issue floated at home or abroad?) and on whether the issue was floated in gold, credit rubles, or in a foreign currency. Most studies of the pre-1893 period[33] (Ol', Gindin, Bovykin) assume that the public loans floated either in gold or in foreign currencies were indeed purchased by foreigners, and, accordingly, that the percentage of public debt denominated in metal or foreign currencies could serve as an indicator of the distribution of public debt between internal and external holders.

In sum, the major problem is to establish the breakdown of the public debt owned internally and externally during the period 1885 to 1913 from these data sources. Insofar as the percentage of bank payments abroad on public debt represents an underestimate and the percentage of public debt on deposit (*nalichnost'*) in Russian banks yields an overestimate of the percentage of debt held abroad, I have chosen to take an unweighted average of the two percentages. In 1913, for example,· the percentage of payments on public debt going abroad was 44% and the percentage of public debt not deposited in Russian banks (*ne nalichnost'*) was 52%. Thus the percentage used in this study is the average, or 48%, where the margin of error is ±4%. To establish a time series of the percent of public debt owned by foreigners, I use the percentage of debt *ne nalichnost'* to backcast the 1913 figure. The backcast figures coincide almost perfectly with the percentages backcast using the bank payments abroad figures (available to 1904); so this backcasting method appears to be reasonably reliable. For the pre-1893 period (before *nalichnost'* data), I use an index of the percentage of public debt denominated in metal and foreign currencies to backcast the percentage of foreign public debt. This backcasting shows a minor decrease in the percent of foreign public debt between 1885 and 1893.

To calculate interest payments abroad on imperial government debt, I multiply the estimated percentages of foreign public debt to total public debt (where public debt includes state-guaranteed railroad bonds and the debt of the Noble Land Bank and the Peasant Land Bank) by the annual interest payments of the imperial government (again including interest payments of the Noble and Peasant land banks). These calculations are shown in Table M.2. In column 1, I supply the annual interest payments on public debt taken directly from the annual budget reports. In column 2, annual interest payments by the Noble and Peasant land banks are given, and the sum in column 3 represents total interest payments on public debt. In column 4 I supply the estimated percentages of public debt held by foreigners, the calculation of which is described above, and in column 5 total interest payments abroad (the product of the percentage times total interest payments) are given.

As table M.2 indicates, public interest payments abroad increased steadily between 1885 and 1913, rising from 134 million rubles in 1885 to 221 million rubles in 1913. Comparing these figures with the merchandise balances for the entire

Table M.2. *Interest payments abroad, public debt of imperial government, including guaranteed railway bonds and mortgages of the Peasant and Noble Land Banks (million credit rubles)*

	(1) Interest payments, public debt, official budget figures	(2) Interest payments, Peasant and Noble Land banks	(3) Total interest payments (1 + 2)	(4) Proportion of public debt held by foreigners (%)	(5) Interest payments abroad on public debt (4 × 3)
1885	223	1	224	60	134
1886	223	4	227	60	136
1887	227	5	232	59	137
1888	233	6	239	59	141
1889	234	9	243	59	143
1890	230	11	241	58	140
1891	216	11	227	58	132
1892	219	15	234	58	136
1893	235	16	251	58	146
1894	238	17	255	57	145
1895	250	17	267	58	155
1896	234	17	251	56	141
1897	246	23	269	57	153
1898	248	20	268	57	153
1899	246	23	269	57	153
1900	248	26	274	57	156
1901	249	29	278	55	153
1902	258	33	291	55	160
1903	267	49	316	55	174
1904	265	40	305	54	165
1905	285	43	328	54	177
1906	315	43	358	51	163
1907	359	50	409	52	213
1908	374	62	436	52	227
1909	372	70	442	51	225
1910	383	74	457	50	229

1911	374	78	452	50	226
1912	368	83	451	49	221
1913	372	89	461	48	221

Sources: Column 1: The official budget figures on interest payments on public debt are from *Entwurf des Reichsbudgets der Einnahmen und Ausgaben für das Jahr . . .,* 1907 to 1914 annual editions; *Ezhegodnik ministerstva finansov,* 1905, 1906–7; *Bericht des Finanzministers für das Jahr . . . ,* 1894, 1896, 1902 editions; *Les Finances de la Russe D'Apres les documents officiels,* Paris, 1896–7, 1888; *Bulletin Russe de Statistique financiere et de Legislation,* 1901 edition, p. 60; "Allgemeines Reichsbudget der Einnahmen und Ausgaben für das Jahr 1886," *Russische Revue,* 26:1–21.

Column 2: Data on the indebtedness of the Noble Land Bank and Peasant Land Bank are incomplete. For the Noble bank, interpolations must be made for the period 1893 to 1898, but the amounts involved are small and there was apparently not much change during the interpolated period. Data on the outstanding debt obligations of the two banks in circulation (v obrashcheniu) are drawn from *Ezhegodnik ministerstva finansov,* 1905 to 1911 editions (sections *Gosudarstvenny dvorianski bank* and *Krestianski pozemel'ny bank*); *Statisticheski ezhegodnik Rossii,* 1911 to 1914 editions, same headings; *Entwurf des Reichsbudgets,* 1913, part 2, p. 155; *Vestnik finansov,* no. 23 (April–June):442–445; *Sbornik svedenii po Rossii,* 1890, p. 204. In many of these publications, the debt portfolios of both banks are given so that one can calculate their average annual interest rates. In the case of the Noble bank, the interest rate rounded to 4% for the entire period, and for the Peasant bank, the interest rate varied from 4.5% in the early period, dropping to 4% in the mid-period, and then rising to almost 5% after 1906. Annual interest payments are calculated by applying these interest rates to the outstanding debt of both banks.

Column 4: Data for the calculation of the proportion of foreign debt are taken from The figures on the percent of government debt instruments in circulation and on deposit in Russia (v nalichnost'i) are supplied in I. F. Gindin, *Russkie kommercheskie banki* (Moscow: Gosfinizdat, 1948), pp. 452–3, and in the *Ezhegodnik ministerstva finansov* series (section *kassovy otchet Ministerstva Finansov*). The figures on interest payments to foreigners through Russian banks are supplied by A. L. Vainshtein, *Narodnoe bogatstvo i narodno-khoziaistvennoe nakoplenie predrevoliutsionoi Rossii* (Moscow: Gosstatizdat, 1960), p. 435; *Russki denezhny rynok 1908–1912* (Petersburg: Osobennaia kantseliaria po kreditnoi chasti, 1914), diagram 3, and Gindin, *Russkie,* pp. 446–7. Data on the change in the share of payments in metal currencies between 1884 and 1893 are given in V. I. Bovykin, "K voprosu o roli innostranogo kapitala v Rossii," *Vestnik Moskovskogo Universiteta,* no. 1 (1964):62. Because Bovykin gives figures for only 1884 and 1893, the intervening percentages are interpolated. For a more complete discussion of the derivation of column 4, consult the text.

period, we find that interest payments abroad for public debt canceled approximately
three-fourths of the positive merchandise balance (given in table M.1).

Interest and dividend payments abroad of Russian corporations and repatriated pro-
fits of foreign-owned nonincorporated enterprises
Corporations: For the calculation of dividend payments by Russian corporations to
foreigners, I rely heavily upon the noted study by P. V. Ol' of foreign capital in
Russia.[34] The only adjustment I make in Ol's figure is to raise the equity capital
figures by the 10% suggested by Bonwetsch in his evaluation of the Ol' study.[35]
This upward adjustment is fully consistent with Ol's own view of his work as likely
understating the extent of foreign capital in Russia.[36] In his study of foreign
capital, Ol' has estimated the value of corporate equities owned by foreigners,
annual dividend yields, and corporate bonds owned by foreigners. Thus one can
calculate annual interest and dividend payments abroad by Russian corporations by
multiplying the annual dividend yield by the value of foreign-owned equities and the
annual average interest rate on corporate bonds by the value of corporate bonds held
by foreigners. All of this information, with the exception of average interest
rates on corporate debt, is supplied by Ol'.

Because of the important role played by the Ol' foreign capital estimates in
this study, it is important to consider their reliability. Several scholars have
subjected the Ol' study to considerable scrutiny[37] and have concluded that Ol's
figures are reasonably reliable, although there is some controversy over whether he
understated or overstated foreign capital for the immediate prewar period.[38] Nevertheless, the consensus opinion is that the Ol' estimates are reliable, especially as
indexes over time. One problem with the Ol' study is that the actual details of his
calculations are not supplied. Rather, what Ol' does is to outline his general
methodology, state his sources, and then give his overall results. The absence of
detail is explained by the fact that Ol' was working primarily from annual corporate
reports, accounts of shareholder meetings, and so on, and it would have been virtually impossible for him to describe in detail the specifics of his calculations.
One can, however, get some feel for his methods from his earlier work (1897) on the
Russian balance of payments.[39] The point is that one must, to a great extent,
simply trust Ol's work, as it represents an enormous effort, much of which was based
upon unpublished data available to him in the Finance Ministry, which an outsider
could not duplicate.

A few words are in order concerning the general methodology of Ol'. To determine the share of foreign equity capital, Ol' subdivided corporations into nine
categories according to the degree of foreign participation in equity capital. For
example, the first two categories-direct Russian affiliates of foreign corporations,
and corporations set up entirely by foreigners for work in Russia-represented corporations in which virtually 100% of equity capital was foreign owned. The other
seven categories represent corporations in which equity capital was both foreign and
domestic owned, and for these categories foreign capital shares are established by
various means, such as the composition of the boards of directors, where stock

prices were quoted, affiliations with foreign banks, and so on. To determine foreign participation in obligation capital, Ol' subdivided corporate debt into five categories, where the categories were determined by whether the debt was floated in foreign currencies or gold and whether the corporation was a direct affiliate of a foreign corporation.

Using this general methodology, Ol' studied detailed data on corporations published in journals such as *Vestnik finansov, Torgovo-Promyshlennaia gazeta, and Pravitel'stvenny Vestnik* as well as unpublished data to separate corporations into these various categories and then establish, in the case of mixed foreign and domestic capital, the shares of each. The reader interested in viewing some of the raw data with which Ol' worked, should look at the various special issues of the *Vestnik finansov* devoted entirely to annual corporate reports.

Ol's calculations of average annual dividend yields are subject to less controversy, for it was a fairly easy (though time-consuming) task to establish average yields from the mass of published stock market data.

In Table M.3, I supply (columns 1-3) the value of corporate equities owned by foreigners, average dividend yields on such equities, and foreign-owned obligation capital of Russian corporations. In column 4 I supply the estimated average annual interest rate paid on corporate obligation capital. I have estimated these rates by assuming a ten-year average maturity for corporate debt and then using the official discount rate plus 1% (on twelve-month notes).[40] The annual dividend rate is then applied to the value of foreign equity holdings to yield annual dividend payments abroad (column 5), and the average annual interest rate is applied to foreign-held corporate debt to yield annual interest payments abroad (Column 6).

Nonincorporated enterprises: Payments abroad to owners of nonincorporated enterprises cannot be estimated with any degree of precision, but the amount involved is relatively small. I begin with Vainshtein's estimates of the value of nonincorporated capital stock owned by foreigners,[41] which he estimates to be approximately 215 million rubles in 1913. Vainshtein's figure is based upon a 1908 survey conducted by the Ministry of Trade and Industry, and he counts as foreign-owned all those enterprises in which the owner was a foreigner. Vainshtein believed that this figure was likely an underestimate because it included only enterprises having fifteen or more workers and consequently subject to factory inspection. Vainshtein further makes a rough adjustment to include trade establishments, assuming equivalent proportions of foreign ownership of nonincorporated trade establishments.

The 1913 figure of foreign capital in nonincorporated enterprises is backcast using Strumilin's estimates of nonincorporated capital in industry and trade establishments.[42] Thus I assume a constant share of foreign ownership throughout the 1885 to 1913 period. In this manner, foreign-owned capital in nonincorporated enterprises is established for the entire period, and I then assume the repatriated profit rate to equal the dividend rate on corporate equities. The basis for this assumption is that this dividend rate represents the opportunity cost to the foreign owner of the nonincorporated enterprise. These figures are given in Table M.4.

Table M.3. *Interest and dividend payments abroad of Russian corporations (million credit rubles)*

	(1) Foreign-owned stock (Ol' figure)[a]	(2) Average dividend yield (%)	(3) Foreign-owned corporate debt (Ol' figure)	(4) Average interest rate, corporate debt (2 × 4)	(5) Annual[a] foreign dividend payments 1.1 (1 × 3)	(6) Annual foreign interest payments, corporate debt	(7) Total (5 + 6)
1885	147	6.3	12	7.1	10	1	11
1886	159	6.8	14	7.0	12	1	13
1887	161	6.8	16	6.9	12	1	13
1888	178	6.5	17	7.1	13	1	14
1889	179	7.1	19	7.0	14	1	15
1890	186	6.4	29	7.0	13	2	15
1891	198	6.1	33	7.1	13	2	15
1892	202	6.4	34	7.2	14	3	17
1893	203	7.2	35	7.1	16	3	19
1894	210	7.8	35	7.1	18	3	21
1895	244	8.9	36	6.9	24	3	27
1896	321	7.5	48	7.9	27	4	31
1897	379	7.2	63	8.0	30	5	35
1898	476	7.4	87	8.3	39	7	46
1899	644	5.8	118	8.5	41	10	51
1900	762	4.8	149	8.9	40	13	53
1901	814	3.8	161	8.8	34	14	48
1902	815	3.9	167	8.8	35	15	50
1903	829	4.1	179	9.0	37	16	53
1904	851	4.0	172	9.0	37	16	53
1905	850	3.8	188	9.3	36	18	54
1906	905	3.9	183	9.2	39	17	56
1907	945	4.3	190	9.2	45	18	63
1908	989	4.3	199	9.3	47	19	66
1909	1027	5.1	216	9.3	58	20	78
1910	1126	5.8	233	9.0	72	21	93
1911	1288	6.5	247	8.8	92	22	114
1912	1482	7.2	257	8.7	117	22	139
1913	1701	6.8	260	8.7	127	23	150
1914	1856	4.0	269	8.7	82	23	105
1915	1939	5.3	267	8.7	113	23	136

[a]The Ol' figure is adjusted upward by 10%. See text.

Interest payments abroad of Russian cities: Information on the indebtedness of Russian cities is incomplete. Figures on their total indebtedness are available for the periods 1888-1893, 1900, and 1908-1914 from various sources.[43] Moreover, it is difficult to gather information on the average interest rates paid by Russian cities for municipal debt, but there is evidence that it remained around 5% for the entire 1885 to 1913 period,[44] that is, slightly above the average rates paid by the imperial government. The share of municipal debt owned abroad also cannot be established with any precision, although most sources agree that existing regulations made it difficult for Russian cities to float bond issues at home and that the major municipal bond flotations occurred in the European capitals.[45] In fact, it was likely that between 80% and 90% of municipal bonds were owned by foreigners.[46]

My calculation of interest payments abroad by Russian municipalities proceeds as follows: I begin with Vainshtein's estimate of foreign-owned municipal debt for the period 1912 to 1914. To arrive at his figures, Vainshtein takes the average of municipal bonds floated abroad between 1908 and 1912 (75%) and applies this percentage to the total indebtedness of Russian cities in 1913 (445 million rubles) to arrive at a figure of 334 million rubles. To this Vainshtein adds on another 40 million rubles for foreign-owned bonds purchased in Russian bond markets; this yields a 1913 total of 420 million rubles, or 83% of municipal debt in 1913. This percentage is much higher than that estimated by Gindin,[47] but other sources appear to support the higher Vainshtein estimate.[48] I backcast this figure by assuming that this percentage of foreign to total municipal debt remained constant throughout the period. This assumption is likely reasonably accurate back to 1900. Prior to 1900, the estimated values are quite small anyway. To obtain annual interest payments abroad, I use a 5% yield for the entire period. These final figures are given in column 3 of Table M.4.

NET TOURIST EXPENDITURES

An important, yet most difficult to estimate, item in the Russian balance of payments is net tourist expenditures abroad. Not unlike other historical series, the net tourist account of Russia must be derived from various indirect sources, and the end result incorporates a fairly wide margin of error. Various estimates have been made of the Russian net tourist expenditure account, and all agree that it was large and passive and contributed to Russia's passive *raschetny balans*. The reasons for this passive account are fairly obvious: Russia was definitely not a tourist attraction, and returns from incoming tourists were small. Foreigners who did travel to Russia typically did so for business reasons and more often than not entered Russia in order to earn a livelihood. Thus even those entering Russia did not necessarily bring foreign currencies to spend but counted instead on earning rubles through employment in Russia. In some instances, foreign specialists would accumulate ruble savings, which they would then take with them on annual visits home or when they left Russia for good. On the other hand, there is reason to believe that tourist expenditures by Russians traveling abroad were indeed substantial. Wealthy and middle-class Russians typically vacationed in Europe (often on extended visits),

Table M.4. *Repatriated profits of foreign-owned nonincorporated enterprises and foreign interest payments of cities (million credit rubles)*

	(1) Foreign-owned capital	(2) Payments abroad repatriated profits	(3) Interest payments abroad, Russian cities	(4) Total (2 + 3)
1886	75	5	1	6
1887	88	6	2	8
1888	82	5	2	7
1889	82	6	2	8
1890	82	5	2	7
1891	80	5	3	8
1892	82	5	3	8
1893	88	6	3	9
1894	97	8	3	11
1895	105	9	3	12
1896	110	8	4	12
1897	116	8	4	12
1898	123	9	4	13
1899	142	8	4	12
1900	142	7	4	11
1901	138	5	5	10
1902	131	5	5	10
1903	131	5	5	10
1904	140	6	6	12
1905	144	6	6	12
1906	140	6	7	13
1907	148	6	8	14
1908	159	7	9	16
1909	155	8	11	19
1910	176	10	13	23
1911	191	12	15	27
1912	206	15	16	31
1913	215	15	19	34
1914	220	9	21	30

and Russian students often attended European universities, all of which led to an outflow of Russian currency. To this, one must add the substantial emigration of Poles, Jews, and Lithuanians, which took place in the late nineteenth and early twentieth centuries. Although such emigrants were typically from lower income brackets, they nevertheless took with them whatever savings they had accumulated.[49]

Several estimates of net tourist expenditures have been made for the Russian Empire. Ol' estimated that average annual net tourist expenditures between 1881 and 1895 were approximately 65 million credit rubles, but a reading of his methodology indicates his estimates apply to the early 1890s. Vyshnegradski placed such expenditures between 30 million rubles and 80 million rubles between 1888 and 1895. Migulin estimated them between 75 and 100 million rubles at a time of the introduction of the gold standard (1897), and Engeev placed them around 100 million rubles in the first years of the twentieth century and between 150 and 200 million rubles in 1913.[50] Bukovetski places the 1913 figure at 172 million rubles.[51] All of these figures are generally consistent with one another, as I indicated above.

These estimates rest upon a generally common methodology: They begin with the official figures on Russian and foreign citizens passing through Russian borders with either passports or *legitimatsionnye bilety* (for border residents, good for one to two days). Then the average length of stay of Russians abroad is estimated and multiplied by the presumed average per diem expenditures abroad by Russian tourists. Russian travelers are typically divided into two groups: those traveling temporarily abroad and those living permanently abroad, the latter category being estimated from the excess of travelers leaving over those returning.[52] In this manner, gross tourist expenditures are calculated. Net expenditures are derived by subtracting foreign tourist expenditures in Russia; the net figure is approximately 90% of the gross figure.[53] It would require a great deal of discussion to describe the Ol', Vyshnegradski, and Engeev calculations in detail, but I should note that the firmest figures upon which they are based are the data on travelers crossing the Russian border in both directions.[54]

I now turn to a description of my calculation of the net tourist account. Unfortunately, it requires a lengthy explanation, which must be included because of the importance of this account. My procedure for calculating net tourist expenditures abroad is also based upon physical numbers of travelers passing through Russian borders, but it also employs three additional sources of information: data on the average length of stay abroad of Russians returning from foreign travel; information on the average incomes of middle- and upper-class Russians; and the social composition of Russian travelers. All these data sources pertain to the period 1904 to 1906, and the first indicates that the average stay abroad of returning Russian travelers was approximately one hundred days,[55] and the second that the average income of Russian citizens earning 1000 rubles or more per year was 4300 rubles (1904).[56] Moreover, survey data from the same period indicate that some 45% of Russian travelers were in the "middle" or "upper" income category,[57] although these concepts are not defined.

My method is as follows: First I estimate average daily expenditures of Russians abroad in 1913 to apply to the number of Russians traveling abroad (with passports). This I do by assuming that the average annual expenditure per adult (husband and wife) equaled 2150 rubles in 1904 (one half of the 1904 income figure cited above) for middle- and upper-class travelers. This represents a figure of 6 rubles per day; thus 45% of the travelers in 1904 are assumed to spend 6 rubles per day while traveling abroad. The remainder (55%) are assumed to spend one-half as to two days). Then the average length of stay of Russians abroad is estimated and multiplied by the presumed average per diem expenditures abroad by Russian tourists. Russian travelers are typically divided into two groups: those traveling temporarily abroad and those living permanently abroad, the latter category being estimated from the excess of travelers leaving over those returning.[52] In this manner, gross tourist expenditures are calculated. Net expenditures are derived by subtracting foreign tourist expenditures in Russia; the net figure is approximately 90% of the gross figure.[53] It would require a great deal of discussion to describe the Ol', Vyshnegradski, and Engeev calculations in detail, but I should note that the firmest figures upon which they are based are the data on travelers crossing the Russian border in both directions.[54]

I now turn to a description of my calculation of the net tourist account. Unfortunately, it requires a lengthy explanation, which must be included because of the importance of this account. My procedure for calculating net tourist expenditures abroad is also based upon physical numbers of travelers passing through Russian borders, but it also employs three additional sources of information: data on the average length of stay abroad of Russians returning from foreign travel; information on the average incomes of middle- and upper-class Russians; and the social composition of Russian travelers. All these data sources pertain to the period 1904 to 1906, and the first indicates that the average stay abroad of returning Russian travelers was approximately one hundred days,[55] and the second that the average income of Russian citizens earning 1000 rubles per year or more was 4300 rubles (1904).[56] Moreover, survey data from the same period indicate that some 45% of Russian travelers were in the "middle" or "upper" income category,[57] although these concepts are not defined.

My method is as follows: First I estimate average daily expenditures of Russians abroad in 1913 to apply to the number of Russians traveling abroad (with passports). This I do by assuming that the average annual expenditure per adult (husband and wife) equaled 2150 rubles in 1904 (one half of the 1904 income figure cited above) for middle- and upper-class travelers. This represents a figure of 6 rubles per day; thus 45% of the travelers in 1904 are assumed to spend 6 rubles per day while traveling abroad. The remainder (55%) are assumed to spend one-half as much, or 3 rubles per day. This latter figure was well above 1904 per capita daily income, but I assume that the poor were practically precluded from foreign travel by the prohibitive cost of a passport (14 rubles per year). Combining the two per diem figures yields a per diem average of 4.4 rubles in 1904. If one further assumes constant real expenditures between 1904 and 1913 (a modest assumption), this translates to a per diem figure of 7.2 rubles in 1913, or for an average stay of 100 days, 720 rubles per traveler.

How does this figure compare with the estimates of others? Engeev used a much lower figure.[58] but he apparently used Ol's per diem estimate for the early 1890s and thus, in effect, is assuming no real growth and is making no adjustment for inflation. I therefore believe that one can dismiss Engeev's per diem figure as much too low. One can compare my per diem 1913 estimate with that of Ol' for circa 1890. Ol' arrives at a per diem figure of 4.5 rubles, which translates into 6.4 rubles in 1913 prices. A modest real growth of per diem expenditures would make the Ol' 1890 figure generally consistent with my own. In general, I believe my estimate of per diem expenditures to be an understatement, if anything, for if one applies a real annual growth rate of more than .6 percent to the Ol' perdiem figure, then one arrives at a higher 1913 per diem rate than my own figure.

Having established a 1913 per diem figure, it then remains to calculate 1913 tourist expenditures by Russian travelers. In 1913, 404,000 Russians traveled abroad (with passports) for less than one year. I multiply this number by the calculated expenditure per traveler (7.2 rubles times 100 days) to obtain a figure of 291 million rubles. Of those traveling with passports, 125,000 remained abroad longer than one year. To avoid any overstatement of their expenditures, I assume that only 1/10 of these were Russians living permanently abroad and not earning income abroad (spending at an annual rate of 2628 rubles).[59] yielding a figure of 33 million rubles for Russians living permanently abroad. The 1913 total is therefore 324 million rubles.

There remains the difficult matter of emigrant expenditures abroad and transfers of earlier emigrants to relatives in Russia. After a rather lengthy investigation of the available data on Russian emigrants.[60] I have decided that substantive errors would not be introduced into the accounts if one assumes that emigrant expenditures canceled emigrant transfers from abroad, thus rendering a net emigrant account of zero. The small intertemporal bias introduced by this assumption can be readily adduced: Emigrant transfers from abroad would have become extensive only in later years as the numbers of emigrants abroad grew; so it is likely that the net emigrant account was passive in the early years and then tended toward zero in later years as emigrant transfers increased. In this manner, the assumption of a zero net emigrant account will likely result in a small under-statement of the negative tourist expenditure account in the earlier years.

Having established 1913 expenditures by Russian tourists abroad, it remains to convert this into a net account by subtracting foreign tourist expenditures in Russia. This I do, for lack of further information, by using the ratios suggested by Ol' and by Engeev, who indicate an approximate ratio of net to gross tourist expenditures of between .8 to .9. I use the .9 ratio for 1913.

Finally, a time series of net tourist expenditures must be established for the entire period 1885 to 1913. I calculate two series using simplifying assumptions. The first series represents net tourist expenditures in constant 1913 prices. It is derived quite simply by applying the 1913 average expenditure figures (for returning travelers and for those living permanently abroad) to the numbers of Russian travelers returning and living permanently abroad in each of the years. From this first series, I calculate a current price series using the Podtiagin index of retail prices.

These calculations are shown in Table M.5: In column 1 the number of Russian travelers (with passports) remaining less than one year abroad is shown; in column 2 the number not returning within one year is given. In column 3 net tourist expenditures in 1913 prices are shown, and in column 4, net tourist expenditures in current prices are given. Finally, in column 5 the current price estimates of other researchers are supplied for purposes of comparison.

A comparison of my current price estimates with those of earlier researchers indicates a general agreement for the period before 1905, but with a slight tendency for my figures to fall below the contemporary estimates. This could easily be the consequence of my ignoring net emigrant outlays, but I simply do not have enough data to attempt a correction for emigrant outlays in the early years. In any case, the discrepancies between my figures and the contemporary figures do not appear serious enough to warrant a further correction of my figures, especially given the crude nature of the contemporary estimates. It should be noted further that my figures fall within the bounds established by Migulin and Engeev for the early gold standard era. The most serious discrepancies are for the end of the period: For 1913, I estimate net tourist expenditures at 292 million rubles, Engeev at 150-200 million rubles, and Bukovetski (after generous adjustment for emigrant transfers) arrives at a figure of 172 million rubles. My own figure is less than Khrulev's estimate of 406 million rubles, which most researchers dismiss as too high. In view of these discrepancies, it is worth considering why these differences have arisen. Bukovetski fails to supply any explanations of his calculations, but I imagine his methodology is quite similar to that of Engeev (as his figure is the average of the bounds set by Engeev). The Engeev figures are so low, as I mentioned earlier, because he takes the 1890 per diem expenditure figure of Ol' and applies it to 1913 expenditures, ignoring the fact that prices had risen substantially since the 1890s and that real expenditures themselves may have risen. Thus I believe that the Engeev and Bukovetski estimates must be regarded as too low. Another way to demonstrate this would be to use the Engeev figures as the 1913 base for the intertemporal index of net tourist expenditures. If one does this, then the resulting figures fall well below the contemporary estimates of Ol', Vyshnegradski, and Migulin. For instance, the 1892 figure calculated in this manner would be only one-half of the Ol' figure.

In sum, I would argue that my estimates of net tourist expenditures likely capture appropriate orders of magnitude and are supported by contemporary estimates of net tourist expenditures. They must, however, be regarded as approximate, as one has little solid information on the social composition of Russian travelers and their per diem outlays. The only firm figures are on physical numbers of travelers, and if average lengths of stay abroad or average per diem outlays abroad changed dramatically in real terms during this period, then my estimates will be off target. What I have assumed, in effect, is that Russian travelers were indeed drawn exclusively from the upper and middle classes and that they spent abroad per diem roughly what they would have spent at home. I believe the first assumption is quite realistic, as the cost of passports was prohibitive to lower income groups, and the second assumption is, if anything, a conservative one. It is not possible, in my view, to get more reasonable or accurate estimates of the net tourist account, and this is unfortunate because of the importance of this account.

Table M.5. *Calculation of net tourist expenditures abroad in 1913 and current year prices (million credit rubles)*

	(1) Russians travel-ing abroad with passports, stay-ing less than one year (1000)	(2) Russians travelling abroad staying longer than one year	(3) Net tourist expenditures .9 (720R × col. 1) + (.1 x 2630R × col. 2)	(4) Net tourist expenditures, current prices	(5) Other esti-mates, current prices
1885	59	10	41	33	
1886	54	15	39	29	
1887	45	18	33	25	
1888	51	12	36	28	30[a]
1889	79	37	60	47	
1890	65	41	52	39	
1891	95	42	71	55	
1892	87	40	67	54	65[b]
1893	87	49	68	54	
1894	85	27	61	46	
1895	112	30	80	58	80[a]
1896	128	28	89	63	
1897	133	26	102	75	
1898	137	39	98	76	75-100[c]
1899	142	45	103	80	
1900	195	35	134	106	
1901	193	40	135	107	
1902	175	38	122	98	80-100[d]
1903	177	70	131	104	
1904	—	—	144[g]	117	
1905	239	5	156	130	
1906	266	64	188	175	
1907	208	96	158	155	
1908	207	38	143	137	
1909	215	58	153	147	
1910	292	75	207	195	
1911	336	67	234	220	164[e]
1912	367	96	260	257	164[e]
1913	404	125	292	292	150-200[d]
					172[e]
					406[f]

Note: Dash indicates not available.
[a]Vyshnegradski.   [b]Ol'.   [c]Migulin.   [d]Engeev.   [e]Bukovetski.   [f]Khrulev.
[g]Midpoint between 1903 and 1905 values taken.
Sources: Column 1 and column 2: *Obzor vneshnei torgovli Rossii po evropeiskoi granitzam za . . . g.,* section *passazhirskoe dvizhenie,* various years; *Ezhegodnik ministerstva finansov,* various years, same section heading, *Ezhegodnik Rossii,* various years, same section heading; *Entsiklopedicheski slovar' Brokgauz-Efron,* heading *Emigratsiia,* vol. 80. Column 2 is calculated by subtracting the number of Russian travelers returning from the number leaving in a particular year. Column 1 is calculated by subtracting column 2 from the total number of Russian travelers leaving with passports in a particular year.
    Column 3: See text for an explanation. The .9 represents the ratio of net to gross tourist expenditures. The 720R is the estimated per passenger expenditure of Russian travelers spending less than one year abroad in 1913. The .1 is the assumed proportion of Russian travelers not returning within one year living permanently abroad (not emigrating) and not earning income abroad. Finally, the 2630R is the calculated annual expenditure abroad in 1913 of Russian tourists living permanently abroad.
    Column 4: Column 3 inflated by the consumer price index for Moscow and Petersburg in appendix A.

Table M.5 (*cont.*)

Column 5: These estimates are summarized in T. K. Engeev, "O platezhnom balanse dovoennoi Rossii," *Vestnik finansov*, no. 5 (1928):72-84. The Bukovetsky figures are in A. I. Bukovetsky, "'Svobodnaia nalichnost' i zolotoi zapas tsarskogo pravitel'stva v kontse XIX nachale XX v," in M. P. Viatkin, ed., *Monopolii i innostrany kapital v Rossii* (Moscow: Nauka, 1962), pp. 359-76.

MINOR ACCOUNTS: REPARATIONS, INSURANCE, FREIGHT, INTEREST RECEIVED FROM ABROAD, FOREIGN MILITARY EQUIPMENT

To complete the net foreign investment account, some minor items are supplied in Table M.6. The first item represents the reparation payments the Russian government received from Turkey, Bulgaria, and China between 1885 and 1913 (column 1). The second item represents payments by Russian insurance companies for reinsurance to foreign insurance companies. The third column supplies interest payments received from Russian public investments abroad. The fourth column represents expenditures abroad for military equipment (ships, artillery, etc.), which fail to appear in the import account.

Insofar as Russian imports are valued c.i.f. and exports f.o.b., it is necessary to include receipts by Russian ships from transporting exports and imports to foreign ports, and to net out receipts of foreign carriers from interport transport within the Russian Empire. After a careful examination of the massive data on Russian and foreign maritime activity,[61] I was able to conclude that the net freight account was roughly zero. This is true because only a small percentage of Russian imports and exports (about 10%) was carried in Russian bottoms and because interport transport within the Russian Empire by foreign ships was substantial. In both cases, the amounts involved were small and they likely cancel each other anyway.

Table M.6. *Miscellaneous items: reparations, insurance, interest received from abroad, foreign military equipment (million credit rubles)*

	Reparations received from foreign governments (+)	Reinsurance payments to foreign companies (-)	Interest received from abroad (+)	Military equipment purchased abroad (-)	Total (1-4)
1885	2	3	1	7	- 7
1886	2	5	1	7	- 9
1887	2	5	1	7	- 9
1888	1	3	1	7	- 8
1889	4	3	1	3	- 1
1890	7	1	1	4	+ 3
1891	4	1	2	9	- 4
1892	3	1	2	11	- 7
1893	4	5	2	12	-11
1894	3	5	2	14	-14
1895	3	5	3	11	-10
1896	2	6	3	11	-12
1897	2	6	3	10	-11
1898	5	6	3	10	- 8
1899	6	6	3	11	- 9
1900	3	7	3	12	-13
1901	3	7	3	12	-13
1902	16	7	4	(14)	- 1
1903	8	7	2	(16)	-13
1904	12	7	4	(18)	- 9
1905	12	8	3	(20)	-13
1906	10	8	2	22	-16
1907	11	8	2	18	-12
1908	11	8	3	18	-12
1909	11	9	5	19	-12
1910	7	9	5	19	-16
1911	8	9	6	17	-12
1912	8	9	7	16	-10
1913	8	9	6	18	-13

Note: A plus indicates a credit item, a minus indicates a debit item. Figures in parentheses are interpolated values.

Sources: Column 1: Entwurf des Reichsbudgets, 1907 to 1914 annual editions, *Sbornik svedenii po Rossii*, 1896, p. 255; *Les Finances de la Russe, D'Apres les documents officiels*, 1888 edition; *Bulletin Russe de statistique financiere et de legislation*, 4th ed. (1888), p. 473.

Column 2: S. F. Sharapov, *Tsifrovoi analiz raschetnogo balansa Rossii za 15-letie*, Doklad Obshchestvu dlia sodeistvii russkoi promyshlennosti i torgovli na osnovanii tsifrovykh dannykh P. V. Olem (Petersburg: Bernshtein, 1897); A. I. Bukovetsky, "'Svobodnaia nalichnost' i zolotoi zapas tsarskogo pravitel'stva v kontse XIX nachale XX v.," in M. P. Viatkin, ed., *Monopolii i innostrany kapital v Rossii* (Moscow: Nauka, 1962), p. 374. The years 1896 to 1910 are interpolated (increasing from 5 to 8 million rubles).

Column 3: Same sources as column 1. Budget item: interest received from assets held abroad.

Column 4: 1885 to 1895 from Sharapov, *Tsifrovoi*, pp. 23-26. After 1896, the series is extrapolated using an index of expenditures on military equipment by the War Ministry. These figures are taken from the budgetary sources in column 1.

1   In this appendix, by *raschetny balans* I mean net foreign investment or, in other words, the balance of trade including invisibles and services, such as freight charges, interest and dividend payments abroad, and tourist expenditures abroad. The conceptual definition is that adopted by the League of Nations in 1938 and is described in L. I. Frei, *Osnovnye problemy mezhdunarodnykh raschetov* (Moscow: Mezhdunarodnaia kniga, 1945), pp. 30-3.

2   For summaries of these discussions, see P. P. Migulin, *Reforma denezhnago obrashcheniia v Rossii i promyshlenny krizis* (Kharkov: Pechatnoe delo, 1902), Chaps. 1-3, and T. K. Engeev, "O platezhnom balanse dovoennoi Rossii," *Vestnik finansov*, no. 5 (1928):72-84.

3   Ol's estimates are found in S. F. Sharapov, *Tsifrovoi analiz raschetnogo balansa Rossii za 15-letie, Doklad obshchestvu dlia sodeistviia russkoi promyshlennosti i torgovli na osnovanii tsifrovykh dannykh P. V. Olem* (Petersburg: Bernshtein, 1897), introduction. Vyshnegradski's figures are in A. Vyshnegradski, *Mezhdunarodny raschetny balans Rossii*. Because I have not been able to obtain a copy of this work, I must assume it is an internal unpublished document, available only in archival form. The findings of Vyshnegradski are summarized in V. I. Bovykin, "K voprosu o roli inostranogo kapitala v Rossii," *Vestnik Moskovskogo Universiteta*, no. 1 (1964):74.

4   S. S. Khrulev, *Finansy Rossii i ee promyshlennost'* (Petrograd: N.P., 1916). The author was unable to obtain a copy of the original Khrulev study. His results are summarized, however, in A. Sidorov, "Zur Finanzlage Russlands vor 1914: Staatshaushalt und Staatsschuld," in D. Geyer, ed., *Wirtschaft und Gesellschaft im vorrevolutionären Russland* (Cologne: Kiepenheuer and Witsch, 1975), pp. 277-301.

5   L. Pasvolsky and H. G. Moulton, *Russian Debts and Russian Reconstruction* (New York: McGraw-Hill, 1924), Appendix D.

6   For examples, see P. L. Lyaschenko, *History of the National Economy of Russia to the 1917 Revolution*, trans. by L. M. Herman (New York: McGraw-Hill, 1949), p. 718; Sidorov, "Zur Finanzlage Russlands," p. 264.

7   A. I. Bukovetsky, "'Svobodnaia nalichnost' i zolotoi zapas tsarskogo pravitel'stva v kontse XIX nachale XX v." in M. P. Viatkin, ed., *Monopolii i inostrany kapital v Rossii* (Moscow: Nauka, 1962), pp. 359-376.

8   Paul Gregory, "The Russian Balance of Payments, the Gold Standard, and Monetary Policy: A Historical Example of Foreign Capital Movements," *Journal of Economic History* 39, no. 2 (June 1979):379-400.

9   *Balance des Payments*, 1938 League of Nations, (Geneva: 1939).

10   *Obzor vneshnei torgovli Rossii po evropeiskoi i aziatskoi granitzam za g.* (Petersburg: Departament tamozhennykh sborov, 1885 to 1914, annual editions).

11   Margaret Miller, *The Economic Development of Russia 1905 to 1914*, 2nd ed. (London: Cass, 1967), pp. 40-5; John Sonntag, "Tsarist Debts and Tsarist Foreign Policy," *Slavic Review* 27, no. 4, (December 1968):529-41.

12   V. I. Pokrovsky, ed., *Sbornik svedenii po istorii i statistike vneshnei*

torgovli Rossii (Petersburg: Departament tamozhennykh sborov, 1902), 1:14-35.

13   The most detailed study of regional price variation is I. D. Koval'chenko and
     L. V. Milov, *Vserosiisky agrarny rynok XVIII nachalo XX veka* (Moscow: Nauka,
     1974). For data on seasonal price differences, see the *Svod tovarnykh tsen*
     series published annually by the Ministry of Trade and Industry.

14   For such comparisons, see Sonntag, "Tsarist Debts," pp. 536-8.

15   E.g., see *Obzor vneshnei torgovli za 1908 g.*, pp. 5-7.

16   *Obzor vneshnei*, p. 6.

17   Sonntag, "Tsarist Debts," pp. 537-8.

18   Bernd Bonwetsch, "Das ausländische Kapital in Russland," *Jahrbücher für die
     Geschichte Osteuropas* 22, no. 3 (1974):419.

19   B. V. Avilov, ed., "Prilozhenie k st. Ekonomicheskoe razvitie Rossii v XIX i v
     nachale XX veka," *Entsiklopedicheski slovar' Granat*, 7th ed. vol. 36, sections
     4 and 66.

20   E. V. Dvoretski, *Rossiiskaia statistika vneshnei torgovli kak istoricheski
     istochnik*, Ph.D. abstract (Moscow: Akademiia nauk, Institut Istorii SSSR,
     1974).

21   For a discussion of the foreign policy implications of the Russian balance of
     payments, see Bernd Bonwetsch, "Handelspolitik und Industrialisierung. Zur
     aussenwirtschaftlichen Abhängigkeit Russlands," in Geyer, ed., *Wirtschaft*,
     pp. 277-301.

22   For S. Witte's own assessment of the potential contribution of foreign capital
     to Russia's economic development, see Theodore H. Von Laue, "A Secret Memo-
     randum of Sergei Witte on the Industrialization of Imperial Russia," *Journal
     of Modern History* 26, no. 1 (March 1954).

23   The reader is referred to the discussions cited in note 2.

24   V. I. Lenin, *Razvitie Kapitalizma v Rossii, Polnoe sobranie sochinenii, vol. 3*
     (Moscow: Gossizdat, 1958); *Imperializm kak vyshaia stadiia kapitalizma, Polnoe
     sobranie*, vol. 27.

25   See, e.g., Lyaschchenko, *History of the National Economy.*

26   Bonwetsch, "Das ausländische Kapital in Russland," p. 415. In particular, the
     various works of Bovykin and Gindin are viewed as a revision of the
     "half-colony" view of the Stalin era.

27   The French, in particular, with their massive holdings of Russian debt, kept a
     close watch on Russian capital markets and published numerous surveys of the
     Russian economy. An example is the *Les Finances de la Russe, D'Apres les
     documents officiels* series, published by the central library of the French
     railroads.

28   E.g., Pasvolsky and Moulton, *Russian Debts.*

29   The budget account on expenditures for public debt account contained
     considerable detail; such payments were generally divided into interest pay-
     ments, principal payments, and service charges. For the earlier years, pay-
     ments were broken down into payments in metal currencies and payments in

credit rubles, where the metallic payments were converted into credit rubles using prevailing exchange rates between metal and credit rubles. Moreover, debt payments were typically broken down into payments for general government and railroad debt.

30 The *nalichnost'* data were reported in the *Ezhegodnik ministerstva finansov* series, section *kassovy otchet*. A time series of *nalichnost'* data is provided in I. F. Gindin, *Russkie kommercheskie banki* (Moscow: Gosfinizdat, 1948), pp. 452-3.

31 For a discussion of why the *nalichnost'* data would result in an overstatement of the share of foreign capital, see Bovykin, "K voprosu."

32 These data are discussed in Bovykin, "K voprosu," and are given in *Russki denezhny rynok, 1908-1912* (Petersburg: Osobennaia kantseliaria po kreditnoi chasti, 1914), diagram 3, and in A. L. Vainshtein, *Narodnoe bogatstvo i narodnokhoziaistvennoe nakoplenie predrevoliutsionnoi Rossii* (Moscow: Gosstatizdat, 1960), p. 435.

33 For a discussion of this matter, see Bovykin, "K voprosu."

34 P. V. Ol', *Inostrannye kapitaly v narodnom khoziaistve dovoennoi Rossii, Materialy dlia izucheniia estestvennykh proizvoditel'nykh sil SSSR*, no. 53 (Leningrad: N.P., 1925).

35 Bonwetsch, "Das ausländische Kapital in Russland," p. 416. Bonwetsch comes to this adjustment by comparing detailed studies of French and German capital with Ol's own estimates.

36 Ol', *Inostrannye kapitaly*, p. 9.

37 For analyses of the Ol' data, see Bonwetsch, "Das ausländische Kapital in Russland," John McKay, *Pioneers for Profit* (Chicago: University of Chicago Press, 1970), pp. 28-36; Bovykin, "K voprosu," Vainshtein, *Narodnoe bogtstvo*, pp. 439-40; Gindin, *Russkie*, pp. 395-403.

38 Bonwetsch, "Das ausländische Kapital in Russland," pp. 412-15.

39 Sharapov, *Tsifrovoi*, statistical appendix prepared by Ol'.

40 Gindin, *Russkie*, p. 260.

41 Vainshtein, *Narodnoe bogatstvo*, pp. 441-3.

42 S. G. Strumilin, *Statistiko-ekonomicheskie ocherki* (Moscow: Gosstatizdat, 1958), pp. 519, 686.

43 See notes to the accompanying table.

44 This conclusion is drawn from the sporadic interest rates quoted in the *Bulletin Russe* series and the *Ezhegodnik ministerstva finansov* series, section *birzhy*.

45 N. J. Astrov, *The Municipal Government and the All-Russian Union of Towns* (New Haven: Yale University Press, 1929), pp. 148-9.

46 Astrov, *Municipal Government*, p. 148, Vainshtein, *Narodnoe bogatstvo*, p. 437.

47 Gindin gives a foreign capital percentage of approximately 50%. Vainshtein's proportion is 83%.

48 Astrov, *Municipal Government*, p. 148.

49 See Ol's discussion of these points in Sharapov, *Tsifrovoi*, pp. 17-20.

50 These figures are discussed in Engeev, "O platezhnom," p. 77 and in Sharapov, *Tsifrovoi*, pp. 17-20.

51 Bukovetski, "'Svobodnaia nalichnost,'" p. 374.

52 Rough assumptions are made concerning nonreturning travelers for the percent emigrating and the percent living permanently abroad.

53 This is the percentage used by Engeev, "O platezhnom," p. 82.

54 Numbers of Russian and foreign travelers crossing Russian borders in both directions were reported regularly in various official publications (*Obzor vneshnei torgovli, Ezhegodnik ministerstva finansov, Ezhegodnik Rossii*) under the heading "Movement of passengers."

55 S. Patakov, "Vneshnee passazhirskoe dvizhenie mezdu Rossiei i drugimi gosudarstvami," in *Ezhegodnik Rossii 1909 g.*, p. 73.

56 *Opyt priblizitel'nogo ischisleniia narodnogo dokhoda po razlichnym ego istochnikam i po razmeram v Rossii* (Petersburg: Ministerstvo finansov, 1906), p. 91.

57 Patakov, "Vneshnee passazhirskoe," p. 72.

58 Engeev, "O platezhnom," p. 82, uses a figure of 5 rubles per diem.

59 Engeev, "O platezhnom," p. 81, uses a higher percentage (1/4).

60 The two best sources on Russian emigration are found in *Entsiklopedicheski slovar' Brokgauz-Efron*, heading *Emigratsiia*, vol. 80, and in an article by Patakov on emigration in *Ezhegodnik Rossii 1909 g.*, pp. 177-82.

61 Most of these data are reported in the *Obzor vneshnei torgovli* series, heading *zagranichnoe plavanie*.

Anfimov, A. M. "Nalogi i zemel'nye platezhi krestian Evropeiskoi Rossii v nachale XX veka." In Akademiia Nauk SSSR, *Ezhegodnik po agrarnoi istori Vostochnoii Evropy, 1962 g.* Minsk: Nauka i tekhnika, 1964.

Antsiferov, A. N. *Russian Agriculture During the War.* New Haven: Yale University Press, 1930.

Asalkhanov, I. A. *Sel'skoe khoziaistvo Sibiri kontsa XIX-nachala XX v.* Novosibirsk: Nauka, Sibirskoe otdelenie, 1975.

Astrov, N. J. *The Municipal Government and the All-Russian Union of Towns.* New Haven: Yale University Press, 1929.

Avilov, B. V., ed. "Prilozhenie k st. Ekonomicheskoe razvitie Rossii v XIX i v nachale XX veka." *Entsiklopedicheski slovar' Granat,* 7th ed. Vol. 36, sections 4 and 66.

Baedeker, Karl. *Russland, Handbuch für Reisende,* 4th, 7th, and 1st eds. Leipzig: Baedeker, 1897, 1912, 1914.

Bairoch, Paul. *The Working Population and Its Structure.* New York: Gordon and Breach, 1969.

Balance des Payments, 1938, Geneva: League of Nations, 1939.

Barkai, Haim. "The Macro-Economics of Tsarist Russia in the Industrialization Era: Monetary Developments, the Balance of Payments and the Gold Standard." *Journal of Economic History* 33 (June 1973).

Baykov, Alexander. "The Economic Development of Russia." *Economic History Review* 7 (1954).

Becker, Abraham. *Soviet National Income, 1958-1964.* Berkeley and Los Angeles: University of California Press, 1969.

Bergson, Abram. "Conclusion," *The USSR in the 1980s.* Brussells: NATO Directorate of Economic Affairs, 1978.

Bergson, Abram. "Index Numbers and the Computation of Factor Productivity." *Review of Income and Wealth,* ser. 21, no. 3 (September 1975).

Bergson, Abram. *The Real National Income of Soviet Russia Since 1928.* Cambridge: Harvard University Press, 1961.

Bergson, Abram, and Kuznets, Simon, eds. *Economic Trends in the Soviet Union.* Cambridge: Harvard University Press, 1963.

Berlin, P. A., ed. *Entsiklopediia russkogo eksporta,* vol. 1. Berlin: Torgovoe predstavitel'stvo SSSR v Germanii, 1924.

Bobrov, C. P. *Indeksy Gosplana.* Moscow: Gosplan, 1925.

Bonwetsch, Arnold. *Der Handel mit Landwirtschaftlichen Maschinen und Geräten in Russland.* Berlin: Ebering, 1921.

Bonwetsch, Bernd. "Handelspolitik und Industrialisierung. Zur aussenwirt-schaftlichen Abhängigkeit Russlands." In D. Geyer, ed., *Wirtschaft und Gesellschaft im vorrevolutionären Russland.* Cologne: Kiepenheuer and Witsch, 1975.

Bonwetsch, Bernd. "Das ausländische Kapital in Russland." *Jahrbücher für die Geschichte Osteuropas.* 22, no. 3 (1974).

Bovykin, V. I. "K voprosu o roli inostranogo kapitala v Rossii." *Vestnik Moskovskogo Universiteta,* no. 1 (1964).

Bukovetsky, A. I. "'Svobodnaia nalichnosť" M. P. Viatkin, ed., *Monopolii i inostrany kapital v Rossii.* Moscow: Nauka, 1962.

Bulletin Russe de statistique financiere et de legislation, 1891, 1898, 1899.

Cairncross, A. K. *Home and Foreign Investment, 1870-1913.* Cambridge University Press, 1953.

Carr, E. H., and Davies, R. W. *Foundations of a Planned Economy, 1926-1929,* vol. 1, pt. 2. New York: Macmillan, 1969.

Chekhov, N. W. *Narodnoe obrazovanie v Rossi.* Moscow: Levenson, 1912.

Cohn, Stanley. "The Soviet Path to Economic Growth: A Comparative Analysis." *Review of Income and Wealth,* ser. 22, no. 1 (March 1976).

Cole, W. A. *British Economic Growth, 1688-1959.* Cambridge University Press, 1962.

Creamer, Daniel. "Measuring Capital Input for Total Factor Productivity Analysis: Comments of a Sometime Estimator." *Review of Income and Wealth* 18, no. 1 (March 1972).

Crisp, Olga. "Labor and Industrialization in Russia." *Cambridge Economic History of Europe,* vol. 7, pt. 2. Cambridge University Press, 1978.

Crisp, Olga. *Studies in the Russian Economy Before 1914.* London and Basingstoke: Macmillan, 1976.

Davies, R. W. "Soviet Industrial Production, 1928-1937: The Rival Estimates. *Centre for Russian and East European Studies Discussion Papers,* no. 18. University of Birmingham, 1978.

Davies, R. W. "A Note on Grain Statistics." *Soviet Studies* 21, no. 3 (January 1970).

Davis, Lance, Easterlin, Richard, and Parker William. *American Economic Growth.* New York: Harper and Row, 1972.

Davis, Lance, and Gallman, Robert. "Capital Formation in the United States during the Nineteenth Century." *Cambridge Economic History of Europe,* vol. 7, pt. 2. Cambridge University Press, 1978.

Davydova, L. G. *Ispol'zovanie elektricheskoi energii v promyshlennosti Rossii.* Moscow: Nauka, 1966.

Deane, P. M., and Cole, W. A. *British Economic Growth, 1688-1959.* Cambridge University Press, 1962.

Denison, Edward. *Accounting for United States Economic Growth 1929-1969.* Washington, D.C.: Brookings, 1974.

Denison, Edward. *Why Growth Rates Differ, Postwar Experiences in Nine Western Countries.* Washington, D.C.: Brookings, 1967.

Denison, Edward. "Theoretical Aspects of Quality Change, Capital Consumption and Net Capital Formation." In National Bureau of Economic Research, *Problems of Capital Formation*, vol. 19, Studies in Income and Wealth. Princeton: Princeton University Press, 1957.

Department zemledeliia, *Sel'skokhoziaistvenny promysel v Rossii*. Petrograd: Golike, 1914.

Dikhtiar, G. A. *Vnutrenniaia torgovlia v dorevoliutsionnoi Rossii*. Moscow: Nauka, 1960.

Dobb, Maurice. *Soviet Economic Development Since 1917*. London: International Publishers, 1948 (rev. ed. New York: International Publishers, 1966).

Dvoretski, E. V. *Rossiiskaia statistika vneshnei torgovli kak istoricheski istochnik*. Ph.D. abstract. Moscow: Akademiia nauk, Institut Istorii SSSR, 1974.

Ekonomicheski Biulleten Koniunkturnogo Instituta, no. 2 (February 1926).

Elster, Karl. *Vom Rubel Zum Tscherwonjez*. Jena: Fischer, 1930.

Emery, B. J., and Garsten, G. J. "The Measurement of Constant Price Aggregates in Canada." *Review of Income and Wealth*, ser. 15 (1969).

Engeev, T. K. "O platezhnom balanse dovoennoi Rossii." *Vestnik finansov*, no. 5 (1928).

Entsiklopedicheski slovar' Granat, 7th ed., vol. 36, pt. 4, statistical appendix.

Entwurf des Reichsbudgets für das Jahr 1914, pt. 1, Petersburg: Bohnke, 1913.

Erlich, Alexander. *The Soviet Industrialization Debate, 1924-1928*. Cambridge: Harvard University Press, 1960.

Ezhegodnik ministerstva finansov, annual editions, 1900-12. Petersburg: Izdania Ministerstva finansov, 1909.

Falkus, M. E. *The Industrialization of Russia, 1700-1914*. London and Basingstoke: Macmillan, 1972.

Falkus, M. E. "Russia's National Income, 1913: A Revaluation." *Economica* 35, no. 137 (February 1968).

Feinstein, Charles. *National Income, Expenditure and Output of the United Kingdom, 1855-1965*. Cambridge University Press, 1972.

Les Finances de la Russe, D'Apres les documents officiels. Paris: Imprimerie et Libraire centrales des Chemins de Fer, 1892.

Firestone, O. J. *Canada's Economic Development, 1867-1953*. Vol 7. *Income and Wealth Series*. vol. 7, London: Bowes and Bowes, 1958.

Frei, L. I. *Osnovnye problemy mezhdunarodnykh raschetov*. Moscow: Mezhdunarodnaia kniga, 1945.

Gallman, Robert. "Gross National Product in the United States, 1834-1909." In National Bureau of Economic Research, *Output, Employment and Productivity in the United States after 1800*, vol. 30, *Studies in Income and Wealth*. New York: Columbia University Press, 1966.

Gerschenkron, Alexander. "Agrarian Policies and Industrialization: Russia, 1861-1917." *Cambridge Economic History of Europe*, vol. 6, pt. 2. Cambridge University Press, 1965.

Gerschenkron, Alexander. *Economic Backwardness in Historical Perspective.* Cambridge: Harvard University Press, 1962.

Gerschenkron, Alexander. *A Dollar Index of Soviet Machinery Output, 1927-28 to 1937.* Rand, Report R-197, April 1961.

Gerschenkron, Alexander. "The Rate of Growth of Industrial Production in Russia Since 1885." *Journal of Economic History* 7, supplement (1947).

Gerschenkron, Alexander. "The Soviet Indices of Industrial Production." *Review of Economics and Statistics* 29, no. 4 (November 1947):217-26.

Geyer, Dietrich. *Der russische Imperialismus.* Göttingen. Vandenhoeck and Ruprecht, 1977.

Gindin, I. F. *Russkie kommercheskie banki.* Moscow: Gosfinizdat, 1948.

Girault, Rene. *Emprunts russes et investissements francais en Russie 1887-1914.* Paris: Colin, 1973.

Goldsmith, Raymond. "The Economic Growth of Tsarist Russia, 1860-1913." *Economic Development and Cultural Change* 9, no. 3 (April 1961).

Gordon, Robert. "Measurement Bias in Price Indexes for Capital Goods." *Review of Income and Wealth,* ser. 17, no. 2 (June 1971).

Gosplan SSSR. *Kontrol'nye tsifry narodnogo khoziaistva na 1928-29 g.* Moscow: Izdatel'stvo Planovoe Khoziaistvo, 1929.

Gozulov, A. I. *Istoriia otechestvennoi statistiki.* Moscow: Gosstatizdat, 1957.

Greenslade, Rush. "The Real Gross National Product of the USSR, 1950-1975." Joint Economic Committee, *Soviet Economy in a New Perspective.* Washington, D.C.: U.S. Government Printing Office, 1976.

Gregory, Paul. "A Note on Russia's Merchandise Balance and Balance of Payments During the Industrialization Era." *Slavic Review* 38, no. 4 (December 1979):655-62.

Gregory, Paul. "The Russian Balance of Payments, the Gold Standard, and Monetary Policy: A Historical Example of Foreign Capital Movements." *Journal of Economic History* 39, no. 2 (June 1979).

Gregory, Paul. "Grain Marketing and Peasant Consumption, Russia, 1885-1913." *Explorations in Economic History* 17, no. 2 (March 1979):135-64.

Gregory, Paul. "Russian Industrialization and Economic Growth: Results and Perspectives of Western Research." *Jahrbücher für die Geschichte Osteuropas* 2, no. 25 (1977).

Gregory, Paul. "1913 Russian National Income: Some Insights into Russian Economic Development." *Quarterly Journal of Economics* 90, no. 3 (August 1976).

Gregory, Paul. "Some Empirical Comments on the Theory of Relative Backwardness: The Russian Case." *Economic Development and Cultural Change* 22, no. 4 (July 1974).

Gregory, Paul. "Economic Growth and Structural Change in Tsarist Russia: A Case of Modern Economic Growth?" *Soviet Studies* 23, no. 3 (January 1972).

Gregory, Paul. *Socialist and Nonsocialist Industrialization Patterns.* New York: Praeger, 1970.

Gregory, Paul. *Socialist Industrialization Patterns.* Ph.D. diss., Harvard University, 1969.

Gregory, Paul, and Kuniansky, Anna. "The Value of Agricultural Structures in Russia, 1885-1913," mimeographed, 1978.

Gregory, Paul, and Sailors, Joel. "Russian Monetary Policy and Industrialization, 1861-1913." *Journal of Economic History* 36, no. 4 (December 1976): 836-51.

Kahan, Arcadius. "Government Policies and the Industrialization of Russia." *Journal of Economic History* 27, no. 4 (December 1967).

Karcz, Jerzy. "Back on the Grain Front." *Soviet Studies* 22, no. 2 (October 1970).

Katz, V. "Narodny dokhod SSSR i ego raspredelenie." *Planovoe khoziaistvo*, no. 11 (1929).

Kendrick, John W. *Productivity Trends in the United States.* Princeton: Princeton University Press, 1961.

Kennard, Howard, ed. *Russian Yearbook 1912.* London: Eyre, 1912.

Khrulev, S. S. *Finansy Rossii i ee promyshlennost'.* Petrograd: N.P. 1916 (2nd ed. Petersburg: Brokgauz-Efron, 1916).

Klein, L., and Ohkawa, K., eds. *Economic Growth: The Japanese Experience since the Meiji Era.* Homewood, Ill.: Irwin, 1968.

Konüs, A. A. "The Problem of the True Cost of Living." *Economic Bulletin of the Institute of Economic Conjuncture*, no. 9-10. Moscow, September-October 1924, translated in *Econometrica* in 1939.

Koval'chenko, I. D., and Milov, I. V. *Vserossiisky agrarny rynok, XVIII - nachalo XX veka.* Moscow: Nauka, 1974.

Kovalevski, V. I., ed. *Rossiia v Kontse XIX veka.* Petersburg: Ministerstvo finansov, 1900.

Kuznets, Simon. *Economic Growth of Nations.* Cambridge: Harvard University Press, 1971.

Kuznets, Simon. *Modern Economic Growth.* New Haven: Yale University Press, 1966.

Kuznets, Simon. "A Comparative Appraisal." In Abram Bergson and Simon Kuznets, eds., *Economic Trends in the Soviet Union.* Cambridge: Harvard University Press, 1963.

Kuznets, Simon. *Capital in the American Economy.* Princeton: Princeton University Press, 1961.

Kuznets, Simon. *National Income and Its Composition, 1919-1938.* New York: National Bureau of Economic Research, 1954.

Lebergott, Stanley. "Labor Force and Employment, 1800-1960." In National Bureau of Economic Research, *Output, Employment and Productivity in the United States after 1800*, vol. 30, *Studies in Income and Wealth.* New York: Columbia University Press, 1966.

Lenin, V. I. *The Development of Capitalism in Russia.* Moscow: Foreign Languages Publishing House, 1956.

Liashchenko, P. I. *Ocherki agrarnoi evolutsii Rossii.* Petersburg: N.P., 1908.

Lorimer, Frank. *The Population of the Soviet Union: History and Prospect.* Geneva: League of Nations, 1964.

Martiny, Albrech. *Der Einfluss der Duma auf die Finanz-und Haushaltspolitik (1907-1914)*. Ph.D. diss., Freiburg, 1974.

Migulin, P. P. *Reforma denezhnago obrashcheniia v Rossii i promyshlenny krizis*. Kharkov: Pechatnoe delo, 1902.

Ministerstvo torgovli i Promyshlennost. *Tamozhennye tarify po evropeiskoi torgovle*. Petersburg: Kirshbaum, 1913.

Mints, L. E. *Trudovye resursy SSSR*. Moscow: Nauka, 1975.

Mints, L. E. "Ocherki razvitiia chislennosti i sostava promyshlennogo proletariata v Rossii." *Ocherki po istorii statistiki SSSR*, vol. 2. Moscow: Gosstatizdat, 1957.

Mitchell, B. R. *European Historical Statistics, 1750-1970*. London: Macmillan, 1975.

Moorsteen, Richard. *Prices and Production of Machinery in the Soviet Union, 1928-1958*. Cambridge: Harvard University Press, 1962.

Mulhall, M. G. *Dictionary of Statistics*, various editions, 1884-99.

Nötzold, Jürgen. *Wirtschaftspolitische Alternativen der Entwicklung Russlands in der Ära Witte und Stolypin*. Berlin: Duncker and Humblot, 1965.

Nove, Alec. *An Economic History of the USSR*. London: Penguin, 1969.

Nutter, G. Warren. "The Soviet Economy: Retrospect and Prospect," in *Conference on "Fifty Years of Communism."* Stanford: Hoover Institution, 1976.

Obzor vneshnei torgovli Rossii po evropeiskoi i aziatskoi granitzam za g. Petersburg: Departament tamozhennykh sborov, 1885 to 1914, annual editions.

Ocherki istori Leningrada, vol. 2. Moscow-Leningrad: Akademiia nauk, 1957.

Ofer, Gur. *The Service Sector in Soviet Economic Growth*. Cambridge: Harvard University Press, 1976.

Ohkawa, Kazushi, and Rosovsky, Henry. *Japanese Economic Growth*. Stanford: Stanford University Press, 1973.

Ol', P. V. *Inostrannye kapitaly v narodnom khoziaistve dovoennoi Rossii, Materialy dlia izucheniia estestvennykh proizvoditel'nykh sil SSSR*, no. 53 (Leningrad: N.P., 1925).

Opyt priblizitel'nogo ischisleniia narodnogo dokhoda po razlichnym ego istochnikam i po razmeram v Rossii. Petersburg: Ministerstvo finansov, 1906.

Pasvolsky, L., and Moulton, H. G. *Russian Debts and Russian Reconstruction*. New York: McGraw-Hill, 1924.

Patakov, S. "Vneshnee passazhirskoe dvizhenie mezdu Rossiei i drugimi gosudarstvami," In *Ezhegodnik Rossii 1909 g.*, 73.

Pokrovsky, V. I., ed. *Sbornik svedenii po istorii i statistike vneshnei torgovli Rossi*, vol. 1. Petersburg: Departament tamozhennykh sborov, 1902.

Polferov, Ia. Ia. *Sel'skokhoziaistvennyia mashiny i orudiia, ikh proizvodstvo i vvoz v Rossi*. Petrograd: Ministerstvo finansov, 1914.

Popkin, Joel, and Gillingham, Robert. "Comments on 'Recent Developments in the Measurement of Price Indexes for Fixed Capital Goods.'" *Review of Income and Wealth*, ser. 17, no. 3 (September 1971).

Popov, P. I., ed. *Balans narodnogo khoziaistva Soiuza SSSR, 1923-24.* Moscow: Ts. S. U., 1926.

Prokopovich, S. N. *The National Income of the USSR,* Memorandum No 3. Birmingham Bureau of Research on Russian Economic Conditions, November 1931.

Prokopovich, S. N. *Krestianskoe khoziaistvo po dannym biudzhetnykh isledovanii i dinamicheskikh perepisei.* Berlin: Kooperativenaia mysl', 1924.

Prokopovich, S. N. *Opyt ischisleniia narodnogo dokhoda 50 gubernii Evropeiskoi Rossii v 1900-1913 gg.* Moscow: Sovet Vserossiiskikh Koopertivnykh Sezdov, 1918.

Rashin, A. G. *Formirovanie rabochego klassa Rossii.* Moscow: Sotsekizdat, 1958.

Rashin, A. G. *Naselenie Rossii za 100 let.* Moscow: Gosstatizdat, 1956.

Rosefielde, Steven. "The First Great Leap Forward Reconsidered: The Lessons of Solzhenitsyn's Gulag Archipelago." *Slavic Review* 39, no. 4 (December 1980).

Rosovsky, Henry. *Capital Formation in Japan, 1868-1940.* New York: Free Press, 1961.

Rosovsky, L. "Perepisi russkoi promyshlennosti 1900 i 1908." In Akademiia nauk SSSR, *Ocherki po istorii statistiki SSSR, Sbornik III.* Moscow: Gosstatizdat, 1960.

Rostow, W. W. (ed.) *The Economics of Takeoff into Sustained Growth.* New York: St. Martin's, 1963.

Russki denezhny rynok 1980-1912. Petersburg: Osobennaia kantseliaria po kreditnoi chasti, 1914.

Rybnikov, S. *Ocherki sovremennogo polozheniia v Rossii strakhovaniia ot ognia.* Petersburg: N.P., 1912.

Sbornik statistiko-ekonomicheskikh svedenii po sel'skomu khoziaistvu Rossii i inostrannykh gosudarstv, vol. 7. Petrograd: Ministerstvo Zemledeliia, 1915.

Sbornik svedenii po Rossii, 1884-85, 1890, 1896 editions. Petersburg: Tsentral'ny Statisticheski Komitet, 1887, 1891, 1897.

Sharapov, S. F. *Tsifrovoi analiz raschetnogo balansa Rossii za 15-letie, Doklad obshchestvu dlia sodeistviia russkoi promyshlennosti i torgovli na osnovanii tsifrovykh dannykh P. V. Olem.* Petersburg: Bernshtein, 1897.

Shchebrina, F. A. "Krestianskie biudzhety i zavisimost' ikh ot urozhaev i tsen na khleba." In A. I. Chuprov and A. S. Posnikov, eds., *Vliianie urozhaev i khlebnykh tsen na nekotoryia storony ruskkago and narodnogo khoziaistva,* vol. 2. Petersburg: Kirschbaum, 1897.

Shebalin, Iu. "Gosudarstvenny biudzhet tsarskoi Rossii," *Istoricheskie Zapiski,* T65, 1959.

Strumilin, S. G. *Statistiko-ekonomicheskie ocherki.* Moscow: Gosstatizdat, 1958.

Studenski, Paul. *The Income of Nations: Theory, Measurement and Analysis, Past and Present.* New York: New York University Press, 1958.

Svavitski, Z. M., and Svavitski, N. A. *Zemskie podvornye perepisi 1880-1913.* Moscow: Izdanie Ts.S.U., 1926.

Svod tovarnykh tsen na glavnykh russkikh i inostrannykh rynkakh za 1913 god. Petersburg: Ministerstvo torgovli i promyshelnnosti, 1915.

Tilly, R. H. "Capital Formation in Germany in the Nineteenth Century." *Cambridge Economic History of Europe,* vol. 7, pt. 2. Cambridge University Press, 1978.

Trakhtenberg, I. A. *Denezhnye krizisy.* Moscow: Nauka, 1963.

Tsentral'noe Statisticheskoe Upravlenie. *Statisticheski Spravochnik SSSR za 1928.* Moscow: Izdatel'stvo Ts.S.U., 1929.

Tsentral'noe Statisticheskoe Upravlenie. *Statisticheski sbornik za 1913-1917 gg., Vypusk vtoroi.* Moscow: Ts.S.U., 1921.

Tsentral'ny Statisticheski Komitet. *Goroda Rossii v 1904 g.* Petersburg: Ts.S.K., 1906.

Tsentral'ny Statisticheski Komitet. *Urozhai khlebov po ukazaniiam krest'ian-starozhilov iz obsledovaniia 1893 g. 46 gub. Evropeiskoi Rossii.* Vremenik Tsentral'nogo Statisticheskago Komiteta, no. 30 (1893).

Tugan-Baranovsky, M. I. *Statisticheskie itogi promyshlennago razvitiia Rossii.* Petersburg: Tsepov, 1898.

U.S. Bureau of the Census. *Historical Statistics of the United States, Colonial Times to 1970,* pt. 1. Washington, D.C.: U.S. Government Printing Office, 1975.

U.S. Department of Commerce. *Historical Statistics of the United States from Colonial Times to the Present.* Washington, D.C.: U.S. Government Printing Office, 1975.

Vainshtein, A. L. *Narodny dokhod Rossii i SSSR.* Moscow: Nauka, 1969.

Vainshtein, A. L. "Ischisleniia i otsenka narodnogo dokhoda Rossii v dorevoliutsionnoe vremia." Akademiia nauk, *Ocherki po istorii statistiki SSSR,* vol. 7. Moscow: Gosstatizdat, 1961.

Vainshtein, A. L. "Iz istorii predrevoliutsionnoi statistiki zhivotnovodstva." *Ocherki po istorii statistiki SSSR,* vol. 3. Moscow; Gosstatizdat, 1960.

Vainshtein, A. L. *Narodnoe bogatstvo i narodnokhoziaistvennoe nakoplenie predrevoliutsionnoi Rossii.* Moscow: Gosstatizdat, 1960.

Veselovski, V. V. *Istoriia zemstva za sorok let,* 4 vols. Petersburg: Popov, 1909.

Volin, Lazar. *A Century of Russian Agriculture.* Cambridge: Harvard University Press, 1970.

Von Laue, Theodore H. *Sergei Witte and the Industrialization of Russia.* New York: Columbia University Press, 1963.

Von Laue, Theodore H. "A Secret Memorandum of Sergei Witte on the Industrialization of Imperial Russia." *Journal of Modern History* 26, no. 1 (March 1954).

Vzaimnoe strakhovanie ot ognia, guberskoe i gorodskoe, 1889-1892. Vremenik Tsentral'nogo Statisticheskago Komiteta, 1893.

Wattenberg, Ben J., (ed.) *The Statistical History of the United States from Colonial Times to the Present.* New York: Basic Books, 1976.

Weitzman, M. L. "Soviet Postwar Economic Growth and Capital-Labor Substitution." *American Economic Review* 60, no. 4 (September 1970).

Westwood, N. *Geschichte der russischen Eisenbahnen.* Zurich: Füssli, 1964.

Wheatcroft, S. G. "Soviet Agricultural Production, 1913-1940," mimeographed, 1979.

Wheatcroft, S. G. "Grain Production Statistics in the USSR in the 1920s and 1930s."

Centre for Russian and East European Studies Discussion Papers, no. 13. University of Birmingham, 1977.

Wheatcroft, S. G. "The Reliability of Russian Prewar Grain Output Statistics." *Soviet Studies* 36, no. 2 (April 1974).

Yaney, George. *The Systematization of Russian Government*. Urbana: University of Illinois Press, 1973.

Zaionchkovski, P. A. *Pravitel'stvenny apparat samoderzhavnoi Rossii v XIX v.* Moscow: Mysl', 1978.

Zaionchkovski, P. A. *Spravochnik po istorii dorevoliutsionnoi Rossii.* Moscow: Kniga, 1971.

Zaitsev, V., and Groman, V. G., eds. *Vliianie neurozhaev na narodnoe khoziaistvo Rossii.* Moscow: N.P., 1927.

SANTA CLARA UNIVERSITY

3 5098 20140684 3